European Integration and National Identity

The four Nordic countries, Denmark, Finland, Sweden and Norway, have all held referenda on their relationship to the European Union in the 1990s. These referenda generated heated debate: Should Finland and Sweden give up neutrality? Should Denmark follow the European Union's move towards higher degrees of integration? And, had there been enough change in Norway to reverse the rejection of European Community membership in 1972?

The background for the contested nature of European integration in Scandinavia is addressed in this highly topical book which examines the crucial role played by national identity. The authors argue that the discussion of the European Union drew upon ideas of the nation as well as of the state. In each national context these ideas have been connected to each other in a particular manner, which comes to structure how a country can imagine Europe and the European Union.

European Integration and National Identity lays out a new framework for studying European integration. This framework – developed by Ole Wæver – uses discourse analysis and applies it to foreign policy. The empirical chapters on each of the four countries adopt this framework and identify first, the key ideas of nation and state; and, second, how these ideas influenced the debate over the European Union.

Lene Hansen is an Associate Professor in the Department of Political Science, University of Copenhagen.

Ole Wæver is Professor of International Relations in the Department of Political Science, University of Copenhagen. He is the joint author of *Security: A New Framework for Analysis*, 1998; and co-editor of *The Future of International Relations: Masters in the Making*, 1997.

The New International Relations
Edited by Barry Buzan, *University of Westminster*
and Richard Little, *University of Bristol*

The field of international relations has changed dramatically in recent years. This new series will cover the major issues that have emerged and reflect the latest academic thinking in this particular dynamic area.

European Integration and National Identity

The challenge of the Nordic states

Edited by Lene Hansen and Ole Wæver

London and New York

First published 2002 by Routledge
11 New Fetter Lane, London EC4P 4EE

Simultaneously published in the USA and Canada
by Routledge
29 West 35th Street, New York, NY 10001

Routledge is an imprint of the Taylor & Francis Group

Typeset in Baskerville by Keystroke, Jacaranda Lodge, Wolverhampton
Printed and bound in Great Britain by The Cromwell Press, Trowbridge,
Wiltshire

British Library Cataloguing in Publication Data
A catalogue record for this book is available from the British Library

Library of Congress Cataloging in Publication Data
European integration and national identity : the challenge of the Nordic states /
    edited by Lene Hansen and Ole Wæver.
    p. cm
    — (The new international relations series)
    Includes bibliographical references and index.
    1. European Union—Scandinavia. 2. Europe—Economic integration.
    3. Nationalism. I. Hansen, Lene, 1968– II. Wæver, Ole, 1960– III.
    New international relations
HC240.25.S34 E92 2001
337.4048—dc21
    2001034986

ISBN 0–415–26184–8 (pbk)
    0–415–22093–9 (hbk)

Contents

Figures

Contributors

Lene Hansen is an Associate Professor of Political Science at the University of Copenhagen. Her main research interests include European integration, security studies, gender and International Relations theory. She has published articles in *Journal of Common Market Studies*, *Millennium*, *International Feminist Journal of Politics*, *Journal of Peace Research* and *Alternatives*.

Ole Wæver is a Professor of International Relations in the Department of Political Science, University of Copenhagen. He is the author (with Barry Buzan and Jaap de Wilde) of *Security: A New Framework For Analysis* (1998) and (with Barry Buzan) of *Regions and Powers: The Structure of International Security* (2002). He is a member of editorial boards for several international journals as well as policy advisory bodies in Denmark.

Iver B. Neumann, DPhil (Oxon), is on leave from the Norwegian Institute of International Affairs and works as a policy planner in the Norwegian Ministry of Defence. His latest book is *Uses of the Other. 'The East' in European Identity Formation*, Minneapolis, MN: University of Minnesota Press, 1999.

Lars Trägårdh is Assistant Professor at the Department of History, Barnard College, Columbia University. His research has been focused on the comparative history of political culture in Sweden and Germany. More recently he has written on the subject of rights and the juridification of politics in the United States and Europe.

Pertti Joenniemi is a Senior Research Fellow and a Programme Director for Nordic-Baltic studies at Copenhagen Peace Research Institute (COPRI). His research agenda includes Nordic co-operation, region-building in Northern Europe, the North and South in the construction of the European Union, regionalisation in Russia as well as the external relations of Russian regions located at the Northwestern part of the country.

Series editor's preface

This book offers more than just a sophisticated comparative approach to understanding why the four main Nordic countries relate to the European Union in the way they do. In addition, it offers three other things: 1) a challenge to the liberal intergovernmentalist approach to explaining the EU exemplified by the work of Andrew Moravcsik; 2) a method of analysis that could fruitfully be applied to other members and would-be members of the EU; and 3) a discourse analysis theory of foreign policy. For those who have been sceptical about the ability of poststructuralists to do anything except criticise and deconstruct, this study will come as a welcome (or in some cases unwelcome) demonstration of a well-structured analytical comparison rooted in poststructural epistemology and methods.

The book is most easily read as a set of theoretically coherent and historically informed essays about EU politics in Denmark, Finland, Norway and Sweden. The importance of the Nordic states in the widening and deepening politics of the EU by itself justifies a close look at the social and historical underpinnings of their responses to the EU. The novelty in the study is the authors' use of discourses about state, nation and Europe as the main analytical lens through which to gain insight into the policies that these states have and have not adopted towards the EU. These discourses are viewed as historically sedimented layered structures of greater and lesser depth and durability, whose interplay shapes and constrains the legitimacy of various policy options towards Europe. The approach through discourse structures offers both a new angle on understanding the relations of the Nordics and the EU, and some important insights into vital turning points for the whole European enterprise such as the Danish rejection of the EMU. The very effective link that the authors form between theory and history, and the powerful comparative analysis that results, suggests that they have developed a method that should be applied in a similarly systematic study to Britain, France, Germany and others. There is a host of potential Ph.D. projects here. It is all too apparent that the future development of the EU hangs on how the relationship between concepts of state, nation and Europe gets worked out. The main barrier to both further expansion and integration lies not within the political and economic elites, but with the peoples of Europe, and their attitudes towards, and understandings of, the relationship between state and nation. If getting a grip on this clarifies the position of the Nordic states, it could also pay dividends in understanding the same set of dynamics within the major powers that lie at the heart of Europe.

So in addition to its insights into the Nordic–EU relationship, this book also offers a general methodology for understanding the whole attempt to construct and develop a post-Westphalian international politics in Europe. Although on the surface, the book seems most obviously to be pitched at those interested in the Nordic countries and those interested in Nordic–EU politics, this wider implication means that it should be of interest to the wider community of those concerned with the European project as a whole.

Beyond that, the book has relevance for two further circles of interest: foreign policy analysis, whose shortcomings over the past decades are all too well known; and International Relations theory more generally. The foreign policy analysis community will find here a well-developed theory of foreign policy with both a novel approach and an exemplary set of cases demonstrating the method. The IR theory community will find a structural theory that can, with a bit of imagination, be placed in complementary tension with neo-realism's three tiers of structure as a parallel set.

Barry Buzan

Preface

This book seeks to bring together discourse analysis, conceptual history and post-structuralism in a study of the debates on European integration in the Nordic countries. In this respect, it sides with the so-called reflectivist turn in International Relations theory in taking the construction of national identity and the importance of legitimacy as its starting point. Yet, it is also a study with a clear structuralist ambition which might come as a surprise to those who tend to think of post-structuralism as an intellectual playing ground devoid of any rules or rigour.

The theoretical framework of our book was initially developed by Ole Wæver in a collaborative project with Ulla Holm and Henrik Larsen which examined the German and French approaches to European integration. The first motivation behind this book was to use this framework in a study of the Nordic countries, all of which have held referenda on their relationship to the EU in the 1990s. Lene Hansen had worked as a research assistant to the Wæver, Holm and Larsen project and Iver Neumann and Pertti Joenniemi also had strong ties to the 'Copenhagen coterie' as Iver Neumann had called this 'school'. It was our hope and ambition that this would allow us to produce an edited book which pursued a common theoretical approach throughout the empirical chapters. Lars Trägårdh came on board relatively late in the process, and the ease with which he, a 'real historian', became part of the group speaks highly of both his intellectual flexibility as well to the fertile ground between the fields of IR and history.

Our second motivation was to offer a thorough understanding of what was at stake in the discussions of the European Union in our Nordic countries. When reading the debate on the EU's legitimacy crisis, or studying the discussions of how the EU should develop in countries like France and Germany, we discovered that both the academic and the political discourse seemed jarring to a Nordic ear. Efforts to strengthen the European Parliament, or to equip the EU with a cultural identity, or to move the EU in more federal directions were likely to meet with Nordic resistance. As the outcome of the referenda showed, the Nordics were, with the exception of Finland, less than enamoured with the thought of being part of an increasingly integrated Union. And we found that materialist and rationalist explanations had difficulties capturing the importance of arguments which highlighted national identity and the fears of losing the Scandinavian welfare state. The alternative route we pursue in this book goes through centuries of history to trace the formation of the concepts of state, nation and *Folk* ('the people'), not 'only' because we wish to uncover conceptual history, but because we claim that these concepts have a structuring influence on the present construction of 'Europe' and the way in which the debates have unfolded in each of the Nordic countries.

Acknowledgements

This book would not have been possible without the financial support and critical encouragement of a large number of people. The Copenhagen Research Project on European Integration (CORE) funded authors' meetings in 1995 and 1999 as well as valuable research assistance. The Copenhagen Peace Research Institute (COPRI) made it possible to invite Lars Trägårdh for a two week research visit, and the Danish Foreign Policy Institute (DUPI) supported a visit by Iver Neumann in August 1999. We are extremely grateful for the support from all three institutions, none of which bear any responsibility for the final product.

This manuscript has been a long time in the making and we have benefited enormously from many presentations and discussions of our key ideas over the years. While it would be impossible to thank each and every one individually we would like to extend our special thanks to the following people: first and foremost Ulla Holm, who worked with Ole Wæver on the original theoretical framework and wrote the French part of the Franco-German case study in *Struggles for Europe*; Jutta Weldes and Jef Huysmans who acted as extremely thoughtful discussants at our first presentations of the theory chapter, and of the Danish, Norwegian and Finnish chapters at the ISA's annual conference in San Diego in 1996; the European Security Group at the Copenhagen Peace Research Institute, which discussed parts of the manuscript several times and the entire manuscript in August 1999 (present on that occasion were Barry Buzan, Thomas Diez, Ulla Holm, Karen Lund Petersen and Gearóid Ó Tuathail). We would also wish to thank the three anonymous readers for their useful comments as well as our editor at Routledge, Craig Fowlie, and his staff.

On the logistical side, Jesper Hybel Pedersen provided valuable research assistance at the final stage of the process. We would also like to thank the Swedish Labour Movement Archives and Library (Arbetarrörelsens Arkiv och Bibliotek) for the right to reproduce illustrations 1 and 2, Robert Nyberg for the right to reproduce illustrations 3–5, and Leif Zetterling for the right to reproduce illustration 6.

1 Introduction*

Lene Hansen

European integration became one of the most salient issues in Nordic foreign policy in the 1990s. Finland, Norway and Sweden applied for EU membership and held referenda on accession in the fall of 1994 and Denmark witnessed no less than three EU-related referenda, one on the Maastricht Treaty in 1992, one on the Edinburgh Agreement in 1993, and, finally, one on the Amsterdam Treaty in 1998. In all four countries, the governments were in favour of integration – and with the exception of Norway, they had the support of almost the entire political and economic establishment – yet, with the partial exception of Finland, this was a policy which confronted serious opposition among the Nordic voters. The Maastricht Treaty was rejected in Denmark in June 1992 by a 50.7 per cent no vote; Norwegian accession was turned down with 52.2 per cent against membership; and in Sweden only a slim majority of 52.3 per cent voted in favour. In Finland, by contrast, a, by Nordic standards, comfortable 57 per cent voted 'yes' (Arter 1995; Tiilikainen 1996). At the turn of the millennium, the Nordic EU members continued on their sceptical track: the rejection of Denmark's accession to the third phase of the EMU in September 2000 was the most spectacular incident, but opinion polls published in July 2000 in the 53rd *Eurobarometer* supported this trend: Sweden had the highest number of any member country arguing that membership was a bad thing, and in Finland only 40 per cent were in clear support of membership.[1]

This book seeks to understand the reserved approach to 'the European question' in Norden.[2] Why in three out of four countries did the vote split almost exactly in half? What were the major points of contestation and how did the opposing sides represent their European policy? Or, in the case of Finland, even if less than a majority expressed outright support for membership by the end of the 1990s, why was integration perceived as less of a contested issue than in the rest of Norden?[3] Answering these question leads us to a study of the debates preceding the referenda in each of the Nordic countries. While those supporting integration fought to present membership of the EU as a precondition for political influence and continued economic growth – and as not seriously compromising national sovereignty – the no-side adopted sometimes a nationalist rhetoric, sometimes the argument that the Scandinavian welfare state would be seriously threatened inside an integrated Europe. Peter Lawler has argued that 'Scandinavian scepticism about European integration exhibited a significant, if intellectually unfashionable, attachment to a positive understanding of the sovereign state which a generic term such as nationalism cannot fully capture' (Lawler 1997: 566). Or, one could argue along similar lines that Norden exhibits dual nationalisms, that a 'state nationalism' which fears the demise of the Scandinavian welfare state co-exists alongside a traditional 'cultural nationalism' centred on the concern for national identity. This produces a political terrain where opposition to the EU has been argued mostly from the parties located at the two ends of the political spectrum, while social democrats, conservatives and liberals have been – as a general rule and with Norway as an exception – in favour (Sæter 1996: 143–5; Dahlerup 1997).

As the analysis of the four countries in Chapters 3 to 6 will show, the Nordic debates over Europe have evolved around the importance of national identity and the role of the state (Ingebritsen and Larson 1997; Lawler 1997). If we wish to fully understand the Nordic reluctance towards European integration we need, as a consequence, to study the way in which the political concepts 'nation' and 'state' are deployed in the debate on Europe. But our approach moves beyond studying the impact of national identity in some important ways. First, the analysis of a particular country will most often begin by tracing how the concept of the nation is related to the state, and how these constructions influence the current debate on Europe. But other concepts refering to larger collectivities such as 'society' and 'the people' (or *Folk*) may also be of relevance for fully comprehending the structure of the debates.

Second, it is our claim that these 'crucial concepts' are tied together in *conceptual constellations*, that the specific constructions of each concept – for example of the nation along cultural/German or political/French lines – are linked to one another in a particular way, and that this constellation is constitutive for the way in which European integration can be constructed politically. It is, in short, the central claim of this book that these concepts have a structuring influence on the way in which 'Europe' can be articulated in a particular, national context. Or, put differently, when political actors argue in favour of a certain policy towards Europe, they do so through a presentation of how this 'Europe' fits with a particular construction of 'Finland', 'Norway', 'Sweden' and 'Denmark'. Specific constructions of Europe are thus constrained – and enabled – by the way in which the concepts of state, nation, etc. have been formed historically. A pro-EU project articulated within a given national context has to include a vision of how 'Europe' strengthens the idea of the nation and the state – or at least of how it does not pose a threat to these ideas. Those opposing integration attempt, on the other hand, to convince the public that the EU does indeed involve a threat to national identity and/or political independence. This is not to say that one will find an explicit use of the word 'nation' or 'state' in every single argument over Europe, for it might be that the concept of the nation is taken for granted to such an extent that it does not need to be directly referred to.

Although the discourse analysis approach to foreign policy presented by Ole Wæver in Chapter 2, as well as the specific methodological principles accompanying it, are applied to a specific set of states, namely the Nordic ones, it should be emphasised that this theoretical framework has a more general applicability. Ole

Wæver's discourse analysis foreign policy theory was, in fact, originally conceived in a project which took the debate on Europe in France and Germany as its empirical case in point (Wæver and Holm, forthcoming). This project included, besides Ole Wæver, who also wrote the analysis of Germany (Wæver 1992b, 1996, 1998b), Ulla Holm and Henrik Larsen, both of whom have modified and applied the theoretical framework to France (Holm 1993, 1997, 1999) and France and Britain (Larsen 1997). Although not following the detailed methodology of discursive levels, presented in Chapter 2, to a similar extent to the chapters in this book, two of the contributors, Iver B. Neumann and Lene Hansen, have used significant parts of it in studies of Russia (Neumann 1996a) and Slovenia (Hansen 1996).[4]

This chapter proceeds in the following way: first, it presents the debate on the EU's legitimacy crisis; second, it defines our poststructuralist approach and discusses the difference to alternative constructivist studies of national conceptualisations of Europe; third, it addresses the challenge to constructivism which has been presented by Andrew Moravcsik, the leading scholar within the liberal intergovernmentalist approach; and, fourth, it argues the relevance of the 'Nordic choice' and presents a brief history of the Nordic region and the difference between the way in which 'Norden' and 'Europe' have been constructed.

The legitimacy debate

The four Nordic countries are interesting 'Europeans' not least because they include – together with Britain – some of the most reluctant integrationists (Miljan 1977). The Nordic cases are in this respect highly relevant for those beyond the Nordic area who are interested in the ongoing debate over the legitimacy crisis of the EU. This debate seeks to understand why a gap has developed between the attitudes of national elites on the one side and a significant part of the electorate on the other. National governments and the EU's own representatives have in general constructed existing and increased levels of European integration in more positive terms than large parts of the populations. Indeed the 'break on integration' currently in evidence can, in most cases, be located at the level of the EU members' populations rather than – as traditionally expected – in the states' unwillingness to give up sovereignty. Opinion polls such as those compiled in the *Eurobarometer* provide one useful indication of the degree of legitimacy crisis across the EU as a whole, as well as inside each of the member states. But referenda have the advantage over polls in that they not only provide us with a concrete measure of the degree of support for integration, but also tend to generate *debate*: they force political actors to argue *why* a particular policy towards integration is called for. Polls might allow one to identify a legitimacy crisis, but they cannot in and of themselves be used to identify *why* integration is seen as unwanted by a large part of the electorate.[5] Debates surrounding referenda – or other high profile events such as the sanctions imposed on Austria in 2000 – facilitate, on the other hand, a study of the reasons why the EU is seen as legitimate or not.

Throughout the 1990s a debate over the causes and solutions to the legitimacy crisis has taken place (Hansen and Williams 1999). One set of authors has taken a liberal political position claiming either that a European citizenry already exists, and that the EU's crisis stems from the absence of adequate structures of political representation at the European level (for example Featherstone 1994: 151; Lodge 1994; Wiener and Sala 1997: 597), or that a European political community can and should be created through the introduction of these structures (Howe 1995). Another set of authors argues in response that the precondition for a solution of the crisis is the construction of a European cultural identity and that attempts to follow the liberal political route will aggravate the crisis, not resolve it (Smith 1992; Obradovic 1996). A major weakness of this debate has been, however, that it has taken place almost exclusively at the general European level. The implicit assumption has been that the legitimacy crisis is the same throughout the whole of the EU, that, for example, the strengthening of political representation at the EU level through the European Parliament would lead to increased legitimacy in all member states. In contrast, the analyses in this book argue that 'the' legitimacy debate is composed for the most part of a set of *national* debates, and it might well be that while some initiatives undertaken at the EU level might ameliorate the legitimacy crisis in one country, they might exacerbate it in another.

The field of European studies needs therefore to draw more attention to the specifics of particular national debates on Europe. Seen in this light, it is particularly beneficial to study those countries which have held referenda and where the 'crisis perceptions' are apparently biggest, namely the Nordic states. Do those critical of the EU seem most concerned with the absence of all-European representative political institutions, as held by the liberal position, or do they think that those institutions already in place pose a threat to national sovereignty and identity? The Nordic referenda provide a 'test' not just of the public's 'yes or no attitude' to integration, but also of the assumptions about integration, national sovereignty or cultural autonomy that have underpinned the debate.

Presenting poststructuralism

The debate between rationalist and constructivist approaches to International Relations (IR) has recently reached the field of European integration studies, adding to the already lively debate between liberal intergovernmentalists and institutionalists (Jørgensen 1997; Christiansen *et al.*, 1999; Diez 1999; Moravcsik 1999a and 1999b; Puchala 1999; Kelstrup and Williams 2000). A similarly vibrant debate over the difference between constructivism and poststructuralism (or postmodernism as it is often labelled by those who do not sympathise with this position) is now on offer. (See, for example, Adler 1997; Campbell 1998a: 216–22; Katzenstein *et al.* 1998: 674–8; Ruggie 1998: 35; Wæver 1998a.) It is clearly beyond the scope of this chapter to go through each of these controversies; we would, however, if pressured, define ourselves as poststructuralists in the sense that our primary and most abstract concern is with the production of structures of meaning. More concretely, this implies that our research is focussed on national discourses on European integration, and we are in this respect close to the work done by other authors who have carried out discourse analysis of foreign policy (for example Jutta

Weldes (1996; 1999), Roxanne Lynn Doty (1996), and David Campbell (1998a)).[6] We might, however, be more *structuralist* than some of these authors in our claim that key political concepts of state, nation, society and 'the people' are highly influential – indeed structuring – for the way in which policies of 'Europe', and European integration, can be argued. This is not, however, as will be explicated in more detail by Ole Wæver in Chapter 2, to make the structurally determinist claim that these constellations can never be rearticulated. The most basic layer of discourse, that comprising the concepts of state and nation, is assumed to be highly resilient to change, not least because it has a historical trajectory which tends to give it a 'taken for granted', sedimented quality. But resilience should not be mistaken for impossibility, and our theoretical framework does therefore incorporate the possibility of change, even at the most deeply institutionalised level. The pressure for change can arise from external developments which challenge existing representations, as in the Danish case where the deepening of European integration in the 1990s has made a construction of the EU as pure intergovernmental cooperation increasingly difficult to sustain, thus challenging the basic state–nation construction. Or, one might trace change to individuals or institutions which seek to make an inroad into the debate by adopting an approach to Europe which implies a rearticulation of state and nation. While change is thus both possible and traceable the importance of the structure implies that attempts to construct a European policy which simply ignore the dominant constellation will in all likelihood fail to attract serious recognition within the debate. There is furthermore the difference between our theoretical approach and other related poststructuralist-constructivist studies that parts of our analysis build upon conceptual history as we trace the historical formation of those concepts which are important in the contemporary debate on Europe.[7]

Our reliance upon (broadly conceived) poststructuralism implies that we take key concepts from IR theory like 'the national interest' to be a point of contention rather than given prior to discursive and political processes (Weldes 1996). This position implies a break with rationalism's argument that state action is to be explained by states' pursuit of their preferences according to a particular utility function which weighs up the influence of important societal groups. The problem with this assumption is that even if a state, or more correctly its leaders, had successfully defined its utility function vis-à-vis European integration, and even if the government wished to act towards Europe on the basis thereof, the views of the electorate might differ significantly from those of the political and financial elites. In a democratic system this can cause problems for the elites in question, as, for example, has been experienced by Social Democratic parties which have had difficulties convincing their traditional voters of the virtues of adopting a pro-integration policy. The political elite is in this situation struggling to have its interpretation of what is in the national – or working-class – interest accepted by its electorate. The point is that the very identification of what constitutes 'the national interest' or 'the utility function' has itself become a contested issue.

As we shall see in the chapters dealing with the individual countries, this contestation takes place at several levels. First, there is often disagreement concerning the economic consequences of membership as well as whether particular groups are going to benefit over others. Second, whenever there is a heated debate in a given country, it is very likely to involve not only economic issues, but also whether the loss of *political* independence associated with membership or increased integration is offset by the possible *economic* gains. It is the latter form of political debate in particular – where economic and political factors are intertwined – which makes the determination of state preferences a very difficult matter (Wind 1997: 19), and it is not, as a consequence, possible to separate economic interests from political ones (Diez 1999: 361). A construction of Europe as a 'free market' with a limited set of institutions whose purpose is restricted to facilitating the transfer of information between states and monitoring compliance is, for example, also a political project in that it advocates a particular political-economic form of organisation. The fact that it does so by explicitly advocating a minimal degree of political control and institutionalisation does not make it less of a political project.

Our focus on how political actors seek to generate support for their constructions of 'Europe' should indicate that our approach involves a break with materialist explanations, but the point is not simply 'that ideas are important, too'. Liberal rationalism and parts of conventional constructivism acknowledge that ideas are at work in political debates, but treat them as separate from (material) interests (Laffey and Weldes 1997: 200). As a consequence their research becomes focussed on deciding which of the two factors, ideas or interests, is more influential. Our strategy, to be described in more detail in Chapter 2, is to investigate the way in which political discourses represent material interests *as well as* arguments about the desirability and validity of certain ideas, in this case ideas about the nation, Europe and European integration (Campbell 1998b: 25; see also Laclau and Mouffe 1985).

Before turning to a more thorough discussion of the challenge issued by neo-liberal intergovernmentalism, it may therefore be useful to point to where our approach differs from two prominent constructivist examinations of national constructions of Europe: those offered by Jachtenfuchs *et al.* (1998), and by Marcussen *et al.* (1999). The former constructs four ideal types of polity ideals for the EC/EU, and proceeds to identify which of these have been the choice of the major political parties in Germany, France and Britain in three phases between 1950 and 1995. Our analysis, by contrast, does not establish ideal types to which the individual countries are compared, but proceeds from the assumption that the meanings of concepts of 'state', 'nation' and 'Europe' are generated in specific national debate, and our analysis traces therefore the constructions of Europe as they have developed within national debates. Second, while our goal is to analyse the debate on European integration, our analytical starting point is not the conceptualisation of 'Europe', but the constructions of nation, state, people and society. To put it differently, even if Jachtenfuchs *et al.*'s mapping of dominant polity ideas is correct, it does not tell us why certain 'Europes' were put forward in a particular national context, how easily they might be changed, and what structures within a domestic discursive field govern these processes. The approach suggested by Marcussen *et al.* comes closer to our approach in that they, too, locate a nation-state identity to which the construction of Europe must conform. Their identifications of nation-state identity are, however, limited to a rather brief and descriptive characterisation – 'state-centred republicanism' in the case of France, 'parliamentary democracy and external sovereignty' in Britain, and 'federalism, democracy and social market economy' in Germany – whereas ours consist of more structurally explicit and detailed examinations of prevailing constructions.[8]

Liberal intergovernmentalism and the state of Denmark

Although constructivism, at least in its conventional form, has been on the rise within IR as well as within European Studies, there is still little doubt that liberal intergovernmentalism – and particularly the form associated with Andrew Moravcsik – occupies a central, if not *the* central place within the discipline (Wind 1997: 28). Liberal intergovernmentalism's insistence on the importance of state power, and social scientific epistemology and methodology, challenges the field in general and critical constructivism in particular. This challenge also, incidentally, illustrates a divide between the positivist tradition of American social science and the more sociological and humanistic tradition of Western Europe (Wæver 1998a). Moravcsik has on two recent occasions tied his criticism of constructivism specifically to our approach and we would therefore like to elaborate on the difference between his theory and ours.[9]

In an article entitled '"Is something rotten in the state of Denmark?" Construct-ivism and European integration', which reviews a constructivist special issue of *European Journal of Public Policy*, Moravcsik identifies the 'Copenhagen School', and argues that 'the force of continental constructivist theories appears to radiate outward from the Danish capital, where it is the hegemonic discourse' (Moravcsik 1999a: 669).[10] Judging from Moravcsik's review, not just some things, but most things are rotten in Denmark. To select the most prominent problems: construct-ivism does not formulate claims which can be empirically tested (Moravcsik 1999a: 670), it has no distinctive, testable hypotheses, and it does not test its claims against plausible alternatives (Moravcsik 1999a: 677). These are all problems concerning the choice of epistemology, and we doubt if we would be capable of fully living up to Moravcsik's scientific challenge. Our strategy has not been to proceed by generating testable hypotheses in the sense proposed by Moravcsik, nor have we constructed the individual chapters as a set of tests of our approach against liberal intergovernmentalism or, for example, in relation to adaptation theory which has been quite influential in the study of Nordic foreign policy (Petersen 1977 and 1996; Goldmann 1988; Mouritzen 1988). Our ambition has, on the contrary, been to present our analytical framework and a set of detailed applications of this framework to four Nordic countries. One might disagree with that choice, but we have thought it more important to develop the actual analysis itself rather than a detailed comparison of theoretical 'models'.

But if we leave the epistemological debate aside for a moment and engage instead with the substantial content of our the theories,[11] it might be asked why one should focus on debates, as we suggest, rather than on the Nordic governments' influence within EU negotiations, or, following Moravcsik, on which and how domestic actors successfully influence the formation of national preferences (Moravcsik 1993, 1997, 1998). Put bluntly, should not a study of debates be secondary to the prior goal of determining patterns of influence and power? Is there not some truth to the saying that 'talk is cheap' and consists mainly of rhetorical window-dressing covering the pursuit of interests? Our pragmatic answer is, first, that the liberal inter-governmentalist study of negotiations (by, for example, tracing concrete channels of influence from corporate interest groups) and our constructivist study of debates on European integration are simply analysing two different aspects of European integration; that we ask and answer different types of questions. Moravcsik's aim is to uncover what has been the *cause* of European integration, and he concludes that 'commercial interest provides the only empirically robust explanation for the long-term evolution of the EU' with ideas having only a secondary importance (Moravcsik 1999b: 373). European integration has proceeded because of governments pursuing their interests, not as an 'unintended consequence'. As Moravcsik wants to identify the causes of European integration he is concerned largely with the most influential – or powerful – states in the West European arena: France, Germany and Britain. As a consequence of his research design's focus on the causes of integration, he is not particularly concerned with the question of legitimacy. Individuals are presumed to adopt a particular attitude towards the EU depending on their economic interests; legitimacy then becomes a matter of satisfying most of the people, or social groups, most of the time (see also Majone 1996: 285–300).

Our focus on the debate on European integration in the Nordic countries implies that we are not concerned with what has *caused* the development of the EEC/EC/EU, the key issue in the intergovernmentalist–institutionalist debate (Puchala 1999: 327). Whether the EU has developed due to (powerful) states' pursuit of their strategic, commercial interest, as argued by liberal intergovernmentalism, or whether an independent institutional dynamic has had – in rationalist terminology – a causal effect, as claimed by the institutionalists, is from the point of view of small states in most situations a minor issue since the EU tends to assume the quality of an external fact in *both* of these cases. What matters is that the small state perceives itself as having a low degree of influence on the trajectory of the EU within both scenarios. Second, a rationalist analysis would want to establish whether the Nordic countries *were* influential or not vis-à-vis the EU. Following the procedure identified by Moravcsik (Moravcsik 1999b: 377), for example, one might first predict Finland's economic interest, then see whether it was held by the Finnish government, and then determine whether, or to what extent, the Finns succeeded in reaching their goals in EU negotiations. Our focus, on the other hand, is on how influence is discursively constituted within domestic debate: to what extent is the government seen as making an impact in Brussels or not, and how does this assessment influence the debate? In a situation where the relationship to the EU is highly politicised, as for instance prior to a referendum, determining the national degree of influence vis-à-vis Brussels might in itself be a contested issue at the heart of the debate. So while we agree with liberalism that a move 'beyond the state' to include the domestic level is necessary, its decision to do so by studying the state–society relations in terms of 'shifting pressure from domestic social groups, whose preferences are aggregated through political institutions' (Moravcsik 1993: 481) involves a different conceptualisation of the domestic 'level' than ours. Our analysis claims to be capable of identifying the most basic 'codes' which structure the way in which constructions of 'Europe' can be argued politically in a given country. These conceptual codes constitute a filter through which policies towards Europe need to travel to improve their chances of being considered legitimate by the wider public. This analysis operates at a higher level of abstraction than neo-liberal intergovernmentalism, and does not, in other words, provide an explanation of why, for example, the influence of particular social groups differs between issue areas.

That said, we cannot fully solve the question of the relationship between liberal intergovernmentalism and rationalism, on the one side, and our poststructuralism, on the other, solely by saying that they pursue different questions. Part of our disagreement stems from more fundamental differences concerning the conceptualisation of interests and ideas. Moravcsik, for example, has portrayed the Copenhagen School as saying that

> In this view . . . European integration is essentially a battle between nationalist and the European ideals, or, more precisely, a battle between various national ideals consistent and inconsistent with a united Europe. This view of integration remains prevalent among pro-European elites in many Continental countries, who are sincerely offended by the notion . . . that European integration is driven primarily by interest rather than idealism.
>
> (Moravcsik 1999b: 374)[12]

In contrast to this assertion, a central point of departure for the analyses in this volume is that there are 'competing Europes' inside (some, if not all) national discourses, and that it is in terms of their nature, and direction, that the desirability of Europe is contested (Wæver 1990). This *analytic* endeavour should not be confused with the adoption of a 'pro-European elite attitude'. While some of the contributors, like Moravcsik himself, have functioned as public and advisory academics this is, as in Moravcsik's own work, separated from the academic and analytical study of the debates on Europe presented in this book (Moravcsik 1999b: 385). Moreover, we are not arguing that European integration is driven by idealism rather than interests; what we are arguing, rather, is that the opposition between ideas and interests is less self-evident than Moravcsik assumes. The conceptual constellations we identify are not to be considered as 'ideas', but as structures which all policies on European integration need to construct themselves within regardless of whether material, economic and strategic interests or ideals of a united Europe are foregrounded.

Liberal intergovernmentalism has, of course, been highly contested within the field of European integration. But the central location of this perspective, and in particular Moravcsik's writings, is not the only reason why we have devoted extensive treatment to it in this introduction. Many of the points apply equally to the only other monograph to treat the Nordic EU debates in the 1990s from an explicitly theoretical point of view, Christine Ingebritsen's *The Nordic States and European Unity* (1998).[13] While located broadly within the same liberal tradition as Moravcsik, Ingebritsen argues that Moravcsik's theory has difficulties in explaining the Nordic cases because it 'assumes that the national interest can be determined exogenously according to the position of states in the international system' (Ingebritsen 1998: 41). To achieve a more adequate theoretical framework, she argues, one needs to 'know more about which economic interests are expected to win and which economic groups are expected to lose in the EC' (Ingebritsen 1998: 41). Liberal intergovernmentalism does, however, as laid out above, take state-society relations and non-state actors into account, and there seems therefore to be little reason to make a distinction between Ingebritsen's approach and the 'classical' one of Moravcsik.[14] Ingebritsen's conclusion is that the ending of the cold war was a precondition for Swedish, Finnish and Norwegian decisions to apply for EU membership. The difference in the Nordic countries' attitudes towards European integration is a cause of the different patterns of sectorial dominance within the countries' economies. 'Interest groups representing the leading sectors had distinct preferences and vital interests at stake in the accession process' (Ingebritsen 1998: 113). These interest groups influenced – directly and indirectly – the governments' position as well as the referenda. In short, 'The diverging paths to Europe conformed to the specificities of sectoral politics, not to the structure of the state, to membership in international institutions, or to class divisions within the society' (Ingebritsen 1998: 115).

Our individual country chapters are not going to conduct rigorous testing of the explanations of liberal intergovernmentalism. However, in contrast to a neo-realist analysis, both liberal intergovernmentalism and the analysis in this volume allocate significant importance to sub-state actors and processes, and we find it therefore useful to engage a couple of the central claims being made by Moravcsik and Ingebritsen. Consider the following three claims representative of the liberal view:

1   Ingebritsen concludes that 'The diverging paths to Europe conformed to the specificities of sectoral politics' (Ingebritsen 1998: 115). We take this to imply that when there is an agreement amongst the key sectors within a country then this should translate into a clear outcome in the referenda. In other words, if there is a high degree of support for European integration amongst leading sectors, then we should expect a high degree of support amongst the population.
2   'The most fundamental influences on foreign policy are, therefore, the identity of important societal groups, the nature of their interests, and their relative influence on domestic policy. Groups that stand to gain and lose a great deal *per capita* tend to be the most influential' (Moravcsik 1993: 483). Moravcsik makes here the claim that influence is a product of relative economic change. This claim is well suited to our focus on European referenda; we would assume that those groups who will experience the largest economic consequences of a given decision will mobilise their resources to be most influential on the outcome.

3   'Liberal theory suggests that fundamental constraints on national preferences will reflect the costs and benefits to societal actors; where these are weak, uncertain or diffuse, governments will be able to pursue broader or more idiosyncratic goals.' And 'The difficulty of mobilizing interest groups under conditions of general uncertainty about specific winners and losers permits the position of governments, particularly larger ones, on questions of European institutions and common foreign policy, to reflect the ideologies and personal commitments of leading executive and parliamentary politicians, as well as interest-based conceptions of the national interest' (Moravcsik 1993: 494). In short, governments will have a higher degree of influence when there is uncertainty concerning the outcome.

We will return to these three claims in the conclusion and discuss to what extent the trajectory in the Nordic cases have confirmed to liberalism's assumptions, and whether our analysis of discourses and concepts might provide a better explanation of the outcome in the four referenda.

Europe and Norden: complementary or conflicting communities?

The selection of 'the four Nordics' as the basis for a study of debates on European integration is, as already alluded to, motivated in part by the high number of referenda in the region and the public debates surrounding them. This provides us with an excellent basis from which to investigate the more precise contours of the EU's so-called 'legitimacy crisis', but the choice is also informed by more rigid comparative and theoretical reasons. First, as pointed out by Ingebritsen, while the Nordic countries do differ significantly in terms of their industrial sectoral organisation, they also share a number of characteristics. In terms of size and geopolitical location – with the possible exception of Sweden – all are small states; with the partial exception of Denmark, all are part of northern Europe; and in terms of political culture, all are Scandinavian welfare states as well as nation-states with high degrees of ethnic homogeneity. These similarities provide an excellent basis from which to conduct a more thorough comparative analysis of why the legitimacy crisis appears. Second, the Nordic countries are also embedded within a discourse about 'the Nordic', a discourse which emphasises the cultural, political and moral distinctiveness of Norden. There is a tradition, to be traced briefly below, of constructing 'Norden' as a particular community standing above the narrow rational and strategic concerns according to which states are normally said to pursue their foreign policies.

The crucial question in our context is to investigate the way in which this constructed community – 'Norden' – is employed within the debates on Europe, that is, to trace the political use of 'Norden' in attempts to legitimise particular approaches to European integration, as well as to investigate how these European debates have affected the belief in a 'common Nordic future'. Speaking more rigorously in terms of the theory advanced in Chapter 2, one might say that 'Norden' functions, or at least has the possibility of functioning, as an intermediate category between the national and the European level. This extra layer in the debates over Europe sets 'the Nordics' apart from states such as France, Germany and Britain who face the EU more directly.

The development of the Nordic community has fallen in two main stages. The first phase ran from the 1830s to 1864 and consisted of the cultivation of a common cultural Nordic identity coupled with calls for political integration. The Danish historian Uffe Østergård argues that this movement was quite similar to the contemporaneous national movements in Italy and Germany, the main difference being that Piedmont and Prussia succeeded in uniting Italy and Germany under their leadership while Sweden, which was assigned a similar role in the Nordic scheme, did not (Østergård 1994: 13). The Danish defeat in the war against Schleswig-Holstein (backed by Prussia and Austria) in 1864 marked the end of the political integrationist Scandinavism and the turn towards the cultural Nordicity which turned out to be strong enough to survive until today.

As it happened, the 'Nordic' developed in conjunction with the same modern nationalisms that underpin the current nation-states, and this inter-linkage between Nordism and nationalism was important in investing 'the Nordic' with a distinctly positive identity (Hastrup 1992: 227). The environment created by students and poets in Copenhagen in the 1830s and 1840s was crucial not only for the establishment of Scandinavism and Nordicity, but also for the development of Norwegian, Icelandic and Faroese nationalisms, all of which were born and nurtured in the capital of the Danish empire (Wåhlin 1994). These nationalisms constructed themselves in opposition to Denmark, but this opposition was rarely extended to 'Norden', which as a universal category was given a more specific interpretation in accordance with the individual nationalist struggles. In Iceland, for example, one could draw on a construction of Iceland as the original, essential Nordic; on the Faroe Islands, we find both the construction of similarity between the Faroese identity and the Nordic one, and later an additional figure: 'the Nordic' as the mediator between the Faroese and the Danish (Wåhlin 1994: 39, 48–9).[15] This entanglement of 'the Nordic' and the national thus provided an elegant solution with both universal and particular elements: 'the Nordic' could keep its universal, transnational appeal at the same time as each nation could construct itself as the quintessential 'Nordic' exemplar. As a consequence, 'Norden' has survived with a cultural Romanticism which is not normally bestowed on non-successful integrationist identities. While political integration failed in the middle of the nineteenth century, a set of 'low level' associations grew up independently from the initiatives at the governmental level. The most well known of these, the Norden Association ('Foreningerne Norden') was formed in 1919 around a programme emphasising cultural similarities and information about Nordic issues (Hansen 1994: 118–19), but also more specific and limited cases of Nordic cooperation took place, like the Nordic female teachers' cooperation from 1898 to 1905 (Hilden 1994).

The second stage in the development of the Nordic community took place after the Second World War when the tradition of cultural cooperation, primarily at the level of civil society, was continued and ambitious plans at the institutional level were introduced. (Østergård 1994: 15) The most notable of these proposals were the Scandinavian Defence Alliance of 1948–9, the Nordic Customs Union of 1947 and the Nordic Economic Union (NORDEK) of 1968 and 1969, but none were brought to a successful conclusion. This led to the description of the dynamics of Nordic cooperation, not as the 'spill-over' or 'spill-back' argued by neofunctionalism, but as 'spill-around', as failed attempts at extensive institution-building were 'compensated' by institutional innovations in other fields, as when the Nordic Council was established in 1951 in response to the failed defence alliance (Sundelius and Wiklund 1979: 65). The character of this integration has been described by Niels Andrén as 'cobweb integration': 'in which the significance and strength of a single thread or mesh is very small but the total result in many fields may be recognised as considerable' (Andrén 1967: 17). This led first Andrén and later Sundelius and Wiklund to suggest that there were perhaps more similarities between Nordic and European integration than commonly assumed (Andrén 1967: 17; Sundelius and Wiklund 1979: 59).

These similarities notwithstanding, the gap between the two communities widened in the 1980s and 1990s. While the EC accelerated its economic integration and developed a stronger political identity expressed in the adoption of the Single European Act and the Maastricht Treaty, Nordic cooperation was left largely on standby as the Nordics approached Europe. A discussion of this process must therefore involve not just an analysis of Miljan's 'reluctant Europeans', but also an appreciation of these countries as 'reluctant Nordics'.[16] Was European integration a threat to regional cooperation and previously successful identities like the Nordic one? Or did it on the contrary pose a new chance for a reinvigoration of a decaying 'Norden'? Could Norden continue to be seen as an alternative community by the opponents to the EU? Or, was Norden's only possible survival strategy to support Europe?[17] Opinions on these questions differed, amongst politicians as well as amongst academics (Joenniemi 1994; Wæver 1997: 319–24). Regardless of the answers to these questions, it was evident that the future of 'Norden' as a political, strategic, economic and cultural entity could not be debated outside of the European context. This is the case not because Europe in and of itself is more important, but because the political construction of 'Norden' within the four Nordic countries takes place *through* the debates on Europe. Even those who argue for 'Norden' as an alternative to the EU present this option *in opposition to* Europe, not in isolation from the European question. Put differently, since the early 1990s, it has been 'Europe' which conditions 'Norden', not 'Norden' which conditions 'Europe'. This, however, does not mean that 'Norden' is unimportant within the debates over Europe. While Norden is *dependent on* the articulation of Europe it is still *crucial* to the success of the competing national European projects, and a project which does not have a Nordic vision will be seriously weakened. This is not to say that a common construction of 'Norden', or a common set of contending 'Nordens', will necessarily be found in each of the countries in question. Nor would we expect identical 'Europes' to prevail across the region. Moreover, it is also quite likely that the importance of 'Norden' itself will differ between the different countries.[18]

The continuing success of Norden as a 'political card' is intimately related to the history of Nordicity and its inter-linkage with the evolution of nationalism. A similar romantic connection between the nations of Norden and Europe has never, on the other hand, been forged. The European movements of the inter-war period, like Coudenhove-Kalerghi's pan-European movement, or the Monnet and Schumann of the post-war era, did not find Nordic counterparts (Hansen 1969: 15 on Denmark in this context; Neumann in this volume). The absence of a political European federalist tradition meant, as will be shown in the country chapters, that those arguing in favour of European integration had no 'emotional Europeanism' to draw on in the 1990s. Those arguing in favour of Nordic cooperation as an alternative to Europe could on the other hand not only invoke the traditions of 'Nordicity', they also had much easier access to the classical nationalism than the disadvantaged yes-sides.

The structure of the book

The structure of this book is a relatively simple one. Chapter 2 presents the theoretical framework of the book in greater detail. It describes the relationship between our approach, poststructuralism and structuralism and locates the discourse analysis approach within the field of foreign policy theory. Viewing discourses as composed of a set of layered structures, it seeks also to address the question of change within and between discursive structures. The first layer consists of the basic constellation of the concepts of state and nation and possible other core, 'we', concepts, the second layer of the concept of Europe, and the third layer of the more concrete policies towards the EU.

Chapters 3 to 6 analyse the debates over European integration in each of the Nordic countries. They begin by presenting the situation vis-à-vis European integration in the 1990s and point to the core positions within the debate. The chapters then turn to the historical formation of the key concepts of state, nation and, in most cases, 'the people', describing how they came to be linked to one another in particular constellations which form the structuring reference point for the current debates on Europe. The third section of each chapter traces the significant developments in the post-war period. The fourth section of each chapter provides an analysis of the debates in the 1990s with a specific focus on the way in which the conceptual constellations have structured the construction of 'Europe', and the question of how the debate might continue to unfold is, finally, discussed.

The Conclusion consists of three parts: first, it sums up and compares the analyses of the four countries; second, it turns to the claims of Moravcsik and Ingebritsen presented above and discusses whether or not those claims have been supported by the four case studies; and, third and finally, the chapter reflects upon the future of 'Europe' in the Nordic countries.

Notes

*   A number of people have offered comments on and criticism of early versions of this chapter. I wish to thank the following in particular: my co-contributors, Barry Buzan,

Thomas Diez, Ulla Holm, Ian Manners, Karen Lund Petersen, Gearóid Ó Tuathail, Richard Whitman and Michael C. Williams.

1 The answers to the question 'Generally speaking, do you think that (our country's) membership is . . . ' are as follows: 'A good thing' (DK: 53 per cent; FIN: 40 per cent; S: 34 per cent); 'A bad thing' (DK: 24 per cent; FIN: 22 per cent; S: 38 per cent); 'Neither good nor bad' (DK: 20 per cent; FIN: 34 per cent; S: 25 per cent); 'Don't know' (DK: 4 per cent; FIN: 4 per cent; S: 3 per cent). *Eurobarometer*, no. 53, Spring 2000.

2 The term 'Norden' refers to the following countries: Denmark, Finland, Iceland, Norway and Sweden. It is commonly used within the Nordic area.

3 As illustrated by the opinion polls quoted in note 1, the main difference between Denmark and Finland is not that the level of EU support in Finland is higher, but that the question of European integration fails to take on the significance in Finland that it does in Danish politics.

4 For a comprehensive list of studies with theoretical and empirical resemblance to ours, see note 8 in Chapter 2 (p. 43).

5 Another limitation concerning polls, as for example those referred to in note 1, is that a negative view of the EU might not amount to a legitimacy crisis – or to a crisis for a pro-integration government – if the EU is not considered a very important issue. There are in other words two components to a legitimacy crisis: a negative view of the EU/integration amongst a 'large part' of the electorate and a location of the European question relatively high on the political agenda.

6 We might also mention a couple of works by the contributors to this book, which deal specifically with national discourses on Europe: Hansen (1996), Neumann (1996a, 1999), Trägårdh (1997) and Wæver (1990, 1996).

7 Our study is also focussed on competing discourses whereas, for example, Campbell's path-breaking study of US foreign policy focusses on the dominant one only. However, despite the differences between our work and Campbell's, there are also similarities in terms of the common emphasis on history and the development of discursive structures over time (Campbell 1998a: 222–5).

8 Since both Jachtenfuchs *et al.* and Marcussen *et al.* are articles, and thus briefer presentations, one should, of course, be cautious about drawing too clear-cut conclusions. And differences notwithstanding, we applaud the development of a variety of constructivist and poststructuralist analyses of European integration.

9 As noted in the Acknowledgements, this book project has been long in the making, but its theoretical approach has been launched in a series of working papers and unpublished manuscripts since 1989, which explains why Moravcsik engages the core argument of our book prior to its publication.

10 Strictly speaking, Moravcsik's use of the term 'Copenhagen School' is not quite accurate. The 'Copenhagen School' is normally used to identify the work on security carrried out by Barry Buzan and Ole Wæver (see Wæver *et al.* 1993; McSweeney 1996; Buzan *et al.* 1998; Huysmans 1998; Williams 1998), and while all of us, except Lars Trägårdh, have been closely associated with that school, we are also, to different extents, critical of it (Neumann 1998; Hansen 2000). The specific foreign policy theory used in this book has previously been labelled 'the Copenhagen coterie' (Neumann 1996b: 162).

11 I take Moravcsik's argument that 'meta-theory is not the solution but the problem' as a justification for engaging more with his key conclusion as to what has caused (the form of) European integration than with the question of what constitutes social science (Moravcsik 1999a: 678).

12 Moravcsik makes this point as a comment on Thomas Diez's presentation of the Copenhagen School.

13 Miles (1996) offers an extensive discussion of the policies of the Nordic countries, but does not apply a particular theoretical framework throughout.

14 It should be noted though that it is questionable whether Ingebritsen's analysis conforms to the high social scientific standards Moravcsik advocates. She does not, most importantly, test alternative explanations.
15 There is, however, also an example of the 'Nordic' as a negative frame of reference, namely in (not yet independent) Finland, where 'Nordic orientations' were associated with the Swedish speaking minority in Finland (Østergård 1994: 16).
16 If the 'crisis of Norden' lies in the problems of keeping together a Nordic political block in global politics, of giving political content and cohesion to a cultural community, the 'crisis of the EU' lies in one account, the liberal political one, in the absence of legitimate institutions of participation and in the other, the romantic account, in the absence of a European cultural identity (Wæver 1992a: 77). In this respect it seems as if the one community presides over exactly that which the other one lacks.
17 For an example of this position see the article by the heads of the Liberal parties in Finland, Denmark and Sweden, 'Skapa nordiskt EU-block' (Leijonborg, Norrback, and Ellemann-Jensen 1998), which argues in favour of overcoming the divisions between the Nordic countries in the EU.
18 It has been argued by two historians that 'The Nordic element was less conspicuous in the young nations such as Norway and Finland' than it was in Denmark and Sweden (Sørensen and Stråth 1997: 22). However, this 'historical inclination' might be offset by other factors, for example the strong European opposition in Norway.

References

Adler, E. (1997) 'Seizing the Middle Ground: Constructivism in World Politics', *European Journal of International Relations* 3, 3: 319–63.
Andrén, N. (1967) 'Nordic Integration', *Cooperation and Conflict* 2, 1: 1–25.
Arter, D. (1995) 'The EU Referendum in Finland on 16 October 1994: A Vote for the West, not for Maastricht', *Journal of Common Market Studies* 33, 3: 361–87.
Buzan, B. *et al.* (1998) *Security: A New Framework for Analysis*, Boulder, Col.: Lynne Rienner.
Campbell, D. (1998a) *Writing Security: United States Foreign Policy and the Politics of Identity*, revised edn, Minneapolis: University of Minnesota Press.
—— (1998b) *National Deconstruction: Violence, Identity, and Justice in Bosnia*, Minneapolis: University of Minnesota Press.
Christiansen, T., Jørgensen, K. E. and Wiener, A. (eds) (1999) *The Social Construction of Europe, special issue of Journal of European Public Policy* 6, 4.
Dahlerup, D. (1997) 'Amsterdam – en station på vejen', 24 September, <http://www.junibevaegelsen.dk/sturm/juninet/politik/art/24.09.97.11.07.html>.
Diez, T. (1999) 'Riding the AM-track through Europe; or, The Pitfalls of a Rationalist Journey Through European Integration', *Millennium* 28, 2: 355–69.
Doty, R. L. (1996) *Imperial Encounters: The Politics of Representation in North–South Relations*, Minneapolis: University of Minnesota Press.
Featherstone, K. (1994) 'Jean Monnet and the "Democratic Deficit" in the European Union', *Journal of Common Market Studies* 32, 2: 149–70.
Goldmann, K. (1988) *Change and Stability in Foreign Policy*, Princeton, NJ: Princeton University Press.
Hansen, L. (1996) 'Slovenian Identity: State Building on the Balkan Border', *Alternatives* 21, 4: 473–95.
—— (2000) 'The Little Mermaid's Silent Security Dilemma and the Absence of Gender in the Copenhagen School', *Millennium* 29, 2: 285–306.

Hansen, L. and Williams, M. C. (1999) 'The Myths of Europe: Legitimacy, Community and the "Crisis" of the EU', *Journal of Common Market Studies* 37, 2: 233–49.

Hansen, P. (1969) 'Denmark and European Integration', *Cooperation and Conflict* 3, 1: 13–46.

Hansen, S. O. (1994) 'Foreningene Norden 1919–94 – ambisjoner og virkelighet', *Den Jyske Historiker* 69–70: 114–31.

Hastrup, K. (1992) 'Nordboerne og de andre', in K. Hastrup (ed.) *Den Nordiske Verden*, Copenhagen: Gyldendal.

Hilden, A. (1994) 'Nordisk lærerindesamarbejde omkring 1900', *Den Jyske Historike* 69–70: 98–113.

Holm, U. (1993) *Det Franske Europa*, Aarhus: Aarhus University Press.

—— (1997) 'The French Garden is not what it used to be', in Knud-Erik Jørgensen (ed.) *Reflective Approaches to European Governance*, London: Macmillan.

—— (1999) 'The French Europe: A Discourse Analysis of the Relation between the Concept of State-Nation and Europe', Ph.D. thesis, University of Aarhus.

Howe, P. (1995) 'A Community of Europeans: The Requisite Underpinnings', *Journal of Common Market Studies* 33, 1: 27–46.

Huysmans, J. (1998) 'Revisiting Copenhagen: Or, On the Creative Development of a Security Studies Agenda in Europe', *European Journal of International Relations* 4, 4: 479–505.

Ingebritsen, C. (1998) *The Nordic States and European Unity*, Ithaca, NY: Cornell University Press.

Ingebritsen, C. and Larson, S. (1997) 'Interest and Identity: Finland, Norway and European Union', *Cooperation and Conflict* 32, 2: 207–22.

Jachtenfuchs, M., Diez, T. and Jung, S. (1998) 'Which Europe? Conflicting Models of a Legitimate European Political Order', *European Journal of International Relations* 4, 4: 409–45.

Joenniemi, P. (1994) 'Norden – En europeisk megaregion?', in S. Karlsson (ed.) *Norden är död – Länge leve Norden!*, Stockholm: Nordiska Rådet.

Jørgensen, K. E. (ed.) (1997) *Reflective Approaches to European Governance*, London: Macmillan.

Katzenstein, P. J., Keohane, R. O. and Krasner, S. D. (1998) '*International Organization* and the Study of World Politics', *International Organization* 52, 4: 645–85.

Kelstrup, M. and Williams, M. C. (2000) *International Relations Theory and the Politics of the European Union*, London: Routledge.

Laclau, E. and Mouffe, C. (1985) *Hegemony and Socialist Strategy: Towards a Radical Democratic Politics*, London: Verso.

Laffey, M. and Weldes, J. (1997) 'Beyond Belief: Ideas and Symbolic Technologies in the Study of International Relations', *European Journal of International Relations* 3, 2: 193–237.

Larsen, H. (1997) *Foreign Policy and Discourse Analysis: France, Britain, and Europe*, London: Routledge.

Lawler, P. (1997) 'Scandinavian Exceptionalism and European Union', *Journal of Common Market Studies* 35, 4: 565–94.

Leijonborg, L., Norrback, O. and Ellemann-Jensen, U. (1998) 'Skapa nordiskt EU-block', *Dagens Nyheter*, 17 February.

Lodge, J. (1994) 'Transparency and Democratic Legitimacy', *Journal of Common Market Studies* 32, 3: 342–68.

McSweeney, B. (1996) 'Identity and Security: Buzan and the Copenhagen School', *Review of International Studies* 22, 1: 81–93.

Majone, G. (1996) *Regulating Europe*, London: Routledge.

Marcussen, M. *et al.* (1999) 'Constructing Europe? The Evolution of French, British and German Nation State Identities', *Journal of European Public Policy* 6, 4: 614–33.

Miles, L. (ed.) (1996) *The European Union and the Nordic Countries*, London: Routledge.

Miljan, T. (1977) *The Reluctant Europeans: The Attitudes of the Nordic Countries towards European Integration*, London: C. Hurst.

Moravcsik, A. (1993) 'Preferences and Power in the European Community: A Liberal Intergovernmentalist Approach', *Journal of Common Market Studies* 31, 4: 473–524.

—— (1997) 'Taking Preferences Seriously: A Liberal Theory of International Politics', *International Organization* 51, 4: 513–53.

—— (1998) *The Choice for Europe: Social Purpose and State Power from Messina to Maastricht*, London: UCL Press.

—— (1999a) '"Is something rotten in the state of Denmark?" Constructivism and European integration', *Journal of European Public Policy* 6, 4: 669–81.

—— (1999b) 'The Future of European Integration Studies: Social Science or Social Theory?', *Millennium* 28, 2: 371–91.

Mouritzen, H. (1988) *Finlandization: Towards a General Theory of Adaptive Politics*, Aldershot, UK: Avebury.

Neumann, I. B. (1996a) *Russia and the Idea of Europe: A Study in Identity and International Relations*, London: Routledge.

—— (1996b) 'Collective Identity Formation: Self and Other in International Relations', *European Journal of International Relations* 2, 2: 139–74.

—— (1998) 'Identity and the Outbreak of War: Or why the Copenhagen School of Security Studies should include the Idea of "Violisation" in its Framework of Analysis', *International Journal of Peace Studies* 3, 1: 7–22.

—— (1999) *Uses of the Other: "The East" in European Identity Formation*, Minneapolis: University of Minnesota Press.

Obradovic, D. (1996) 'Policy Legitimacy and the European Union', *Journal of Common Market Studies* 34, 2: 191–221.

Østergård, U. (1994) 'Norden – europæisk eller nordisk?', *Den Jyske Historiker* 69–70: 7–37.

Petersen, N. (1977) 'Adaptation as a Framework for the Analysis of Foreign Policy Behavior', *Cooperation and Conflict* 12, 2: 221–50.

—— (1996) 'Denmark and the European Union 1985–96', *Cooperation and Conflict* 31, 2: 185–210.

Puchala, D. J. (1999) 'Institutionalism, Intergovernmentalism and European Integration', *Journal of Common Market Studies* 37, 2: 317–31.

Ruggie, J. G. (1998) *Constructing the World Polity: Essays on International Institutionalization*, London: Routledge.

Sæter, M. (1996) 'Norway and the European Union: Domestic Battle Versus External Reality', in L. Miles (ed.) *The European Union and the Nordic Countries*, London: Routledge.

Sørensen, Ø. and Stråth, B. (1997) 'Introduction: The Cultural Construction of Norden', in Ø. Sørensen and B. Stråth (eds) *The Cultural Construction of Norden*, Oslo: Scandinavian University Press.

Smith, A. D. (1992) 'National Identity and the Idea of European Unity', *International Affairs* 68, 1: 55–76.

Sundelius, B. and Wiklund, C. (1979) 'The Nordic Community: The Ugly Duckling of Regional Cooperation', *Journal of Common Market Studies* 18, 1: 59–75.

Tiilikainen, T. (1996) 'Finland and the European Union', in L. Miles (ed.) *The European Union and the Nordic Countries*, London: Routledge.

Trägårdh, L. (1997) 'European Integration and the Question of National Sovereignty: Germany and Sweden, 1945–1995', *Working Paper Series* no 2.50, Berkeley, Calif.: Center for German and European Studies.

Wåhlin, V. (1994) 'Island, Færøerne, Grønland og det nordiske', *Den Jyske Historiker* 69–70: 38–61.

Wæver, O. (1990) 'Three Competing Europes: German, French, Russian', *International Affairs* 66, 3: 477–99.

—— (1992a) 'Nordic nostalgia: Northern Europe after the Cold War', *International Affairs* 68, 1: 77–102.

—— (1992b) 'Det "nye" Tysklands internationale profil', *GRUS*, no. 36: 18–41.

—— (1996) 'The Struggle for "Europe": A Discourse Analysis of France, Germany and European Union', paper presented to the 'Rethinking Security Seminar' at the University of Southern California, 23 October.

—— (1997) 'The Baltic Sea: A Region after Post-Modernity?', in P. Joenniemi (ed.) *Neo-Nationalism or Regionality: The Restructuring of Political Space Around the Baltic Rim*, Stockholm: NordREFO.

—— (1998a) 'The Sociology of a not so International Discipline: American and European Developments in International Relations', *International Organization* 52, 4: 687–727.

—— (1998b) 'Explaining Europe by Decoding Discourses' in Anders Wivel (ed.) *Explaining European Integration*, Copenhagen Political Studies Press, pp. 100–46.

Wæver, O., Buzan, B., Kelstrup, M. and Lemaitre, P. with D. Carlton *et al.* (1993) *Identity, Migration and the New Security Agenda in Europe*, London: Pinter.

Wæver, O. and Holm, U. (forthcoming) *The Struggle for 'Europe': French and German concepts of state, nation and European Union*.

Weldes, J. (1996) 'Constructing National Interests', *European Journal of International Relations* 2, 3: 275–318.

—— (1999) *Constructing National Interests: The United States and the Cuban Missile Crisis*, Minneapolis: University of Minnesota Press.

Williams, M. C. (1998) 'Modernity, Identity and Security: A Comment on the "Copenhagen Controversy"', *Review of International Studies* 24, 3: 435–9.

Wiener, A. and Sala, V. D. (1997) 'Constitution-making and Citizenship Practice – Bridging the Democracy Gap in the EU?', *Journal of Common Market Studies* 35, 4: 595–614.

Wind, M. (1997) 'Rediscovering Institutions: A Reflectivist Critique of Rational Institutionalism', in K. E. Jørgensen (ed.) *Reflective Approaches to European Governance*, London: Macmillan.

2 Identity, communities and foreign policy

Discourse analysis as foreign policy theory

Ole Wæver

An analysis of domestic discourses on 'we' concepts like state, nation, 'people' and Europe can explain – and up to a point predict – foreign policies. When applied to the major European powers, it can explain and predict the development of European integration and security; when applied to medium and minor states like the Nordics, it explains mostly their dilemmas and problems – but occasionally they too impinge on overall European developments, not least via their referenda on European questions. This chapter presents the general conjecture of discourse analysis as foreign policy theory as applied in this book. The first section discusses briefly the attempts by different IR theories to integrate identity into explanations of foreign policy and argues the need for a modified poststructuralist approach (over a neo-realist, a neo-liberal or a mainstream constructivist one). The second section discusses different forms of poststructuralism in IR and thereby clarifies the meta-theoretical position of our theory, not least in relation to its – controversial – use of structure and explanation. Then, in the third section, it is spelled out how this can become a theory of foreign policy, that is, how discourse matters to policy and why it can therefore be utilised analytically. A crucial element in the present theory is the layered conception of discursive structure. The more exact components of these layers are presented in the fourth section, and drawing on a brief presentation of the analysis of France and Germany, a list of questions and distinctions are set up as a guidance for the study of our four Nordic cases. Finally, some more practical questions of methodology and operation are briefly dealt with before the book is mercifully allowed to proceed to its main matter: the study of the four countries.

Identity and foreign policy according to IR theory

National identity, new foreign policy theory, security – these themes are in demand and quite a few offerings are on the market, but none that convincingly combines these elements. Explanations from identity and culture have experienced a general revival in IR theory recently, sometimes as part of the constructivist turn (Finnemore 1996; Hudson 1997; Katzenstein 1996; Lapid and Kratochwil 1996a), sometimes within more rationalist frameworks (Posen 1993a, 1993b; Van Evera 1994). But the shared focus on culture and identity has, unsurprisingly, not led to agreement on how identity and culture should be studied or how they can inform a general theory of international politics.

The current debate within IR thus features a set of different theoretical arguments and ambitions with regards to identity. Neo-realists aim at integrating sub-state conflicts between antagonistic ethnic and nationalist groups within a structural theory of the international system, but without revising the 'identity of the constitutive unit' as being that of self-help (Posen 1993a, 1993b; Van Evera 1994; Kaufmann 1996). It has therefore been argued that neo-realism's lack of a theory of the state is repeated in its attempt to theorise about nationalism: as the coherent state/national identity is the ontological foundation for theory-building neo-realism becomes unable to theorise about the construction and re-construction of these identities (Krause and Williams 1996: 239–42; Lapid and Kratochwil 1996b: 123–4).[1] Neo-liberals like Keohane have challenged neo-realism's conclusions about the possibility of international cooperation beginning from the same construction of state identity; the neo-liberal argument has been that even with the self-help identity as the starting point, cooperation beyond and above the realist predictions is possible (Keohane 1989). Yet, while neo-liberalism has recently argued the importance of ideas, norms and the transparency of information, these are only factors which intervene between the self-help seeking state and the ensuing state action, not factors which change state identity itself (for an excellent critique of neo-liberalism's embrace of 'ideas', see Laffey and Weldes 1997). As a consequence, neo-liberalism does not seem to offer a compelling starting point for the development of a theory of how particular national and state identities are constructed, re-articulated and modified in the face of the evolving European integration.

If we are searching for a theory which unites a concern with identity, an attempt to provide a general foreign policy theory and a non-fixed concept of identity we might begin in the constructivist corner of International Relations where the most noticed identity-related, constructivist approach is probably Alexander Wendt's. He, however, concentrates on international systemic theory and thus on identities in the sense of the general meaning of 'state', of 'sovereignty' or of 'anarchy' (Wendt 1992, 1999). But for the purpose of understanding meanings generated from within (Onuf 1989; Ringmar 1996) – how each state, nation or other 'unit' has to create its own terms and rationales, its identity and foreign policy – this theory offers little advice. As argued by Erik Ringmar, Wendt's theory of identity formation is

> fundamentally one-sided: the problem of identity formation is constantly seen from the perspective of the system and never as a problem each state and each statesman has to grapple with. He can tell us why a certain identity is recognized, but not *what that identity is* . . . What Wendt needs, but cannot provide with the help of the theoretical perspective he has made his, is an account of how states *interpret* the structures of international politics and how they use them in interaction with others.
>
> (Ringmar 1997: 283)

Katzenstein's (1996) collection of essays tries to address this shortcoming by focussing on the construction of national identity in particular cases, for example the Soviet Union/Russia (Herman 1996), Japan and Germany (Berger 1996) and China (Johnston 1996). However, these analyses have not led to the development of a more general, systematic foreign policy theory, perhaps because constructivism seems committed to accepting a division between ideational and material explanations. This dichotomy leads many constructivists to confine 'identity' to the realm of ideational factors, which as a consequence tends to produce a theoretical design, where 'identity' explanations are measured against non-ideational, material factors. In the end the choice becomes one of either 're-integrating' the material explanations or, an even less attractive option, confining oneself to only explaining parts of the world of international politics. Furthermore, as foreign policy theory constructivism easily becomes a culturalist and/or cognitivist explanation for inertia and continuity. The set-up typically becomes a debate where on the one side a structuralist neo-realist argues that, for example, Germany or Japan ultimately will adapt to their position in the power structure and turn more power political and maybe acquire nuclear weapons, and on the other side a constructivist argues why a continued policy of relatively low profile is to be expected from Germany and Japan: it reflects deeper cultural factors (although the same culture could also cause militarism at another stage), and politics is path-dependent, so *now* a self-understanding has been created that sustains this policy (Berger 1993, 1996, 1998). Thus, typically, there is no constructivist suggestion for likely change, but a very strong theory of non-change, which stands well until change happens and it can then explain the firmness of the new status quo. This theory is unable to explain in a systematic way – beyond historical narrative – why the same cultural and historical background can sustain highly contradictory foreign policies, or to explain change, especially discontinuous change. It is necessary to have a view of identity that is both more *structured* and more *unstable*.

To achieve a shift towards more fully respecting the contingent, self-producing meaning systems of different actors (addressing the problems of the Wendtian perspective) and to break with the ideational problem of constructivism, the approach easily turns more poststructuralist. Poststructuralism is not, despite statements to the contrary, an ideational enterprise. Emanuel Adler argues, for example, in an attempt to distinguish constructivism from poststructuralism that the latter 'concedes too much to ideas; unless they are willing to deny the existence of the material world, they should recognize, as constructivists do, that "a socially constructed reality presupposes a nonsocially constructed reality" as well (Searle)' (Adler 1997: 332). But the poststructuralist understanding of identity is not an unreflected idealism; on the contrary, as has been pointed out by Laclau and Mouffe, for example, it is an attempt to resist the very dichotomous construction of idealism–materialism as those options from which we can explain the world: 'we will affirm the *material* character of every discursive structure. To argue the opposite is to accept the very classical dichotomy between an objective field constituted outside of any discursive intervention, and a discourse consisting of the pure expression of thought' (Laclau and Mouffe 1985: 108).

Poststructuralism(s) in International Relations

This is not to suggest that poststructuralism, as one big, coherent programme, has solved all the questions of IR and foreign policy analysis. Rather, that the challenge lies not in continued discussions of idealism versus materialism, but in more elaborate and systematic understandings of identity, in our case national identity, which work their way out of this distinction. This implies that the work in which most of the theory for the approach used in this book was developed – *The Struggle for Europe: French and German Concepts of State, Nation and Europe* (Wæver and Holm forthcoming) – takes the somewhat unorthodox position of combining on the one hand a view of language and meaning which is more poststructuralist and semiotic than it is constructivist and sociological, and on the other hand striving for an explanatory theory with quite a dose of structuralism. In relation to the history of (French) poststructuralism this is maybe not so surprising after all. Poststructuralism does not mean 'anti-structuralism', but a philosophical position that developed out of structuralism (in the French sense of the word), a position which in many ways shares more with structuralism than with its opponents (for instance, one of the celebrated, defining books of structuralism, Foucault's *Les Mots et les choses* is now seen as poststructuralist, and Derrida started publishing his poststructuralism in 1967 before the culmination of structuralism). In present day IR, poststructuralism has a quite different reputation which has a lot to do with the intra-disciplinary roles it performs: as a leading critical position, it is known more for its attacks, not least on (structural!) neo-realism, than for its own analyses (for a hostile counter-attack, see Østerud 1996, 1997; and responses by Patomäki 1997 and Smith 1997). If one turns to the main works of French, mainly philosophical, poststructuralists, there is, however, a possibility of a more disciplined, more strictly textual approach.

In our definition of discourse, we draw primarily on the tradition influenced by Michel Foucault, including notably Ernesto Laclau and Chantal Mouffe. (The understanding of language is primarily from Jacques Derrida, and again, Laclau and Mouffe.) If one needs labels, this might be called 'early poststructuralism'. It will be spelled out below – and has probably already become apparent above – that we deviate from much of what is currently seen as poststructuralist in IR, primarily through our conceptions of explanation, theory, causation and structure; here we are clearly more 'structuralist' than (what is now seen as) 'poststructuralist' (Weldes 1996 should be mentioned as an example of a text with a related ambition). However, we share with poststructuralists first of all an insistence on the contingency and fragility of all conceptual closure, of all discursive systems; this in contrast to Saussure who posited stable (if arbitrary) relationships between signifier and signified (Derrida 1978), and even more in contrast to the structuralism of Lévi-Strauss, which strives for ahistorical truths about human beings.[2] The view of language as paradoxical and a system with its own oddities and meaning, as ever fragile and contingent, is what ultimately sets poststructuralists apart from constructivists in IR, because the latter will be more inclined to possibly stable situations and take less interest in language as such (Zehfuss 1999, n.d.; Wæver 1999). On the other hand, with their shared roots in Saussure and close relationship to semiotics, structuralism

(French type) and poststructuralism are not incompatible. The prevalent American conception of poststructuralism as *anti*-structuralism is thus hard to reconcile with the way poststructuralism emerged as a radicalisation of structuralism by authors who were at the time (late 1960's) seen as structuralists.[3]

A large part of poststructuralist work on 'identity' in IR has concentrated on self/other relations. Although it is undoubtedly true that identities are often engaged in such contrasting games, it definitely does not follow from a poststructuralist starting point that antagonisms should be the main source of meaning. Quite the contrary – pure dichotomies are not very information rich in contrast to differentiated systems of difference. To put things very simply: the big difference between poststructuralist (and a few of the more philosophically minded constructivists) and mainstream IR (including mainstream constructivism) correlates with the subscription to either a *differential* or a *referential* view of language: language is to be approached as a system of meaning (i.e. from its internal mechanisms) or as a way of representing external reality (i.e. as more or less accurate). From a differential approach to meaning it follows that most identity will need complex, multidimensional systems to make sense, and difference only collapses into opposition in special situations (the ultimately impossible limit case). Then the pure contrast of self/other has a strong energising and entrenching capacity, but due to its circular nature (the Other is the opposite of us; we are the opposite of Him), the meaning of 'us' will usually involve other distinctions as well.[4] In addition to Others (cast as radically different and potentially threatening enemies) there are, for instance, friends and relatives – highly relevant in the present study, where the Nordics exactly enter each other's identity construction as something different from both self and Other, as close and yet different.

The tendency for poststructuralist identity writings to focus on self/other often brings them depressingly close to traditional peace research writings on 'enemy images'.[5] This is again a reflection of the intra-disciplinary role played by poststructuralism in IR (Wæver 1998b, unpublished). With an interest in non-antagonistic systems of differences, the problem is the opposite: to delimit a core constellation and thereby avoid having to represent the whole network in its total complexity as 'the meaning'. Our task is therefore to find small constellations of concepts that produce a nucleus of meaning from which much of a national discourse can be generated. Granted that identity is a relational concept, that it is produced through – and produces – juxtapositions between selves and others, we argue that it is both possible and necessary to identify specific concepts which historically have come to take on particular importance as 'vehicles' of identity production. While several poststructuralist analyses have shown the importance of the Other for the construction of the identity of the self, we turn the focus to investigate more systematically, theoretically as well as empirically, the elements involved in the construction of the self.[6]

This book's focus on national debates on Europe and European integration leads us to place the concepts of state and nation at the centre of analysis. The reason for selecting state and nation (and Europe) as central categories is that these are the forms the 'we' take. Thus, the claim for pre-eminence of state/nation over, say, conceptions of international relations or concepts of security is that they turn out to be particularly useful 'lenses of identity' through which to enter the Europe debates in specific national contexts.[7] Overall policies involve the question of how communities project themselves into the future. Therefore our key categories are the collectives, the 'we's': state/nation, but also Europe which has to be thought of as another 'we'. In the case of 'smaller' countries like the Nordics, a sub-regional category like Scandinavia/Norden enters in-between state/nation and Europe, and for a global power like the United States, the collective above state/nation will not be regional but either global or quasi-global like 'the West' (cf. Ruggie 1997). The analysis is thus focussed not simply on 'who' we are, but on the *way(s)* one conceives this 'we' through the articulation of different layers of identity in complex constellations of competition and mutual definition.[8]

Identity questions in international relations are too often translated into sociological questions about how people *are* or *live*, for example the question of the viability of European integration is seen as contingent on how different or alike the member nations are.[9] But as it is argued by most of the contemporary literature on nationalism, political identity is a discursive and symbolic construction (e.g. Anderson 1983). It is furthermore a second-order concept, where belonging to a nation means to identify with *the idea* of being, for example, French, and to assume that others do so as well – not to feel that one is 'identical' to other French (Gellner 1993; Wæver 1998a). By emphasising this, the current approach offers an alternative to the usual discussions about 'European identity', which turn into a discussion of the relative power of loyalty to Europe versus that to the nation/state (where the latter is still likely to win out and thus make 'Europe' seem irrelevant). More interestingly, one can ask how the nation/state identification is upheld by way of narratives on Europe, and conversely how Europe as a politically real concept is stabilised by its inner connections to other – maybe more powerful – we's. Thus we avoid a return to old discussions such as, are cosmopolitan loyalties really stronger than (or strong enough to withstand) nation/state identity in the case of crisis (the answer remains, probably not). This simply is not the question, because *what* the nation/state identity is has been transformed. This is not primarily the Wendtian question of how the meaning of statehood or nationhood (or sovereignty as such and identity as such) has changed, it is the question of how the different state/nations in *different* ways have 'Europe' integrated into their we's. Competitions between different political constructions of state and national identity thus typically play themselves out through debates on 'Europe'.

It is a crucial part of any foreign policy vision for any country in Europe (and some outside it) to imagine a Europe compatible with a vision of the nation/state in question. Europe can be simply a context shaped so that it is hospitable to 'us' – community being only our own nation/state conceived in narrow terms – or parts of our identity can be projected on to 'Europe' as such. In either case, Europe has to be conceived as a political construction drawing on the national traditions for how to think politics, that is, how to think state and nation. We therefore expect that Europe is not (in a logical sense) an external 'issue' but holds an internal relationship to state/nation. A basic grasp of national modes of conceiving state/nation can therefore be extended to understanding the way Europe is articulated in national contexts.

In the opening line of the section on 'identity and foreign policy', we called for a perspective that combines identity, foreign policy theory and security. The last component enters in this way: the identity–foreign policy linkage is sealed by a focus on security (in the sense of high politics, big questions). It delineates the sphere of validity for the theory and inside this field of overall policy existential concerns about 'the general direction' in which things are developing, and about identity and foreign policy, become tightly linked because here it is always necessary for policy makers to be able to present a convincing narrative of how the present trends (and thus one's own present foreign policy orientation) point towards a future which is hospitable to an attractive vision of the self. Therefore, it must always be possible to articulate the core idea of the nation/state in some acceptable way that fuses with a vision of Europe which both politically seems to leave space for 'us' and discursively makes sense in the national political lexicon. If such an articulation becomes unconvincing, the general policy becomes unstable, and change is imminent (to which we return below). If the state in question is one of the leading members of the EU (read, France and Germany) such a turn is always a risk to the project as such. In some cases (the Intergovernmental Conference (IGC) on a new treaty and not least the ratification of this through national referenda), the smaller states can upset the process too (read, Denmark 1992). This positive role of 'security' for the theory is a surprise due to the line-up of competitors in IR theory. The general prejudice is that the more traditional the theory, the better it is suited to dealing with security, the more constructivist and radical it is, the more difficulties it will have with security. To us it is quite the contrary: security and high politics form the existential pressure that makes the theory work.

Discourse analysis as foreign policy theory

Structures of meaning can explain and elucidate foreign policies. Finding and presenting in a systematic way patterns of thought in a specific country will always be helpful in making the debates and actions of that country more intelligible to other observers. Discourse analysis shares this endeavour with many writers coming out of the humanities or traditional(ist) IR. Explaining how political thought makes sense in, for example, France and Germany hopefully makes it easier for foreign observers in particular to *understand* these two countries. However, we try to go one step further: foreign policy can be partially *explained* (*how* partial and *why* only partially will be discussed below) by a *structural* model of national discourses.

Discourse analysis works on public texts. It does not try to get to the thoughts or motives of the actors, their hidden intentions or secret plans. Especially for the study of foreign policy where much *is* hidden, it becomes a huge methodological advantage – and one inherent in the approach – that one stays at the level of discourse. If one sticks rigorously to the level of discourse, the logic of the argument remains much more clear – one works on public, open sources and uses them for what they are, not as indicators of something else. What interests us is neither what individual decision makers really believe, nor what are shared beliefs among a population (although the latter comes closer), but which codes are used when actors *relate* to each other. Thus, the German discursive structures are in the last instance properties neither of the German people, nor of German politicians but of the German political arena.

A central feature of our theory is to be conscious about this and not slide between discourse and speech on the one hand and perceptions and thought on the other. If one stretches discourse analysis to telling us what people think, and why they do what they do, at first one gains a lot in explanatory reach, but then numerous problems and unjustified inferences emerge. What is often presented as a weakness of discourse analysis – 'how do you find out if they really *mean* what they say?', 'what if it is only rhetoric?' – can be turned into a methodological strength, as soon as one is conscientious in sticking to discourse as discourse. One often finds a confusion of discourse analysis with psychological or cognitive approaches, or a commonsensical assumption that the 'real' motives must be what we are all interested in, and texts can only be a (limited) means to get to this. Not so! Structures within discourse condition possible policies. *Overall* policy in particular must hold a definite relationship to discursive structures, because it is always necessary for policy makers to be able to argue where 'this takes us' (who they have to argue this to depends on the political system, but they are never free of this obligation) and how it resonates with the state's 'vision of itself' (Kissinger 1957: 146).

It is a not overly well-guarded secret that the discipline of International Relations is disappointed with its sub-discipline Foreign Policy Analysis. And that the grand theorists have not been very good at integrating domestic and international explanations. While domestic factors are usually involved in empirical studies as part of the explanation, most IR *theorists* have found it very difficult to see how the two sides can be linked in a coherent way. Stanley Hoffmann, as someone who has actually done both – written about IR theory as well as (French and American) foreign policy – frankly admits that he has been unable to bring the two together and has adopted a dual personality doing sometimes the one, sometimes the other (Hoffmann 1989: 266–7). Often, IR theorists send off 'domestic' explanations to be dealt with separately, allegedly by the sub-discipline FPA, Foreign Policy Analysis (previously CFP, Comparative Foreign Policy). This is done with a certain ambivalence as it is widely felt that CFP/FPA has not only been unable to deliver what it promised, but also that it is unlikely to do so in the future. Robert Keohane and Joseph Nye argued, for instance, in 1987, that they felt it unsatisfactory that they had concentrated their theoretical work at the level of the international system; that it was necessary to include the domestic arena. On the other hand, they added that they were afraid that opening up to the domestic arena would forfeit the cogency of their theory. This they believed was the experience of earlier attempts to integrate a theory of domestic politics into an international relations theory (Keohane and Nye 1987: 739–40; Nye 1988; cf. Waltz 1979).[10]

Our intention is in response to suggest a *structured* analysis of the domestic arena, which is consciously 'minimalist' in a way not unlike Kenneth Waltz's neo-realism:[11] we want to say a few important things from a limited, maybe even elegant, set of premises (see Wæver 1990a, 1990b, 1994, and in preparation). As Robert Keohane has argued (1989: 30), 'the next major step forward in understanding international co-operation will have to incorporate domestic politics fully into the analysis – not on a merely ad hoc basis, but systematically'. Such a minimalism has its price: we could often 'explain' more easily some specific policy change by taking in specific domestic factors, but this would take structure out of the study and reduce it to *ad hoc* explanations.

Traditional Foreign Policy Analysis usually falls in one of two categories: a set of causal explanatory factors (the tradition from Rosenau's pre-theory) or a decision-making model (the model of Snyder *et al.*). For such theory to be structured or even elegant, the first type needs to specify a hierarchic set of domestic 'factors' and the second needs a formalised decision-making model. This has usually not materialised. Our minimalist, structured approach is very clear about *how* it produces its explanations (by clarity about variables and their relationship), and therefore has the potential for producing more clear-cut conclusions and thus knowledge about general patterns.[12] Thereby, it aspires to make something close to predictions (to be specified and qualified in the pages following).

We want to show that the longer lines of foreign policy can actually be explained without making use of the incoherent pool of *ad hoc* domestic 'causes'. The basic thesis is that although not every single decision fits the pattern to be expected from the structures used in the analysis, there is sufficient pressure from the structures that policies do turn within a certain, specified margin onto the tracks to be expected. At some junctures the situation will be very open, but discourse analysis can then specify what the options are – even if it cannot say which is the more likely – and it can make sense of each of them in the light of the general structure. To moderate the theoretical claims made here: this is not a general theory of foreign policy in the sense that it will be able to deal with every and all foreign policy issues. Narrow, compartmentalised issues will often be better explained by more classical decision-making theories. Discourse analysis will have its value first of all for 'overall' policies, whereas a decision on the approved level of nitrite in salami is likely to be more unpredictably influenced by issue specific lobbying interests.

The basic idea is to let discourse analysis deliver the coherent, well-structured constraints on foreign policy that have been missing in Foreign Policy Analysis by zooming in on discourse and the structures that organise it. The first precondition for doing this is to clarify one's basic assumptions about *language*. To see structures in language is not easy as long as one works from a traditional (referential) understanding of language, where words and concepts are names used in order to make reference to objects out there in reality and where the structure and logic of language therefore is to be captured by studying these relationships between words and things. A referential understanding will not have much more to work with than the degrees of deviation from the ideal of language as a transparent medium. Works in this tradition therefore often draw on psychological explanations of how words get stuck in specific meanings and how certain images or perceptions get used as filters for future impressions (the psychological approach to foreign policy; more on this below). Here language itself does not really become a separate object of analysis and focus typically moves on to the psychological level which leads to questions on how we know what people *really* think and how misperceptions can be corrected.

Studies of 'perceptions' or 'belief systems' or 'images' in Foreign Policy Analysis have a basically referential concept of language. Therefore, their various insights become disjoined instances of how a subject relates to the world out there; there is no place in these theories for overarching codes that regulate what is meaningful at a given place and time. Furthermore, it is difficult to avoid a hierarchy of importance where the view held by the actors is somehow more important than what they say. As soon as one opens up to an interest in what people really think (which we consciously bracket completely), this becomes the criterion to judge all texts.

If, however, in contrast, we work from a differential understanding of language, meaning is located in the differences among concepts – we know how to use the term horse by the distinctions differentiating it from other animals, from other means of transportation as well as through other sets of distinctions (Saussure 1959). Then language is a system, and we can study its structure as a separate stratum of reality. It is not everything – the world is more than language and other meaning systems – but it is hard to do much of what we as scholars are interested in doing without drawing on this layer. Everything that includes statements about meaning has to involve an understanding of these systems, and thus there is a discursive element to more or less all we could find interesting. It is not the only element, but it is possible to focus on this. (How important – and explanatorily 'efficient' – it is depends on the degrees of autonomy, structuredness and obligations, one imputes to it. We return to this below.)

Discourses organise knowledge systematically, and thus delimit what can be said and what not. The rules determining what makes sense go beyond the purely grammatical into the pragmatic and discursive, linking up to some extent to the traditional studies of 'history of ideas' in terms of 'how did they think in different periods', or more precisely: how is the conceptual universe structured into which you have to speak when acting politically? Subjects, objects and concepts cannot be seen as existing independent of discourse. Certain categories and arguments that are powerful in one period or at one place can sound non-sensible or absurd at others. Instead of starting in the referential way by taking the link between subjects and objects as the starting point, discourse analysis is about easing those ties and treating language as an independent system, and studying its connection to what is 'outside' as contingent on the operations internal to language as discourse. As summed up nicely by Jens Bartelson: 'a discourse is a system for the formation of statements'[13] (Foucault 1972; Dreyfus and Rabinow 1982; Bartelson 1995: 70).

Discourse analysis looks for the rules governing what can be said and what not. It argues – in our version at least – that discourse forms a system which is made up of a layered constellation of key concepts. Discursive practice has a duality of depending on (and thereby actualising) as well as reproducing/reformulating the various levels of the discursive system. Discourses are made up of statements, and what makes for the unity and coherence of a discourse is simply the regularities exhibited by the relations between different statements. This sounds like discourse is only a kind of afterthought, an empirical registration of a coincidental pattern. But Foucault was insistent that discourse is the *precondition* for statements: a discourse is a system for the formation of statements, and not every statement can be made as rules govern the formation of statements. These rules on the other hand cannot be observed independently of the statements.[14] Thus, the discourse is the regularity of dispersion. When do we then say that we confront a particular discourse? And when is one discourse different from another? A discourse is the set of variations it is possible to generate from a given structure, and the answer to the question of what discourses there are, and how to systematise them, follows from the models we invent in our attempt to make sense of the Europe debates in our four case studies.

Discourse analysis moves one away from a focus on 'things' as well as from one on 'words' (or on their relationship) towards an interest in 'a group of rules proper to discursive practice. These rules define not the dumb existence of a reality, nor the canonical use of a vocabulary, but the ordering of objects' (Foucault 1972: 49). Foucault's interest is thus not linguistic in the sense that he analyses the meaning given to this or that word, what he wants to investigate is, on the contrary, how, for instance, 'criminality' or 'sexual deviation' come to appear as objects for specific medical or psychiatric discourses (Foucault 1972: 48).

This approach has advantages and disadvantages in terms of its necessary assumptions. This is most clearly seen by stressing that it stays at the level of discourse: what is read is text, and what is constructed from it is a model of a structure in discourse, and explanations work if discourse is important. The approach searches for structure and meaning exactly at the level where meaning is generated: in the discursive universe. In a specific political culture there are certain basic concepts, figures, narratives and codes, and only on the basis of these codes are interests constructed and transformed into policies. Basing a study on this level rests on three assumptions: 1) these codes put relatively narrow limits on possible policies; 2) the codes are sufficiently inert so that they can be seen as 'causal' factors in relation to policies (together with other causes) and so that one can study the way they are transformed as an effect of changing political constellations; and 3) it is possible to locate the most important discursive space in which the actor in question is operating. In the case of the particular study undertaken in this book it is claimed that the codes, cultures and concepts are still primarily following national lines. Therefore, we are studying the national political discursive structures dominant in the four countries in question. As regards the relationship between 'interests' and discourse, it is our argument that interests cannot be presented by political actors outside of the discursive structure, that an interest-based argument is always made on the basis of a particular distribution of layered identities (see also Weldes 1996 and Jepperson, Wendt and Katzenstein 1996).

Public, discursive activity constitutes a realm with its own coherence, logic and meaningful tensions and by studying this one can capture strong structuring logics at play in foreign policy. Foreign policy discourse – as 'public logic' – is limiting for future moves, and it has deep connections to conceptual constellations in other arenas involving the same core concepts, such as state and nation. Thus, instead of the customary image of political speech as haphazard and offhand, we substitute an idea of politics as a constant and relatively tight loop, where the political argumentation on a specific issue is strongly dependent on the basic conceptual logic which is available in a society, and at the same time reproduces or modifies this conceptual code, thereby setting the conditions for the next political struggle.

A main problem with much structuralism and to a large extent also with Foucault's theory of discourse is that change appears in the form of incomprehensible jumps between synchronic and structural orders. From one order everything is suddenly different and we are in another constellation of mutual conditioning. This is to some extent a necessary price to be paid for upgrading synchronic analysis. Foucaultian discourse analysis studies logical spaces; how meaning is governed by specific rules, and thus how a number of seemingly contradictory and opposed enunciations can be seen as regulated by some system defining possible, meaningful speech. A logical space can be constructed as a whole age, and we have concepts like Foucault's episteme where it is assumed that a certain age is marked by a specific mode of reflection. The discursive space can also be more limited and in competition with other discourses, but still kept together by its own internal rules of formation: thus its rules are basically synchronic. In any case, the perspective becomes synchronic, and in the last instance change either presupposes the Lévi-Straussian kind of ahistorical and comprehensive structuralism where there is one system covering it all and therefore transformation rules internal to the system bring us from one system to the other, or we must assume some kind of Hegelian self-transformation according to the inherent logic of contradictions, or finally point at some external and then incomprehensible force. It is hard to conceptualise change as stemming either from an interaction of competing discourses (since the source of contradictory coherence is *in* the separate discourses) or from non-necessary internal features.

One of the advantages of the *layered* discursive structure we suggest is that it can specify change within continuity. Change is not an either/or question, because we are not operating at one level only. This further has the effect that the question of what is the 'dominant' discourse in a sense becomes tricky, in a sense less controversial. That something is in 'opposition' or even 'marginalised' means only that it is 'outside' and 'different' at the level of manifest politics, most likely it *shares* (essential) codes at the next (deeper) level of abstraction. The 'dominant' political line and the main opposition most often share a lot (except *the* question on the agenda), and the more marginalised opposition shares less, but still some basic codes etc. This follows from the fact that political opponents relate to each other, and therefore almost always deal with some of the same issues and use some of the same concepts and images while struggling to reformulate and conquer other key terms (Laclau and Mouffe 1985: Chapters 3 and 4).

This is no complete solution. Since we do not make the Lévi-Straussian assumption of an over-arching structural logic, our systems are all contingent, and it is – and *should* be – possible to imagine a change beyond the system. In that case, we can say very little of how things would look. We have not solved the logical problem that structural analysis of logical spaces inevitably orders its material into a synchronic pattern. We have only placed a set of Foucaultian boxes within each other which enables us to perform a dynamic analysis up to a certain limit.

The metaphor of 'depth' is not to imply that the deeper is truer or that the surface is eternally contained within the deep structure which it can only continue to repeat.

Rather it refers to *degrees* of sedimentation: the deeper structures are more solidly sedimented and more difficult to politicise and change, but change is always in principle possible since all these structures are socially constituted.[15] When a pressure is building up in a system – when the discourse does not easily handle a problem anymore – it is possible at first to make 'surface changes' which keep all the deeper levels intact, but this might be more and more uncomfortable, more and more unstable; and therefore at some point a deeper change might be carried out by the same actor or through the replacement of the actor with someone representing a different position (Goldmann 1988: 5–13). If this happened, it would be costly to the original actor, and it would mean that a number of other issues – beyond the one causing the change – would suddenly be cast in a new light.

Discussing 'change' we are therefore not addressing the question, 'is it possible or not possible to change something?' It is only a question of how much pressure is necessary, what degree of political cost can be tolerated in breaking a certain code – in the last instance anything is possible. Some changes are just very unlikely, or would if they happened imply very dramatic changes of many other issues. And adjustments made on the 'surface level' might have unforeseen consequences as the costs materialise at a deeper level (cf. Holm 1993, 1996, 1997).

Understanding discursive systems makes it possible to predict in the following way:

- If the dominant policy and discourse seems to be well functioning, if no major pressures or anomalies are present, one can take this system as *basis* and make rather precise and strong predictions (i.e. the German situation at present). These derive from both knowing which position in the 'map' of the structure is in charge and from knowing what are the other currently powerful positions.
- If the system is under pressure, one cannot take the specific position in the system as such as premise but can only move one level down and say what other combinations are possible on the basis of the deeper elements. And if the crisis is tough, then move down one more level.

In the first case the theory puts itself at a risk by suggesting rather far-reaching predictions (deductions), and thereby making some kind of soft 'test' possible, because a given position in the structure is sufficiently specific that it constrains in quite rigorous ways. In the second case, the theory does not make specific predictions about future policy; but it does make two other kinds of predictions, first that there will be more dramatic change, and second that there are certain possible directions this can take (but not which one is most likely). In the second case it can therefore happen that several policies are presented as possible although they are at the surface level (concrete issues) extremely far from each other; what they share is the trait of being logically possible constructions on the basis of the available basic discursive elements. The model basically makes 'negative predictions', it tells what is impossible given a certain structure (and what would therefore only become possible with a deep structural change).[16]

This concept of structure can be thought of as parallel to the one of international political structure in (modified) neo-realism. According to John G. Ruggie, the three tiers (or levels) of the international political structure are to be seen as successive depth levels, and the concept of structure is generative, meaning that

> They are not visible directly, only through their hypothesised effects. [The second tier] mediates the social effects of the deep structure [first tier], but within a context that has already been circumscribed by the deep structure . . . [The third tier] comes closest to the surface level of visible phenomena, but its impact on outcomes is simply to magnify or modify the opportunities and constraints generated by the other (two) structural level(s).
>
> (Ruggie 1983: 266, 280)

Every new layer adds specifications and variations on the deeper one, but one cannot take a gradual change at, for instance, the third layer and say that it starts to weigh heavier than the second one; either one is still inside the frame set by the prior 'choice' at the first and second level, and then the changes at level 3 are variations on this basic premise, *or* pressure becomes sufficiently great to generate a change at the first or second level. Change will in the latter case be to a radically new agenda, where several basic premises have changed and one will not be able to see this new situation as an extrapolation of the change happening with the factor at level 3: the system makes a 'jump' when there is a change at a deeper level.

State, nation and Europe: the layered framework

What are then more concretely the layers that make up the domestic discursive structure? We suggest a three-tiered structure built on the general principles of discourse analysis and the relational understanding of identity laid out above: a structure which step-wise adds specificity and constraints to the analysis of the European debates, not only in the Nordic countries, as discussed in this book, but in other European countries as well.[17] The three-tiered framework should not be understood as implying that distinct discourses are located on either of the three different levels: that some discourses on Europe are located on the first, most basic, level while others are to be found on levels 2 or 3. Rather, each discourse on Europe comprises – or articulates itself around – all three levels simultaneously. In other words, a specific European policy (level 3) will involve a construction of a particular 'Europe' (level 2), building on a construction of the state–nation constellation (level 1). While the specific policies are often the most manifest level within a debate (few people discuss explicitly primarily at the first level), they are not in other words what structure the deeper layers of the debate.

First layer: the basic conceptual constellation of state and nation

The first layer consists of the basic constellation of the concepts of state and nation; it asks the questions, what is the idea of the state, what is the idea of the nation, and how are the two tied together? It is often useful to begin the 'mapping' of the basic state–nation idea with a look to the two 'ideal types': the French and the German constructions.[18] France's first layer consists of a *fusion* of state and nation, not a specific concept of state or a specific nation but the very fact that the two have to stand in a mutually constitutive relationship.[19] This construction is also known under the rubrics of the 'Western' type of national identity (in Kohn's classical distinction between Eastern and Western nationalism), or a 'political or civic' national identity (Smith 1991). Two more elements are present in this very general 'French' model of the state–nation: the necessity of *some* external – preferably European – role (attached to the state), and the necessity of a foundation for the nation in the *patrie* (elaborated in Holm 1997 and Wæver and Holm, forthcoming).

This constellation of state and nation provides a specific set of constraints and possibilities, both in terms of how foreign policy has to be presented, how 'Europe' can be thought, and whether and how one can become 'French'. One of the key structuralist points of our framework is that the constellation of state and nation at the first level exerts considerable constraining power; thus while it is possible to initiate political projects which involve a different nation–state construction, this is a much more difficult endeavour than remaining within the basic constellation. One of the most important constraining features in the French case is that the 'French interlocking' of the nation and the state implies a limited range of manoeuvres in terms of how 'Europe' can be approached: 'Europe' has to be articulated as not threatening the bond between the nation and the state. In the case of France itself, this has meant that recent 'France–Europe constructions' have come in three forms: 1) an external relationship between 'France' and 'Europe', with Europe as the scene on which France acts; 2) through a 'doubling of France' where Europe is created as a larger France which takes on the tasks and ideals of France because France has become too small to project its universal values itself; and 3) to execute the typical French state–nation operation on Europe as such, that is, to create a Europe that is French in its form, but not with a distinct France in it (Holm 1993). But a similar set of 'country-Europe' constructions are not necessarily as easily available in non-French cases; as the next chapter will show, Danish discourses operate with a tight link between the nation and the state which resembles the French construction, but French politicians have, because France is a European great power, the possibility of envisioning, for example, a 'doubling of France' or to create a French-type Europe – Danish political actors on the other hand simply cannot construct similar 'Danish directed' Europes as realistic scenarios.

The German basic constellation entails a rather different construction of the state and the nation as well as the relationship between them. The original German nation differs from the political nation of the French lineage (which is, in principle, open for those who wish to belong to it) by its emphasis on culture, language and blood: one has to be born into the *Kulturnation* to be a member. The classical praise for this criteria of nationhood came from Herder who not only heralded the organic nature of the nation, but also, at least initially, was highly suspicious of the necessity and desirability of the state. His fear was that the organic essence of the nation would be threatened by the intervention of the non-organic state. This view was obviously not going to dominate German history: rather than Herder's absent state, the Hegelian 'power state' became victorious (Wæver 1992; Wæver and Holm forthcoming). The Hegelian 'power state' was not only involved in turning the German Association into a German state, it also involved strong external power projection. Crucially though, for our purpose of establishing a more general theoretical framework, the German trajectory exemplified by Herder and Hegel did not lead to the tight coupling of the idea of state and nation as found in the French case. Even when the dominant concept of the state was a Hegelian power state, the state and the nation could still be thought of as two independent entities.

The post-war era implied a break with the Hegelian state, a whole generation of intellectuals insisting on what could be called 'the anti-power state' – the Hegelian idea of the state reversed 180 degrees – as the necessary response to the disasters the Hegelian German state had brought the world. The Kulturnation was divided into two (or in some sense three and a half) states, but because of its ability to exist independently of the state, this was not as problematic as if a similar division had occurred in France. The German construction of state and nation as two separate ideas implies that the 'European question' can be answered through a combinatorics of the typical state idea and the typical nation idea: power state or non-power state can be combined with Kulturnation or absence of Kulturnation, producing four combinations (Wæver 1996: 14) – it is not constrained by the reliance on one particular construction as in the French case.

These two constellations, the French and the German, have been developed and analysed by Ulla Holm, Henrik Larsen and Ole Wæver (Holm 1993; Wæver 1996; Larsen 1997; Wæver and Holm forthcoming). However, they also have a general relevance beyond their concrete, empirical instantiations in the French and German political discourses. On the one hand, since the meanings of the concepts of state and nation are discursively constructed as part of each individual, national history, it is not possible to make an overall typology of possible state–nation concepts or a very systematic definition of what to include at layers 1, 2 and 3, and one has therefore to find each individual country's unique constellation through concrete empirical textual work. On the other hand, while particular constellations cannot be deduced abstractly from the French and German cases, these cases can nevertheless be used as a first theoretical heuristic device as one might use these two different constructions to trace the historical construction of the idea of the nation and the state, and their relationship in one's own case.

First, one may ask whether the country in question spins its identity around a tight coupling between the nation and the state, as in the French case, or whether the two can be thought of independently of each other as in the German one. Second, one should look more carefully as part of this exercise at the construction of the nation; is the path one of a Kulturnation where membership is dependent on birth and culture, or is it a political nation which is open, at least in principle, to assimilating new members as long as they sign up to the political project as materialised in the state? Third, turning towards the idea of the state, one should investigate more closely how it is constructed along two 'dimensions': an external and an internal one. The external part of the state idea refers to the state's projection of itself onto the world; a rough distinction can be made here between the Hegelian power state, which sees itself as engaging in a classical balance of power politics and raison d'état logic, and the anti-power state, which constructs itself as the (positive) negation of this stance, making foreign policy either a moral enterprise leading to, for example, peacekeeping and support for development policies, or an absence of engagement. The internal dimension refers to the state idea as projected 'backwards' onto its constituency; different examples of the internal dimension include the welfare state, the socialist state and the liberal-capitalist state. It should be kept in mind that the distinction here is a *discursive* one: one is tracing the country's own discursive construction of itself, one is not trying as an analyst to decide what a given state is according to a set of external, objective criteria.

The internal dimension of the idea of the state is clearly not as analytically sharp as either of the previous ones, it lacks the dualistic character of the French–German, the Kulturnation–political nation, and the Hegelian–anti-power state distinctions. Yet, while this might make it both more difficult to 'apply' in practice, and possibly in need of more theoretical elaboration in future studies, this does not in and of itself make it a less important distinction when it comes to understanding political debates on Europe. As will be shown in the case of Sweden, for example, the overall analysis clearly needs to incorporate the internal idea of the state as being a welfare state, an idea which developed as the institutionalisation of the organic link between 'the people', the nation and the state itself. The distinction between an internal and an external dimension of the state idea does not, however, imply that each of these two dimension will always be equally important – in fact, it might be that only one of the two offers the crucial structuring power within a given Europe debate. However, in terms of the establishment of a general framework, both of them have to be pointed out as worthy of attention.

Fourth, there might be an 'attachment' to the idea of the nation. In the French case, this attachment comes in the form of the *patrie* which refers to the emotional bond to the past and cultural roots (the cultural 'back-up' for the political nation without which it would be a 'cold political monster'; Holm 1993: 26). In the Swedish, Norwegian and Danish cases, it is 'the people' (*Folket*) which provides the state–nation constellation with a particular twist. The French *patrie* and the Scandinavian *Folket* are not identical – again, one has to be careful not to deduce the specific conceptual construction in one country on the basis of other countries or ideal types – but they both introduce complication and dynamism in the state–nation constellation. The key here is that the *patrie* and *Folket* can be constructed as underpinning and supporting the nation and the nation–state construction; but they might also be articulated by political actors as being in tension – or maybe even in conflict – with the nation and/or the state–nation (on France see Holm 1993: 26).

Finally, it is possible that one might find other concepts which describe the actual linkages being made between the state and the nation, or the nation and its 'attachment'. In Sweden, for example, argues Lars Trägårdh in Chapter 5, the words 'state' and 'society' are used interchangeably, and 'society' is simultaneously very close to 'nation' with the former being used much more than the latter. 'Society' thus functions – if one is to put this very schematically – as the conceptual and ideational link, or 'fusion', between 'state' and 'nation'. It is crucial for the proper determination of the basic constellation of state–nation on level 1, that such a 'transmission concept' is taken into the analysis: if a debate over the content of 'society' is taking place, we would assume that the 'pact' between the state and the nation was simultaneously under scrutiny.

These five very general principles provide a first theoretical 'toolbox', or set of guidelines as to what one should look for in developing an analysis of a particular country. However, these are no more than exactly this. In making a particular analysis it is necessary to embark on a historical evaluation of how the current basic constellation was produced, and each of the four chapters in this book include therefore readings of how ideas of the state, the nation, and their possible 'attachments' and 'linkage concepts' were produced. It should also be repeated that these are *discursive* analyses of the way in which political actors have constructed the concepts at hand. In other words, we are not going to present what we think the idea of the state should be or argue that the current construction of the Danish/Swedish/Norwegian/Finnish nation is 'wrong' either because it no longer corresponds to an (always) imagined past or because it does not accurately reflect current reality.

Second layer: the relational position of the state /nation vis-à-vis Europe

The second layer is made up of the relational position vis-à-vis Europe. The question at this level is how the basic constellation from level 1 is related to 'Europe'; this relation between the 'country construction' and 'Europe' can be seen to comprise two moves. The first move involves a particular articulation of the constellation at level 1. The point here is that while the basic construction of state-nation is providing a highly structuring impact on the discourse on Europe, it is not without room for manoeuvre; there is often flexibility or ambiguity connected to the way in which the constellation has been fused. As was argued above, the French and Danish cases show that even when a tight coupling between state and nation has been made, it is still the case that the *patrie* and *Folket* are connected to the nation and the state in such a way that a tension within the constellation itself – as well as harmony – can be produced. There is also room for manoeuvre in the sense that the basic constellation might lend itself to different combinations within a discourse on Europe. In the case of Germany, for example, the twin concepts of power state and romantic nation are constitutive, but not fused (as in the French concept) and one (the power state) can be put as layer one, whilst the other comes in at the second level where it is decisive for the formation of the specific concept of Europe or vice-versa. The second level includes therefore the combination of yes/no in relation to these two concepts. One could also put this differently and say that the basic constellation in the German case is less rigid than in the French one where no similar 'negotiation' of level 1 is occurring in the Europe debate. The German constellation of state and nation is thus structuring in the sense that political discourses have to answer the question of whether one supports a power state or whether one works against it, and the question whether one operates with a cultural nation or the absence of this. Clearly, the overall

'German room for manoeuvre' vis-à-vis Europe is larger than the French one, with the former involving a debate and re-articulation centred on the basic constellation, and the latter 'only' involving the ambiguity which resides in the state–nation–*patrie* construction itself. In any particular historical situation, the relevant 'room for manoeuvre' can be smaller or larger in one or the other country.

The second move concerns the relationship established between the particular articulation of the state–nation construction at level 1 and 'Europe'. 'Europe' is here defined at a very general level: is Europe an arena for intergovernmental cooperation between sovereign states? Is Europe a market ungoverned by state intervention? Is Europe integrating around a Western core? Is Europe all-European? These are the not necessarily mutually exclusive questions which go into the construction of the state–nation–Europe relationship. The key is for a political discourse to construct a compelling and 'logical' narrative which couples a state–nation with a 'Europe' in such a way as to present 'Europe' as in accordance with the state–nation construction. For example, if a discourse articulates a strong concern for the protection of 'its' cultural nation, the ensuing 'Europe' has to argue how it is delivering this protection. Or, to take another example, if a discourse constructs the external dimension of the idea of the state as one of power politics, then 'Europe' has to either offer the possibility of this country's own pursuit of power politics, or, alternatively can itself be the one pursuing the power politics on the country's behalf.

Third layer: concrete policy for Europe

The third layer is made up of the more specific European policies pursued by specific groups of actors, often political parties, thereby adding more specificity to the very general level of abstraction of level 2. First, it is at the third level that concrete political actors are found. This implies, methodologically, that it is often at this level that one would begin working towards one's analysis. The key puzzle which faced the authors in this book was thus how to explain the way in which positions on European integration unfolded and competed at level 3.

Second, the third layer is important in terms of integrating a dynamic element into the structural model. Levels 1 and 2 consist of the constructions as they are argued within political discourses, level 3 adds specific projects and actors who not only argue their own position and construction, but also – because they are engaged in a debate – pass judgement on other positions and constructions. Actors might in short contest each other in three important ways: first, by arguing that their opponents fail to offer an appropriate construction of level 1, that they offer a misleading – or even dangerous – interpretation by not paying sufficient attention to, for example, the cultural identity of the nation, or the necessary bond between the state and the nation. Second, actors argue that the 'Europe' their opponents construct will pose a threat to the proper construction of the state–nation constellation. And, third, they claim that their opponent's interpretation of the character of the EU is out of touch with the reality of the EU, that the competing position, in principle, operates with a proper construction of the basic state–nation constellation, and that there is, again, in principle, a sufficient correspondence between this construction and its 'Europe', but that this is an unrealistic construction given the realities of European integration. The so-called 'federalist threat' is here a case in point: in the debates in Denmark, Norway and Sweden, it was argued by the 'no side' that the EU was on its route to a federalist state – thus contesting the rendition of integration of the 'yes side' which adamantly denied that federalism was what the EU did or would amount to.

These contestations, not only of the proper interpretation of the concepts of state and nation and their coupling to 'Europe', but also of the actual character of the current Europe, imply that the debate – and the layered model – is not static. Change and rearticulations come about through adjustments, either to changing internal power positions (like, for example, the growth of the working class's political power in the early twentieth century) or to changing external European conditions as when the increasing momentum of the EU in the early 1990s made representing it as a 'normal' inter-state cooperation more and more unsustainable. It is here worthwhile noticing the difference between the European great powers, most importantly France and Germany, and minor powers like Denmark and Finland in terms of their ability to influence 'Europe' – or, more correctly, their belief in their ability to influence it. French and German debates on Europe operate on the premise that their choices as to the construction of European integration have serious impact, whereas a smaller country like Denmark does not see its actions and constructions as capable of having the same kind of impact on the overall 'Europe'. Europe and France/Germany are mutually dependent: the European project is only possible if France and Germany participate (and non-integration is therefore a policy option to them). At the same time, the currently dominant policy lines in both countries are dependent on a crucial European component in their narrative of 'who are we and where are we heading'. Thus, the actual European development has to be such that it enables leaders in these countries to tell convincing (but possibly divergent) stories about their future. It is due to this mutual dependence of European integration and national political orientation that the theory when applied to the big countries becomes a theory able to explain European integration and security.

   Each country constructs in principle its own Europe on the basis of its individual constellations of state and nation. One might then ask to what extent these 'Europes' are politically compatible, to what extent they can unfold simultaneously. Again, there is a difference between the small and the great powers: it is in most cases essentially the former's own problem if their 'Europe' is at odds with the logic of European integration; if the great powers' Europes collide, the problem, on the contrary, has much wider ramifications. If a major power cannot project a Europe in which it can imagine itself (in a recognisable form which instantiates the basic idea of the nation/state) it will not pursue this policy. And with an abrupt change of policy in a major power, the whole project of European integration is threatened. This, however, does not mean that their 'Europes' have to be identical. Possibly, it is even a condition for European stability, that the major powers think *differently* about Europe (Wæver 1990c, 1995). If they all thought in the same logic – and, for example, wanted a French kind of role – there might not be room for all of them! Political scientists and international relationists have a general predisposition to think that the condition for cooperation and institution building is that the different parties *agree* and come to define concepts identically (cf. the explanation of the demise of superpower détente as caused by conflicting definitions), but probably there are important cases where the condition is the opposite: that they pursue policies that are *compatible* (and, for instance, agree on building an institution), but that the story sustaining this policy is very different from one country to another.[20]

The goal is thus to create a theoretical model which by being layered is capable of incorporating change and confrontation. The smallest changes – the ones closest to the surface – are those on level 3 which can be made without changing level 2. A more radical change would be to change to one of the other main options at level 2. And the most radical would be a change away from the basic concept of the state–nation. This situation would be so radically different that speculating about possible actualisations would in most cases be too hazardous.[21]

Those who assume that 'talk is cheap' will say that you can always come up with a different narrative. If, in contrast, one believes there is structure to language and that a large part of politics is about structuring the national conceptual landscape, options are not so abundant. For a specific country there will be a certain number of structural routes, and each of these can be given different concrete policy formulations. But there are so many suggested policies (for instance most of the roles allocated to France in American plans for Europe) that are completely unrealistic because they would require a reconstruction of the basic state–nation constellation. As such a shift would demand a thorough re-articulation of a range of key concepts and thereby resonate far into a number of societal issues as well as European-wide ones, we would expect it to meet with fierce resistance. Conversely, if one line of policy breaks down (due to changed external pressure or a recon-figuration of domestic power), at least for a medium or major power, it is likely that one would not just live with the ensuing vacuum. The question about the meaning of and future for the nation/state will generate a new construction of 'Europe' and its relation to the state–nation that can lead to discontinuous developments in foreign policy. The politicians would have, so to say, to 'go one level down', pick up the concept of state–nation and give it a different articulation, which could easily mean very different policies on level 3.

Finally, one might ask where one is to find those different discursive constructions of state, nation and Europe; which texts should, in short, be read? In terms of the historical analysis of how the present constellation of state and nation became formed, the question might depend to some extend on the availability of historical studies which adopt a perspective similar to our own; if such studies exist they can be drawn on (as in the Danish chapter), if not a more independent study of historical documents has to be undertaken. In terms of the studies of the current debates, one needs to uncover both the dominant positions and those new ones which might give an indication of where the debate might move next. While the former should be more easily identifiable, there is always a likely risk that one might overlook some of the latter ones (Neumann 1996b: 3).

The toolbox should not be understood as implying that with this in hand you can go to a Nordic or any other case and 'generate' a structure for the country at hand. There is a creative element in the drawing up of the structure in each case. The theory posits a number of general features: the model should be layered, the three layers contain this and that, and the way actors interact with the structure is so and so. But the content of each layer in a specific case cannot be discovered by any formalised method. In contrast to, for example, the work of Hayward Alker (1996), which shares many ideas about discourses, texts and methods but tries to create computer-based methods for getting from text to structure, we do not think you can get mechanically from text to structure. Naturally, you get ideas for the structure from reading texts, but generating the structure is – as suggested by Waltz (or Marx or Popper) – a creative act. You have to have a good idea and then put it forward as your starting point (whether in strict tests with Popper or by deductively developing a larger story that has in the last instance to be convincing due to its rationalisation of complex reality when it finally reaches the surface, as practised by Marx in *Das Kapital*). Thus, these various questions and distinctions can produce fragments and independent insights for a country, but to define a *structure* involves creativity.

Therefore, this discourse analysis has a synchronous and diachronous part, each with its characteristic usage of texts. The first establishes a model by fitting together material from different contexts, actors and years into a structure, while the second moves through time with specified actors and studies how the structure shapes and how it is reproduced and modified. In the first, the task is to create a clear logic by finding powerful examples from quite different contexts but with the aim of getting the pattern as clear as possible – quotes that express the 'typical French' in a more typical way than any other, and quotes that bring out the internal links between different typical traits. The second part pays much more attention to context and interaction: who tries to do what, how do they draw on the structures or resist them thereby trying to change them?

The two parts draw to some extent on different kinds of sources. For the construction of the model (synchrony), the sources are primarily politicians in official positions but also others who contribute to the formation of the national discourse. Often the logic is found most explicitly with intellectuals or even researchers, and these can then be checked to see whether the same textual operation – maybe more implicitly – is employed by politicians. When reading the politicians, it is useful to select 'difficult situations': not negotiated, unclear expressions like party programmes. At interventions in heated debates (for instance in parliament), the politicians need to mobilise rhetorical power, and they draw therefore on the semiotic structures that generate most power in relation to their aim.[22]

In the explanatory part (diachron) the task is to show how these structures constrain or suggest arguments and positions. Therefore, one has to explore how actors acted linguistically to change discursive structures when they needed to, and when they conducted counter-intuitive foreign policies that can be explained from the constraints that the discursive structure constituted. Thus, this part of the analysis must follow the political process and the political actors in a more traditional way while the structures created in the first part of the analysis are used as analytical instruments.

'Covering' a national discursive space is in principle impossible: one cannot read everything which has been written – or stated – within a debate as broad as the national debates on Europe. However, accepting a pragmatic stance we suggest the following points: first, our focus on the construction of foreign policy from a discourse analysis perspective gives us a 'bias' towards texts by leading political figures; we are not, as argued above, pursuing a methodological strategy aimed at uncovering what 'ordinary people really think about Europe' but on the contrary looking for the structures within which 'one' has to argue about Europe. Those who define these structures are to a large extent leading political actors, that is, politicians and spokespeople from large social movements. It would thus be very unlikely that we would miss a dominant position if we examine the parliamentary debates, discussion programmes on TV, the programmes distributed by parties and social movements, the debate in leading newspapers and books on European integration which have been discussed within the debate itself. The parliamentary debates in particular turned out – to our slight surprise! – to provide very clear representations of constructions of the key positions. As Neumann stated in his discourse analysis of the Russian debate on Europe: 'In this sense, there is such a thing as reading enough' (Neumann 1996b: 3). And while it can always be contested when, exactly, 'enough' has been reached, it is also helpful to consider what we could call 'the opposite burden of evidence' which goes as follows: 'I claim that on the basis of my reading of the debate in country X, the discursive structure looks like this . . . If you show me a text I have not included, it should be possible for me to read this text through the structure I have constructed. If not, my reading of the debate needs to be revised.' Working comparatively, as in this book, also offers the simple methodological advantage that the analyses produced in other countries lead one to consider possible re-articulations and more detailed conceptual shifts one might not have identified otherwise.

Notes

1 Huntington's civilisational thesis offers another example of adopting 'culture' as the explanatory variable (Huntington 1993, 1996). Yet, Huntington's goal is not to explain particular foreign policy 'details', like Denmark's shifts in attitude to European integration, but to generate policy prescription on the basis of (almost) objective definitions of civilisations.

2 On this matter, Saussure would stress that each language articulates or organises the world differently, but to the extent that Lévi-Strauss defines the structuralist movement, the search for deep structures in the human brain can be said to be a defining characterisation. Then we are not structuralists (Lévi-Strauss 1963; Leach 1970; Kurzweil 1996 [1980]).

3 Involved here is the more general question of the politics of poststructuralism in IR. There are marked differences between the development of poststructuralist IR in the USA and in continental Europe (and maybe Scandinavia in particular) for a number of reasons having to do both with the general development of poststructuralism in academia (before IR) and with the structure of the IR discipline (Wæver 1998b). Because poststructuralism in the USA became elevated to a temporary status as official challenger to the dominant neo-neo synthesis, poststructuralist IR became locked into

playing a particular game of mostly critique and disciplinary politics. A number of possible uses of poststructuralism became tabooed (Wæver unpublished and in preparation).

4 Iver B. Neumann has pointed out how this stress on complex differences together with an emphasis on internally contested identities differentiate what he calls 'the Copenhagen coterie' from most other poststructuralist works on self/other relations and identity in general (Neumann 1996a: 162).

5 This relates to the fact that most poststructuralist studies of the relationship between identity and foreign policy are not at all interested in *explaining foreign policy from identity*. As epitomised by the most celebrated work in the genre, Campbell 1992, the aim is rather to show how foreign policy is implicated in the reproduction of identity – foreign policy is one of the more important arenas where struggles are fought to shore up the ever-fragile national identity. Therefore, it is not very surprising when identity and discourse is in practice reduced to the one dominant one, not competing ones, and the relations to others reduced to that of Others, that is, self–Other relations where the monolithic self reproduces itself, rather than complex relations where different versions of the national self fight and re-articulate themselves. For criticisms of such poststructuralist identity-foreign policy studies see Hansen (1997) and Wæver and Holm (forthcoming).

6 Hudson (1997) argues the need for a theory of foreign policy which explores the effects of culture. She does not, however, offer such a developed theory, 'only' eight questions which should form a research agenda (Hudson 1997: 15–19).

7 This also implies, conversely, that other concepts might be more appropriate for other kinds of studies. Lene Hansen has, for example, analysed the debate about policies concerning Bosnia with a similar 'structuring poststructuralism' ambition, but she adopts the concept of security as her theoretical focus (Hansen 1998).

8 Studies of specific states and their foreign policies are starting to emerge along lines more or less similar to the ones outlined here: France: Holm 1993, 1996, 1997, 1998; more fully developed in Wæver and Holm, forthcoming; Germany: Wæver 1994, 1995; and Wæver and Holm, forthcoming; Russia: Neumann 1996b; Turkey: Kazan 1994, Kazan and Wæver 1994 and Kadayifei 1996; Finland: Joenniemi 1993; UK: Larsen 1997, Diez 1999; Egypt and India: Banerjee unpublished; Slovenia: Hansen 1996; Greece: Stauersböll 2000; the Nordic Countries, this book!; Algeria: Holm in preparation; USA in European security: Sørensen 1998; the US as a global power: Ruggie 1997.

9 How problematic this approach is becomes immediately visible in the case of the conflicts in the former Yugoslavia. The underlying assumption of much identity/culture based thinking about conflict is that the propensity for conflict correlates with difference and cultural distance. However, Croats, Serbs and Bosnians are quite close for most purposes, including language. And this closeness is actually part of the reason for the conflict. Identity driven conflicts are often caused or spurred by the Other making one's own identity insecure, which is done more by making it unclear and problematic than by presenting it with a comfortable opposition. The 'narcissism of minor differences' thus makes a lot of sense in the light of both theories of societal security and psycho-analytical theories of politics (Lacan, Zizek).

10 This problem is, however, not inherent in the nature of domestic level explanations (as especially Waltz explicitly assumes; 1979). It is rather caused by the birth marks of CFP/FPA as part of the behaviouralist movement, and therefore with an enduring proclivity to empiristically bring the domestic level in all its complexity into our IR outlook.

11 The main candidate these days for a successful, structured theory including domestic as well as international factors is probably the 'two level games' approach (Putnam 1988). Also some of the developments of neo-realism (so-called neo- and post-classical

realism) attempt to merge foreign policy theory and IR theory (Rose 1998). Finally, the, in this book, often mentioned Moravcsik grounds his general liberal theory of IR (1997) in the generation of interests from groups in societies, that is, as a domestically based foreign policy theory which as a second step adds a bargaining element which allegedly makes it an IR theory.

12 As argued by Kuhn, the criterion of *science* is not that it puts up testable hypotheses (even medieval astrology did that), nor that the theory itself is given up in the case of the failure of the test (theory never is, unless a general crisis is in play), but that hypotheses should be derived from theory in a sufficiently close manner, that failure creates *puzzles*, which foster further work on data or theory (Kuhn 1970: 8–10).

13 Bartelson here skips Foucault's distinction between discourse and discursive formation.

14 This point – which should now be familiar to readers of the structure–agency debates – was made by Foucault in order to avoid the ahistorical deep structuralism of the Lévi-Strauss type of structuralism. In this kind of structuralism an absolute matrix exists that controls *all possible* instantiations. Foucault's theory in *The Archaeology of Knowledge*, in contrast, works with contingent, 'local' discursive systems that *happen to exist*. There are no ultimate structures that control the whole, all possible forms and the transformation from one to another – the rules are internal to contingent and bounded systems. This is the 'empiricist' and 'positivist' element that Foucault provocatively claims for his work. On this see the very helpful discussion by Dreyfus and Rabinow 1982.

15 A hierarchy of depth over surface definitely exists in many structuralisms and is related to the fact that the code is seen as constant, only to be transformed in correspondence to its own rules of transformation. The relationship between code and manifestation is seen as one of perfect correspondence (or isotopy), and thus these structuralisms contain assumptions about stable, self-present meaning which are – as argued on p. 23 – drastically subverted by various forms of poststructuralism. Generally, structuralism can be seen as a science of the sign and poststructuralism as a critique of the sign. Structuralism operates on the basis of an optimism regarding the possibility of finding the codes and mechanisms that actually produce the manifestations we meet, whereas poststructuralism works from the attitude that meaning is always precarious, transient and self-contradicting. Poststructuralism is, however, not (as often implied in American playful postmodernisms) a negation of structuralism – it is poststructuralism because it has grown from and through structuralism. The various mechanisms of meaning generation analysed by structuralists can be registered but they will never be seen as full, complete or self-confirming. Meaning is always an attempt, a process, a move that temporarily counters the indeterminacy of signification. The present concept of discourse is therefore simultaneously process and structure, realisation and precondition. One can qualify and talk about discursive practice and discursive structure, but 'discourse' as such is still a meaningful term both as a level of analysis (a dimension of the social) and as a count noun: a specific discourse (say German discourse on the state) is practice and structure simultaneously. This is not very far from the way the term is used by Foucault, although he probably emphasises structure a bit more, and practice a bit less, at least in those texts where the term discourse is most central.

16 Can we predict whether change will happen and then what change it will be? No, we can only register that change is becoming more and more likely, and point out what changes are more or less likely in the sense that the more likely changes are less demanding, and the less likely ones demand deeper and more costly change. Then the theory cannot explain the origins of change? No, this is not a theory of ultimate causes. Generally, there are no theories of ultimate causes. As soon as one moves into an interdisciplinary terrain it is always possible to keep asking 'but why, what caused *this*?' To answer the question of ultimate causes would demand a total theory of everything. Theories – to the extent that they are theories at all – are a screen that is well enough

defined to register whenever something crosses its plane, that is, there is one step in all relevant processes that involves crossing this screen and at this point it is registered in a clearly specified model which is conscious of operating at this and only this level (cf., for example, Waltz 1979).

17 The framework is not in principle limited to the study of Europe debates; one can think of its relevance in other geographical settings or for different questions of foreign policy. However, it is probably no coincidence that the theory was developed in the European context, as the European question has become so contested and has led to a heightened focus on national identity and states' 'visions of themselves'. The most obvious extension would be to the global powers and their visions of world order.

18 Our usage of the term 'state–nation idea' should not be understood to the effect that an ideational account of 'France' should be juxtaposed to a material one (see the discussion of idealism–materialism on p. 22).

19 This specific interpretation of France is the work of Holm 1993, 1996, 1997; and Wæver and Holm forthcoming.

20 The questions of state influence and mutual compatibility would pose themselves differently for the Nordics if the 'higher-order category' we investigated was 'Norden' rather than 'Europe'. The actual development of 'Norden' is shaped by the Nordics and a politically useful concept of 'Norden' has to be made meaningful in the Nordic states in a way that parallels the status of Europe to the French and the Germans.

21 See Wæver 1998c for another presentation of the current approach, which partly overlaps with this chapter, partly develops some dimensions further and not least presents the empirical analysis of France and Germany.

22 For more detailed discussions of the selection of texts, see Sørensen 1998: 44–6; Holm 1999; Agersnap 2000: 26–9; Neumann 2001; Wæver and Holm forthcoming.

References

Adler, E. (1997) 'Seizing the Middle Ground: Constructivism in World Politics', *European Journal of International Relations* 3, 3: 319–63.

Agersnap, L. (2000) 'Fra Dagsorden til Verdensorden: En poststrukturalistisk analyse af Danmarks udenrigspolitiske identitet', MA thesis, University of Copenhagen.

Alker, H. (1996) *Rediscoveries and Reformulations: Humanistic Methodologies for International Relations*, Cambridge: Cambridge University Press.

Anderson, B. (1983) *Imagined Communities: Reflections on the Origins and Spread of Nationalism*, London: Verso.

Banerjee, S. (unpublished) 'National Identity and Foreign Policy'.

Bartelson, J. (1995) *A Genealogy of Sovereignty*, Cambridge: Cambridge University Press.

Berger, T. U. (1993) 'From Sword to Chrysanthemum: Japan's Culture of Anti-militarism', *International Security* 17, 4: 119–50.

—— (1996) 'Norms, Identity, and National Security in Germany and Japan', in P. J. Katzenstein (ed.) *The Culture of National Security: Norms and Identity in World Politics*, New York: Columbia University Press, pp. 317–56.

—— (1998) *Cultures of Antimilitarism: National Security in Germany and Japan*, Baltimore, Mass.: Johns Hopkins University Press.

Campbell, D. (1992) *Writing Security: United States Foreign Policy and Politics of Identity*, Manchester: Manchester University Press.

Derrida, J. (1978 [1967]) 'Structure, Sign, and Play in the Discourse of the Human Sciences' in *Writing and Difference*, Chicago: University of Chicago Press.

Diez, T. (1999) *Die EU lesen: Diskursive Knotenpunkte in der britischen Europadebatte*, Opladen: Leske + Budrich.

Dreyfus, H. L. and Rabinow, P. (1982) *Michel Foucault: Beyond Structuralism and Hermeneutics*, New York: Harvester Wheatsheaf.

Finnemore, M. (1996) *National Interests in International Society*, Ithaca, NY: Cornell University Press.

Foucault, M. (1972) *The Archaeology of Knowledge*, London: Pantheon.

Gellner, E. (1993) 'Nationalism and the Two Forms of Cohesion in Complex Societies', Radcliffe-Brown lecture in social anthropology, 3 February 1982, British Academy.

Goldmann, K. (1988) *Change and Stability in Foreign Policy: The Problems and Possibilities of Détente*, Princeton, NJ: Princeton University Press.

Hansen, L. (1996) 'State Building on the Balkan Border', *Alternatives* 21, 4: 473–95.

—— (1997) 'A Case for Seduction? Evaluating the Poststructuralist Conceptualization of Security', *Cooperation and Conflict* 32, 4: 369–97.

—— (1998) 'Western Villains Or Balkan Barbarism? Representations and Responsibility in the Debate over Bosnia', Ph.D. dissertation, Institute of Political Science, University of Copenhagen.

Herman, R. G. (1996) 'Identity, Norms, and National Security: The Soviet Foreign Policy Revolution and the End of the Cold War', in P. J. Katzenstein (ed.) *The Culture of National Security: Norms and Identity in World Politics*, New York: Columbia University Press, pp. 271–316.

Hoffmann, S. (1989) 'A Retrospective', in Joseph Kruzel and James N. Rosenau (eds) *Journeys through World Politics: Autobiographical Reflections of Thirty-four Academic Travelers*, Lexington, Mass.: Lexington Books, pp. 263–78.

Holm, U. (1993) *Det Franske Europa*, Aarhus: Aarhus University Press.

—— (1996) 'Den franske nationalstat: en urolig magt', i *Militært Tidsskrift* 125, 1: 53–68.

—— (1997) 'The French Garden is not what it used to be', in Knud-Erik Jørgensen (ed.) *Reflective Approaches to European Governance*, London: Macmillan, pp. 128–145.

—— (1998) 'Algeria: France's Untenable Engagement', *Mediterranean Politics* 3, 2: 104–14.

—— (1999) 'Metode og teori: en retrospektiv udviklingshistorie', part of a Ph.D. thesis, University of Aarhus.

—— (in preparation) Study on Algeria.

Hudson, V. M. (1997) 'Culture and Foreign Policy: Developing a Research Agenda', in Hudson (ed.), *Culture & Foreign Policy*, Boulder, Col.: Lynne Rienner, pp. 1–26.

Huntington, S. P. (1993) 'The Clash of Civilizations?', *Foreign Affairs* 72, 3: 22–49.

—— (1996) *The Clash of Civilizations and the Remaking of World Order*, New York: Simon and Schuster.

Jepperson, R. L., Wendt, A. and Katzenstein, P. J. (1996) 'Norms, Identity, and Culture in National Security', in P. J. Katzenstein (ed.) *The Culture of National Security: Norms and Identity in World Politics*, New York: Columbia University Press, pp. 33–75.

Joenniemi, P. (1993) 'Euro-Suomi: rajalla, rajojen, välissä vai rajaton?' in P. Joenniemi, R. Alapuro and K. Pekonen, *Suomesta Euro-Suomen: Keitä me olemme ja mihin matkalla*, Tampere: Occasional Papers of Tampere Peace Research Institute, No. 53, pp. 13–48.

Johnston, A. I. (1996) 'Cultural Realism and Strategy in Maoist China', in P. J. Katzenstein (ed.) *The Culture of National Security: Norms and Identity in World Politics*, New York: Columbia University Press, pp. 216–68.

Kadayifei, A. (1996) 'Discourse Analysis and Conflict: Turkish Identity Creation', Ph.D. thesis, University of Kent at Canterbury.

Katzenstein, P. J. (1996) (ed.) *The Culture of National Security: Norms and Identity in World Politics*, New York: Columbia University Press.

Kaufmann, C. (1996) 'Possible and Impossible Solutions to Ethnic Civil Wars', *International Security* 20, 4: 136–75.

Kazan, I. (1994) 'Tyrkiets udenrigspolitik – en diskurs udfordret af EFs integration og Sovjetunionens opløsning', MA thesis, Institute of Political Science, University of Copenhagen.

Kazan, I. and Wæver, O. (1994) 'Tyrkiet mellem Europa og europæisering', *Internasjonal Politikk* 52, 2: 139–75.

Keohane, R. O. (1989) *International Institutions and State Power: Essays in International Relations Theory*, Boulder, Col.: Westview.

Keohane, R. O. and Nye, J. (1987) 'Power and Interdependence Revisited', *International Organization* 41, 4: 725–53.

Kissinger, H. A. (1957) *A World Restored: Castlereagh, Metternich and the Restoration of Peace, 1812–1822*, Boston: Houghton Mifflin.

Krause, K. and Williams, M. C. (1996) 'Broadening the Agenda of Security Studies? Politics and Method', *Mershon International Studies Review* 40, 2: 229–54.

Kuhn, T. (1970) 'Logic of Discovery or Psychology of Research', in Imre Lakatos and Alan Musgrave (eds) *Criticism and the Growth of Knowledge*, Cambridge: Cambridge University Press, pp.1–24.

Kurzweil, E. (1996 [1980]) *The Age of Structuralism: From Lévi-Strauss to Foucault* (with a new introduction), New Brunswick, NJ: Transaction Books.

Laclau, E. and Mouffe, C. (1985) *Hegemony and Socialist Strategy: Towards a Radical Democratic Politics*, London: Verso.

Laffey, M. and Weldes, J. (1997) 'Beyond Belief: Ideas and Symbolic Technologies in the Study of International Relations', *European Journal of International Relations* 3, 2: 193–237.

Lapid, Y. and Kratochwil, F. (eds) (1996a) *The Return of Culture and Identity in IR Theory*, Boulder, Col.: Lynne Rienner.

—— (1996b) 'Revisiting the "National": Towards an Identity Agenda in Neorealism?' in Y. Lapid and F. Kratochwil (eds) *The Return of Culture and Identity in IR Theory*, Boulder, Col.: Lynne Rienner, pp. 105–26.

Larsen, H. (1997) *Foreign Policy and Discourse Analysis: France, Britain, and Europe*, London: Routledge.

Leach, E. (1970) *Claude Lévi-Strauss*, New York: The Viking Press.

Lévi-Strauss, C. (1963) *Structural Anthropology*, New York: Basic Books.

Moravcsik, A. (1997) 'Taking Preferences Seriously: A Liberal Theory of International Politics', *International Organization* 51, 4: 513–54.

Neumann, I. B. (1996a) 'Collective Identity Formation: Self and Other in International Relations', *European Journal of International Relations* 2, 2: 139–74.

—— (1996b) *Russia and the Idea of Europe: A Study in Identity and International Relations*, London: Routledge.

—— (2001) *Mening, materialitet, makt: Innføring i diskursanalyse*, Oslo: Fagbokforlaget.

Nye, J. (1988) 'Neorealism and Neoliberalism', *World Politics* 40, 2: 235–51.

Onuf, N. G. (1989) *World of Our Making: Rules and Rule in Social Theory and International Relations*, Columbia: University of South Carolina Press.

Østerud, Ø. (1996) 'Antinomies of Postmodernism in International Studies', *Journal of Peace Research* 33, 4: 285–390.

—— (1997) 'Focus on Postmodernisms: A Rejoinder', *Journal of Peace Research* 34, 3: 337–8.

Patomäki, H. (1997) 'The Rhetorical Strategies and the Misleading Nature of Attacks on "Postmodernism": A Reply to Østerud', *Journal of Peace Research* 34, 3: 325–9.

Posen, B. (1993a) 'The Security Dilemma and Ethnic Conflict', *Survival* 35, 1: 27–47.

—— (1993b) 'Nationalism, the Mass Army, and Military Power', *International Security* 18, 2: 80–124.

Putnam, R. D. (1988) 'Diplomacy and Domestic Politics: The Logic of Two-level Games', *International Organization* 42, 3: 427–60.

Ringmar, E. (1996) *Identity, Interest and Action: A Cultural Explanation of Sweden's Intervention in the Thirty Years War*, Cambridge: Cambridge University Press.

—— (1997) 'Alexander Wendt: A Social Scientist Struggling with History', in I. B. Neumann and O. Wæver (eds) *The Future of International Relations: Masters in the Making?* London: Routledge, pp. 269–89.

Rose, G. (1998) 'Neoclassical Realism and Theories of Foreign Policy', *World Politics* 51: 144–72.

Ruggie, J. G. (1983) 'Continuity and Transformation in the World Polity: Towards a Neorealist Synthesis' (Review Essay on Waltz, *Theory of International Politics*), *World Politics* 35, 2: 261–85.

—— (1997) 'The Past as Prologue? Interests, Identity, and American Foreign Policy', *International Security* 21, 4: 89–125.

Saussure, F. de (1959), *Course in General Linguistics*, New York: Philosophical Library (these lectures of 1906–11 were published posthumously in 1916).

Smith, A. D. (1991) *National Identity*, London: Penguin.

Smith, S. (1997) 'Epistemology, Postmodernism and International Relations Theory: A Reply to Østerud', *Journal of Peace Research* 34, 3: 330–6.

Sørensen, J. M. (1998) 'The Coming Hegemony? A Constructivist Interpretation of the Future Direction of the US Security Role in Europe', MA thesis, University of Copenhagen, Institute of Political Science.

Stauersböll, H. (2000) 'Between Byzantium and Hellas: Understanding the Greek Policy Towards Macedonia in the 1990s', MA thesis, University of Copenhagen, Institute of Political Science.

Van Evera, S. (1994) 'Hypotheses on Nationalism and War', *International Security* 18, 4: 5–39.

Wæver, O. (1990a) 'The Language of Foreign Policy' (Review Essay on Carlsnaes, *Ideology and Foreign Policy*), *Journal of Peace Research* 27, 3: 335–43.

—— (1990b) 'Thinking and Rethinking in Foreign Policy' (Review Essay on Goldmann, *Change and Stability in Foreign Policy*), *Cooperation and Conflict* 25, 2: 153–70.

—— (1990c) 'Three Competing Europes: German, French, Russian', *International Affairs* 66, 3: 477–94.

—— (1992) 'Det "nye" Tysklands internationale profil', *GRUS*, no. 36: 18–41.

—— (1994) 'Resisting the temptation of post foreign policy analysis', in Walter Carlsnaes and Steve Smith (eds) *European Foreign Policy*, London: Sage, pp. 238–73.

—— (1995) 'Power, Principles and Perspectivism: Peaceful Change in Post-Cold War Europe', in Heikki Patomäki (ed.) *Peaceful Change and World Politics*, Tampere Peace Research Institute, Research Report 71, pp. 208–82.

—— (1996) 'The Struggle for "Europe": A Discourse Analysis of France, Germany and European Union', paper presented to the 'Rethinking Security Seminar', University of Southern California, 23 October.

—— (1998a) 'Insecurity, Security, and Asecurity in the West European Non-war Community', in Emanuel Adler and Michael Barnett (eds) *Security Communities*, Cambridge: Cambridge University Press, pp. 69–118.

—— (1998b) 'The Sociology of a not so International Discipline: American and European Developments in International Relations', *International Organization* 52: 4: 687–727.

—— (1998c) 'Explaining Europe by Decoding Discourses' in Anders Wivel (ed.) *Explaining European Integration*, Copenhagen Political Studies Press, pp. 100–46.

—— (1999) 'Does the English School's *Via Media* equal the Contemporary Constructivist Middle Ground? – or: on the difference between philosophical scepticism and sociological theory', paper presented at the annual meeting of the British International Studies Association, Manchester, December.

—— (in preparation) *The Politics of International Structure*.

—— (unpublished) 'The end of poststructuralist IR', article in draft.

Wæver, O. and Holm, U. (forthcoming) *The Struggle for 'Europe': French and German Concepts of State, Nation and European Union*.

Waltz, K. N. (1979) *Theory of International Politics*, New York: McGraw-Hill.

Weldes, J. (1996) 'Constructing National Interests', *European Journal of International Relations* 2, 3: 275–318.

Wendt, A. (1992) 'Anarchy is what States make of it: The Social Construction of Power Politics', *International Organization* 46, 2: 383–92.

—— (1999) *Social Theory of International Politics*, Cambridge: Cambridge University Press.

Zehfuss, M. (1999) 'Constructivist Theories in International Relations and German Military Involvement Abroad', Ph.D. thesis, Dept of International Politics, University of Wales, Aberystwyth.

—— (n.d.) 'Constructivism in International Relations: The Approaches of Wendt, Onuf and Kratochwil', in Knud-Erik Jørgensen (ed.) *The Aarhus-Norsminde Papers: Constructivism, International Relations and European Studies*, papers presented at a workshop, October 1997, printed in Århus, pp. 37–42.

3   Sustaining sovereignty

The Danish approach to Europe*

Lene Hansen

Denmark adopted for almost a quarter of a century a unique position within the EC/EU. It was the only Nordic country to join the EC in the 1970s, yet as Danish politicians in favour of integration often pointed out, Denmark had not abandoned Norden in favour of the EC, it was, on the contrary, acting as a 'bridge-builder' between the two. But the history of Denmark's participation in the EC/EU has not only been one of balancing or, in the best cases, uniting the 'emotional attachment to the North' with 'the economic attractions of the EEC' (Miljan 1977: 169). It has also been the story of what Miljan aptly termed an 'anxious European' with a European record in referenda over EC/EU related questions: the referendum on accession in 1972 was followed by one in 1986 on the Single European Act, and then in the 1990s no less than three were held: one in June 1992 on the Maastricht Treaty, the defeat of which led to one on the Edinburgh Amendment on 18 May 1993; the Amsterdam Treaty was accepted on 28 May 1998. More recently, on 28 September 2000, a Danish accession to the third stage of the EMU was rejected by 53.2 per cent. This frequent use of referenda, and their close and shifting results have contributed to making the European issue one of the most contested, polarised and sensitive in current Danish politics.

But the EU is not only contested in terms of traditional party politics. The European integration project has increasingly involved a split between the politicians and the electorate: the Single European Act was defeated in 1986 by an opposition foreign policy majority including the Social Democratic Party, the Radical Liberal Party and the Socialist People's Party. However, the ensuing referendum resulted in a 56.2 per cent approval. In 1992 the pattern was reversed: although the European question was hotly debated within the Parliament it was only the small Christian People's Party, the most left-wing and the most right-wing parties, the Socialist People's Party and the Party of Progress, which argued against the Maastricht Treaty. Yet the result was a slim 'no', in no small part due to the successful mobilising strategies of the social movements against the EC/EU and the Maastricht Treaty. But the pattern of EU support in the Parliament and the population was not the only thing which changed between 1986 and 1992. The parliamentary rejection in 1986 was in large part due to domestic political conflicts unrelated to the EC. While those against European integration pointed to the federal ambitions inherent in the EC, the dominant construction on the yes-side was of the EU as an economic project whose main advantage to Denmark had been its agricultural policies (Worre 1988; Schou 1992).

By 1992, the cold war, bipolarity and the Soviet Union were history, and West European institutionalisation had made a huge leap forward. As symbolised by the word 'Union' in the Maastricht Treaty, the construction of European integration as confined to the economic sphere became increasingly untenable. In Danish politics, this expansion and intensification of the European project meant that those opposed to it argued that the outcome would be the double loss of political sovereignty and cultural identity. Conversely, pro-European forces held that although the EU had become a political project, it was one located at the intergovernmental, not the federal, level and constituted little or no threat to Danish sovereignty and identity. These increasingly clear divisions regarding the political importance of the EU made the 1992 debate a milestone in the history of Denmark's debates on Europe, and it set the terms for the 1993 Edinburgh Agreement, the so-called National Compromise, as well as the subsequent debates in 1993, 1998 and 2000.

Attempts to explain Denmark's European anxieties have not been lacking. One group of analysts interpreted the result in 1992 as an expression of a European-wide disjuncture between the goals of the political elites and their populations (Laffan 1996; Obradovic 1996; Hansen and Williams 1999). For those supporting the move towards a stronger EU, Denmark stood out as a warning of the need to secure the legitimacy of the EU in the minds of ambivalent populations; for those working against membership of the EU or against the tighter character of its cooperation, the Danish case promised the success of popular 'resistance' against initiatives 'from above'. Still others argued that to interpret the referenda as a result of deeper opposition to Europe was misleading, that it was the popularity of the governments which caused the difference: the government in 1992 was widely perceived as unpopular whereas the new government in 1993 had much broader support (Franklin, Marsh and McLaren 1994). The 'no' vote was thus not about European integration, but about domestic politics. This attempt to read the European question out of the EU votes is, however, misleading. The EU issue is so solidly established in Denmark as a *sui generis* issue that most voters find it too important for such signalling and the Social Democrats (who took over before the 1993 vote) were as entangled in the 'yes' vote of 1992 as the government,[1] and the rejection of the Maastricht Treaty was surely not interpreted as a victory for this party.

Since the EU has been the subject of frequent referenda, the field of election studies has been one of the major contributors of EU analyses. The main conclusion of probably the most extensive Danish study of the 1992 referendum was that the outcome of the referendum should be explained by attitudes to European cooperation: those who voted 'no' wanted the EU to remain a solely economic organisation whereas those who voted 'yes' were ready to concede political power to the EU. The bottom line was that 'A majority preferred political freedom for economic gains, if they had to choose. The electorate voted in accordance with their interpretation of the direction of the cooperation in the EU. The most important thing was how the EU was perceived' (Siune, Svensson and Tonsgaard 1992: 131–2).

But how do we get to a deeper understanding of how the EU was perceived? Why, in other words, did the choice ifself become constructed as one of making a trade-off between political independence and economic gains? And why did the debate take a turn in the 1990s, highlighting possible threats not only to Danish political independence, but also to Danish cultural national identity? The argument of this chapter is not that, for example, Finn Laursen's characterisation of Denmark as a 'minimalist' in EU issues or Torben Worre's conclusion that even the Maastricht Treaty's supporters were against supranational developments are wrong (Laursen 1993: 120; Worre 1995: 257).[2] My point is rather, in accordance with the general theoretical framework laid out in Chapters 1 and 2, that an understanding of why Denmark has come to adopt a minimalist position which rejects supra-nationality requires a study of how modern Danish national identity has been constructed, of how the idea of the state, the nation and the people has evolved into a particular conceptual constellation, and of the influence of this constellation on the conceptualisation of 'Europe'. The key argument to be advanced is that a particular Danish combination of a French state–nation and a German conception of the nation has situated the construction of 'Europe' within a logic of states. The EU debate has, as a consequence, unfolded between a pro-integration construction of the EU as an intergovernmental form of cooperation between sovereign nation-states on the one side, and the no-side's construction of the EU as a new European superstate on the other.

This chapter falls into four sections. The first section presents a reading of the historical developments which went into the production of the state–nation constellation. The second section analyses the European debate from the 1950s to the beginning of the 1970s. The third section shows the importance of this constellation for the debate over the Maastricht Treaty, in which the main positions were consolidated in the 1990s. The fourth, and final, section examines the development of the debate in the 'post-Maastricht' phase until the referendum on the third stage of the EMU in September 2000.

Towards the Danish nation-state[3]

The story of how the basic discursive structures underpinning contemporary Danish politics were formed begins in the 1750s and ends with the formation of the social democratic welfare state in the twentieth century. It is a story composed of three sets of interlinking elements: external developments (lost wars and countries, and imported ideologies); internal political movements (the strengthened positions of the peasants, the liberals and the socialists); and internal material developments.

The Whole-state and the fatherland debate

Compared to the rest of Europe the first movements towards a modern Danish national identity took place relatively early, namely in the last half of the eighteenth century. This is not to suggest that there were no earlier expressions of patriotic sentiment towards 'Denmark', both medieval sources and later statements made by the aristocracy heralded the Danish past and the king's achievements. Denmark was governed by the monarch and the aristocracy until 1660 and the intellectual and emotional attachment to Denmark as an *amor patriae* espoused by the latter group functioned as a way in which they could justify the privileges bestowed upon them, arguing that 'it was their duty to risk their lives in defence of their king and their country, so that the common people could live undisturbed and in peace' (Feldbæk 1996: 132; Ilsøe 1991) The introduction of absolutism in 1660 changed the aristocracy's status. It no longer shared power with the king, and the concept of *amor patriae*, which had ranked above the king and put him on an equal footing with the aristocracy, was discarded by the absolutist power. The king institutionalised himself at the top of an unchallenged hierarchy, and praise for the Danish fatherland now came mainly from academics or poets in the service of – or seeking support from – the king himself. Thus, as Ole Feldbæk concludes, a medieval and early modern Danish identity did exist, but only among very small and privileged groups (Feldbæk 1996: 133).

The Danish absolutist state, the *Whole-state*, by the 1750s covered Denmark and Norway (the so-called Dual Monarchy) as well as the duchies Slesvig and Holstein. The first crucial battle of 'nation–state construction' was fought over how to define the concept of *fædreland*, which can be translated as fatherland or *patrie* (Feldbæk 1991: 131). The key theme of this 'pre-nationalism' debate was first, who were to be considered citizens of the fatherland, and, second, what kind of attachment these citizens should bestow upon the state: their loyalty to the king could not be questioned, but to what extent should this be followed by an emotional attachment, not only to the king, but to the state?

Tyge Rothe, who after a grand tour of Europe had become the teacher of the young Prince Frederik, initiated this debate in 1759 (Feldbæk 1991: 131–6). Inspired by Montesquieu and the philosophy of the Enlightenment, and at the same time keeping within the bounds of political acceptability (loyalty to the king), he defined the fatherland as the land where one chose to live, 'where I live well'. 'The fatherland is the people, not the earth on which they walk. The fatherland is the people with whom we are united as citizens, not those amongst whom we were born' (quoted in Feldbæk 1991: 133; my translation). Everyone who would be loyal to the Danish king, could therefore in principle become a member of the fatherland. This concept of the fatherland was clearly influenced by French thinking, as shown by Rothe's use of the French *patrie* for fatherland, but it was also well suited to the political reality of the absolutist monarchy: the king was surrounded by a large number of 'foreigners', especially Germans who held important political posts, and direct criticism of this group might both threaten and provoke them and indirectly amount to a questioning of the king's judgement.

Although one distinguished between Danes, Norwegians and the Germans from the two duchies (Holstein was also a member of the German Association), this had not yet been translated into an idea of these groups as distinct politically important entities. Rothe was therefore not compelled to point out what the relationship was between the three national groups, or between these national groups and the fatherland; the aim of Rothe's exercise was simply to define the relationship between the Danish Whole-state and the fatherland on one side, and 'the rest of Europe' on the other. One can, however, find signs of the sentiments which were to be further developed by nationalism: Rothe's call that 'everybody should love their fatherland' (Feldbæk 1991: 132) shows that political loyalty was no longer enough, the fatherland called for *emotional* loyalty, it deserved to be loved rather than simply obeyed.[4]

Rothe's 'cosmopolitan' definition of the fatherland was not to stand unquestioned. Eiler Hagerup, the son of the bishop of Trondhjem, published in 1767 a short but very influential pamphlet, which directly challenged the position of Rothe: the fatherland was not where one 'lived well' and where one chose to be loyal to a ruler, it was where one was born (Feldbæk 1991: 153–65). The king should as a consequence only appoint men who were born within the territorial realm of the fatherland. The battle between Rothe's voluntarism and Hagerup's genealogical reasoning ended ten years later with the latter's victory. This was not only an intellectual triumph; the birth definition advanced by Hagerup resonated with the material concerns of the small, but growing, Danish bourgeoisie who strove to secure a better place for itself within the state administration.

In this climate of awakening intellectual and material dispute, one of the most spectacular incidents in modern Danish political history took place. Struensee, the German born physician of the mentally ill Christian VII, gained control of the state by becoming the highest ranking minister from 1770 to 1772. He exploited the situation to create a freer press, but he also engaged in an increasingly open affair with Queen Caroline Matilde, who gave birth to a daughter who looked un-mistakably like Struensee. Ultimately, Struensee was outmanoeuvred in a coup, arrested and executed. Caroline Matilde was sent to Hanover without her children, where she died three years later. In political terms the main result of the short reign of Struensee was a heightened hostility towards those not born in the state, predominantly those identified as *Germans*. But while the Struensee period acceler-ated the development towards a fatherland criteria of birth, it did not bring about the change itself (Feldbæk 1991: 180). The interpretation of Struensee as a *German* traitor rather than simply a traitor was an outcome of the anti-German mood, not the cause of it. Nonetheless, rising anti-German sentiment led to the Law of Indigenous Rights in 1776, a remarkable phenomenon in European history as this was the first time a law declared that all official positions within a state were to be given to citizens born within the state. The 1776 solution was to close the fatherland off to the outside, but at the same time to stress that the fatherland consisted of all the king's possessions including Norway, Slesvig and Holstein.

The late eighteenth century was characterised by two trends. Parts of the intellectual strata had started to promote a sense of Danishness which praised the Danish language and Denmark's glorious past. 'The foreigners' whom this growing Danish identity was constructed against were increasingly singled out and identified as 'the Germans' (Feldbæk 1991: 181). The second trend of this period was to promote a state patriotism based on the fatherland of the Whole-state. These two trends could potentially come into conflict as Holstein and parts of Slesvig were

German speaking; the Whole-state was in other words a dynastic, multinational construction which could be threatened by a heightened emphasis on the Danish nation. While this was not yet the case – nationalism had not yet transformed Danes, Norwegians and Schleswig-Holsteiners[5] into Danes, Norwegians and Germans with cultural awareness and political goals – it was still something which concerned those supporters of the Whole-state who could envision such a trajectory (Feldbæk 1991: 187–8). The reigning state–fatherland construction solved the problem of several national groups by identifying the fatherland as the entity which encompassed all three of them, yet this was by no means going to be a stable solution.

The continuing debate over the status of 'the Germans' and Slesvig-Holstein highlighted the importance of Norden. A Nordic identity began to figure as part of the construction of the difference between the Whole-state and 'Germany': Denmark and Norway belonged to the glorious Norden, it was argued, Germany to an inferior 'Europe' (Feldbæk 1991: 220). This use of 'Norden' did not, however, amount to the romantic and political advocacy of a unified Norden which was to develop in the nineteenth century, in no small part because the contacts between Denmark and Sweden were few at this time.[6] Rather, 'Norden' was a symbolic background which bestowed a particular identity on Denmark and Norway.

The Slesvigian Wars

The fifty years from 1814 to 1864 were devastating for the Whole-state. Norway was lost to Sweden in 1814 due to Denmark's engagement in the Napoleonic Wars on the losing side, and Lauenborg, a small duchy south of Holstein given to Frederik VI by the Congress of Vienna, was only a meagre compensation. In terms of identity formation, however, the loss of Norway and the end of the Double Monarchy played a minor role compared to that which Slesvig and Holstein were to acquire. As noted, the tension between 'Germans' and Danes had been growing since the late eighteenth century, and the conceptualisation of the Whole-state which granted all groups within the state equal opportunities came increasingly under pressure in 1789–90.[7] Although the official position held that everybody born within the state was equal regardless of nationality, there were voices who argued that the Holsteiners should only be granted official positions within Holstein. 'The Germans' became identified, in this discourse, as those who (despite the Law of Indigenous Rights) kept the growing Danish bourgeoisie out of office, and it became therefore increasingly difficult to see the Schleswig-Holsteiners' role in the Whole-state as unproblematic: if they were 'Germans' should their equal status in the Whole-state not be reconsidered? This discussion went to the core of the relationship between the Danish state and the Danish nation – and the difference between the two began to be clearly articulated. The Danish state went as far as the Elbe, and the Holsteiners, who spoke German, were obviously not Danish in a cultural sense. But what about Slesvig, the large duchy in-between Denmark and Holstein which was divided into a Danish-speaking and a German-speaking half?[8]

The question of Slesvig's national and political status became intertwined with the liberal fight for a democratic constitution, a question which by the 1840s had been forced onto the political agenda (Feldbæk and Winge 1991; Rerup 1991; Winge 1991). The position of the Danish king was not surprisingly to fend off the calls for liberal democracy and to rearticulate the conception of the traditional Whole-state – that all three parts of Denmark were equal within the state – avoiding the question of which nation Slesvig belonged to. The 'National Liberals' were the driving force behind the transformation from absolutism to liberal democracy (Gundelach 1988: 188), but their classical liberalism nevertheless implied an elitism which made them sceptical of granting too much power to the 'uneducated' common people (Rerup 1992: 353). The 'national' component of the National Liberals referred to a burgeoning accentuation of a distinct Danish identity – in which linguistic criteria played a crucial part – and an ensuing distinction between Holstein and Slesvig. The river separating the two, 'Ejderen', thus lent its name to the 'Ejder programme' which stipulated that the connection between Denmark and Holstein was open to discussion, but that Slesvig was a part of Denmark that could not be surrendered.

The Schleswig-Holsteiners argued in contrast to both the Whole-state patriots and the National Liberals that the two duchies were a single political and economic unit. These visions came into open conflict in 1848. At the same time as the Danish constitution was drafted the Schleswig-Holsteiners organised themselves against the Whole-state. They wanted to secede, and whereas Holstein might have been able to leave Denmark, the demand that Slesvig should follow triggered Danish resistance. With the traditional Whole-state programme shattered, the predominant attitude in Copenhagen was that Slesvig should not be divided. There had been some negotiations between the Schleswig-Holsteiners and the Danish ministers Orla Lehmann and D. G. Monrad, both National Liberals, about a possible division of Slesvig based on a linguistic criteria, but the pressure against such a solution was too strong.

These competing Danish conceptualisations of Slesvig's relationship to Denmark implied different ideas of state and nation. The Whole-state programme, supported mainly by conservatives, insisted on the inclusion of several national groups in one state. The Ejder programme built upon a cultural nationalism and articulated a strong concern for the Danish population in Slesvig, but it was not so 'nationalised' that it granted the indigenous population the right to decide on the location of the boundary. Some expressed concern and willingness to protect the rights of the German-speaking population, others probably took a more assimilating route expecting that most of the German-speaking Schleswigers would realise that they were in fact Danish once they were strongly linked to a Danish state. A division based on a linguistic border – a policy which did not gain any prominence at this point – started with the nation rather than the state. Here the correspondence between nation and state – as well as a more benign and/or realistic view of the integrationist possibilities than the first two programmes – was granted higher priority than getting a larger state.

The war between Schleswig-Holstein and Denmark lasted from 1848 to 1851, when Austria and Russia forced Prussia to accept that Holstein was to be returned to the Danish king. The great powers had restored the Whole-state, but the problems between the Danish governments and the German Association – of which Holstein and Lauenborg were members – continued, and the second Slesvigian war broke out in 1863. This time neither luck nor the great powers were on Denmark's side. The Schleswig-Holsteiners had the military support of both Prussian and Austrian troops and advanced quickly into Jutland. A compromise was suggested, but the Danish prime minister Monrad declined, the war continued, and Denmark ended up losing Holstein, Lauenborg and Slesvig. Denmark had not only been substantially reduced, for the first time parts of the Danish nation were located within another state.[9] The Slesvigian wars had contributed to creating a general feeling of national identity, and now the nation was divided. Thus neither the Ejder nor the linguistic programme ended up, at the end of the Slesvigian wars, seeing its project fulfilled. Both were, however, to adapt and continue as competing discourses between 1864 and 1920.

The Slesvigian wars not only dealt a serious blow to Danish ambitions towards Slesvig-Holstein, they also brought an end to Scandinavism as a political project (see Chapter 1). Copenhagen had been a stronghold of Scandinavism since the 1830s. Indeed, when war broke out in 1848, the Swedish king sent 15,000 men (but only 4,000 reached Funen, the remaining 11,000 stayed in Scania). With the lack of official Scandinavian support for Denmark in 1864, the vision of a unification or a very close union was dead in Denmark. This, however, did not mean that 'Norden' lost its significance, but it turned from an actual political possibility to a cultural family of nations. As 'Norden' did not challenge national identities on political grounds, it could be freely articulated within national self-constructions as both an organic part of the Danish nation and a larger cultural space around Denmark.

The consequences of 1864: the development of the Kulturnation

Although a Danish national identity was articulated from the end of the eighteenth century, it was not until the Slesvigian wars that romantic nationalism became a mass phenomenon. The loss of Slesvig led to an inward turn; one of the most well-known figures of post-1864, Dalgas, led the cultivation of the hitherto uncultivated moor of Jutland, under the slogan 'What is lost on the outside should be gained on the inside'. What Denmark had lost in Slesvig and Holstein should be found territorially as well as symbolically inside herself.

The National Liberals had been crucial in putting the national question on the political agenda, but their nationalism was, broadly defined, primarily a political one (Rerup 1992: 343). Their belief in popular sovereignty was circumscribed by a delineation of who were deemed cultured and educated enough to exercise democratic rights – and they held no romantic vision of the peasantry, as they were situated within the liberals' 'general discontent for everything which took place outside of Copenhagen' (Gundelach 1988: 189; my translation). Yet, the formation of *Bondevennernes Selskab* (Association for the Friends of the Peasants) in 1846 was in part a result of the wish to build an alliance between urban liberals and the discontented peasants, with the goal of fighting the absolutist state (Rerup 1992: 350–1). After the adoption of the constitution in 1848, this alliance was, however, broken, and Bondevennerne developed into an independent political force, which helped create a space to the left of the rather elitist liberalism of many National Liberals. It also broke the ground for a nationalism which took the peasants and the 'common people' as its positive starting point – and which helped build an argument in favour of an extension of the political rights of these groups.

The influence of Grundtvig on the development of a critique of the liberal elite can hardly be overrated. Grundtvig is *the* figure in the history of modern Danish identity, and the only one to get his own chapter in the four volumes of *Dansk Identitetshistorie* (History of Danish Identity) (Lundgreen-Nielsen 1992). Not only is he the author of an overwhelming number of shorter poems, speeches, sermons, psalms and journalistic notes, he and his ideas also played an important role in the development of the Danish Folk High Schools and the Danish *andels-movement*.[10] Grundtvig's conceptualisation of the Danish nation resembled the Kulturnation Herder had applauded in the German context, and his central concept was 'the People', '*Folket*', or 'Volk' in German. He believed – in contrast to a number of other more liberal thinkers of his time – that 'the people' were in natural contact with the true meaning of the nation, that 'the people' did not have to be educated by the academics from Copenhagen about how to be real Danes.

The central Romantic category in Danish political discourses, for Grundtvig and today, is thus not 'the nation', but 'Folket' as can be witnessed by numerous examples: the parliament is called 'Folke-tinget'; the word is part of the name of political parties from Socialistisk Folke-parti (Socialist People's Party) over Det Konservative Folke-parti (The Conservative People's Party) to Dansk Folke-party (Danish People's Party); Folke-bevægelsen mod EF (The People's Movement Against the EC); the state church is 'den danske folke-kirke' (The Danish people's church); primary school is called 'Folke-skolen' (people's school), and so on. But more importantly, the Grundtvigian view has been continued as a normative position: 'Folket' inhabits a superior position, and if one can successfully construct oneself as speaking on behalf of 'Folket', then one has, as a consequence, gained the upper hand in a political debate.[11]

The period from the end of the Slesvigian wars to 1920 was characterised by a competition between three different political programmes, each drawing on a different conceptualisation of the relationship between the Danish state and the Danish nation.[12] The nationalism promoted by *Højre* ('Right'), a party of conservatives, the nobility and National Liberals was centred around the 'defence movement': Denmark and Copenhagen should be ready to defend themselves until the great powers came to their support. The hope was that Russia and/or France would force Prussia/Germany to hand back the northern part of Slesvig, or Southern Jutland as it was also called (which is the name that the Danish part of Slesvig has in Danish today). *Højre*'s line of thinking was to a large extent a continuation of the 'Denmark to Ejderen' policy of 1848 and 1864, and it argued that the future revision of the border between Denmark and Schleswig-Holstein/Germany should be based on (Danish) strength, not on the nationality of the (German) people living in the area. The Danish state did not have to be limited to the Danish nation – *Højre* was quite willing to extend Denmark into predominantly German areas – yet one difference to the earlier Whole-state patriotism lay in the recognition of the existence of nations: one was no longer emphasising the common traits inside the state which made nationality irrelevant as Whole-state patriotism had done; one believed instead in incorporating and assimilating Germans of a different nationality.[13]

Venstre ('Left'), the political party that developed out of *Bondevennerne*, followed a different route. They put 'the people' at the centre, and 'peoples' were assumed to have their individual characteristics which one should not or could not easily change. *Venstre* believed not only in the people's right to self-determination, but also that Southern Jutland would be allowed to join Denmark when Germany eventually became democratic. This 'nationality policy' had already been promoted during the war in 1864 when Lehmann and Monrad suggested a division of Slesvig according to linguistic criteria, and no matter how idealistic this 'wait and see' logic may have sounded, this was nevertheless close to how Southern Jutland eventually 'came back' to Denmark in 1920.

The third programme adopted the last logical possibility: that the Danish state would be smaller than the nation and since this was also the actual state of affairs, the policy was labelled 'a realistic foreign policy' by its supporters. The most prominent spokesman for this position, the journalist and politician Hørup, held that it was in Denmark's best interest to make friends with Germany, that this would strengthen Denmark even if it meant that Slesvig would have to be written off.[14]

At Versailles after the end of the First World War the German question was reopened and Denmark asked for a revision of the border based on a plebiscite. *Venstre*'s line had won and Denmark became for the first time a nation–state. The Conservative Party (*Højre*'s successor) and a part of the Left had not wanted to give up some of the areas with a German majority, amongst them Flensborg, one of the largest towns with a Danish majority in 1864. The border has remained where it was drawn in 1920, but the period from 1920 to 1955 did witness controversies over its sanctity. The most noticeable one came after the end of the Second World War when the first post-war prime minister, Knud Kristensen from the Liberal Party (Left), had to step down in 1947 after his unsuccessful attempt to reopen the Slesvigian question (sources collected in Hoffmeyer and Koch 1959).

The disaster of 1864 and the rewarding of the neutrality of the First World War with the reacquisition of Southern Jutland led to the construction of the *external* idea of the state as one of *anti-power politics*. Denmark, it was believed, was to pursue a low profile foreign policy based on negotiations and patience towards the great powers, a policy which, for example, manifested itself in the lack of resistance when German troops occupied Denmark in 1940 (Branner 2000). From the 1970s onwards this anti-power politics position turned increasingly in a more active direction with Denmark taking on a leading role in peacekeeping operations and development aid, issues which were presented as an antidote to the egoistic power politics of the superpowers (Agersnap 2000).

1920 and beyond: the Scandinavian welfare state

From 1920 onwards the line of thinking on the nation–state relationship which the Liberal Party and Grundtvig had articulated went from being one possible project to being the hegemonic one. The Danish nation and the Danish state became so closely knit together that Denmark could enter the textbooks as one of the few true nation–states of the world: it had gone in less than a hundred years through three stages, from a multinational, dynastic state over a divided Kulturnation to a nation–state. The result was a somewhat peculiar combination of the French and the German conceptualisations of state and nation: the state and nation are so tightly knit together that it seems impossible to think of the nation without the state – as in the French conceptualisation – and the nation is at the same time defined according to descent – as in the German model.

Taking a closer look at the internal idea of the state, 'Denmark' became a social democratic Scandinavian welfare state formed by the Social Democratic Party, a non-revolutionary socialist party who wanted control of the state in order to create a decent life for the working class and to protect its rights, not to promote a centralised communist system (Gundelach 1988: 192). These more modest ambitions notwithstanding, there is, however, no doubt that the more interventionist state constructed by the Social Democratic Party triumphed over the more limited liberal state supported by the Liberal and the Conservative parties. And 'the welfare state' became so successful that even current liberals and conservatives operate with political programmes which rarely, especially to a non-Scandinavian observer, question the fundamental social democratic vision of the state. When the prominent Danish sociologist Peter Gundelach argues that one can read the last 100 years of Danish history as the battle between the movements of the working class and the peasants, it is thus tempting to add that one can also read this period as a story of the increasing acceptance within these two groups of the battles won by the opposing side (Gundelach 1988: 296).

The Social Democratic struggle for the welfare state did not dispense with 'the People', rather it articulated this important concept into its own, slightly different terms. Feldbæk argues that by the mid-1930s, the workers' movement had developed a national identity which 'was built not upon the "God, King and Country" of the conservatives, nor the Grundtvigian programme of the folk high schools, but upon a feeling of a common attachment to the land and the language and to the new Danish society which the working class had built with their own hands' (Feldbæk 1996: 130). And as in the case of the Grundtvigian programme, the link to the nation and the (welfare) state went through 'Folket'. The idea that 'the People' formed the emotional and essential core of the nation, and that 'the People' should underpin and be represented by the state was symbolised in 'Danmark for Folket' ('Denmark for the People'), the title chosen by Stauning (one of the most influential Social Democratic prime ministers) for his new programme in 1934.[15] Stauning's 'People' was thus different from the victorious 'People' of the Grundtvigian movement in the sense that it was the working class, not the farmers, who formed the core of 'Folket'. Yet, a rearticulation of 'Folket' allowed the Social Democrats to negotiate the concept of the nation while simultaneously accessing selected parts of the cultural romanticism of the nineteenth century: 'Folket' had traditionally formed the 'true' core of the nation, and the two concepts were closely related yet at the same time distinct.

The replacement of the peasantry 'People' with the working class 'People' meant that the organic core of the nation changed, but that the relationship between 'the People' and the nation remained intact and there was therefore no direct antagonistic onslaught on a number of the Romantic elements associated with the nation.[16]

This commonality turned out to be very important for Danish political thinking: both the Grundtvigian and the Social Democratic construction of 'the People' evolved around an opposition between 'the People' and the 'elites' and an organic link between 'the People' and the nation. For the Social Democrats, the opposition ran between the working class 'People', who had provided the material foundations for Denmark on the one side, and the capitalist class on the other. For the Grundtvigians, the opposition was between 'the People' as the unspoilt, authentic peasantry (in cooperation with the liberal intellectuals), and the exploiting, modernised and de-cultured elites. The fact that both the Social Democrats and the Grundtvigians (through the Liberal and the Radical Liberal Party) came to have decisive impacts on the Danish state of the twentieth century did not cause this opposition to dissolve into an unproblematic correspondence between 'the People', the nation and the state. Rather, the relationship between 'the People' and the state was ambiguous: 'the People' both provided the true foundation for the nation (the working class or the peasants forming its organic core), and were at the same time potentially in opposition to the state. This opposition was of course more or less outspoken depending on who was in power, but it never disappeared and the insistence on a disjuncture between 'the People' and the political elite has remained a feature of the Danish discursive landscape. The correspondence between 'the People', the nation and the state might be fully accomplished, but 'the People' hold the power if this balance is seen as being upset. Politicians are as a consequence sensitive to events which can successfully be constructed as actions of 'the People'.

Summing up, we have in the Danish case a conceptual constellation which involves three elements. First, the tightness of the state–nation coupling: state and nation were fused and the nation was constructed as a German-type cultural nation. Second, the victorious internal state identity was constructed as the welfare state, the external identity in terms of anti-power politics. Third, the core of the nation is 'the People', and politics based on 'the People' implies that the state is the nation's state, that the state is legitimate and that the nation is secured. If the elite, however, is seen as the basis, the state gains an undue independence and becomes an apparatus of power and ambition. In Danish political thought, 'the People' and the state are thus *potentially* closely linked in terms of the state's ability to generate legitimacy, but they are also in a potential tension. The consequence for the debate on Europe has been that the 'Denmark' which confronted the European integration experiment has been a nation–state sensitive to, first, threats to political independence as this would easily be seen as constituting threats not only to the state, but also to the nation; and second, that it has had a state which due to its extended welfare scope would more easily be seen as threatened by an EC/EU moving into an increasing number of policy areas.

Introducing Europe: from the 1950s to 1972

Post-Second World War Western Europe witnessed an unprecedented degree of institutionalisation with the Council of Europe and NATO in 1949 and the EEC in 1957 organising different combinations of countries around different issues. Denmark was a founding member of the two former institutions, but abstained from the economic integration of the EEC for as long as Britain because of the large Danish agricultural exports to Britain. EFTA became instead the Danish free market framework in 1959 and it also offered a strong Nordic dimension as both Norway and Sweden were founding members. The Danish debate in the 1960s was thus centred on how to tackle a potential choice between the British and the Nordic options; and on the economic benefits of an EEC membership if Britain did join versus the loss of political independence entailed by membership (Hansen 1969). When the British application was finally accepted after two French vetos, Denmark decided to join after a referendum in 1972 with 63 per cent in favour and 37 per cent against. The 'yes – no' divide followed to a large extent a traditional left–right division with the Conservatives and the Liberal Party in favour, the Radical Liberal Party and the Social Democratic Party in favour but with 'no' minorities, and the Socialist People's Party voting against. The debate preceding the referendum was heated and set out two key elements which have remained important in the debate on Europe until today. First, although the two positions differed in their assessment of the political consequences of the EC, they nevertheless agreed on a negative view of European federalism. As Peter Hansen wrote in 1969, 'The Danish attitude towards the federalist plans of the early fifties was one of a curious mixture of reassuring disbelief and discomfort at the prospect of further division of Europe' (Hansen 1969: 17). Second, both agreed on the desirability of 'Norden': Denmark's position should be compatible with the protection of Nordic unity and the interests of the other Nordic countries. What the two positions disagreed on then – as they do today – was whether the EEC/EU entailed a federalist programme and how the Nordic option was to be secured in practice.

The heated debate in 1971–72 featured a yes-side which pointed to the economic benefits of a Danish membership and a no-side which argued, first, that these analyses were mistaken and, second, and more importantly, that the loss of political independence would be unacceptable. As Gert Petersen from the Socialist People's Party argued in the debate on Danish accession in the parliament, *Folketinget*, in December 1971:

> The continuing tendency to view the Common Market as a matter of cattle and how much butter we can sell is amazing. The Common Market is a lot more than that. It is also narrow political cooperation, including foreign policy cooperation, and one can blame the Common Market for a lot of things, but not that it is trying to hide its political nature, because it isn't.
>
> (*Sådan sagde de om Danmark og EF* 1972: 96–7; my translation)

As a consequence Denmark's degree of self-determination in the area of foreign policy would be seriously diminished (*Sådan sagde de om Danmark og EF* 1972: 99). But the no-side's argument was not only that Denmark would lose sovereignty vis-à-vis other countries; the EEC would also force Denmark to change its domestic policies within areas such as labour law, industrial policy and the rights of foreigners to buy land. The entire foundation of the welfare state was in short seen as being threatened by the loss of political sovereignty.

Turning to the conceptualisation of 'Europe', the yes-side argued that 'Europe' was not going to become a federation, that it would be unrealistic to expect the ambitions of the most integrationist states to become reality, especially when the institution came to include such 'moderates' as Denmark, Norway and Britain. 'Europe' was an association of independent states and was thus not going to encroach fundamentally on the sovereignty of the member states. 'Europe' would benefit politically and possibly also morally from Denmark's participation, and Denmark would benefit economically. Norden was important, but it was not, and could not be, a real alternative to Europe and Denmark should try to protect her own interests as much as she could. Fortunately, Danish membership would facilitate the creation of better conditions between the EEC and the Nordic non-members, and Danish membership would therefore, paradoxically, strengthen Norden rather than weaken it. This way the emotional affection for 'Norden' could be united with the practical, economic advantages of 'Europe' through the construction of a 'Norden (e.g. Denmark and Norway) in Europe'.

The no-side argued on the contrary that economic benefits notwithstanding, it was a fact that European integration *did* pose a threat to Danish political independence and thereby to the Danish (welfare) state. Even though Aksel Larsen from the Socialist People's Party called Europe 'a mysterious concept', it was clear that this 'Europe' was deeply politically integrated; that it threatened the Danish state; that it would support a capitalist liberal economic order; and that it would function as a bureaucratic superstate internally and externally. The latter superpower capability was perhaps most strongly suggested by Aksel Larsen, who compared it to Hitler's '*Neuropa*' and '*Das heilige römische Reich deutscher Nation*' (*Sådan sagde de om Danmark og EU* 1972: 90; Aksel Larsen's own spelling). In the light of the debates in the 1990s it is worth noticing that at the beginning of the 1970s the entity being threatened by a European federal state is 'only' the state whereas the 'no' position came to argue in 1992 that the nation was also threatened by European integration. Certain implicit cultural elements existed in the 'no' argument in 1971: the influx of guest workers – predominantly from Turkey through Germany – and the fear of Germans taking over Danish summer cottages, but cultural issues of national identity were not at the centre of the debate to the extent they were to become in the 1990s.

The no-side also tried to play the Nordic card by arguing that one had to make a choice between Norden and Europe. Although the NORDEK negotiations had recently stalled it was still possible to construct a Nordic economic union, and Aksel Larsen concluded that 'it is the choice between saying yes to a dubious Europe led by certain great powers who have never wished us well, and saying yes to Norden'

(*Sådan sagde de om Danmark og EF* 1972: 92). While 'Europe' threatened political independence, 'Norden' was not to be feared: there were no great powers in Norden, and the other countries were more 'like Denmark'.

The standard account of the debate in the 1960s and early 1970s emphasises the centrality of economic and material arguments, especially on the winning side (for example Pedersen 1996: 88), and economic advantages, in particular for the agricultural sector, were definitely the most frequently advocated argument in favour of membership. It is, however, also worthwhile to qualify this representation of the debate as solely 'economic' (Worre 1988: 362–3; Schou 1992: 335). While the yes-side emphasised the economic advantages of Danish membership, it was not devoid of political arguments in favour of membership. These took three different forms. First, it was argued that an enlargement with two Nordic countries (Denmark and Norway) and Britain and Ireland would change the internal political composition of the EEC in a more democratic direction and have a 'good political influence' on 'Central Europe'. Second, it was held that there were as many political interests that united certain political groups across the EEC countries as there were national interests. As Hilmar Baunsgaard of the Radical Liberal Party argued,

> More important [than legal issues] is the political understanding – or if one likes, political division – which increasingly cuts across borders. There are in all countries progressive as well as reactionary positions. Increasingly, political views have cut across borders, also across the borders of smaller and larger countries.
>
> (*Sådan sagde de om Danmark og EF* 1972: 77; my translation)

Third, and finally, one finds the 'security argument' in favour of integration: that economic and political integration was a precondition for a transformation of the traditional military rivalry between France and Germany. Jens Christensen, former head of the Foreign Ministry's EEC secretariat, writes about then Prime Minister Krag that 'His conclusion was that we would probably be a part of the United States of Europe in the next century. However, [Krag thought that] this was not such a bad thing taking into account what we had experienced in the first half of the century' (Christensen 1993: 147; my translation).

It is important to notice these political arguments, even if they were infrequently made, because they point to where the next debate would be centred when political arguments came more strongly to the fore in the 1990s. It is not the case that the politicians were lying about the nature of European integration in 1972 as has been subsequently claimed. But the fact that the integration process stalled at the moment when Denmark joined made an assessment of the potentials – and threats – of political integration much less pressing. When European integration picked up speed in the 1980s and early 1990s, Danes had become used to viewing integration as something which the yes-side could easily explain as a project of grand, but unrealistic, ambitions, which 'we', in the more 'down to earth' Nordic part of Europe, had not needed to concern ourselves with.

1992: the fall of Maastricht and the return of the nation

The successful attempts to reinvigorate European integration in the late 1980s and early 1990s, culminating in the adoption of the Maastricht Treaty in late 1991, confronted Denmark with a new situation. As argued in the introduction to this chapter, the debate over the Single European Act in 1986 did not constitute a new phase. The context was still that of the cold war, domestic politicking unrelated to the EC was a major factor in provoking the referendum, and the positions on the conceptual terrain followed by and large those of the 1971–72 debate. The no-side pointed to the political threat to independence and the liberal-capitalist character of the single market, and the yes-side pointed to the economic benefits and argued that sovereignty was not at stake.

The most important difference between the debate in 1992 and the two previous ones was that the Maastricht Treaty made it very difficult for the yes-side to construct the EC/EU predominantly as an economic institution and argue that the political implications of the EC/EU were few, insignificant and in the interest of Denmark. As the debate became centred around the political importance of European integration, it moved onto the political terrain which the no-side had tried to privilege since the early 1970s. The yes-side's strategy was to represent the EC as an intergovernmental form of cooperation taking place within a 'normal' international institution, but the no-side kept insisting that the EU was a superstate in the making. While the threat to political independence had always been the key argument of the no-side, its next move, carried out in 1992, was to claim that cultural, national identity was also being threatened by European integration.

This section will focus on the three main positions within the 1992 debate: the 'yes' advocated by the centre parties from the Social Democrats on the left, to the Liberal Party on the right; the 'no' argued by the most right-wing party, the Party of Progress; and the traditional 'no' of the left wing represented by the Socialist People's Party and the two social movements: the People's Movement against the EU and the June Movement (in 1992 called Denmark '92). (For a more detailed analysis of the individual parties, see Haahr 1992, 2000a, and 2000b.) Compared to the 'no' and 'yes' positions of the 1970s, we have a division of the 'no's' into a left-wing and a right-wing no.

The broad 'yes': 'Europe of the nation-states'

The key argument of the 'yes' position was that even if the EC was becoming a more *political* institution, it was still based on sovereign states; the European Union as outlined in the Maastricht Treaty, is not, in other words, a federation or a superstate. As Niels Helveg Petersen, the leader of the centrist Radical Liberal Party, and Minister of Foreign Affairs from 1993 onwards, put it: 'the nation-state will continue to be the decisive stone in the European construction', one should see the European Union 'not as a way to dispose of the nation-states, but as a framework for their closer cooperation' (9973).[17] The Liberal Party was definitely more in favour of an integrated Europe than the Radical Liberal Party and the Social Democrats. The Liberals supported, for instance, the development of a common foreign and defence policy within the EU, whereas the Radical Liberal Party and the Social Democrats had been against Danish membership of the WEU and the creation of stronger links between the EU and the WEU. But not even the Liberal Party argued in favour of a European federation modelled after, for example, Germany or the USA. The USA is on the contrary explicitly mentioned as that which the EU is *not*. The Prime Minister Poul Schlüter, from the Conservative Party, argued that 'Europe is not a state, it is not the USA.' Europe – in contrast to the USA – consists of nations and peoples who live *by themselves* not scattered *among* each other ('hulter til bulter'), and this is the way that it should be and will continue to be (Presentational programme of the Conservative Party).[18] Unfortunately, Schlüter said, the word 'Union' makes it sound as if Europe is moving in the American direction, when the reality is one of independent countries, nations and people interacting – as coherent and separated wholes – in a 'Europe of the Fatherlands'. The Danish 'fear of federalism' went so deep that when confronted with the 'no' argument that the EU was moving towards a more tightly integrated, federal Europe the response from the yes-side was not simply that the EU of the 1990s was identical to the EU of the 1970s and 1980s, but that it had in fact become *less* federal. Schlüter had stated in 1986 that 'the Union is stone-dead', a statement which was now constantly thrown back at him and the yes-side. Schlüter argued, however, that he was right in 1986, that the European federalists were strong in the 1980s but that they had suffered a setback at Maastricht. A similar reasoning was adopted by the Social Democratic Party in its defence of its change from a 'no' to the Single European Act in 1986 to a 'yes' in 1992, but this was a tricky and not fully convincing argument. It might be true that the early 1990s lacked the integrationalist reports of the previous decades, like those by Spinelli and Werner, but in practical terms the EC/EU had moved into a larger number of political issues. This disjuncture between the declaratory and the practical political levels was not explicated by the yes-side whose emphasis on the former level made them open to critique on the latter.

Probably the most successful move of the no-side was to construct all attempts towards further integration as 'federalism' thereby blocking a discussion of how a 'non-federal, but post-sovereign Europe' might be constructed. 'Federalism' was, in fact, used as a synonym for 'state', where 'state' came to imply a state built on the Danish nation-state model and with a similar degree of centralisation. The possibility that federations might differ significantly in terms of the degree of autonomy allocated to the sub-state level was thus a point which was not allowed to surface in the debate. The yes-side was also weakened by the lack of a Danish 'Europeanist' tradition. It is possible to think and argue romantically about the Danish nation; it is also possible to think and argue romantically about Norden – it is not, however, possible to draw on a similar romanticism in the case of Europe.

The choice of the yes-side was thus to leave the strong link between the nation and the state in the Danish conceptual constellation intact, 'Europe' is made up by nation–state constructions similar to the Danish one and a consideration of political constructions which are not (nation) states is blocked. But the fact that pro-integration politicians had to provide continued reassurance that the EU did not disturb this link shows that the link *was* under pressure. The fate of the nation was also addressed defensively, for example in the 10 minute presentation movie by the Conservative Party, which began with a Viking ship and a lecture by the famous Danish historian Thorkild Kjærsgård on the Danish nation's ability to survive just fine in Europe and ended with a Danish beech forest, the national tree and a key national-romantic symbol. Turning to the *external* idea of the state it follows from the traditional, Danish aversion to power politics that 'Europe' has to be constructed as not undertaking power political endeavours vis-à-vis the rest of the (non-western) world. The construction of the external identity of the Danish state as one of *anti-power politics* was in short lifted onto the external identity of 'Europe'. Proponents of the Maastricht Treaty mentioned on rare occasions that stronger cooperation between the EU members was necessary in order to compete economically with Japan and the USA, but the 'great power image' was in general avoided. The concept of 'Europe' of the broad 'yes' position was composed of nation-states on the one hand, but it was also one which argued that this nation-state based 'Europe' had to have a strong centre and a clear distinction between insiders and outsiders if security and economic issues were to be dealt with in a satisfactory way.

The broad 'yes' went from the Liberal Party on the right wing to the Social Democratic Party on the left. The Social Democrats were, however, careful on several occasions to distinguish themselves from the more pro-EU Liberal Party and its charismatic Foreign Minister Uffe Ellemann-Jensen. In the words of Ivar Nørgaard, spokesman on foreign policy:

> The Liberal Party is as far as I know in favour of taking steps, quick steps, and as many steps as we can possibly get the population to accept, towards a European federative state – this is what it writes in its programmes. We are definitely against this.
>
> (9901)

The Social Democrats were more concerned with the pace of the integration process than the Liberals, they were more troubled by the attempt to develop a strong foreign and security identity of the Union, and they were more worried about the impact of European social and environmental policies on Danish standards and legislation. The debate shows the Social Democratic Party as susceptible to the challenge from 'its' 'People' in the sense that the threat at the level of the state – in both its internal and external dimension – risked disturbing the assurance that 'the People' were being adequately represented by the state. What is put under pressure is in other words the Social Democrats' willingness to protect the welfare state which they themselves have created. The Liberal 'yes' is not in the same way troubled by 'the People' – here the main challenge comes from the claim that the EU is built upon a planned and highly regulated economy which runs counter to liberal principles.

Norden also played quite an important role in the debate with the yes-parties arguing that an independent/isolated Norden could not be seen as a proper alternative to Europe. According to Karl Hjortnæs from the Social Democratic Party: 'In 1972 there was a Nordic perspective outside the EC; today there is only a Nordic perspective inside the EC' (10008). Finland and Sweden had at this point applied for membership – Norway not yet – and this was used in support of the 'Norden in Europe' argument,[19] which held that the Nordic countries might possibly make a difference inside the EU, but that they did not constitute an alternative in and of themselves. Nor was that what the other Nordic countries wanted, they wanted to become members of the EU. This put Denmark in an advantageous situation, argued Poul Nyrup Rasmussen, the leader of the Social Democrats:

> Remember that Denmark right now adopts a unique geographical and political position, which can be the new opening for broader European and Nordic cooperation. We can find each other again in the Nordic welfare model after 20 years of separation, and we should hang on to this vision.[20]
>
> (10031)

As was argued above, 'Norden' is a Romantic construction which resembles, and supports, Danish national identity; it is also coupled to 'the People' so that the 'Nordic Peoples' stand in an organic relationship to each other as well as to their nation-states. The intimate relationship between 'Norden' and 'Denmark' is also forged at the level of the idea of the state: the 'Nordic welfare state' and the 'Nordic anti-power political state' conducting enlightened and moral foreign policy are seen as confirming the similarity of the Nordic states. The result is a construction of 'Norden' as an organic category similar to the nation, and it is therefore important for the yes-side to convince voters that 'Norden' can continue on organic terms within (the non-organic) 'Europe'. Thor Pedersen, Minister of the Interior, wrote that 'we cannot preserve a common Nordic set of values without a European association' (Pedersen 1992: 7). The non-organic 'Europe' thus becomes the guarantee of an organic 'Norden'.

The 'no's'

The left-wing 'no' contested the 'yes' argument on several accounts. It argued first of all that the Maastricht Treaty was a federalist, superstate project – the yes-side was either trying to deceive the population by deliberately constructing the EU in a digestible, non-federal form, or it had not yet grasped the full consequences of the Treaty and the Union. The more detailed logic of the no-side went as follows: Denmark is confronted by Europe, another state-in-the-making. At first the threat is political as increased political integration at the European level threatens sovereignty and the Danish state. But since the Danish state and the nation are so tightly coupled, a threat to the state comes to imply a threat to the nation and its cultural identity. With the protecting state gone, the defenceless Danish nation will be dissolved within 'Europe' and the Danish nation-state will have been completely replaced – politically and culturally – by the European nation-state. As argued above, the strategy of the yes-side was mostly a defensive one which remained within this logic, accepting the either/or logic of 'Denmark' versus 'Europe', only constructing a different picture of the actual EU: the political threat to the state was played down as it was argued that EU after Maastricht was composed of sovereign states.

The no-side's invocation of the threatened cultural nation also brought in the authentic 'People' of Grundtvigianism and the Social Democratic tradition; and this 'People' was constructed in opposition to the manipulating political elites. The fact that almost the entire establishment – the political parties, the trade unions, the employers unions and the mass media – recommended a 'yes' was turned against the yes-side itself in accordance with the negative connotations 'elites' have in Danish political discourses. If 'over-Denmark' was so keen on getting the Maastricht Treaty through there had to be something wrong, the argument went. Both the left-wing and the right-wing 'no's' emphasised the anti-elite identity of 'the People', but the left-wing 'no' was more concerned than the right wing with the future of the welfare state as an inclusive and social(ist) project and with the activist anti-power politics identity of the state. These arguments were close to the concerns of the more sceptical part of the Social Democratic Party who also feared cut-backs in the Danish level of social support, environmental standards and legislation of the labour market. The perceived threat to the Danish welfare state was, however, not only a threat to the state; because state and nation have become so tightly connected, the welfare state is constructed as representing a particular *Danish* choice where a unique relationship between nation and state has been forged. The left-wing 'no' as it was argued by the Socialist People's Party largely followed this construction; but other parts of the left-wing 'no', in particular as it was articulated from within the social movements, were more ambiguous in terms of its relationship to the traditional, introverted cultural nationalism of the right-wing 'no'.

This introverted, cultural nationalism was brought out by the right-wing 'no', which argued that immigration would be substantially higher with increased integration, that the more open borders envisioned by the Maastricht Treaty would cause an influx of radically different and threatening non-Danes. What should be protected from immigrants was first and foremost the Danish nation and Danish cultural identity, second, the – preferably deregulated – Danish state from the abuse of foreigners. The right-wing 'no's' coupling of Romantic nationalism and a neo-liberal economic programme also drew on a construction of 'the People' as anti-elite. 'The People' are being deceived by the state which steals 'the People's' taxes, and allows waves of immigrants to move to Denmark without caring for the elderly and sick who 'built Denmark'. Right-wing politicians, most predominantly Pia Kjærsgård, were thus very careful not to touch the welfare state as a guarantee of the life of the Danish People, but the right-wing welfare state is one which is highly restricted in terms of to whom it applies.

Turning to the conceptualisation of Europe, the Socialist People's Party, Denmark '92 and The People's Movement against the EC (the two most influential no-side social movements)[21] argued that Maastricht-EU was turning Western Europe into a great power – sometimes even a superpower – which would raise barriers against the outside world, most importantly against Eastern Europe, discipline the countries on the inside, and engage in neo-imperialist, military adventures especially in the areas with ex-colonial ties to France. The left-wing 'no' was not against 'Europe', they argued, but instead of building the yes-side's 'fortress Europe' which would exclude Eastern Europe, one should rather re-negotiate the whole institutional structure of Europe. 'An open Europe' was the catchword for this vision – later the Socialist People's Party launched the slogan 'A Europe in several dimensions' which entailed a similar vision – where a strongly integrated Western Europe was seen as damaging to the development of Eastern Europe, the third world, employment and the environment.[22] Again, as noted above, this not only fit with a traditional set of left-wing concerns, it also argued around the need for the state (alone or as part of 'Europe') never to be associated with traditional (exploitive, as it is seen here) power politics. In keeping with this 'open vision' and the strong emphasis on anti-power politics as the Danish foreign policy mode, security should be taken care of by a strengthened CSCE (now OSCE) because it is a purely interstate cooperation based on 'voluntary', sovereign decisions, not supra-national majority decisions, and because it includes all European countries – East and West, small and large – as equals. Even NATO, despite its traditional reputation as power politics incarnated, got stronger support from the Socialist People's Party as a security organisation than the EU, as it was not bound up with the 'deep integration' of the latter.

The right-wing Party of Progress was the only right-wing party that advocated a 'no' in 1992. The only dimension of European integration that they supported was economic. The Single Market should be the one and only aim of the EC/EU: 'We are saying no to a super-state with a planned economy controlled by Brussels where Danes cannot make any decisions without asking the EU' (Zeus, Oplysningsavis om Den Europæiske Union). The Maastricht Treaty was, as in the left-wing 'no' representation, seen as the beginning of the United States of Europe. It entailed centralisation and socialism; it was, in short, like the Soviet Union (Annette Just 9952). The right- wing 'no model' is self-proclaimedly anti-political – free market forces will solve the problems if they are left undisturbed – and its European vision is therefore, despite the attempt to phrase it as 'Europe of the Fatherlands', only economic. 'Economic Europe' does not involve an opening towards Eastern Europe, it does not involve development aid, and it does not involve a strong insistence on the necessity of the OSCE. Both of the two 'no-Europes' articulate in other words the external identity of the state as one of anti-power politics, but they interpret this identity to radically different effects when it comes to policy: 'Open Europe' argues an extroverted, active foreign policy; 'Economic Europe' argues an introverted, passive foreign policy whose main goal is to secure the European free market.

The emphasis on the neo-liberal market and (non-Nordic) foreigners by the right wing had little need or room for a Nordic vision. Norden played on the other hand a crucial role for the left-wing 'no'. Holger K. Nielsen, head of the Socialist People's Party argued that:

> It has been said that the other Nordic countries are on their way into the EC-Union. The truth is that there is an increasing resistance against the Union in

the other Nordic countries. A Danish 'no' would therefore lead to a completely new Nordic discussion of the relationship between the Nordic countries and the European cooperation. We could help develop this Nordic perspective into something constructive.

(10032)

The Socialist People's Party as well as the Denmark '92 movement did not advocate that Denmark leave the EC altogether, but they constructed Norden as the means to slow down the speed of integration within the EC/EU. The Nordic countries would support Denmark's attempts to counter the more pro-integrationist countries within the EC if they chose to become members, the no-side said, a point they substantiated by pointing to the growing 'no' in polls in the three prospective Nordic members.[23] The Europe–Norden issue was radicalised by EC opponents more critical of European integration than the Socialist People's Party, most clearly by the People's Movement Against the EC, a social/political movement dating back to 1972. Their construction of the choice followed the logic of 1972: Norden was *the* alternative to the EC/EU (Nissen 1992), a possibility raised by the no-side on the eve of the referendum. If the yes-side played the governmental side of the Nordic card, arguing that 'Sweden is applying for membership', the no-side played the 'people side' of the Nordic card, arguing that the polls were showing a larger and larger percentage against membership in Finland and especially in Sweden (Norway had not yet applied).

It is hard to understand the no-side's insistence on 'Norden's' importance if one looks at institutional structures: political integration in Norden has never been particularly successful, as described in Chapter 1, and it would seem unlikely – probably even to the no-side itself – that Nordic integration could form an institutional alternative to the EU. But the main attraction of 'Norden' is not as an institutional alternative – the clue of using 'Norden' in the 'no' discourse is rather to argue the organic character of 'Norden' versus the non-organic character of Europe. The EU is seen as a state ahead of the emergence of any people, it is power at the cost of spirit whereas 'Norden' and Denmark make up logical sequences from people(s) over nation(s) to (welfare) state(s). It is 'Norden' as a romantic cultural community underpinned by different, yet similar, peoples which allowed the no-side to construct the 'yes' in Sweden and Finland as manipulating elite projects unattuned to their peoples.

Post-Maastricht

The Edinburgh Agreement

The referendum in 1992 was a very close race with 49.3 per cent voting 'yes' and 50.7 per cent voting 'no'. While celebrating their victory the no-side attempted to construct the Danish people as a singular entity (despite the almost 50 per cent who had voted 'yes') and, simultaneously, to present a particular picture of Danish traditions, that is, to turn the result into an expression of a deep truth or essence of Danishness. The no-side argued that the outcome was a vindication of Danish traditions (Pedersen 1993: 69–70) and democracy: 'It is not an overstatement to say that this was a historic demonstration of the forces behind real democracy with active participation of informed people' (Meyer 1993: 15). The pride factor was re-enforced into an almost unbeatable Danish self-assuredness when Denmark one month later won the European football championship.[24] It was important for the social movements to construct themselves as *movements*, not political parties; as part of 'the People', not as elites,[25] and one of their main claims was that 'upper-Denmark' (including the political parties) was out of touch with the real Denmark, which the movements on the other hand were a part of. As a consequence, the winning side came close to saying that all real Danes who belonged to 'the People' had voted no. The construction of a strict dichotomisation between elites and the establishment versus the People and the movements allowed the no-side to articulate the anti-elite, anti-state potential of the basic people–nation–state constellation. The yes-project on the other hand was per definition blocked from making these appeals.

But the Grundtvigian tradition with its emphasis on information, dialogue and the equality between the expert and the ordinary citizen influenced the view of the debate beyond the ranks of the 'no' camp: the 'Danish way of dealing with the Maastricht Treaty' was seen in general as uniquely Danish. Not only was Denmark one out of only three EU members to make the Treaty the subject of a referendum, but the emphasis on having a long and thorough public (*folkelig*) debate was seen as embodying the essence of Danish political culture. Hundreds of thousands of copies of the Maastricht Treaty were picked up at the public libraries, the Edinburgh Agreement was printed in a newspaper which was sent to all Danish homes, and Danish newspapers were proud to report how journalists from abroad were impressed by the general level of knowledge amongst the public on the Maastricht Treaty and the EU. When 'no' became the result, the yes-side usually interpreted this as a sign that more information might have been needed, but this with praise for the people, and hopeful statements about the signal sent to the EU.

After the 'no' it remained to be seen whether the other members of the EU would continue their plans, as claimed by the yes-side, or would go back to the negotiation table and start all over again, as argued by the no-side. It turned out that the yes-side had been right in predicting the other members' unwillingness to stop the entire process of ratifying the Treaty, but in contrast to their predictions Denmark did in fact get a 'second chance' and some accommodation by the rest (for a longer account of the negotiations, see Petersen 1993). The Socialist People's Party – from the no-side – initiated the drafting of the document which Denmark would present at the next EU Summit in Edinburgh in December 1992. The Social Democrats and the Radical Liberal Party were invited and the three wrote the so-called National Compromise, entitled *Denmark in Europe*, which was handed over to the Government, who accepted it with some minor revisions. In Edinburgh the most important parts of the National Compromise were approved by the other EU members, and Denmark had another referendum in front of her. According to the Edinburgh Agreement, Denmark got the (in

Denmark) famous 'four exemptions': no to union citizenship, no to the third phase of the EMU (including the common EU currency), no to common justice and police affairs, and no to common defence policy including not least that Denmark would not join the WEU. The Edinburgh Summit also agreed on some declarations about subsidiarity and a more open EU. The exact meaning of the four no's as well as the role of the principle of subsidiarity became a central part of the debate before the referendum on 18 May 1993. Most of the debate concerned the difference between the Edinburgh Agreement and the Maastricht Treaty and the no-side was largely right when it claimed that the substantial differences were small. But it is more important to grasp how these small differences could make the crucial difference between 'no' and 'yes' (not only by moving the necessary 0.7 per cent, but by actually shifting the vote by 7 per cent as 56.7 per cent voted in favour of the Edinburgh Agreement). Obviously, some of the basic categories of how Danes construct Denmark and Europe were influenced and the four exceptions therefore offer a unique possibility for getting a deeper understanding of the structure of Danish political discourse.

First, the exemption from union citizenship was followed by Danish declarations that despite the exemption Denmark would fulfil the substantial part of what was envisioned in the idea of a union citizenship: foreign residents were already able to vote and be candidates at local elections, and Denmark would not deny EU residents in Denmark the right to vote in elections for the European Parliament. The problem it seemed was that these guarantees could not be called 'union citizenship'. Clearly, the *name* citizenship was crucial here – not the content. As Ivar Nørgaard said in the first parliamentary debate on the Edinburgh Agreement, the union citizen-ship was or could be perceived as a move towards a United States of Europe (Folketingstidende IV, 1992–93, 5318–19). Citizenship was seen as tightly linked to Denmark, and Denmark only, and the introduction of another citizenship was constructed as a threat not only to the Danish state but also to the Danish nation.

Second, Denmark would not participate in the third phase of the EMU, which would involve the introduction of one single currency throughout the EU. The Maastricht Treaty had, however, already stipulated that Denmark would make its participation in the third phase of the EMU dependent on the result of a new referendum, and since only a few of the EU members met the criteria for entering the third phase of the EMU anyway, it was altogether hard to judge how much of a difference this point would make. But the debate did not revolve primarily around the economic implications of the EMU, rather it was centred on whether the EMU implied a move towards a federal Europe where Danish national identity would be dissolved. No-proponents in 1992 had argued that the EMU would put an end to the Danish coin with the Danish Queen's portrait; in 1993 the yes-side would tap into the same theme pointing out that the coin and the Queen were now definitely out of danger.

Third, justice and police affairs were also a source of contention. The Edinburgh Agreement declared that Denmark could not agree on these affairs being trans-ferred from the area of interstate (the so-called third pillar of the Maastricht Treaty) to supra-national cooperation (the first pillar) (Petersen 1993: 93). However, the Maastricht Treaty already provided Denmark with the possibility of blocking the development of EU justice and police cooperation, so the exact importance of the exception was also in this case unclear.

Fourth, probably the most significant difference between the Maastricht Treaty and the Edinburgh Agreement was within the area of defence policy. Denmark would neither join the WEU, nor participate in EU discussions and decisions on defence matters. The WEU had been an easy target before the Maastricht referendum as the no-side had constructed the common defence policy as evidence that the EU was becoming the United States of Europe: a European army would be the ultimate symbol of this European state.[26]

The debate over whether the Edinburgh Agreement was radically different was inconclusive: if one looked for elements which were not already included in or possible according to the Maastricht Treaty, then one was left with a meagre result. But to argue that nothing had changed would be to miss the crucial point that the perhaps small changes nevertheless pointed at important symbolic areas as far as national identity was concerned: citizenship, currency/coin, defence and police. The Edinburgh Agreement was thus primarily important as an agreement between 'the elite' and 'the people' in Denmark, not as an agreement between Denmark and the other EU members and it was therefore crucial that the government/'elite' promised that any future change of any of the four reservations would have to pass a new referendum.

In terms of the state–nation–Europe constellation the yes-side's strategy was to reinforce the argument that the EU was only intergovernmental cooperation, and that sovereignty was not really as threatened as seemed to be believed by 'the public'. The no-side continued where it had left the Maastricht Treaty on 3 June 1992, arguing that the Edinburgh Agreement notwithstanding, the whole package was still leading in the direction of a superstate with ensuing threats to the Danish state and the Danish nation. When the Edinburgh Agreement was approved by a 56.7 per cent majority it was not the Vikings or the successful Danish football team who made it to the international media: fighting broke out between the police and young anti-EU protesters in Copenhagen resulting in the police firing, for the first time since the Second World War, at a demonstration. Fortunately, no one was killed, but pictures of injured youngsters and burning barricades presented both the Danes and the outside world with a very 'non-Danish' scene. Even if the violent means of the protesters were highly criticised, the incident was still interpreted as a striking sign of the gap between the EU optimism of the political establishment and the reluctance of the electorate.

Amsterdam and the EMU

The debates over the Amsterdam Treaty in May 1998 and the EMU in September 2000 have continued along the basic positions outlined in 1992 and 1993. The debate on Amsterdam was quite brief and the outcome was, by Danish standards, a relatively secure win for the yes-side with 55.1 per cent in favour (see also Friis 1999 and Petersen 1999). The EMU referendum on the other hand became a thriller. Polls had shown substantial support for a 'yes' over the spring and summer, but in the last month before the referendum the no-side suddenly gained strength and won a 53.2 per cent victory. In terms of themes, substance and the concept of the state, the two debates came to supplement each other. The first focussed on the overall political direction of the EU, in particular its foreign policy dimension and enlargement, and the external aspect of the state, that is, the EU as a peace project, and the borders of Denmark. The second debate centred on the economic nature and consequences of the EMU and the internal aspect of the state, more specifically the possible threats to the welfare state and whether the EMU was a social democratic or a liberal project.

An important change from 1993 to 1998 was the appearance of a more diversi-fied pattern of EU support: the Socialist People's Party had argued against the Maastricht Treaty in 1992, yet as they were included in the drafting of the National Compromise, they recommended a 'yes' in 1993. After heated internal debate – and the inability to convince its voters of the changed and positive nature of the redrafted treaty – the party returned to its traditional EU-sceptical position and recommended a 'no' to the Amsterdam Treaty. A minority centred around Sten Gade and his 'New Europe' campaigned, however, in support of a 'yes' arguing that globalisation required a transnational response inside the EU.

The Social Democratic Party had had problems convincing its voters of the positive nature of the EU, but more resistance was now found amongst liberal and conservative voters as well (Haahr 2000a: 312–13). One of the outcomes was the creation of the group 'Europe of the Nations', which drew upon a traditional conservative construction of the nation-state as the protector of 'God, King and Country' in a Europe made up of similar nation-states. This organisation had no ambition of becoming a mass movement and drew much less on the rhetorical strength of 'the People' than did the right- and left-wing 'no's'.

These important changes notwithstanding, the 'no' was still found primarily on the wings of the political spectrum, and its key argument was still that the EU is a superstate project threatening political sovereignty and national identity. The yes-side, on the other hand, argued defensively that it was unrealistic to expect a European federal state to emerge, and that Danish sovereignty was therefore not fundamentally at stake. As Anders Fogh Rasmussen, the leader of the Liberal Party, the most pro-integrationist of the larger parties, argued in the first round of parliamentary debate on accession to the EMU 'our vision is an EU where sovereign nation-states cooperate voluntarily'. This illustrates how almost ten years after the negotiation of Maastricht, even the most pro-integrationist politicians still had difficulties breaking with the nation–state construction. Another apt illustration of this came two days before the EMU referendum when Fogh Rasmussen in an interview under the headline, 'Fogh suggests a more offensive EU policy', argued that the fear of federalism in the Danish population should be countered through the creation of an EU document which clearly delineated which issues were to be dealt with by the nation-states and which ones by the EU.[27] Clearly, this suggestion was strategically aimed at securing a 'yes' in the referendum, but its defensive character is still noteworthy.

The yes-side's reliance upon, and inability to rethink, the basic state–nation constellation implies that it cannot take the offensive at the level of the basic conceptualisation of Europe and Denmark's relationship to the EU. This, however, did not prevent yes-proponents from attacking the arguments of the no-side more aggressively in 1998 than they had done in 1992 and 1993. The debate was to a large extent focussed on the political future of the EU, in particular on the question of enlargement to the East and the first move of the yes-side was to invoke 'the security argument'. It claimed that the initial idea behind European integration had been to overcome the rivalries of the nation-states which had caused two world wars, that this had now been accomplished inside Western Europe, but that the EU had a moral as well as a strategic interest in extending this logic to Eastern Europe and to overcoming the division of the continent. Since East European enlargement depended upon the acceptance of the Amsterdam Treaty, Denmark had a responsibility for not creating a major crisis within the EU. The no-side argued in response that the Amsterdam Treaty was problematic inasmuch as it limited the first round of enlargement to five countries and, second, that peace between states was not achieved, but threatened, by forced integration.

The Danish People's Party, a party formed by a breakaway group from the right-wing Party of Progress, had had a very good general election in March and constructed its 'no' around immigration and border control. Kristian Thulesen Dahl argued that 'we will receive an increasing number of illegal immigrants, and we will without question experience increased criminal activity' (*Folketingstidende I, 1997–98*, p. 203). The yes-side sought to exploit this in an offensive strategy which argued that the 'no' of the left wing was indistinguishable from the one of the right wing, and that voting 'no' therefore equalled support for an exclusivist nationalism most socialists would normally object to. The June Movement in particular came under the yes-side's attack in April 1998 when a number of campaign posters for the upcoming referendum were sent to several newspapers for a preview. One of the posters featured the headline 'Welcome to 40 million Poles in the EU!', and although the smaller prints presented a pro-East European messages, the poster was eventually withdrawn before its release.[28]

The argument that the two no's were in fact one was made even more emphatically in the debate over the EMU. This time the key target was the Socialist People's Party who argued, of course, that their programme was radically different from that of the right wing. The problem in making that claim in a convincing manner was, however, implicitly acknowledged by the decision of the Danish People's Party to adopt a more withdrawn stance in the final weeks of the debate in order not to jeopardise the left wing's no-support. While the yes-side tried to play the nationalist card against the left wing 'no', the no-side on both wings responded by drawing out one of its traditionally strongest weapons: it argued that increased integration would lead to the abolition of central features of the Danish welfare state, in particular the retirement pension, incidentally called *Folke-pension* in Danish, and granted to everybody over 67 regardless of income and fortune. In making this argument, the left-wing welfare 'no' was espousing a certain 'state nationalism', for example that Denmark would always have superior standards concerning democracy, environment, gender equality, handicapped people and so on, even if this was not identical to the cultural, romantic national- ism of the right wing. The no-side's pressure on the welfare state became so successful that the yes-side's argument that the EMU concerned only the common currency, not fiscal policy, did not stick and the government saw no other option but to issue a guarantee that the retirement pension would not be touched in the future. The left-wing no-side argued, second, that the EMU represented a neo- liberal mode of organisation which amongst other things would postpone the full inclusion of Eastern Europe even further. This claim presented the yes-side with something of a dilemma. On the one hand, the Social Democrats were trying to convince their – and other socialist – voters of the social democratic character of the EU,[29] on the other hand, there was a limit to how much this argument could be played up without making liberal voters sceptical. A similar logic applied to the Liberal Party which had to counter its voters' fear that Europe would become too tightly regulated and social democratic.

The rejection of the EMU by 53.2 per cent caused celebration amongst the 'no' parties and movements and concern within the yes camp. This referendum was not, in contrast to the previous ones, forced upon Denmark, but a choice of the Social Democratic government, and the political stakes were therefore considerable: a 'no' in the referendum would block the consideration of any of the four exemptions of the Edinburgh Agreement for a significant period of time. Although the vote made little difference in changing Denmark's position – it continues to fix the crown to the euro – the outcome was nevertheless an affirmation of Denmark's position as a reluctant member of the EU drifting away from the centre of power and influence. The no-side argued very much along the lines of 1992 that the result was a vindication of 'the People's' unwillingness to be manipulated by the elites as well as the resistance against a federal Europe. The yes-side on the other hand tried to take the result in its stride. Most politicians argued that although the result evidently showed the Danish reservations towards the EU, this was also a sign that one needed to have more information on and debate about European integration. Nyrup Rasmussen suggested, for example, that future EU questions should be the subject of *folke-høringer*, that is gatherings to 'hear the People'. This combination of the liberal belief in educating the people couched in the language of Grundtvigian privileging of 'the People' illustrates that while the yes-side's attack on the apparent nationalism of the left wing tries to legitimate a narrow concern with the nation, it does not go as far as trying to destabilise the concept of 'the People' itself. Where to turn in terms of the conceptualisation of the relationship with Europe is, however, an unsolved matter.

Rearticulating the 'yes': Europe of the regions and Federal Europe

The Danish EU debate has been heated since 1992, and the main discourses have, as a consequence, changed their emphases and strategies to better counter their opponents. Yet there is also a remarkable stability within this debate inasmuch as both the yes-side and the no-side construct their European policies around a conceptual constellation which ties state and nation closely together. Both discourses seek, in other words, to protect this state–nation fusion and the final question therefore becomes whether there has been any attempt to break with this basic constellation and more fundamentally rethink 'Denmark' in the context of an integrating Europe. Such an attempt at rearticulation should be found on the yes-side. The no-side's insistence on protecting the nation–state fusion provides no incentive to fundamental rethinking, whereas the yes-side has a problem justifying the representation of the EU as an intergovernmental project in the light of the integration which has been accomplished.

This problem was exactly the starting point of Lars Hedegaard, an editor and journalist, who argued after the 'no' in June 1992, that the yes-side should have acknowledged that the Maastricht Treaty *did* imply the beginning of the dissolution ('afvikling') of the Danish state, *but* that this was a good thing as the state had turned out to be 'a dangerous form of organisation for Europe' (Hedegaard 1992: 17). Instead of attempting to reinforce state sovereignty one should acknowledge that the coming political organisation of Europe would be made up of a network of different levels: regional, national (the states), European and global. Hedegaard did not envision the dissolution of national and regional identities within an integrated Europe, but argued on the contrary that the diffusion of state sovereignty will allow those 'peoples (nations)' who were assimilated by the states (as Brittany for example was forced to assimilate to 'France'), to regain cultural and political status (Hedegaard 1992: 16). In terms of the basic nation–state constellation, Hedegaard de-links the bond between the state and the nation, partially lifts the state to the European level – where the coherence of the state is dissolving – and leaves the nation and 'Folket' at the Danish level.

While Hedegaard does not himself use this term, his Europe accords with what became known as 'Europe of the Regions', a construction which was argued by Peter Duetoft of the Centre Democratic Party in the parliamentary debate in 1992: 'We are moving towards a Europe of the regions, which will be very decentralised and very beautiful. It is a "local democratic" Europe, we are creating, not a central-ised great power, although some are trying to present it that way' (9967). This construction draws upon the traditional Danish superiority bestowed upon decentralisation and 'local democracy'[30] as opposed to centralisation, while simul-taneously claiming that this does not imply the loss of the Danish Kulturnation which could be equally well protected by a 'Europe of the regions' as within the old-fashioned Danish nation-state. Danish culture, argues Duetoft, has a long and strong European heritage. It is not threatened by anybody or anything outside Denmark, such as the Maastricht Treaty; rather 'It is threatened by those people who forget that they are Danish by forgetting their history, their language and their background' (9968). The 'Europe of the Regions' slogan could in principle be an elegant method of getting it both ways: it says that Europeanisation is not only about centralisation, it is about breaking up the larger European nation-states and constructing smaller units. As a model for the reorganisation of Europe, this suggestion has fewer ramifications for Denmark than for countries like

France, Spain and Italy, which have strong regional identities and movements. Denmark is so small that it is not to be divided into 'regions', and the whole of Denmark would be a region in a 'Europe of the Regions' together with Bavaria, Silesia and Catalonia. Actually, argued Duetoft, a 'Europe of the Regions' would allow Denmark to adopt a stronger role in Europe – much like it used to have before the middle of the nineteenth century (9966).

Has anyone advocated a more radical reconstruction of 'Europe' and 'Denmark'? In fact there were a few intellectuals who in 1993 tried to open the debate by consciously referring to a 'Federal Europe', some of them, all known from the EU debates but some from the no-side and most from the yes-side, gathered in the so-called 'Club of Federalists' (Føderalistklubben 1993).[31] One of the (moderate) 'no' advocates, professor of economics at Odense University, Christen Sørensen, argued that the Maastricht Treaty was problematic because it implied a confederal structure rather than a federal one (Sørensen 1992: 17). A federal Union would strengthen the democratic deficit by extending the European Parliament into two chambers modelled on the American Congress. The confederal Europe of Maastricht on the other hand would strengthen the role of the Council of Ministers and the Commission. This federal Europe did not, however, correspond to the 'Federal Europe' constructed by the no-side. Rather the Europe of Sørensen and associates began with de-linking the question of political sovereignty as embodied in the state and cultural identity as embodied in the nation. The main differences between 'Federal Europe' and 'Europe of the Regions' are, first, the conscious choice of the provocative 'federalism' as a strategic move to attack the no-side through its central category of danger; second, its higher degree of concern for the solution of the problems of European democratic accountability; and, third, the claim that national identity would have to supplemented with – although not replaced by – a European identity (Sørensen 1992: 17). The development of a European cultural identity is envisioned as an underpinning of the political level where there has to be enough cultural commonality to prevent representatives in the European Parliament from voting according to national lines. But it is also important to notice that Sørensen abstains from using the term 'folk' ('the People') about the required European identity: while a European 'national type' identity can co-exist with the national ones, the development of one European people (as understood along the lines of the Danish 'Folk') would probably infringe too much on national identities.

As it happens, few people have argued like Hedegaard, Duetoft, and the Club of Federalists. The attempt to dissociate the link between the state and the nation puts too much pressure on the basic state–nation constellation even when it is argued that this does not threaten the cultural nation. Attempts to provide an alternative to 'Europe of the nation-states' have remained sparse throughout the 1990s, and have perhaps even declined since 1993. These discourses are nevertheless important because they would be amongst the likely alternatives to the 'Europe of the nation-states' if this construction comes under increasing pressure from the development of the EU.

Conclusions

This chapter has argued that the key to an understanding of the Danish debate over Europe since the beginning of the 1990s lies in the particular relationship which was forged between the concept of the state, the concept of the nation and the concept of the People. The loss of Norway in 1814 and Slesvig and Holstein in 1864 meant that the Danish state was for the first time not presiding over the whole of the Danish nation. The simultaneous expansion of a Danish Romantic nationalism and the drawing of the border in 1920 produced a unique constellation of a French state-nation, which forged a very tight relationship between the state and the nation, coupled to a German cultural conceptualisation of the nation. To the Danish French–German combination of state and nation were added two important elements. The first refers to the domestic content of the state; the Danish state became in the last three quarters of the twentieth century a welfare state, at first formed and fought for by the Social Democratic Party, but later supported well beyond the ranks of the centre-left. The achievements of the welfare state in terms of social policies, health policies, gender equality and so on have often been at the heart of the disputes between the pro-integration side and their opponents, with the former arguing that these welfare issues were not touched by European integration policies, and the latter arguing that the EU would threaten those standards in the future if it was not already doing so. The specific definition of the internal state project as one of a welfare state made the state more vulnerable in terms of anti-integration arguments than it would have been had it been organised according to more liberal principles. The second element concerned the content of the nation which in the tradition of Romantic nationalism emphasised the unquestionable positive role of 'the People', *Folket* in Danish. The People are differentiated from the elite and defined by an opposition between (rural or working-class) 'ordinary people' and the (urban) elite; between 'those in contact with the soul of the nation' vs. those who have lost that connection (be that because they are cosmopolitans, intellectuals, or pursue narrow, egoistic economic interests). The importance of being close to the 'ordinary people' is crucial to the Danish construction of state and nation (and thereby of possible Europes) as it is through the 'ordinary people' that the soul of the nation is reached.

This conceptual constellation of state, nation, and People has imposed an important set of restrictions on which political projects Denmark could be engaged in vis-à-vis Europe. Specifically, it means, first, that it is very difficult to dissociate the state and the nation, that is, to envision decreased political independence without constructing this as a threat to the nation. Second, as a consequence, it becomes equally difficult to conceive of political constructions in terms other than states, and international institutions are as a consequence perceived in terms of their state-like features and potentials. The EU is therefore presented either as a normal interstate cooperation or as a classical state-building project. The debate in the 1990s became locked into these two options with the yes-side arguing that the EU did not exceed the former, and the no-side claiming that the EU was a new superstate.

One could then speculate whether it is Denmark's 'Frenchness', the inability to think of the nation and the state on separate levels, which has underpinned the consistent high level of no-support from 1992 and onwards. Or, in other words, if Denmark had been more German, would it perhaps have been possible to allocate political authority to Brussels without feeling that cultural, national identity was threatened?[32] Maybe. The situation is, however, that 'Denmark' has been very resistant to embarking on such a change of thinking. A Europe which goes beyond 'Europe of the nation-states' is a threat in Danish political discourses, and being able to construct one's opponent as a proponent of a tightly integrated Europe is a powerful discursive move. Since it is very difficult to construct any models which loosen the link between the state and the nation without then being characterised as federalist, the debate is locked between two choices: the intergovernmental Europe of the nation-states and the United States of Europe.

But neither of these two positions provide a stable point from which to advocate a policy towards an integrating Europe. The yes-side's intergovernmental Europe is under severe pressure as the EU – the exemptions of the Edinburgh Agreement notwithstanding – has moved beyond the traditional interstate cooperation from which sovereignty can easily be retracted. As the integration process continues it becomes increasingly difficult for the pro-EU side to uphold their claim that the EU is never going to infringe upon questions of social and welfare policy. In that case, one could point at two different possible developments. One would be Danish withdrawal from European integration, either completely or to an inferior role within a flexible, or multi-speed, Europe; in other words a victory for the no-side. Another option would be a change of the basic conceptual constellation in order to de-link the state and the nation and reconstruct the meaning of political sovereignty.

But the no-side does not inhabit a stable platform either. For one thing, its argument that in the case of Danish rejections the EU will stop and reconfigure itself according to Danish priorities was proven close to false in the case of Maastricht, as the Treaty was adopted by the rest of the members, and will turn out to be completely unfounded in the case of the rejection of the EMU in September 2000. The integration process might get stalled for a number of reasons, but Danish objections are unlikely to be one of them. Second, it has been the logic of the debate that the no-side has been the negative part within the process, the one rejecting the outcome of the government's negotiations. As the no-side comprises a mixture of left-wing socialists worried about the fate of welfare and democracy within the EU but not seeking a Danish withdrawal, old Marxists aiming for precisely this, conservatives worried about the state of the nation, liberals protesting against a regulated Social Democratic Europe, and right-wing cultural romanticists warning about the influx of immigrants, the task of providing a coherent, positive definition of the alternative Europe one wishes to propose will be a huge and, probably, impossible one. There is thus no sign of the European issue disappearing from the Danish political agenda, and there are no signs that the battle will be over soon either: struggles over the concept of Europe, and Danish policy towards it are likely to continue at full force.

Notes

* A number of people have provided very valuable comments and critique on different versions of this chapter, I wish to thank the following people in particular: my co-contributors, Thorsten Borring Olesen, Barry Buzan, Thomas Diez, Ulla Holm, Jef Huysmans, Karen Lund Petersen, Gearóid Ó Tuathail, Jutta Weldes, and Michael C. Williams. I also wish to thank Kirstine La Cour Rasmussen, Nis Christensen and Jesper Hybel Pedersen for valuable research assistance.

1   Election studies show a correlation between those voting 'no' and those who say they distrust politicians – a distrust aimed at the political establishment in general not at a particular government (Siune, Svensson and Tonsgaard 1992: 110)
2   Knud Erik Jørgensen argues that Danish political science in general 'is characterized by a pronounced behaviouralism, yet of a soft, unorthodox, almost non-committal form' (Jørgensen 1995: 157; see also Branner and Kelstrup 2000: 9–11 and 30–3). As a consequence *Danish* studies of Denmark and European integration have in most cases been located within either the neo-functionalist camp, as Jørgensen notes, or within the Scandinavian school of foreign policy theory known as adaptation theory (Jørgensen 1995: 160; Mouritzen 1993, 1997: 83–9; Pedersen 1996: 96; Petersen 1996). Studies by non-Danes remain so far of limited number (see, however, Miljan 1977 and Ingebritsen 1998). Thus, studies of Denmark are predominantly soft-behaviouralist in the mentioned forms (Haahr 2000a, Hedetoft 2000). The main exceptions are historical explanations with little explicit theorisation (Østergård 1992; Knudsen 1993, 95, or with a stronger emphasis on theory, Branner 2000), and more recently studies of discourses (Larsen 1999, 2000) or the question of legitimacy and democratic theory (Friis 1999, Kelstrup 2000).
3   This section draws extensively on the historical research presented in the four volume *Dansk Identitetshistorie* ('The History of Danish Identity') (Feldbæk 1991–1992). This major work has greatly facilitated the identification of the basic conceptual constellation.
4   The title of Rothe's book was in fact *Reflections on the Love of the Fatherland*.
5   I have in general used the Danish spelling 'Slesvig' but the German 'Schleswig' in 'Schleswig-Holsteiners' because the latter were for the most part German speaking and considered German, although it should be remembered that this was as much a regional identity as it was a German one.
6   Sweden and Denmark had numerous wars in the 1600s – one of which led to the Danish loss of most importantly the three provinces Scania, Halland and Blekinge in 1658, and in addition the until then Norwegian county of Jämtland and the later regained island of Bornholm.
7   This section on the development in 1789–90 draws extensively on Feldbæk and Winge (1991).
8   It is slightly incorrect to speak about 'two sides' over this long span of years. As Germany had not yet developed into a state when the Slesvigian wars were fought, the two sides in the first confrontations were more correctly the Danes on one side and the Schleswig-Holsteiners on the other. The tendency to present this as a battle between Germany and Denmark illustrates, however, that the Schleswig-Holsteinian regional identity did not survive the German and Danish nationalisms which followed. The Danish uproar over a 'Euro-region Slesvig' in 1997 testifies to the successful national projects – and the corresponding unsuccessful Schleswig-Holsteinian one (Johnsen 1997, see also Lammers 2000).
9   When Scania, Halland and Blekinge were lost to Sweden in 1658, they were seen as essential parts of the heartland of Denmark – as Danish as Zealand, Funen or Jutland, for example, with the main Bishop of Denmark being the one in Lund (in Scania). However, Sweden managed to Svedify the population surprisingly quickly (Østergård 1992), and although it retained a clear regional identity (in the case of Scania with

some connotations of Danishness, for example in the colour of the regional flag), an image of 'Danes' living under foreign rule was soon misleading. Furthermore, the cultural meaning of Danishness and Swedishness and their political implications were different in the 1600s than in the 1800s. Some resistance against the Swedes did take place, but due to later (Danish) nationalist myth-making about the nature of this (*Snaphanerne, Gøngehøvdingen*, etc.), it is difficult to assess its contemporary meaning (Linde-Laursen 1995: 42–50 and 79–87).

10 A form of cooperative capitalism; a group of farmers would, for instance, own a dairy together, and each would have one vote independently of the amount of milk he delivered.

11 It is, however, important to remember that this is the result of the work of the National Liberals and the Grundtvigians; in the early nineteenth century, things were different and 'Folket' was perceived as uneducated and the lowest societal class (Gundelach 1988: 14).

12 The first two are described in Rerup (1992: 438–9). The third ideology is most clearly identified by Bagge (1992: 447).

13 It seemed to be the idea that the German areas would gradually become Danish, but I have not yet come across a more detailed study of Right's 'assimilation policy'.

14 According to Povl Bagge is was difficult to say to what extent Hørup had written off North Slesvig altogether; Bagge said that it 'supposedly happened' in the 1880s (Bagge 1992: 447).

15 As an early example of 'buy the movie–book–CD–beer mug–T-shirt' merchandising, Stauning's programme was followed by a song with the same title, which today is one of the most popular socialist songs.

16 One might speculate that this eased an alliance between socialists and Grundtvigian intellectuals in the 1990s debate.

17 Numbers in brackets refers to page numbers in *Folketingstidende* 1992, where all parliamentary debates are published. Translations are mine. The quotes are from the third, and final, discussion in parliament of the Maastricht Treaty. Eight political parties are at this point represented in parliament, and only two of them recommended a clear 'no': the Socialist People's Party on the left wing and the Party of Progress on the right wing; the small Christian People's Party was divided on the question. The proposal is at the end of the day approved by 130 members against 25, a result that reflected that the 'yes' was recommended by almost the entire political and economic establishment.

18 Each political party who was in *Folketinget*, who had the necessary number of signatures to run in the next parliamentary election, or who was represented in the European Parliament was granted a 'presentation package' consisting of, in 1992, a 10 minute movie arguing their case, 27 minutes debate with two journalists, and a 3 minute speech. This set-up is similar to the pre-parliamentary elections, and is a good illustration of the Danish emphasis on debate, information and a civic, public space.

19 'Norden in Europe' was also one of the slogans of the Liberal Party.

20 The Social Democratic Party featured the leaders of the Social Democratic Parties in Sweden and Norway as a testimony to the 'strong Norden in Europe' argument in their presentation programme on national TV.

21 A long tradition of anti-EC/EU movements in Denmark stretches back to the early 1960s. Peter Hansen predicted in 1969 that their leaders had realised, with a few exceptions, that 'the issue has been exhausted and their case lost' (Hansen 1969: 30).

22 When the Central and East European states declared membership a clear objective, it was because they had not realised that membership was not in their own but in the Western countries' interest, argued the no-side. Or because the Eastern peoples had been deceived by their governments.

23 For instance 'Nordisk fodslag på fløjen: Partiledere vil samarbejde' (Nordic agreement on the wing: Party leaders will cooperate), *Politiken*, 28 May 1992, p. 5.

24   Incidentially, Denmark was only admitted at the last minute due to the sanctions imposed on Yugoslavia, who had won Denmark's group. The short preparations and the 'relaxed Danish way of life' were taken to the level of national mythology when Denmark met Germany in the final: the free and creative Danes met the mechanical and over-disciplined Germans.
25   This despite the fact that a large number of the leading 'no proponents' were university professors.
26   It had originally been the negotiating position of the Danish government at Maastricht that defence policy should be kept out of the Treaty.
27   Interview by Rasmus Emborg and Michael Seidelin, 'Fogh foreslår mere offensiv EU-politik', *Politiken*, 26 September 2000, section 1, p. 6.
28   *Politiken's* editorial argued that the June Movement's leader Drude Dahlerup's claim to be unable to see the intolerant message of the poster was hypocritical. 'Drudes ugræs: Junibevægelsens hykleri', *Politiken*, 23 April 1998, section 2, p. 4.
29   A similar objective underpinned 'Nyt Europa' ('New Europe').
30   *Nærdemokrati* in Danish, a word which does not fully translate into English; it means that the democratic process should take place close to 'the people', an idea influenced by Grundtvigianism.
31   The Club of Federalists was not meant to be a popular movement; it was a small group of intellectuals, typically known from the media. Still, this intervention was significant for its attempt to break the hegemony of the two mutually reinforcing combatants and their shared definition of the space of possibility.
32   This conceptualisation has been developed by Ole Wæver in several writings, see for instance Wæver (1995).

References

Agersnap, L. (2000) 'Fra dagsorden til verdensorden: En poststrukturalistisk analyse af Danmarks udenrigspolitiske identitet', MA thesis, Institute of Political Science, University of Copenhagen.
Bagge, P. (1992) 'Nationalisme, antinationalisme og nationalfølelse i Danmark omkring 1900', first published in S. Ellehøj, S. Gissel and K. Vohn (eds) *Festskrift til Astrid Friis på halvfjerdsårsdagen den 1. august 1963*, Copenhagen: Rosenkilde og Bagger, 1963; reprinted in *Dansk Identitetshistorie 3: Folkets Danmark 1848–1940*, Viborg: Reitzels.
Branner, H. (2000) 'The Danish Foreign Policy Tradition and the European Context', in H. Branner and M. Kelstrup, *Denmark's Policy towards Europe after 1945: History, Theory, and Options*, Odense: Odense University Press.
Branner, H. and Kelstrup, M. (2000) 'Denmark's Policy towards Europe in a Historical and Theoretical Perspective', in H. Branner and M. Kelstrup, *Denmark's Policy towards Europe after 1945: History, Theory, and Options*, Odense: Odense University Press.
Carlsen, H. N., Jackson, J. T. R. and Meyer, N. I. (eds) (1993) *When No Means Yes*, London: Adamantine.
Christensen, J. (1993) 'Danmark, Norden og EF 1963–1972', in B. N. Thomsen, *The Odd Man Out? Danmark og den Europæiske integration 1948–1992*, Odense: Odense Universitetsforlag.
Feldbæk, O. (1991–1992) *Dansk Identitetshistorie 1–4*, Viborg: C. A. Reitzels.
—— (1991) 'Fædreland og Indfødsret: 1700-tallets danske identitet', in O. Feldbæk (ed.) *Dansk Identitetshistorie 1, Fædreland og Modersmål 1536–1789*, Viborg: C. A. Reitzels.
—— (1996) 'Is there Such a Thing as a Medieval Danish Identity?', in B. P. McGuire (ed.) *The Birth of Identities: Denmark and Europe in the Middle Ages*, Copenhagen: C. A. Reitzel.

Feldbæk, O. and Winge, V. (1991) 'Tyskerfejden 1789–1790: Den første nationale konfrontation', in O. Feldbæk (ed.) *Dansk Identitetshistorie 2: Et Yndigt Land 1789–1848*, Viborg: Reitzels.

Folketingstidende: Forhandlingerne; Folketingsåret 1992–93, IV, (1994), Copenhagen: J. H. Schultz Grafisk A/S.

Folketingstidende: Forhandlingerne i Folketingsåret 1997–98, I, (1999), Copenhagen: J. H. Schultz Grafisk A/S.

Franklin, M., Marsh, M. and McLaren, L. (1994) 'Uncorking the Bottle: Popular Opposition to European Unification in the Wake of Maastricht', *Journal of Common Market Studies* 32, 4: 455–72.

Friis, L. (1999) 'EU and Legitimacy – The Challenge of Compatibility: A Danish Case Study', *Cooperation and Conflict* 34, 3: 243–71.

Føderalistklubben (1993) *Tag Europa alvorligt: åbent brev til regering og folk*, Copenhagen: Tiderne Skifter.

Gundelach, P. (1988) *Sociale bevægelser og samfundsændringer*, Århus: Politica.

Haahr, J. H. (1992) 'European Integration and the Left in Britain and Denmark', *Journal of Common Market Studies* 30, 1: 77–100.

—— (2000a) 'Between Scylla and Charybdis: Danish Party Policies on European Integration', in H. Branner and M. Kelstrup, *Denmark's Policy towards Europe after 1945: History, Theory, and Options*, Odense: Odense University Press.

—— (2000b) 'The Impact of Globalization and European Integration on the Danish Social Democratic Party', in R. Geyer, C. Ingebritsen and J. W. Moses (eds) *Globalization, Europeanization and the End of Scandinavian Social Democracy?*, London: Macmillan.

Hansen, L. and Williams, M. C. (1999) 'The Myths of Europe: Legitimacy, Community and the "Crisis" of the EU', *Journal of Common Market Studies* 37, 2: 233–49.

Hansen, P. (1969) 'Denmark and European Integration', *Cooperation and Conflict* 3, 1: 13–46.

Hedegaard, L. (1992) 'En stat må have et folk – men hvad skal folk med stater?', *Danmark mellem Norden og Europe*, Copenhagen: Foreningen Norden.

Hedetoft, U. (2000) 'The Interplay Between Mass and Elite Attitudes to European Integration in Denmark', in H. Branner and M. Kelstrup, *Denmark's Policy towards Europe after 1945: History, Theory, and Options*, Odense: Odense University Press.

Hoffmeyer, J. and Koch, B. A. (1959) *Kilder til det sydslesvigske spørgsmål 1945–55*, Copenhagen: Gyldendal.

Ilsøe, H. (1991) 'Danskerne og deres fædreland. Holdninger og opfattelser ca. 1550–1700', in O. Feldbæk (ed.) *Dansk Identitetshistory, bind I*, Viborg: Reitzels.

Ingebritsen, C. (1998) *The Nordic States and European Unity*, Ithaca, NY: Cornell University Press.

Johnsen, P. P. (1997) 'Grænseoverskridende', *Weekendavisen*, 16–22 May.

Jørgensen, K. E. (1995) 'Review Article: European Integration as a Field of Study in Denmark', *Journal of Common Market Studies* 33, 1: 157–62.

Kelstrup, M. (2000) 'Danish Integration Policies: Dilemmas and Options', in H. Branner and M. Kelstrup, *Denmark's Policy towards Europe after 1945: History, Theory, and Options*, Odense: Odense University Press.

Knudsen, T. (1993) *Den danske stat i Europa*, Copenhagen: Jurist og Økonomforbundets.

Laffan, B. (1996) 'The Politics of Identity and Political Order in Europe', *Journal of Common Market Studies* 34, 1: 81–102.

Lammers, K. C. (2000) 'Denmark's Relations with Germany since 1945', in H. Branner and M. Kelstrup, *Denmark's Policy towards Europe after 1945: History, Theory, and Options*, Odense: Odense University Press.

Larsen, H. (1999) 'British and Danish European Policies in the 1990s: A Discourse Approach', *European Journal of International Relations* 5, 4: 451–83.

—— (2000) 'Danish CFSP Policy in the Post-Cold War Period: Continuity or Change?', *Cooperation and Conflict* 35, 1: 37–63.

Laursen, F. (1993) 'The Maastricht Treaty: Implications for the Nordic Countries', *Cooperation and Conflict* 28, 2: 115–41.

Linde-Laursen, A. (1995) *Det Nationales Natur: Studier i dansk-svenske relationer*, Lund: Nordisk Ministerråd.

Lundgreen-Nielsen, F. (1992) 'Grundtvig og danskhed', in O. Feldbæk (ed.) *Dansk Identitetshistorie 3: Folkets Danmark, 1848–1940*, Viborg: Reitzels.

Meyer, N. I. (1993) 'The Danish "No" to Maastricht', in H. N. Carlsen, J. T. R. Jackson and N. I. Meyer (eds) *When No Means Yes*, London: Adamantine.

Miljan, T. (1977) *The Reluctant Europeans: The Attitudes of the Nordic Countries towards European Integration*, London: C. Hurst.

Mouritzen, H. (1993) 'The Two Musterknaben and the Naughty Boy: Sweden, Finland and Denmark in the Process of European Integration', *Cooperation and Conflict* 28, 4: 373–402.

—— (1997) *External Danger and Democracy: Old Nordic Lessons and New European Challenges*, Aldershot, UK: Dartmouth.

Nissen, H. S. (1992) 'Danskeren 1972: Billeder og budskaber', in O. Feldbæk (ed.) *Dansk Identitetshistorie 4: Danmark og Europa 1940–1990*, Viborg: Reitzels.

Obradovic, D. (1996) 'Policy Legitimacy and the European Union', *Journal of Common Market Studies* 34, 2: 191–221.

Østergård, U. (1992) *Europas Ansigter: Nationale stater og politiske kulturer i en ny, gammel verden*, Copenhagen: Rosinante.

Pedersen, K. P. (1993) 'The "No" in the Light of Nordic History', in H. N. Carlsen, J. R. T. Jackson and N. I. Meyer (eds) *When No Means Yes*, London: Adamantine.

Pedersen, T. (1992) 'Norden har alt at vinde', *Danmark mellem Norden og EF*, Copenhagen: Foreningen Norden.

Pedersen, T. (1996) 'Denmark and the European Union', in L. Miles (ed.) *The European Union and the Nordic Countries*, London: Routledge.

Petersen, N. (1993) '"Game, Set, and Match": Denmark and the European Union after Edinburgh', in T. Tiilikainen and I. D. Petersen (eds) *The Nordic Countries and the EC*, Copenhagen: Political Studies Press.

—— (1996) 'Denmark and the European Union 1985–96', *Cooperation and Conflict* 31, 2: 185–210.

—— (1999) 'The Danish Referendum on the Treaty of Amsterdam', in B. Heurlin and H. Mouritzen (eds) *Danish Foreign Policy Yearbook 1999*, Copenhagen: Danish Institute of International Affairs.

Rerup, L. (1992) 'Folkestyret og danskhed: Massenationalisme og politik 1848–1866', in O. Feldbæk (ed.) *Dansk Identitetshistorie 3: Folkets Danmark 1848–1940*, Viborg: Reitzels.

Sådan sagde de om Danmark og EF. Fuldstændig gengivelse af folketingets markedsdebat den 16. december 1971, (1972) Copenhagen: Forlaget Aktuelle Bøger.

Schou, T. L. (1992) 'The Debate in Denmark 1986–91 on European Integration and Denmark's Participation', in M. Kelstrup (ed.) *European Integration and Denmark's Participation*, Copenhagen: Political Studies Press.

Siune, K., Svensson, P. and Tonsgaard, O. (1992)-*det blev et nej*, Århus: Politica.

Sørensen, C. (1992) 'De afgørende spørgsmål ved vor stillingtagen til Maastricht-traktaten', in J. Stubkjær (ed.) *Meninger om Danmark og EF-Unionen. Med 10 bidrag for og imod dansk tilslutning*, Copenhagen: Forlaget Aktuelle Bøger.

Wæver, O. (1995) 'Danish Dilemmas: Foreign Policy Choices for the 21st Century', in N. Petersen and C. Due-Nielsen (eds) *Danish Foreign Policy, 1968–1992*, Copenhagen: DUPI and Jurist og Økonomforbundets Forlag.

Winge, V. (1991) 'Dansk og tysk i 1700-tallet', in O. Feldbæk (ed.) *Dansk Identitetshistorie 1, Fædreland og Modersmål 1536-1789*, Viborg: C. A. Reitzels.

Worre, T. (1988) ' Denmark at the Crossroads: The Danish Referendum 28 February 1986 on the EC Reform Package', *Journal of Common Market Studies* 26, 4: 361-88.

—— (1995) 'First No, Then Yes: The Danish Referendums on the Maastricht Treaty 1992 and 1993', *Journal of Common Market Studies* 33, 2: 235–57.

Zeus, Oplysningsavis om Den Europæiske Union, published by the Party of Progress (n.d.).

4   This little piggy stayed at home

Why Norway is not a member of the EU*

Iver B. Neumann

This little piggy went to market
This little piggy stayed at home
This little piggy had roast beef
This little piggy had none
(English nursery rhyme)

In a referendum held on 28 November 1994, following a divisive debate which had dominated political life for seven years, 52.2 per cent of the electorate voted 'no' to the question of whether Norway should become a member of the European Union (EU). On 25 September 1972, following an even more divisive debate, 53.5 per cent of the electorate had voted 'no' to the question of whether Norway should become a member of the European Community (EC). On these two occasions, the electorates, 'Norway' and the 'EU-EC' were very different entities. This notwithstanding, the 'no' was almost a constant. As of 2001, every European country from Ukraine and Turkey westwards that is not currently a member of the EU is engaged in a debate about whether or not to join. In all of these countries, there is a lively discourse between various shades of integration-friendly and integration-hostile elements (Neumann 1998). As detailed in Lars Trägårdh and Lene Hansen's chapters in this book, similar discourses may be found amongst the member states of the EU themselves. Although the existence of integration-hostile elements is an all-European phenomenon, Norway remains the only country which, given the opportunity of membership, has turned it down, and it has done so twice.

This situation is one which social theorists should be expected to be able to understand. Yet, the literature on the topic is less than convincing. A sizeable but scattered number of contributions by electoral researchers building on the work of comparativist Stein Rokkan try to demonstrate how historical cross-cutting cleavages, dormant in everyday Norwegian politics, have been activated to produce a winning majority for the no side. Certain roles such as those of city-dweller or country-dweller, producer or consumer are supposed to inculcate in individuals certain interests, and because of these interests they are supposed to vote in a certain way. In this way, electoral studies is definitely able to pinpoint patterns of behaviour, but the question of motivation is not explored. It is assumed as a given, on the formula, for example, that a country-dwelling primary producer will presumably vote 'no' because it is in the country-dwelling primary producer's interest to do so.

The only English-language monograph concerned with the variation in the *degree* of European integration between the Nordic countries, by Christine Ingebritsen (1998), builds on this framework, but, drawing on the tradition of political economy, adds an analysis of where these interests may actually come from. Ingebritsen argues that the source of the Nordic variation resides in the sectoral composition of the regional economies, 'not [in] the structure of the state, membership in international institutions, or class divisions within the society' (Ingebritsen 1998: 115). Norway's central sectors, Ingebritsen argues, are petroleum, agriculture and fisheries, and the windfall profits from petroleum have allowed the state to postpone structural change to catch up with other European economies by handing out subsidies. As a result, these sectors have become dependent on a continued state policy of subsidies, and inasmuch as EU membership was seen as a harbinger of change in state subsidy policy, an effect of the state's policy was to entrench sectoral groups which would fight the possibility of change tooth and nail (Ingebritsen 1998: 119).

Ingebritsen (e.g. 1998: 112–13, cf. Matlary 1993: 56) repeatedly insists that petroleum is the reason why the state has delayed structural change. In order to obtain membership, states have to negotiate terms with the EU and, in the case of EU membership, convince their nations to return a 'yes' vote in national referenda. As will be detailed below, however, in the period leading up to the Norwegian referendum of 25 September 1972, the newly discovered petroleum resources were hardly mentioned at all in the political debates, and when they were mentioned, it was as an additional reason to join the Community. Now, this fact does not harm Ingebritsen's argument directly, inasmuch as it pertains to the situation in the 1990s. Nonetheless, we have here a reminder that, only some twenty years before the 1994 referendum, Norwegian agriculture and fisheries interests were able to contribute to a no vote without the existence of petroleum-generated subsidies. At the very least, this should sow some doubt about whether petroleum was as pivotal to the outcome of the Norwegian 1994 referendum as Ingebritsen insists that it was. Furthermore, only a small and shrinking percentage of Norwegians are involved in the primary economic sectors of fishery and agriculture. Thus, the existence of these sectoral interests in and of themselves are not enough to explain Norway's naysayers and Ingebritsen actually acknowledges this when she ends her analysis by stating that 'Some economic interests groups were particularly effective at capturing the heart of the nation during the accession debate' (Ingebritsen 1998: 162).

What is needed, then, is to move beyond Ingebritsen's rationalist premises to an analysis of how the agriculture and fisheries sectors as well as others arguing in favour of a no were able to capture 'the heart of the nation', and thus ensure that people with only the most flimsy material ties to these sectors nonetheless voted 'no' to EU membership in the 1972 and 1994 referenda. In this chapter, I will study the nays not as aggregations of individual rational interests, but as instantiations of identity politics, in terms of the framework of discourse analysis set out in Chapter 2. Such a tack is indeed indirect, inasmuch as it cannot say anything specific about voting behaviour. But it has the strength of investigating so-called interests not indirectly, as an inferred entity emerging from ecological data, but directly, where not only interests but also identities are formulated, namely in language. One crucial presupposition of the analysis, then, is that Norwegian discourse harbours a number of representations of state–nation constellations, and that its subjects will avail themselves of their preferred state–nation constellations when they formulate their representations of Europe. Each intervention about Europe will take a preferred state–nation constellation on the national level as its benchmark (Wæver 1990; Neumann 1996).

Inasmuch as these terms are historical products, every time they were used they carried their history and thus a set of structuring influences with them. Norwegian discourse on European integration played itself out in, and therefore on, the naysayers' own terms. That went particularly for the two terms 'state' and 'nation', but also for the terms 'people' (*folket*) and 'Europe'.

The seventeenth and eighteenth centuries: the making of the Norwegian state and the forging of a Norwegian culture

When books in Norwegian about the High Middle Ages (around 1200) come with titles such as *Norway becomes a State* (Helle 1974), one may of course argue that the use of the word 'state' invites misunderstanding and that 'kingdom' would certainly have been better. Nonetheless, it is a fact that Norway at this time was, by the political standards of the day, a highly centralised kingdom and that the claim to statehood for Norway in the High Middle Ages cannot simply be brushed off as an anachronism. The reason why it is important to point this out has to do with the relative neglect of the states surrounding the Baltic when generalisations are made about what political life in Europe was like prior to the entrenchment of the modern state system. In the extant literature, the presupposition of how European states are supposed to have emerged is first and foremost based on what we may call the Continental experience. The period 1494–1648 is often said to be the chronological crucible, with 1494 marking the onslaught of the French king on Savoy, and 1648 the Peace of Westphalia. But there is a problem here, not only for the case of Norway, but for the North of Europe in its entirety, namely that the enmeshing of sovereignty in a web of cross-cutting allegiances was not uniform throughout Europe. One will recall that it was only as a result of the Thirty Years War (1618–48) that the two power constellations of Europe – that focussing on the Baltic Sea (the North) and that focussing on the Continent – melded into one European system of states. At the end of the sixteenth century, M. S. Anderson (1993: 29–30) writes,

> The Baltic still formed to a considerable extent a distinct and self-contained political world; and to western Europe in general its states seemed too poor and remote to be of much interest. In 1604 a French writer could still speak of Denmark as 'so distant a country where we have scarcely any business'.

The literature on sovereignty has typically focussed on how the states system grew out of the Continental system. This goes for traditional as well as for contemporary literature. For example, John Ruggie's (1998) influential juxtaposition of the EU and medieval Europe as multi-layered polities treats the Middle Ages out of which the European system of states emerged as a clear-cut feudal and catholic affair. The choice of 1494 as a peg is symptomatic in this regard. What is bracketed by this treatment is how state formation in the North did not to the same degree feature a tug-of-war over multi-layered governance as it did on the Continent. There are of course grey areas, such as the question of allegiance owed by local rulers in the Hebrides or in the Crimea – both in political terms more or less tenuous parts of 'the North' due to their political imbrication in a Baltic-centred political system. Power struggles between kings and nobility were commonplace in the North, as they were on the Continent. But the point is that, in pre-Westphalian days, and where Norway is concerned also in the High Middle Ages, state formations in the North tended to be more centralised at an earlier stage than were those on the Continent. The centre of the Catholic church was far away, and not least, there was the question of scale: these parts were not at all densely populated. Given the technology available at the time, sparse population meant a thinner network and less dense contact, which again meant that direct rule was more needed than on the Continent if the king were to rule effectively at all. Inasmuch as knowledge production about the system of states has been based overwhelmingly on Continental cases, we may have here a case of unwarranted generalisation, where systematic differences between state formation in the two sub-systems of what went on to become the European system of states have been occluded. As we shall see, this fact was to become an important resource for Norwegian nation-builders in the nineteenth century.

Where Norway is concerned, the single most discussed event before the con-solidation of modern states and the concurrent codification of the modern states system, which took place around the Thirty Years War, is the unilateral action taken by King Christian III on 30 October 1536. Moving to consolidate his state against the Holy Roman Emperor and other powers at a domestically felicitous moment, the king decreed that Norway, which had come under his sway, should no longer be a separate realm (*rike*), but 'like one of the other counties (*land*)' be 'of the Danish realm, and forever under the crown of Denmark' (quoted in Rian 1997: 15–16). Explicitly, then, the Norwegian 'realm' was subsumed under the Danish 'realm'. What this meant in practice was that the Norwegian Council of the Realm was eliminated, that the previously separate Norwegian church was organised as part of a common state church, and that the administration of Norway happened either directly at the county (*len*) level, or at the level of the king's chancellery in Copenhagen (Rian 1997: 386). As Jespersen (1984: 30) puts it, the locus of sovereignty moved 'from estate meetings to the crown of Denmark, represented by King and council [now in the singular] *in fælli*'.[1]

Up until 1625, Norway was one of the realm's backwaters, run on a shoestring budget by a shoestring administration, whence little income reached the state capital. During the 1600s, however, the state administration expanded, and the part of it which was to be found in the counties located in Norway – a number which was itself in flux, inasmuch as some had to be handed over to the Swedish crown – peaked at 1,200 civil servants (*embedsmenn*). These civil servants formed a core of a stratum of perhaps 5,000 people who ruled the country and were known as *øvrigheten* – loosely 'the authorities'. Between themselves, this cadre administered around 80,000 expanded households known as *almuen* – loosely 'the populace' (Rian 1984: 94). For our purposes, the civil servants which made up the core of 'the authorities' had two particularly interesting sociological characteristics. First, they were part of a structure whose education and hierarchical structure tied their work and their cultural horizon directly to the King's Chancellery. Although the civil servants in Norway were usually not well travelled themselves, then, they were part of a corps where a grand tour of Europe was very much part of the cultured ideal. Second, as the corps expanded, it did so as a result of influx from Copenhagen and other cities in the Continental part of the state (Elsinore, Kiel, etc.).

After the Napoleonic Wars, in 1814, when Norway was handed over from Denmark to Sweden in compensation for the latter's loss of Finland to Russia, the number of civil servants expanded by one-third, to 1,800, and by 1875 there were 2,300 (Seip 1997: 65). Due to the total expansion in the number of people, they and their families still made up around 1 per cent of the population. They were the unquestioned and unchallenged leading group, and in the midst of the transfer of Norway from Denmark to Sweden, they were able to organise and orchestrate a political campaign. This campaign involved calling together a long working session in which they and a few representatives of other societal groups drew up a constitution for Norway, which was later to be confirmed in the main as a legal basis for the personal union with Sweden. Out of a disparate set of immigrant families there had emerged a class *für sich* with state-bearing potential and state-bearing aspirations.

In the case of Norway, then, at this stage the civil servant stratum wanted it to become a country, on a par first and foremost with Denmark and Sweden, but also in certain respects with England and the Netherlands. This required that they differentiate themselves from neighbouring projects of the same kind. Gerhard Schøning, a historian, made it his task to convince Norwegians that they had a common and proud history which flowered particularly in the High Middle Ages. To him, the North had a historical identity which started with Tacitus' 'Germans', out of which Norwegians crystallised during the age of the Sagas (which during the nineteenth century was re-baptised the Viking age). In particular, Schøning focussed on the simple and dour life allegedly led by Norwegians as an ideal to cherish. It might 'characterise us, as a Nation, as an Original, and not turn us into a motley copy of other nations, as we have struggled to become for a while' (quoted in Christensen 1993: 50). As he wrote in the 1770s with reference to a battle in 1611 where Norwegian peasants ambushed and massacred a detachment of Scottish mercenaries, the course of the battle 'may serve as Proof, that the Fire and the Heat, the Bravery and the Endurance, which in olden Days made the Norwegians a Terror, almost for all of Europe, is still glowing in the Hearts of Norwegian Peasants' (quoted in Christensen 1993: 50).

With its invocation of the fighting Norwegian nation, and its stress on the peasants as being the real carriers of the nation, this passage is a typical example of contemporary European discourse. The representation of relative freedom where peasants are concerned quickly became a truth claim in Norwegian discourse – and later on in Nordic discourse as well:

> The core of the peasant myth is a figure that is difficult to conceptualize with the term 'peasant', which connotes subordination in a feudal order. The Nordic peasant is rather somewhere between a yeoman and a freeholder in an English context, moving toward farmer around 1900.
>
> (Stråth and Sørensen 1997: 5)

As Jacob Aall wrote to Christian August in 1809, hot on the heels of two years of hunger following in the wake of the Napoleonic Wars: 'Peasant and Freeman make up the lion's share of the Country's Census, and who can deny that they have possessed a Freedom and savoured a Happiness, which is rare in Europe. Who were freer and less taxed than the Norwegian Peasant' (quoted in Mykland 1997: 10). And representations such as these were recognised and validated by contemporary intellectuals such as Thomas Malthus and Mary Wollstonecraft, who at the end of the eighteenth century visited the country and confirmed the relative wide-ranging freedom of the Norwegian peasant in their writings.

If the civil servants then had a very tangible and materially based representation of 'Norway' and a self-identification as part of a Europe-wide elite, the next question to ask is what that representation of Norway looked like. Certain diacritical markers were mountains, cold climate and the inheritance from the age of the Sagas. To these we may add an interest in local words, which, by dint either of having already appeared in the sagas or of being used in certain parts of Norway, were from the 1770s onwards beginning to be considered typical of *all* of Norway. They were, as it were, nationalised. Whereas at this time throughout Europe it was a general practice to attack specific cultural traits as unwanted and decadent, in Norway the tendency was to criticise culture *tout court*. As an example, one may quote a poem by Andreas Bull from 1774 which exhorts fellow Norwegians 'not sickly to crawl down to the countries of the South, where your ancestors bashed in so many skulls, but to populate your fatherland as a healthy and respected neighbour; and if you have to go [South], then go, but do not call yourself a Norwegian!' (quoted in Christensen 1993: 81).

It is hardly incidental that the production of these celebrations of Norwegian nature and Norwegian language played themselves out among the civil servants in the city of Trondheim, where one may also find the first incident where the Norwegian language was implicated in a discussion concerning who should man the state position of secretary to the bishop. In 1771, Johan Nordahl Brun had to give up his job to a German, the reason being that his German was not strong enough. This sparked a wave of resentment against the use of German speakers in state jobs generally, in a local echo of the waves of resentment of German speakers at the King's court in the capital of Copenhagen (see Chapter 3). Language had always been a professional skill and an asset. What was new was that the question of language was now tied directly not only to the question of specific jobs, but to the question of who the 'we' from among whom civil servants should be recruited actually were. At the outset of the Napoleonic Wars, then, Norwegian culture was already being nationalised, and made relevant to key political questions such as the composition of the state-bearing corps of civil servants.

The long nineteenth century: the making of the Norwegian nation

Having forced the Swedish king to transfer a number of counties which eventually became known collectively as Finland to Russia, the tsar was eager to compensate his fellow monarch for the loss, not least in order to minimise the possibility of revanchism. With Denmark ending up on the losing side of the Napoleonic Wars, the opportunity rose to partition off the Danish king's Northern province, known as Norway, and offer it to Sweden. However, in the brouhaha surrounding the transfer, the local Danish pretender to the throne rallied the state-bearing element of what was about to become the state of Norway, namely the civil servants, and urged them to organise a meeting of representatives including a number of peasants. These representatives duly met and drew up a constitution for Norway. The upshot was that Norway obtained a legal basis from which to insist on more of a separate profile inside the Dual Monarchy than the Swedish king had intended. Qualified statehood was thrust upon the country – qualified, inasmuch as the representation of the state was one which stressed the fact of union with Sweden.

The Norwegian state which came into being in this year was constitutional, which meant that 'two independent powers of state were juxtaposed: the parliament and the king' (Seip 1997: 70). In the first years of the period, this split presents itself as one between the Swedish king in Stockholm on the one hand, and the Norwegian people led by the civil servants wielding the constitution on the other. 1814 is Norway's *annus mirabilis*, when, to use Jens Arup Seip's expression, a 'flame of feelings' melded older identity elements into a new patriotism, whose main carriers were the civil servants, whose main elements were the freedom ideas of the European Enlightenment, and whose main symbol was the free peasant that European intellectuals had sighted in Norway and which the civil servants had made their own. The civil servants programmatically defined their role as being that of running the state, and the role of the state as being that of 'leading and correcting public opinion' so as to bring about progress (e.g. Slagstad 1998: 30 *et passim*).

But dissenting voices came from within the civil servant stratum itself, and they had a clear programme (Neumann 2000). In the extant literature, this programme is often referred to as one of 'national romanticism', but, in the same way that national romanticism co-existed uneasily with the Enlightenment project in European discourse generally, it is hard to pinpoint exactly when and how this position changed from an Enlightenment celebration of the people's potential for learning to a celebration of the people's innate qualities. Henrich Steffens lectured to Norwegian students on romanticism in Christiania as early as 1802–3 and thus planted the philosophical seeds. Early interest in folkways – in the collection of national costumes, old songs, old myths – may also be found during the first decade of the nineteenth century. Even an interest in the old Norse language and the first calls for a 'national language' hail from this decade (Andresen 1994: 48–55). These efforts were not explicitly tied to questions of the state, but other efforts of related interest were. Nicolai Wergeland, a minister, was the author of a philippic against Denmark, and his central idea was that the 400 years of Danish rule had suppressed and usurped Norway and the Norwegians. Wergeland took up a theme which is perennial in politics – whether the balance of contributions and gains made by a particular part of a political entity to its distributional centre comes out in its favour. What made his contribution pivotal for us is, first, that Norway was no longer a member of the political entity in question, namely Denmark. Therefore, his representation of Norwegian history did not have as its goal to change the immediate political set-up (that had already changed), but to brand Danish culture as foreign to Norway. Second, mirroring the interest in folkways, the hero in Wergeland's historical script was not the civil servants, but the populace. The two concepts which figure prominently in Wergeland's account are 'the populace' (*almuen*) and 'the people' (*folket*). The former term was the established one, and it encompassed the perhaps 95 per cent of the population which was not part of the civil service stratum. The concept of 'the people' had a normatively more positive ring to it, but even more importantly, it was undecided whether the civil servant stratum was part of the people or not.

To the dissenting voices inside the civil servant stratum, this new use of the concept of 'the people' was a defining trait. For example, when in the 1830s they formed first a society and then a journal devoted to the study of Norwegian history, their object of interest was 'the language and history of the Norwegian people' (see Storsveen 1998: 230). The representation of 'the people' as the critical subject of a specifically Norwegian history was further sharpened in 1834. Wergeland's son, Henrik, postulated Norwegian history as falling in two parts or two 'half rings': the Viking age and the period after 1814. The Danish period which lay between these two half rings was no more than a bad piece of welding for historians to remove (Sørensen *et al.* 1995: 48). Norwegian culture, which had survived in the nooks and crannies of Norwegian valleys and fjords, had to be resuscitated.

The postulation of a separate and subaltern Norwegian subject, with a culture different from the Danish one, has been called 'perhaps the most important national result of Norwegian nineteenth century historical research' (Storsveen 1998: 232). This 'nation' was postulated by representatives of the civil servant stratum as resting on 'the people', and not on 'the populace'. This is also what makes these moves and this national discourse qualitatively different from the one that existed before the Napoleonic Wars. There exist a number of uses of the term 'nation' from the end of the eighteenth century and even from before (Lunden 1992). There are also a number of uses of the term 'fatherland'. The historical depth intended by these uses, however, seems to be very different from what Wergeland *fils* and others had in mind. Before the Napoleonic Wars, what seems to have been at stake was first and foremost whether one was born in the country, whether one belonged to it by right of birth (indfødsret). The question, then, is literally whether the father, the biological father, was an inhabitant of Norway. For Wergeland *fils* and other dissidents writing from the 1820s onwards, it was no longer enough to be second generation Norwegian, one had to be a pure-blooded Norseman and the point was explicitly to set Norwegians off from the less pure-blooded Swedes and Danes, who, they insisted, hailed from invaders from the south.

The clash between the dominant and the marginal positions came in the 1830s. An intense struggle broke out between two coteries – 'the intelligentsia', 'the troop', 'the danomans' (that is, those who twenty years after the country had been torn away from Denmark saw little difference between Danish and Norwegian culture), and the 'patriots' (characterised by a member of the opposition as 'ultra-Norwegian, mead-drinking, horsemeat-eating, Odin-worshipping'; Aarnes 1980: 140) – over the representation of the nation (Seip 1994). Two things are particularly noteworthy about this clash. First, by the 1840s, the marginal position, as represented by the Wergelands, had moved towards the centre of the discourse and its representation of the nation took over as the dominant one. The diacritica used to mark off a culturally and ethnically defined Norway were all concerned with 'the people's culture', and 'the people' were thus installed as a key referent of the nation. Yet, while this romantic nation was a historical and idealised entity it nevertheless needed the guidance of the civil servant stratum to obtain a satisfactory level of culture. Second, however, it is interesting that the clash was for most practical purposes limited to the relationship between 'the people' and 'the nation'. Representations of the state and of Europe were on the other hand not central to the clash. It was no coincidence that representations of the state and of Europe were not discussed during the 1820s and the 1830s: there was broad agreement inside the civil servant stratum that the state should be run by that stratum, that it should guide the nation, and that it should participate in the common European evolution. What happened in the 1840s was, however, that a different representation of the nation–state nexus emerged, one which had its base not in the civil servant stratum and their capital of Christiania (present-day Oslo), but in the countryside and cities of the western part of the country. Amongst the bearers of this romantic nationalist representation were people who were themselves 'of the people', but it was key to the success of this representation that it was dominated by students and businessmen (Dalhaug 1995: 51). The diacriticon around which this new representation coalesced was language.

The romantic position now argued that the spoken language, as opposed to the written one, should be a diacriticon for Norwegianness. In 1851, Aasen commented on the role of language to nationality in the following way:

> From their civil servant positions, a new stock (*Slægt*) rules the cities, the churches and the schools, a stock (*Een Slægt*) which neither understands nor bothers to read a word of the old language and which does not want to acknowledge the so-called people (*det saakaldte Folk*) except as their servants and creatures . . . The people itself is seen as a strange tribe of savages, their mores abominable, their looks disgusting, their names barbarian. One cherishes names such as

Fischer, Meltzer, Schreiner, but not [the Norwegian peasant variants of the same Germanic roots] Fiskar, Maltar, Skrinar.

(Quoted in Hoel 1998: 310)

Three central features make this the *locus classicus* of the new representation of 'Norway'. First, there exist two cultures in Norway, one autochthonous 'people's culture' and one foreign 'civil servant culture'. Second, the civil servant culture is hegemonic, in a Gramscian sense, but also institutionally, by dint of its control of the state. Third, the civil servant culture is suspect due to its supranational connections to Danish culture (particularly via language) and to German culture (witness the pinpointing of German-sounding names, which were rampant within the civil servant stratum). By the end of the century, this representation had moved to take up centre stage in the discourse and it managed to impose its pedagogical and nationalist ideas onto the educational system of the state.

Mapping nineteenth-century Norwegian discourse we have, on the one hand, the representation of the civil servant stratum which was hegemonic from 1814 and up until the 1840s. In the light of subsequent developments, it may some-what anachronistically be called the statist representation. It was paternalistic in the Enlightenment tradition: the civil servants were the state, and the state led the nation. The nation consisted of a leading civil servant stratum as well as the populace. Norwegian culture was the culture of the civil servants, and the culture of the civil servants was a seamless part of European culture.

Then there was the romantic nationalist representation, the carriers of which made up the marginalised part of the civil servant stratum. To them, the nation was 'the people' and the people consisted of both the civil servant stratum and the populace. Interestingly, this representation does not focus much on the role of the state and the nexus between the state and the nation – in this they are close to the early Herder. This representation stresses how the romantic turn to the people is an all-European phenomenon: Norway is one in the series of European nations. By dint of culture and language, it is particularly close to Sweden and Denmark. Accordingly, some romantic nationalists were avid Scandinavianists. This representation is able to make its idea of the nation hegemonic from the 1840s. Crucially, however, this does not immediately change the hegemonic model of the fit between state and nation, since the romantic nationalists did not actually offer an alternative model for what this should look like. Neither did they offer a model for Scandinavian cooperation. One notes that Norwegian romantic nationalists, contrary to some Scandinavianists in Denmark and Sweden, did not call for cooperation between states through leaders – that is, their kings. The reason is obvious: inasmuch as the Swedish king was also the Norwegian king, such cooperation would not be cooperation between the three Scandinavian nations, but between the two Scandinavian states, and so Norway would be left out as a directly represented entity.

The third representation is that of populist nationalism, where the crucial point is that the nation should take over the state. This is presented as the rule of the people, and 'democracy' is understood unequivocally as rule by the people, by the majority, and not as protection of minorities. What is seen as hindering such a development is the civil servant stratum's hold on the state.

Nowhere were the divisions between the three major representations of the Norwegian nation more clear than in the debates surrounding the crucial diacriticon of Norwegianness, namely language. This was also where the major positions – statism, romantic nationalism and populist nationalism – translated most directly into specific policy stands. Romantic nationalists wanted to weld the nation together under the banner of a common language which was, most fittingly, called 'common Norwegian' (*samnorsk*; the Norwegian root means common as in 'in common', not as in 'simple'). For example, Halvdan Koht, who was later to become foreign minister, gave a rousing speech in 1895, ending by saying that '*The language issue* is going to be the banner under which we are going to unite the Norwegian people. And then, when we really are one people, then we are going to fight for independence, and then we are going to *win*' (quoted in Klippenberg 1998: 366). Populist nationalists and statists, on the other hand, had their specific variants for which they sought hegemony. For the populist nationalists, this was the invented language of Ivar Aasen (*landsmål, nynorsk*), which to them was the real language of the real people, who had survived despite the state-building efforts of the foreign-born civil servants and their descendants. For the statists, it was the language traditionally written and spoken by the civil servant stratum (*riksmål*). The clash between them crystallised in a celebrated and still much discussed battle between the two writers Arne Garborg and Bjørnstierne Bjørnson. To Bjørnson, Norway was split,

> between a 'cultured culture' (*dannelseskultur*) which was state-bearing, and a 'peasant culture', between 'inside' and 'outside', between 'high' and 'low', between 'quick' and 'slow', between 'light' and 'dark', between town and country – particularly between capital-where (*hoved-stad*) and else-where (*annan-stad*). And the decisive and limning criterion for whether one is 'inside' or 'outside' is exactly language – that is, for Bjørnson, 'the language of the realm' ('*Rigsmaalet*').
>
> (Time 1998: 351)

To Garborg and the romantic nationalists, who had been the ones to postulate and insist on such a split as constitutive of everything which was to count as really Norwegian in the first place, it was the other way around. The central binary oppositions were the same, but the distance between the opposites was larger and the prospects for and interest in narrowing it much smaller.

When this incredibly divisive debate did not lead to a full split, it was partly because the three positions made common cause when it came to seeking independence from Sweden, and partly because there was considerable slippage in the romantic nationalist position on the language question and on the relationship between the nation and the state. Actually, Bjørnstierne Bjørnson, who fronted the language issue from within the statist position, was himself a romantic nationalist. Furthermore, even the most well-represented and influential coterie of romantic nationalists, who embraced the idea of a common Norwegian language, still stuck to the idea that the state should lead the nation. The development of this position from the 1840s onwards might have changed their stand on the language issue and made them susceptible to compromises with the populist nationalists on this central point, but they still adopted a paternalistic position on the relationship between the state and the nation (Stenseth 1993). In a word, for sociological as well as ideological reasons, the romantic nationalists took up a mediating position (cf. Sørensen 1997: 219–21).

In our perspective, the second half of the nineteenth century offers two major dramas. The first one is the forging of an alliance between romantic nationalism and populist nationalism. The major triumphs of this alliance, which was institutionalised as the political party of 'the Left' (*Venstre*), were the taking over of Parliament and the breakthrough of parliamentarianism in 1884, and the establishment of a Norwegian nation state as a sovereign subject under international law in 1905.

The second drama concerned how to represent the civil servant stratum, and how to reconcile the existence of a nationalised and democratised part of the state – Parliament – with the continued existence of other parts of the state: up until 1905, the king in Stockholm, and, before and after 1905, the bureaucracy. This was a question which split the victorious alliance between romantic and populist nationalism. The reason for this split was simple enough. As we have seen, the major difference between romantic and populist nationalism concerned the status of the civil servant stratum. The romantic nationalists belonged historically to this stratum, and were, unsurprisingly, unwilling to subscribe to a definition of the nation which excluded themselves and a view of the nexus between the nation and the state which put the traditional livelihood of their stratum into question. The populist nationalists, on the other hand, seem to have held that they had nothing to lose by equating the nation unequivocally to the people, and thus simply exclude the civil servant stratum from the nation, the state and the country. In accordance with this, the civil servant stratum was banished from the Norwegian nation, branded as a separate nation with close ties to the Danish one, and as the enemy of the Norwegian nation: they were, as Arne Garborg put it in 1883, 'failing their duty' to the Norwegian nation, and so they became enemies: 'the enemy is within the country now' (quoted in Dalhaug 1995: 79).

The three representations came to the fore in 1866–7, where the issue was one of how Norway should relate to its king and to the other half of the Dual Monarchy – Sweden. The statists wanted to strengthen the state by strengthening union with Sweden. In the words of the nationalists, they wanted an 'amalgamation' of the two countries. As seen by the populist nationalists, then, the cultural treachery of the civil servant stratum in maintaining linguistic and other ties to Denmark had its parallel in a politically treacherous programme of supporting the king and the union. The 'foreignness' of the civil servants is presented as both cultural and political, both Danophile and Swedophile, and it is confirmed by their lack of interest in independence (Svendsen 1998: 249).

The bearers of the statist representation had feared being banished from the nation ever since populist nationalism made its first appearance. The place where it is most easily spotted is perhaps in the continued debate over Norwegian history, where the statist representation countered the romantic nationalist idea of 'the people' by stressing how Norway's ties to Denmark had secured Norway's partaking of 'the boons of civilisation'. What the bearers of this representation feared was above all isolation – that Norway in its hankering after what was specifically national should rather end up as a province cut off from the rest of European civilisation (Svendsen 1998: 257–61; Danielsen 1998: 379). In this, they were bearers of the entire conservative representation, which consisted of a French understanding of 'civilisation' in the singular with some Germanic trimmings superficially added. Herder's reading of culture had permeated the Enlightenment discourse of the civil servants only superficially. Thus, a conservative historian like Yngvar Nielsen could refute the 'two cultures' theory of the Norwegian nationalists by insisting that the two cultures which they saw in their Norwegian 'fatherland' were really of a kind. It was a question of to what extent Norwegians had been able to absorb culture in general: the civil servants had succeeded to a larger degree than the common people (*almuen*). Thus, Nielsen insisted that there was only one qualitative culture in Norway – and also, interestingly, only one 'people' (*folk*), consisting of the common people (*almue*) as well as the cultured core: the city population, the civil servants and the immigrated stock (*slekter*) (see Danielsen 1998: 380). Nielsen and the other conservative historians were at this stage among the key bearers of the statist representation of Norway, as the newly formed conservative political party *Høire* (the Right) was a key bearer of it in the parliamentarian arena. By the end of the century, then, the statist representation, too, had incorporated the idea of the 'people'. Of course, their representation of the people was specific – it was a very different people indeed.

Furthermore, responding to the pressure of the other representations, it was rapidly incorporating the idea that the Norwegian state was not intrinsically tied to the king in Stockholm. Parliament and the bureaucracy were strong enough to make up the state on their own, and to lead the nation alone. This was a crucial development, inasmuch as it narrowed the difference between nationalist and statist representations of Norway, and made possible a 'united front' against Sweden in the heady days of secession from the Dual Monarchy. The nationalist idea of a separate nation having the right to a separate state very much carried the day in a referendum on independence in 1905, with only 184 votes cast in favour of a continued union with Sweden and the rest voting in favour of establishing a sovereign Norwegian state.

We may now take stock of the situation as it stood when Norway emerged as a fully sovereign state in 1905. Specific foreign policy debate was dominated by relations with Sweden, and also with Denmark. In the role of 'civilisation' in the singular, as well as in the role of a general cultural presence, Europe was explicitly mentioned (Østerud 1996: 31). A crucial duality surrounded the project of establishing Norway as a European nation state. On the one hand, as pointed out by the key nation-building historian Ernst Sars, the idea of the nation was 'the dominating idea in Europe's recent policy' (quoted in Seip 1997: 114). Thus, building a Norwegian nation and inscribing that nation with 'its own' state so that Norway could take its rightful place in the line-up of European nation states was a thoroughly European project. Nation-building equals a Europeanisation of Norwegian politics. On the other hand, in order to stand out in the line-up of European nation states, Norway needed some special characteristic, something to set it apart not only quantitatively as a number in a series, but qualitatively as a unique cultural instantiation of the human spirit. This element was exactly the one presented to Norway and other 'noble savages' by European Enlightenment discourse. As adopted in Norwegian discourse from the late eighteenth century onwards, this is the idea of the 'free peasant', what amongst romantic nationalists was sometimes referred to as Norway's 'special mission', namely to build a people's democracy and hence 'fulfil its mission for itself and for European democracy' (Bjørnson quoted in Sørensen 1997: 50). And it was here, for those who were hankering after the uniquely national, that Europe became 'the Other' to the Norwegian nation-building project. To the populist nationalist position, the European Other was not seen only or even predominantly as an entity which was external, continental and side by side with Norway, but as internal, 'Danish–Norwegian' and hierarchically in charge of Norway through its control of the state apparatus. The central political slogan of the populist nationalists, 'out of the unions', neatly juxtaposed political independence from Sweden with cultural independence from Denmark. Inasmuch as Danish culture was seen as an internal presence in the form of the statist position, this was also a slogan directed against that position's continued hold of the bureaucracy. This control was, crucially, seen as being wielded by the state bureaucracy, and another branch of the state, Parliament, was seen as the natural ally of the nation in the fight to do away with this foreign control. Populist nationalist discourse was inner-driven, in the sense that the delineation of the nation is made into an affair which plays itself out on the inside of Norwegian territory, and not on its borders. The populist nationalists simply did not spend much energy on specifying ideas of how the entity of Norway should relate to other state entities. The exception to this was the arena of Scandinavia, where the representations were clear-cut: direct cooperation between representatives of the nations was in order. For them, international cooperation was quite literally an issue for the nations, and not for the states. The exception was that part of the state which was Parliament, which by dint of its organic connection to the nation was seen as its legitimate representative. Kings or bureaucracies were not represented as legitimate carriers of international cooperation. This raises a key issue in political science, namely to what extent formality is needed in order for successful cooperation to take part. It is interesting that some of the key carriers of the populist nationalist position were also drawn to anarchism, which has a radically negative answer when it comes to the question of how much formality should be involved in politics. At least to these people, resistance to formal political cooperation *on all levels* was a matter or preference, not oversight.

Where the romantic nationalists were concerned, their representation of international cooperation was also predicated on the idea of cooperation between nations, either direct, or through parliaments. The basic premise was cultural: European culture came in the form of a series of nations, and the question of international cooperation had to be a question of how best to order things so that the national spirit could blossom within each of the nation states making up the series.

As to the statist representation, which was clearly on the defensive, its major role was to try and incorporate these elements into a representation of Europe, the basic idea of which was also cultural, but one which stressed the uniform and common form of European culture, not its division into a series of national cultures. A major example of how the statist position became marginalised concerns the way in which the political party *Høire* or 'the Right' accommodated its stance on the question of national sovereignty in the years immediately before 1905, when Norway emerged out of the United Kingdoms as a sovereign state. The force of the other two positions had grown to such a degree that any political party which harboured an aspiration of being state-bearing simply had to accommodate itself to their central policy implication: sovereignty for the Norwegian state.

Subsequent representations of 1905 invariably stressed the dissolution of the union as an act which followed not a military campaign, not even the policy of the Norwegian state, but which came as the peaceful result of *the people's struggle for independence*, as articulated by one part of the state – Parliament. Hence, as a result of the initiative and leading role taken by the nationalists on the issue of independence and the way it was finally achieved, a crucial convocation was established between the terms 'people', 'democracy' and 'independence'. Furthermore, in relation to the outside world, there was added a touch of what we may call baptismal exceptionalism. This exceptionalism was added to an already established idea that Norway was different from what the man who would go on to become Norway's first foreign minister, Jørgen Løvland, had referred to as the 'European warrior states' (*Stortingstidende* 1905/06: 46).

The inter-war period: the re-making of the Norwegian people

What dominates Norwegian discourse from the early 1920s and until the late 1940s is the remaking of the category of 'the people'. Questions which are to do with the representation of state, nation and the relationship between the two are derivative of this. The issue which prompted the remaking was the rise of the working class and the emergence of a workers' movement. The Norwegian detachment of international social democracy underwrote a Leninist analysis of politics: politics was class struggle, and class struggle was primarily an extra-parliamentarian and internationalist activity. 'Europe' was divided into a 'true Europe' of the internationalist working class on the one hand, and a 'false Europe' of the nationalist bourgeois classes on the other (see Neumann 1996). The strong embracement of modernity, seen as an inevitable evolution, meant that free trade between states was a preferred mode of international cooperation in the Norwegian social democratic representation of the world (Fure 1997). In this, they stood in direct contradiction to the three established representations, all of which embraced various shades of national protection in the name of the national interest (see p. 97).

As a result of a series of battles inside the workers' movement throughout the 1920s, however, the Leninist position was forced to the margins, and a hegemonic representation emerged where politics was seen as more of a parliamentarian activity, and the question of the relationship between the working class and the rest of the people became a central concern. In the course of the 1930s, a representation emerged where the workers' movement defined itself not only as the core of the people, but as the arena where that core could enter an intimate relationship with other working strata of the people, particularly the farmers. The Labour Party slogan, 'The whole people at work': *'the whole people,* not just the working class: *work,* not revolution', for the 1933 election captures this entire development (Dahl 1969: 68).

Three sets of countermoves were made by the established political forces in order to meet this appropriation of the concept of 'the people' by the workers' movement. First, some populist nationalists, particularly those belonging to the agrarian party, favoured a policy of accommodation and even collaboration. The workers' movement responded favourably to this. Second, a budding fascist movement emerged from off the margins of both the populist and romantic nationalist ranks. They tried to forge a fascist representation by drawing on their own organic representation of the people and relating it not to the state understood as Parliament or the bureaucracy but rather directly to the state's leader: the *Führer.* It was a central concern of the workers' movement not to pursue a policy which was so confrontational *vis-à-vis* other established positions that these positions should be tempted to evolve towards a fascist position. Third, and most conspicuously, the romantic nationalists and the statists increased their collaboration. They tried to counter the merging of the concepts of 'working class' and 'people' by playing up the concepts of the citizen (*borger*), of the fatherland, and of the nation.

The workers' movement answered by distancing itself from the term 'nation' and playing up the term 'people'. This was often done by denigrating the national credentials of the statist position and their historical bearers, the civil servant stratum. Interestingly, a central technique here was to evoke the tardiness of the statists in breaking the union with Sweden and with the Swedish king (see, for example, Tranmæl quoted in Dahl 1969: 42). However, in the course of the 1930s, as a follow-up on the move from class to people, the workers' movement evolved its position to envelop the idea of the nation. This discursive work was done primarily by people who had previously been bearers of a romantic nationalist position, but who had subsequently joined the social democrats. It thus embodied the very transformation of the workers' movement from being 'of the workers' to being 'of the people'. The central figure associated with this transformation from communism to nationalism was Halvdan Koht, and the central techniques used had already been seen in an article published in 1923 (Koht 1933). Koht's framing of the problem is instructive: there exist many people, particularly amongst peasant youth, who sympathise with communist thinking, but who are alienated by the idea that it is 'non-national or even directly hostile towards all things national' (Koht 1933: 268). It is true enough that the Communist Manifesto held that workers had no country, Koht maintains, but this should be taken as a regrettable fact rather than something to be celebrated. Indeed, the First International followed a practice which was clearly national in spirit.[2] History teaches us that 'peoples' (not countries, not states, not classes, but *folka*) are brought ever closer, but it also teaches the specialisation of these very peoples: 'The national thought has emerged as a living reality everywhere' (Koht 1933: 268). However, only a particular *kind* of national thinking and feeling is thus an organic part of the inexorable march of history:

> the national demands may always be marked by the ruling class, more than by the people's will itself; or the ruling class may force *their* 'national' demands upon the people. We must remember that the national feeling was born amongst the upper classes; in this country, it first emerges amongst the nobility and the civil servants, then amongst the bourgeoisie, and finally amongst peasants and workers, – as these classes grasp power in the state and in society. It is natural, then, that the national feeling still carries the marks of its progeny and is all too used to serving the political needs of the upper classes. This is the kind of national feeling which is called 'nationalism' abroad, and it is small wonder that the working classes rise against it.
>
> (Koht 1933: 269)

This is the kind of nationalism which inexorably leads to war, Koht adds. However, Norwegian history is a reminder that national spirit may also be a peaceful force. Indeed, Koht concludes, growing national feeling in and of itself points towards a communist policy: 'We all need to teach ourselves that the national idea makes a social demand on us, just as all social policy must be inculcated by national spirit. We have here not two separate thoughts, but two manifestations of the same mighty move towards progress' (Koht 1933: 282).

One notes that there is no explicit representation of the state in Koht's innovative amalgamation of different representations of human collectives. Thus, Koht's successful addition to this representation was not only to add the concept of the nation, but also to bring in the romantic nationalist idea that the state is an under-communicated part of an organic nexus with the nation, and most particularly with society. The state, that is, is simply 'us'. This was a move which has been incredibly successful, particularly in putting the difference between 'state' and 'society' under erasure: to this day, Norwegians do not really separate the two. The term which is beginning to be used interchangeably with all three terms – state, society and nation – is 'the people'. A central political slogan, in Norway as elsewhere, was 'rule by the people'. Again, the part of the state upon which Koht and what we may refer to as the socialist representation focusses was Parliament, not the king, and certainly not the bureaucracy. With the change away from a revolutionary policy, it was the policy of the social democrats that 'the people' should take over 'the state' by taking over one specific element of it – Parliament. The argument, which largely proved to be correct, was that the rest of the state would eventually be made to follow the lead of politicians put at the head of various departments and agencies by Parliament.

Comparing the Norwegian case with the other cases in this book, one notes that the workers' movement in Norway allied itself to small farmers, and not to workers in the public sector (Esping-Andersen 1990). Thus, whereas in a number of other countries, the relationship between state and society was reconfigured as a direct result of state employee involvement with their incoming political masters from the workers' movement, in Norway the political preferences of the state employees were changed only after the social democratic political leadership was changed. Thus, there was no radical change, but a gradual one, which made it easier to uphold the already existing representations of people and state. One possible development which could have mellowed the dichotomy between representations of the state in general and the bureaucracy in particular, on the one hand, and the people, on the other, was thus to a large degree warded off.

The success of the social democratic representation of politics may be seen not least by the way it marginalised other representations of the nation. The statist, romantic nationalist and even the populist nationalist positions did not disappear, but they were marginalised. It is true that in terms of state power, this period was the pinnacle for Norwegian nationalists, but a discursive analysis demonstrates that new discursive moves were needed, or else the institutional hegemony would be lost to the representation of the workers' movement. But few of the bearers of the established positions channelled their energies into innovative institutional or intellectual work. The onslaught of the workers' movement had borrowed so much from their own national portfolio that there was little room for manoeuvre. Furthermore, the need to counter was felt as less pressing now that the workers' movement had been nationalised and parliamentarianised. Thus, the task of drawing up a counter-representation was left to the fascists.

The early work of forging a fascist representation took place in the margins of the populist nationalist representation and incorporated racialist thinking. The 1921 Programme from what was to become the Agrarian Party (later the Centre Party), for example, made it clear that the party wanted to bar unwanted racial elements from the country:

> The Norwegian people's tribe (*folkestamme*) must be protected against everything which breaks down family life and the people's character (*folkekarakteren*). Immigration by suboptimal population elements must therefore be prevented. Consolidation of a strong economy must prevent detrimental emigration.
>
> (quoted in Angell 1994: 64)

The second prime minister from the Agrarian Party joined the Nazis during the occupation, and the basic innovative work was done by an Agrarian Government Minister, Vidkun Quisling, who was also the driving force behind the establishment of a Norwegian Nazi Party in 1933. However, in a comparative perspective, the most interesting thing about the budding fascist position is not its genealogical ties to populist nationalism, which are the same in Norway as in most other European countries, but the way it absorbed elements from the two other established representations of the nineteenth century.

In response to the rising workers' movement there emerged an anti-parliamentarian reaction of the kind which the rise of nationalism had not inspired.

The strong anti-parliamentarianism of fascism had an appeal to some within the statist representation, and this appeal was articulated in historical terms, as an opportunity to return to the period before Parliament substituted itself for the government as the claimant for the pinnacle of state power. The point, then, is that the emerging ideas which were to congeal into an aspiring state-bearing representation due to the German occupation of Norway were able to draw on elements from *all three* major representations of the nineteenth century.

The Norwegian people were represented as all persons of pure Norwegian blood and the representation's insistence on the centrality of blood as well as the infatuation with quantifying the extent of it in each individual was a characteristic radicalisation of the populist nationalist representation of the nation. Another characteristic radicalisation concerned the reading of how the Norwegian people had gained independence in 1905. As demonstrated above, all the three major representations that emerged out of the nineteenth-century discourse held that Norwegian sovereign statehood was the result of the people's struggle for independence. The Nazi chief ideologist concurred, but added that sovereignty had been won too easily – presumably since blood had not been shed (see Sørensen 1989: 39).

Where the representation's general view of Norwegian history was concerned, the same tendency to radicalise was in evidence. The Nazi chief ideologist, Gulbrand Lunde, adopted the populist nationalist idea that there were two cultures in Norway. There was a Norwegian 'people's culture', and then there was a 'foreign city culture'. The former, he insisted, was the only real and peasant-based national culture, and it had 'nothing to do with that city culture which has its root in the imposed Danish civil servant rule' (Lunde quoted in Sørensen 1989: 38).

After the war, when the Nazi coterie was removed from the state, a government consisting of all the inter-war parties took over, and before long, Labour had established a hegemony over the state, and a discursive grip on the definition of the nation and the people. The wartime experience had three key effects on the constellation of the other positions. The first has already been mentioned, namely a galvanisation of Labour leadership into Labour hegemony. Second, the diacritica of language and class were marginalised as central to the issue of how to limn the nation. Instead, a 'good Norwegian' came to be defined first and foremost as someone who had not been either a Nazi or a collaborator during the war. With the onslaught of the Cold War, a second diacriticon of this type was added: a good Norwegian was someone who was not a communist. Third, with the coming of peace, those parts of the state which had stuck it out in London during the war came back to Oslo in triumph, and the king was able to maintain the thrust of his role as a symbol of the nation.

This is quite noteworthy to our undertaking, because it shows that the split in the Norwegian state which had been in evidence since 1814 was maintained, but in a new form. From 1814 to 1884, the split had involved the king, his bureaucracy and his government on the one hand, and Parliament on the other. From 1884 to 1905, it involved the king and his bureaucracy on the one hand, with the government in between, and Parliament on the other. From 1905 and into the Second World War, there was the bureaucracy on the one hand, the government and the king hovering between, and Parliament on the other. After the war and with the king's newly won status as symbol of the nation, Parliament, government and the king arrived from London together, and the bureaucracy was at an all-time low and had to be reconstituted. The king had gone from being antithetical to Parliament, which was the part of the state closest to the nation, to be of a kind with it. As the bureaucracy reconstituted itself, it was yet again to take up the discursive position of being antithetical to Parliament and to the nation.

The making of Europe: the post-war years

Norwegian European discourse in the 1950s and 1960s is characterised by its truncated form. Only two major representations existed: the functionalist position and the nationalist position. True, debates about security policy figured prominently in foreign policy discourse during this period, but the major political dramas turned not on Norway's international relations, but on the questions of rebuilding the economy, on the extent to which it should be directly planned, and on the degree of detail in which this planning should be administered. When it reached Norway, then, the question of Europe was framed as a peripheral question inside a peripheral corner of political discourse. Furthermore, contrary to what was the case in a number of other European countries, there was no direct tradition of working in favour of a United States of Europe inside the workers' movement, in pan-European organisations like Coudenhove-Kalerghi's, or in Catholic organisations (Norway being Protestant), or inside the resistance. To the degree that Europe was present, it was not as an organisational question for overtly political debate, but as a cultural question. And inasmuch as there was little or no activity in favour of European integration, neither was there much activity against it.

The functionalist representation originated with people like the poet Arnulf Øverland and the MP Herman Smitt Ingebretsen who showed some positive interest in European integration, commenting on the potential for peace between erstwhile enemies. Smitt Ingebretsen and Wilhelm Keilhau had actually participated at the Haag meeting called by Churchill in May 1948, where they had acknowledged the need for cooperation, but also warned against the idea of supra-nationality (Gabrielsen 1975: 12–13, 24). When the European Movement was formed in the aftermath of this meeting, Smitt Ingebretsen became its first chair. The perspective of the European Movement was one of practical cooperation not first and foremost between sovereign states, not specifically political in kind, but between unspecified entities, in an unspecified manner. When specified at all, the goal of European cooperation was said to be co-operation between the *peoples* of Europe and increased efficiency, but also confidence-building – a peace-building exercise between former adversaries. The functionalist representation of European cooperation was from the very start formed as a positive representation, but in opposition to a rejected, federal representation which was not actually present in Norwegian discourse. Any talk of a Europe of 'states' was alien to Norwegian discourse; and the very few politicians who articulated the functionalist position stuck to what kept them together, not what divided them. The two variants – a social democrat and a bourgeois functionalist position – were present in discourse, but their bearers went out of their way to play down the differences, which were basically a question of key left–right differences recognisable from the national level of politics. The issues were to what extent 'Europe' as an economic project should be primarily market based or interventionist; to what extent its central organs should be redistributive of economic resources etc. Inasmuch as a national compromise had been worked out on these issues at the national arena (the basic idea being that the state could be interventionist as long as it did not favour direct intervention into specific enterprises, whose ownership in most cases remained private), the basic assumption was that they would in due course be negotiable on the European level, too. Thus, they could be de-ferred for the time being, and so it was possible for functionalists of both stripes to undercommunicate their differences, and to agree to disagree when they were in fact communicated.

Even inside the Foreign Ministry, where the question of Norway's approach to European integration arose as a result of the routine work of reporting on political developments worldwide, there were really only a small handful of people who took an interest. The question was framed as an economic one with the Minister of Trade rather than the Foreign Minister initiating coordinating policy. When it became evident that Britain, to which Norway looked for guidance, considered applying, and there arose a need for MPs to be informed, the Foreign Ministry actually had to send two persons over to Parliament to run regular classes on integration in its attic (see Eriksen and Pharo 1997: 328). When the parliamentary Foreign Affairs Committee voted to apply for membership, the majority view set out the economic sides of the issue first, and the political next. Significantly, they wheeled out the view taken by the Parliamentary Foreign Affairs Comm-ittee majority, in 1949, when the following had been taken down: 'The majority stresses that the European Council [that is, the Council of Europe] does not imply that a European federation or *Staatenbund* is formed, but, in common with the Ministry, sees the Council as the first step further to develop that European cooperation which is already a reality in a number of areas' (reproduced in Eriksen and Lundestad 1972: 215).

The main point was the negative tack, the qualified embrace of the idea of mem-bership, the need to spell out at the very outset what one was *not* in favour of. Federalism as an idea did not have any resonance for the Foreign Affairs Committee majority. And how could it, when the Norwegian state–society nexus from which the EEC was so tentatively embraced was one of enmeshment of interchangeable entities? The entire idea was that nations should cooperate on a par, and through their 'own' states, so that cooperation would not change the basic layout of a Europe of nation states. Since everybody embraced this presupposition, the one thing everybody could agree on was that they were against federalism, and since there was no federalist representation present in the Norwegian debate, hostility towards federalism became something which glued together not only different pro-European camps, but *all* the participants in the debates of this period. By the same token, when anti-marketeers would attack pro-marketeers for leaning towards federalism, pro-marketeers would invariably deny that they were in favour of a federalist Europe. The key importance of this is that the anti-marketeers could argue that it was the pro-marketeers who wanted to change things, and that the response of the pro-marketeers would be that what they wanted really was not that bad (meaning that it was not a federalist Europe).

The first major institutionalisation of the nationalist position came in December 1961, when a group of 143 artists and intellectuals, the majority of whom sympathised with the left wing of the Labour Party, formed a 'Movement against Membership in the Common Market – the 143'. The very name of the movement played on an incident of civilian resistance to the Nazi occupation during the Second World War (Bjørklund 1982: 21, 24, 30–38). It also latched on to a Norwegian patriotic tradition by addressing itself to 'Norwegian women and men', by declaring itself to be the defender of the Constitution and to protest 'the abandonment of Norway's independence and sovereignty'. The major point was that membership of the EEC would mean a break with Norwegian history and a bypassing of the people:

> When the large decisions in the history of our country were taken in 1814, in 1905 and in 1940, a united people stood behind them . . . The ties that bind us to European culture are strong. However, Europe is two things. There is a Europe which has inspired our work of freedom, our democracy and our Constitution. Yet there is also a Europe which has been responsible for wars of conquest, colonialism as well as economic and social oppression. The danger is great that it will be the latter of these tendencies that is going to envelop us if we join the Common market . . . As an independent state our country must strengthen the work done in the large worldwide institutions in order to bring all peoples closer to one another, in mutual understanding and cooperation. The new West European union which the Common Market is going to become, does not have such a goal . . . Our property right and right to govern (*råderett*) our own country will be undermined . . . The acting Parliament does not have the people's mandate to relinquish Norway's sovereignty and national independence for a purpose such as this one . . . The will of the people must be brought to the fore.
>
> (From the appeal, which is reproduced in full in Bjørklund 1982: 381–5)

The central concept here is the people. The concepts of 'nation' and 'state' are only mentioned once, and they are used as interchangeable synonyms of 'Norway' and 'country'. But one part of the state, namely Parliament, is given pride of place, and it is stressed that 'the acting Parliament' does not have 'the people's mandate'. The central tie between the people and Norway is said to be that of its right to govern (*råderett*). A distinction is made, then, between Parliament as a direct representative of the people – Parliament as it should be – and Parliament as a congregation of politicians – Parliament as it is. The concluding sentence of the appeal, that 'the will of the people must be brought to the fore', may be read as an appeal to Parliament to act as the direct representative of the people. It is also, however, a recipe for direct action – that Parliament may not be able to rise above its shape as a congregation of politicians, and so the question of Norway's relationship with the EEC should be decided *directly* by the people, in a referendum. One notes, then, that even the part of the state which is seen as being closest to the people, namely Parliament, is being bracketed as standing too far from the people.

A second crucial move is the representation of Europe as being fundamentally dichotomous. There is a benign cultural Europe of peoples, and a malign Europe of imperialist states. The Common Market is an institutionalisation of the latter, and it is on its way to becoming a 'union'. Coming hot on the heels of the historical presentation of the Norwegian people's struggle for independence, the othering of the Common Market is complete. On the one hand, there is the united Norwegian people, who follow the historical 'line' from 1814, 1905 and 1940 by taking a stand in favour of the good Europe, against the false European union. On the other hand, there is the bureaucracy and the government, who try to split the Norwegian people, who were not at the forefront of or even against developments in 1814, 1905 and 1940, and who take a stand in favour of the false Europe, against true European culture.

The second nationalist representation was an agrarian nationalist position which was articulated in Parliament in the early 1960s by Centre Party MP Erik Braadland as follows:

> Some would even insist that by giving away rights in our own country we may win the same rights in other Common Market countries . . . [But do we?] Which country has even remotely the same opportunities to hunt and fish as we do? There is no balance between what we give and what we gain . . . the Norwegian people have built up the modern and affluent society in which we live today. By consistent work and innovation, by going in unison, in national community, we have reached where we are today. It is the feeling of community, popular sovereignty, our national self-government which maintains it, and which is the only thing which can maintain the society we have created . . . we want to maintain the right to preside over what nature has bestowed on us, and what we have accumulated as production capital, not because we are ungenerous or jingoistic, but because we want to remain a nation.
>
> (quoted in Eriksen and Lundestad 1972: 223)

Nature has bestowed on the nation, the people, society, the opportunity to hunt, fish and produce, and the people have diligently ploughed the soil and harvested the waters to produce the riches of modern Norway. This soil–people nexus is under attack, and must be defended, 'because we want to remain a nation'. 'We', that is, the people, therefore say 'no' to the EEC.

Differences notwithstanding, all representations of Europe in the 1950s and 1960s put 'the people' forward as the central concept. Where the functionalist pro-cooperation representation is concerned, however, one notes a silence when it comes to exactly *who* is going to be cooperating with European counterparts. In its stressing of the adherence to a common European culture as a key factor of Norwegian political life, the functionalist position harks back to the nineteenth-century statist representation of Europe. However, that representation was barred from announcing its statism by its association with the union with Sweden. Upon its return, it still cannot speak its name, the main reason for this being that it has to manoeuvre in a discursive space where the concept of 'the people' has become hegemonic.

One sees this most clearly in the way that what we may call the nationalist representation of Europe is able to silence the statist aspect of the functionalist position. The Europe of the functionalists is specified as a false Europe, a union of states, far from the people. Whereas all representations try to present themselves as the logical perpetuators of the 'general line' of Norwegian history, the affinity of the functionalist representation to the state in its bureaucratic aspect and to the union of states renders it ineffective.

However, one also notes the interesting self-silencing of what we may call the nationalist position. The nationalists wanted to create *one* anti-union representation and in order to do this, the historical and nation-based moves were played up, and the anti-capitalist moves were forced to the margins of the representation. The upshot was that anti-capitalists and nationalists succeeded in forging a united representation and a united front – even if most anti-capitalists in terms of practical politics at this stage wanted nothing whatsoever to do with the Common Market, whereas the nationalists favoured some kind of association. As laid out admirably by Tor Bjørklund (1982), it was almost a decade before this united representation materialised in a united front, namely the organisation called 'The People's Movement against the EEC'. One notes that 'the people' was not only the central concept around which the representation was built, but that it was even present in the name of its material expression – 'The *People's* Movement'.

The 1972 referendum

In 1972, Parliament had decided that a referendum on Norwegian EC membership was called for once the result of negotiations was clear. Indeed, the feeling was that nothing could be done if the referendum yielded a no. If the result was a yes, however, it was argued from a number of quarters that 50.1 per cent would not be a clear enough indication. In terms of national decision making and public opinion, the central question to analyse is what people thought they were voting for and against, what they thought they were 'advising' Parliament about and what Parliament thought it was being advised on, in the referendum of 25 September 1972. This question may be illuminated by an analysis of the 30-hour parliamentary debate which took place on 6–8 June 1972. This debate is also crucial to the wider debate in the sense that it was widely covered, commented on and used as a point of reference by the Norwegian media.

Everybody acknowledged that there had to be some relationship to Europe, and that the institutionalisation of this relationship should take the form of either membership or a free trade agreement. A fair share of the debate turned on whether it was possible to forge such an agreement, how quickly it would be possible to negotiate it, and what it should contain. The parliamentary debate reflects strong disagreement not so much about what Norway is, but about what Europe and the EC are. On the yes side, it was argued that Europe and Norway are of the same order: Europe is more of the same. Norway is just another cultural nation in a European order of cultural nations. It may be a bit more advanced when it comes to democratic rights, including women's rights, it may have a somewhat better social policy, but it is basically a variant on a European theme. On the no side, it was argued that Norway is basically different from Europe. Europe is hierarchical, Norway is egalitarian. Europe is centralised, Norway is dispersed. Europe cares about the strong, Norway cares about the weak. The 'no' representation was able to harness history: Norwegian nation-building was successfully portrayed as a question of organising an egalitarian peasant-based stock against a European culture and its local representatives. These representatives are the civil servants who were the state-bearing stratum of the Danish empire of which Norway was a part until 1814, the rightist state-bearing elites who were in charge during the Union with Sweden and, by association, the state-bearing party cadres of the contemporary social democracy which acts in cahoots with big capital and the liberal international right.

We may start with how the prime minister represented the EC. Bratteli's (3368)[3] own take on the EC was close to what we would now (anachronistically) refer to as the principle of subsidiarity and the pooling of sovereignty. The EC should primarily take care of

> tasks which cannot be handled by one state alone, which cannot be handled by the sovereignty of one state alone. We are talking about a sovereignty which states working together are trying to grapple from yet untamed (*ustyrte*) forces, particularly in international economics. There are forces in our closely integrated world which can only be handled (*styres*) by regional or international sovereignty.

Bratteli and the yes side generally almost without fail referred to the EC as *Fellesskapet* – like its German translation *Gemeinschaft*, this word invokes solidarity, togetherness, indeed community. They stressed Norway's role as a cultured nation, with a responsibility for the further evolution of that central feature of European civilisation, a rule of law. If Bratteli is representative in emphasising Norway and Europe's cultural togetherness, his stress on the pooling of sovereignty is unique in the debate. A whole plethora of other voices argue against any possibility of the EC evolving towards a union. In Norwegian parlance, union equalled federation. The leader of the Conservatives, Willoch, was representative of the yes side in juxtaposing an intergovernmental and a federal model, and then denying the possibility that the EC might evolve towards the latter (Willoch 3201). Intergovermentalism secured co-decision (*medbestemmelse*), a free trade agreement did not, and this was even more important than the economic loss that the latter alternative would entail, Willoch concluded. But this was a defensive representation of the EC's future, which could effectively be parried by pointing to the Treaty of Rome's formulation that the goal was 'an ever closer union', that federation was therefore the 'logical result' of the integration process, and that intergovernmental ideas about a Europe of fatherlands were 'a chimera' (Oddleif Fagerheim 3310). It must be added that, in Norwegian debate, formulations in treaties tend to be taken at face value; the Latin approach of '*en principe*' does not come easily either to a Norwegian lawyer or to a Norwegian politician, and much less to the Norwegian voter. There exists an ideal that people do and should 'mean what they say', and variations on this theme are not treated simply as a matter of cultural variation, but as a moral flaw. Indeed, the centrality of the treaty as a legal document created a sub-debate on the question of the Norwegian Constitution.

It was an important part of the argument in favour of membership as co-decision that it would secure continuity in Norwegian foreign policy: that the world had moved on, and that Norway would therefore have to join the new organisational forms by means of which states interacted. Membership, then, was perhaps a question of taking a radical new step, but it was a step which had to be taken in order to keep Norway's position as a normal European state. However, this was a step too far for the no side which argued that if one looked at Norwegian history, one would find that 'both in 1814 and in 1905, there were unionist parties which held that Norway would benefit from joining larger units. It was the right and the civil servants (*embetsverket*) then. Now it is the Norwegian Union of Industrialists, the Banking Union, civil servants and the party functionaries.' On the other hand, there were peasants and leftists, and now a plethora of peripheral groups 'without established positions of power. At the present time, only the proletarians of the periphery are uniting. However, there exist living Peoples' Movements in country after country, ours included' (Bjørn Unneberg 3291).

The centrality of these representations was acknowledged by the yes side which repeatedly stressed that the historical parallels to the times of the Danish empire and the union of Sweden (1814–1905) were bogus, but only one attempt was made to turn the parallelism around. This reading tried to make an alternative narrative: that the Swedish–Norwegian Union consisted of two parties which developed different mercantile orientations, that similar mercantile orientations made for nice cooperation, and that the European Community was a project which would secure that countries maintained similar mercantile orientations. This alternative narrative was ill-conceived and confused, and so a non-starter as a challenger (Per Karstensen 3307).

The yes side's other attempt to shoot down the no side's representation was to short-circuit the tie between the no side and the historical Norwegian nation. The left-based part of the no side was singled out as being fuddy-duddy and bookish, consisting of students and professors, while the yes side could count the working people on its side: 'The common people want growth, it is only the professors and the students which say we can do without it' (Gunnar Berge 3313; cf. Guttorm Hansen 3194; Bodil Aakre 3348). However, this countermove proved ineffective, inasmuch as the articulation of a tie between non-growth and bookishness, EC opposition and intellectuals, growth and folksiness, EC support and common sense, etc. did not register in subsequent debate. The attempted move had no resonance, and so simply did not stick. This is not only of importance in that it demonstrates how it was not up to the yes side to define the connotations of 'the people', the representation of which thus remained a key resource for the no side, but it is also important because it goes a long way to explaining why the difference between a social democratic and a bourgeois yes seems so negligible. In general political discourse, the left could often use the representation of 'the people' to delineate itself from the right by arguing that it was closer to 'the people' than was the right. On EC questions, however, 'the people' was a discursive resource which was not available to *either* of the yes representations. Inasmuch as there were few other resources by dint of which the left and the right on the yes side could set themselves apart from each another, they came across as being rather similar. We have here another example of how central the representation of 'the people' is in Norwegian discourse: in a context where it was not available, differentiation to a large extent broke down.

As already mentioned, the issue of self-government was the common denominator on which nay-saying socialists and nay-saying nationalist conservatives had forged their alliance and their alternative representation of the EC. It was clear that the focus on self-government turned on the entire question of who 'Norwegians' were and what 'Norway' should be. The insistence on this focus implied a wilful and programmatic ontologification of the debate: it was turned into a question of who 'we the Norwegians' were, to a question of identity politics. The yes side resented this, not least because it represented them as traitors to the nation and national history. Tor Bjørklund (1982: 188) argues that 'The EC pros felt that they were marked off as the internal enemy.'

The no side also made a potent pairing of cultural and security concerns in a critique of 'neo-colonialism'. Norway is different from 'EC' countries in this regard, the anti-minority argued in a report to Parliament (Innst. no. 277, 1971–2. p. 523), because 'our country does not find itself in a conflicting relationship with developing countries through colonial or post-colonial investments'. The pros did little to counter this except to gesture vaguely in the direction of Norway being seemingly inevitably part of a European culture which despite its colonial past was positive, not negative: 'The European idea and European cooperation rest on three pillars: common culture, common economy, common security' (Erling Petersen 3252). Furthermore, the point was repeatedly made that the heads of former colonies such as Kenya and Tanzania, with which Norway had fairly close relations through development programmes, actually favoured Norwegian membership of the EC. On religion, Sigrid Utkilen (3390) reported that a number of people were worried about the EC closing down the Protestant Norwegian state church, and also feared what she referred to as a 'Catholic invasion'.

Having remarked that the kingpin of the yes argument had so far been the economic benefits of international cooperation, the no side argued that growth was ecologically harmful and only benefited big capital. Another economic argument against membership was derivative of the sovereignty argument and turned on the need to maintain Norwegian resources for the Norwegians. This, after all, was the major glue of the anti-membership alliance. The slogan here was 'No to the sale of Norway' (*Nei til salg av Norge*) (see Bjørklund 1982: 71). Pros repeatedly objected to this argument, pointing out, for example, that the country most active in 'buying'

Norway was a non-EC member, namely Sweden (Paul Thyness 3264). Antis could then defuse this counter-argument by arguing that 'selling' should not be understood in economic terms only, but was rather a metaphor for 'selling out'; what was at stake was submission in general (Kristian Halse 3309). We see here how the antis subsumed the whole question of economy under what is represented by them as the more basic issue, namely sovereignty.

My interpretation is that the argument of sovereignty, which as the main glue of the anti-membership alliance is central to the debate, comes complete with an argument not only to the effect that 'the people' rather than the state apparatus is the custodian of sovereignty, but that there is an inevitable nexus between 'Norway' understood as the Norwegian people, and 'Norway' understood as Norwegian territory. If the people do not cover all of the territory, Norway cannot be Norway. 'The continent' is the town, 'Norway' is the countryside, and if that countryside is not populated, Norway is no longer Norway. Since EC membership will entail 'concentration' or 'centralisation', it will inevitably lead to a drop in rural population, and then the entire idea of Norway will be in danger. Thus, agriculture and fisheries are about much more than simply money. Inasmuch as they uphold current demographics, they are institutional mechanisms which sustain a certain representation of Norway. This representation is endangered by EC membership, which must therefore be fought tooth and nail. This explains how two parts of the economy which in terms of productivity were rather peripheral to an already heavily industrialised country could become so central to the debate about the EC. Pros did not question the dominating representation of Norway in this particular regard, perhaps because they shared it to such an extent that they did not even question it, perhaps because they saw it as so deeply rooted that they deemed it suicidal to challenge it. Actually, pros seem to have had a hard time understanding that the growth argument might not be seen as crucial. Meanwhile, the antis dominated the debate by hinging the economics question solidly on what they saw as the more basic question of sovereignty and demographics, that is, to an identity politics in favour of a certain idea of Norway, and a Norway which was superior to Europe.

To sum up, the no side was able to win the fight over the past, over how EC membership would fit in with Norwegian history, and it was also able to win the fight over the future. By successfully representing the EC as being on its way to becoming a federation, a United States of Europe (this being the local Norwegian way of reading the word 'union'), membership was seen not only as a question of being dissolved in a larger unit, but also as a question of eradicating Norwegian democracy and identity by returning to a situation which had existed once before, namely a union with stronger parties. The EC was a union in the making, membership of which would put an end to Norwegian sovereign statehood.

Against these powerful representations, the yes side's alternative representations were simply not strong enough. Despite the overwhelming material resources which the yes side was able to muster (the state apparatus, the major media, most major employees, etc.), the no side won out. In a word, the antis won the fight because they were able to differentiate two meanings of 'Norway': that of the nation/the people, and that of the state/the government apparatus, and to privilege the former over the latter. By doing this, they not only nullified the effect of the state using its institutional resources to ram through a yes; they were able to represent the fact that the state was harnessed to the yes cause as positively confirming that it was not only different from the people, but actually opposed to them. In this regard, one should not overlook the symbolic power emanating from the strong net of social movements which were opposed to the EC. These movements distributed leaflets, staged demonstrations and so on, and this was in and of itself of importance. However, their major importance may lie in their power as a symbol of the people's capacity to organise themselves, in opposition to the state. The very existence of the social movements confirmed that the state did not have a monopoly on building institutions which embodied the nation and its will. Not only were 'the people' opposed to 'the state', they were also capable of mustering the institutional resources to prove it.

The parliamentary debate confirms that the major representations which had formed during the two preceding decades were basically unchanged. With the partial exception of Bratteli, who referred to the possibility of a 'pooling of sovereignty', nowhere in the debate is there as much as a trace of a federalist representation. The functionalist representation dominated the yes side. Furthermore, a lot of discursive work continued to be spent on keeping the social democratic and the bourgeois variants of this representation from erupting. Mirroring this situation, the nationalist representation dominated the no side. Not even differences about specific policies allowed the agrarian nationalist and anti-capitalist variants to come into open conflict: when the option of association was mooted, no friendly fire was drawn. Similarly, when the anti-capitalist variant was attacked, it was invariably by pros who in this way wanted to discredit the entire no side, or to make visible a split, but to no avail. What we see in this debate is not the discussion of a wide array of political groupings, but rather two disciplined armies locked in almost ritualised polemics.

The 1994 referendum

For fourteen years after the 1972 referendum, the EC question remained taboo in Norwegian political life (Allen 1979; Slaatta 1999). Only in 1986, when the Labour government made a successful attempt to restart it by initiating work on a White Paper about the overall political and economic situation in Europe, did it slowly begin to reappear. It became a central issue only with the end of the Cold War, reaching a peak with the second referendum on membership on 28 November 1994. For eight years prior to the referendum, the functionalist and nationalist representations and their basic concepts were re-presented once again. In the period 1986–94, political discourse was partly preoccupied with large issues such as the tapering off of industrialisation, increased urbanisation, the end of the Cold War and the Swedish and Finnish membership applications. However, despite attempts by the yes side to link all of these questions to the question of Norway's relationship to the EC, they did not seem to have any basic impact on the representations. Neither did they bring about any major new representations, although some isolated intellectuals founded a tiny chapter of the federalist movement in 1990 – a clear break with the Norwegian tradition of having no federalist presence in European discourse. The federalist representation was so different from the two dominating representations that it hardly registered in the debate. The two dominating representations once again congealed around the European Movement and a counterpart whose very name underlined its catch-all character: 'No to the EU' (*Nei til EU*). The major drama of the run-up to the referendum, therefore, did not turn on the forging of representations and the solidification of representation by dint of institutionalisation. Rather, it was a question of which already existing organisations would take a stand, and what that stand would be. The Labour Party after a long period of internal debate settled on a yes, but an internal no caucus called 'Social Democrats against the EU' thrived inside the party. The Conservatives opted for a yes, as did the People's Progress Party. The rest decided on a no. The largest environmentalist organisation, which had pointedly remained above the fray in 1972, opted for a no, as did the Trade Union Conference, which had been in favour in 1972.

Once again, the nearest thing I have found to a catalogue of arguments or, in the words of Prime Minister-to-be Kjell Magne Bondevik, 'a useful review of the argumentation' (4924) about the EU is the verbatim record of the Storting's 26-hour debate on 29–30 September 1994.[4]

The leader of the major no party, Anne Enger Lahnstein, headed off in the following terms:

> The date for the referendum was fixed by the yes parties, who hoped that a Swedish 'yes' a fortnight earlier would create a so-called Swedosuction (*svenskesug*) and influence people to do what the Swedes do . . . What we are going to vote on is not whether we belong in Europe or not, but whether we are going to become a member of the European Union . . . The PM has insisted that we do not give up on our right to govern ourselves (*selvråderett*), only our egoistic wilfulness (*egenrådighet*). There is no longer any point in insisting that this is totally common cooperation between sovereign nations. What we have here, is deep integration . . . People seek information and knowledge about the Union. However, they are hardly going to let themselves be coerced or threatened to vote in favour of yet again making Norway a part of a Union. And I think many balk at the thought that the Swedes are going to decide for us.
>
> (Lahnstein, C, 4707–10)

In the following exchange, she went on to air her and her party's characteristic constitutional conservatism, about which she had also published a pamphlet, and which to her and her party serves as a bulwark of Norwegian sovereignty. One notes how this key intervention begins and ends with the geographical locus of Sweden, how Sweden and the EU are juxtaposed to Norway as possible partners to avoid, and how the word 'union' performs the job of maintaining the link between Sweden and the EU over time. For Norway, this intervention argues, being in a union with the EU must mean the same thing as being in a union with Sweden: a subaltern partnership with another but stronger entity of the same kind as Norway (also Gjedrem, Chr, 4884). The EU, then, is represented as a state formation; some of the work of making it so is performed by the word 'constitution', which is tied in both with the Treaties of Rome and Maastricht, but also with former and future suggestions for a constitution for Europe emanating from the European Parliament and other loci within the Union. This representation of Norway and the EU as being political phenomena of the same kind and hence alternatives to one another is so strong that it allows an attack on the other dominant representation of the EU not only of being that of the state and of the elite, not only of not daring to speak its name, but of being deceitful. In a cultural setting where honesty is cherished in all spheres of life, including politics, deceitfulness in and of itself is a highly un-Norwegian trait. In addition to substance, then, Lahnstein is able to mark the opposing representation of the EU as being foreign to Norwegianness simply by being dishonest.

The discursive power of this nationalist representation of Norway and the EU was confirmed by the absence of any clear alternatives. Labour's Foreign Minister commented on this intervention and the Centre Party's representation of the EU generally that

> he was left with the impression that the EU is a conspiracy to kill off people's democracy (*folkestyret*), the environment, equality, welfare and all the other things we cherish in Norway. But then I have a question: How come that some of Europe's oldest democracies have conspired to destroy everything that engages ordinary people throughout Europe?
>
> (Godal 4774)

The move here, then, is to equalise Norwegian democracy with member country democracies, and to reproduce the idea of 'the people' on the European level, to move some of the emotional appeal of the idea of 'the people' away from the national level. In other words, an attempt is made to articulate 'the people' as a phenomenon on the European level, the consequence of which is that 'the people' is not an exclusively Norwegian phenomenon, but that there exist other peoples as well, that these other peoples may be tied in with states roughly in the same way as the Norwegian people are, namely by dint of 'democracy', and that it may even be possible to conceive of 'the people' in Europe as one entity. Another response was to agree that Norway is a good place to live in, but to argue that this is due to Norway's already existing involvement in European cooperation (Stoltenberg 4781).

Five, head of the Conservative party, the staunchest of the yes parties, stated that her party said 'absolutely no' to the idea of a Constitution for the Union (4713). Another leading spokesman of the same party confirmed that the Conservatives were against a federal Europe and that

> Norway is one of the best countries of the world to live in . . . It is simply untenable when the no side tries to make people believe that for all practical purposes, the EU is a state formation . . . The heavy stagnation in the rate of

investment in Switzerland after its no to the EEA demonstrates what kind of problems face countries which opt for isolation . . . A yes to Norwegian membership of the EU means a more secure future for Norwegian values.

(Petersen, Con, 4714–17)

When challenged, the vice chair of the Norwegian European Movement would not confirm whether she was a federalist, but preferred to duck the question (Widvey 4821). Again, the stress is on the EU as a safeguard of the already dominant representation of Norway, as a complementary phenomenon to the central phenomenon of the Norwegian nation state. There is no challenge to Lahnstein's position here, only a confirmation of her representation of Norway and an insistence that the EU is not a project of a kind with Norway. The only attempted challenge is to argue that 'the EU is something new in history – one tries to find a power construction which is between the nation state and the purely new federal state on an international level' (Blankenborg 4745). This challenge, however, is ineffective because it still argues in state terms (state, federation), and because it is internally inconsistent (a federation is a state, and thus cannot exist on an 'international' level).

This allowed a leading spokeswoman of the Socialist Left Party, which was against joining the EU, to argue convincingly that

Jan Petersen says that Norway is one of the best countries of the world to live in. That is right, and not only because Norway is a rich country, but because we are the country in Europe where the differences between people are smallest, where we have built a system of welfare on the premise that the differences between people are small, with rights for everybody.

(Halvorsen 4718–19)

This was repeated by two other spokespersons for this party, which also added that the reason why this was so was Norway's 'most important and proudest tradition', namely 'a strong civil society with strong people's movements'. These, he pointed out, were now almost unanimously poised against Norwegian membership of the EU (Solheim 4721). The dichotomy equality/inequality is successfully linked to the dichotomy Norway/EU. A later Minister and head of the Christian People's Party argued that 'We have an EU internal market which among other things consists of the Netherlands and the union town of Maastricht, where narcotics are sold openly', 'we have Spain, with legalisation of hashish, we have the Minister of Trade's German sister party – the Social Democratic Party – which has the legalisation of hashish on its programme' (Svarstad Haugland 4851). The representations attacked here add to the dichotomies of healthy/sick and sound/decadent. Most of all, the EU threatened women: 'If Norway were to become a member of the EU, it would lead to Norwegian women losing the possibility they have today to influence the society they live in' (Øveraas, C, 4910; Fossum, L, 4829).

The spokesman for the Christian People's Party maintained that 'We should remind one another that Europe now consists of 40 countries, the EU of 12, and at a maximum 15–16 from the beginning of next year' (4727). This view – that Europe consists of countries, that Europe is the sum of its nation states and nothing else, was nowhere challenged in the debate. To put the point in a different way: the debate saw no voicing of something approaching a federalist representation (the closest thing being the suggestion noted above that there may indeed exist a 'people' on the European level as well as on a national one). The leader of the Liberal Party (4738) and a number of others focussed on and regretted how EU membership would weaken Parliament and strengthen the Government. This theme dovetailed with the theme of how the EU reached decisions in smoke-filled back rooms, the implication being that Norwegian democracy had an open decision-making structure. As demonstrated above, in Norwegian tradition, Parliament is 'the people's parliament'. The bureaucracy, on the other hand, is seen as alien to the people. The dichotomies people/bureaucracy and open/closed seem to be tied to the dichotomy Norway/EU, where the former is privileged over the latter. When the theme of the EU meeting in closed rooms was repeated later, the point was made that participation in such meetings would be nice for those Norwegians 'who are used to participating in such meetings, reading the documents in English and perhaps chatting in French in the corridors', but that for the others, the distance to the decision-making process would simply increase (Bakke, L, 4756). The dichotomy closed/open is here linked to the dichotomies centre/periphery, mobile/immobile, polyglot/monoglot and, since state personnel are explicitly amongst those charac- terised in this way, people/bureaucracy. Another MP continued with the following elaboration of the dichotomy: 'The EU has no critical common press, therefore no alert and critical opposition. How then can the EU system ever become a democratic one?' (Fossum 4829). Since the federal argument was only present in its negative form, as a bogeyman of the no side, it was not only that the debate was state centric; it was about the no side convincingly arguing that the EU was an alternative to Norway – a clearly inferior and indeed threatening alternative – and the yes side only saying in effect that 'it is not so bad'. Interestingly, this nondescript yes side could equally well be described as conservative as social democratic.

The dichotomies colonial/non-colonial and EU/Norway were introduced by the Parliament's only Maoist representative who registered that the way 'German imperialism is enveloping Eastern Europe and Asia' was characteristic of the EU's *modus operandi,* and therefore a reason to vote no to Norwegian EU membership (Gythfeldt 4744). A leading spokesperson for the Centre Party maintained that Norway as a member of the EU and the WEU could end up in a situation where it 'afforded support to [military] operations outside of the EU area' (4746).[5] These two themes were linked by Solheim of the People's Left Party, who pointed out that old colonial powers like France kept interfering in Africa to prop up 'the most oppressive, undemocratic and corrupt state leaders which exist on the African continent, for example Mobutu' (Solheim 4749). The dichotomy interventionist/ non-interventionist is linked to the dichotomy EU/Norway, and on Norway is conferred the task of bearing witness to the dirty deeds of the warlike European states. Again, the retort is simply that 'Norway does not intend to wage war outside our continent' and that 'one should perhaps be glad that Norway has not been a powerful nation through history, for then perhaps we would have had a double history which would have been much harder to handle than is our own history' (Blankenborg 4749–50; also Berg, Con, 4902–3). Again, this argument simply confirms that there are two histories: a non-colonial Norwegian history and a colonial European history. The no side could elaborate on the theme of the EU as an imperialist bloc by arguing, in the words of the later Minister of Energy, that the 'EU is an answer to the attempt of the rich countries to increase the competition between themselves'. Norway, she maintained, should remain outside the EU so that it could join Nelson Mandela and the poorer countries in the world in standing aside from this competition race (Arnstad 4751). This move effectively reinforces the association of Norway with anti-colonialism and the EU with colonialism. As further embellishment of this dichotomy, it was pointed out that Norwegian development aid was much higher than the EU's, actually the highest in the world per capita, and that the EU's development programmes were piddling and ineffective (Frafjord Johnson 4906). The Foreign Minister responded to the no side's alleged internationalism by alluding to how this internationalism only seemed to affect far-away countries with which contacts were limited, and not the countries with which communication was most intense. The Minister of Trade parodied the no argumentation of 'the odd country' (*annerledeslandet*) by sending it up: 'the odd message: I am best, look at me, learn from me! – For I am the lighthouse' (Knudsen, L, 4848).

The Nordic card was played by the yes side, which argued that Nordic cooperation could flower inside the EU, but would wither if some Scandinavian countries joined and others did not (Syse 4786). However, it was also argued that Nordic cooperation had stagnated, and that the stagnation was due to the countries being too similar: it was within the EU, it was argued, that tensions between opposites were strong enough for new initiatives to flower (Syse 4788) The retort was that Nordic cooperation would disappear inside the EU anyway (Lunde 4787).

Although the yes side tried to contest what they saw as the no side's untenable identification with the people by pointing out that those who used it were themselves elites, for example parliamentarian leaders (Frøiland, L, 4813; also Blankenborg 4845; Jagland 4847), these moves were ineffective. Parliamentarian leaders belong to that part of the state which, given the Norwegian historical constellation of representations, is close to the people. Attempts to represent the EU as being close to its peoples, based on subsidiarity, or, as it was rebaptised by the yes side following its Danish opposite number, 'the closeness principle', were also to little avail (Widvey, Con, 4815; Five, Con, 4853). Neither did it help to make the point that physical distance to decision makers was less important in the jet age (Knudsen, L, 4849). The dichotomy people/state ruled the roost in tandem with the dichotomy Norway/EU. 'It is not without reason that No to the EU has formed the slogan "Yes to people's rule, no to union"' (Dale, C, 4862). The debate was clinched by Erik Solheim, leader of the Socialist Left Party, who argued that

> Historically, in Norway we have had a political and economic elite which has been much weaker than in very many other places. We have no nobility in Norway. The civil servants (*embedsmennene*) received their political counter-thrust

from a strong people's movement at the end of the last century, and during this
century we have had strong people's movements which have dominated our
country in opposition to the elite.

With the exception that the anti-capitalist variant of the nationalist position was
this time allowed to surface thanks to the presence of the Maoist MP, the 1994
debate demonstrates the inertia of the European debate in Norway. However, over
time, there is no such thing as an unchallenged discourse. The question which forces
itself to the fore, is this: how can it be that the bearers of the functionalist representation go into bat with the same concepts, the same strategy and in a number of
cases even the same arguments as in 1972, when this strategy proved itself ineffective
in 1972 and there were no signs that it would prove more effective this time? Three
general answers may be offered to such a question. The first answer is that the stress
on intentionality is misplaced, that participants in discourse occupy their subject
positions without being able first to identify and then to challenge their permanence.
This general answer, that subjects are largely unable to look at their discourse from
the outside, is often a good one, but it is a non-starter in a discursive setting where
the question of what 'went wrong' the last time is being discussed at length, as it was
in this case. Specifically, the inability of the yes side to reflect on its own history
may have had pervasive consequences, and its focus on economistic arguments may
have been so narrow that it occluded many other parts of discourse, but the need
to 'do something' was glaringly obvious. The consequences of these new moves
remain unknown, but the need for making them was very present indeed. It may
be true that subjects are not able to fathom much of the discourse of which they are
the bearers, but at least on the tactical level, an explicit willingness to 'do something'
was in evidence. This general answer may have relevance, but not for this immediate
political situation.

A second general answer may be that new moves are attempted, but that the
inertia of the discourse is such that they are ineffective. In this case, if new moves
were made, they were not made in Parliament, where the concept of 'the people'
in its nationalist tapping remained central to all concerned. The specific problem
with this answer is that (at least to this participant in the debate and to this reader
of all available analyses of the debate), the parliamentary debate does indeed seem
to cover the major available moves. However, some new moves were indeed in
evidence, for example trying to articulate 'the people' to 'Europe' as well as to
'Norway', and they did indeed flounder due to the inertia of the discourse.

A third general answer is that the contenders are indeed able to assess their
situation, but that they are simply not able or willing to come up with new moves
which may change the discourse. Inasmuch as the two former observations seem
not to apply, the reason why discourse remained basically unchanged and few new
moves were made by the yes side must be that they were unable or unwilling to make
new moves. In a word, the pros lost because of their lack of new arguments which
could change a discourse which was stacked against them.

Why it was stacked against them has been demonstrated above: it has to do with
the historical connotations of the terms of discourse. 'The people' is a term which

is tied in with 'Parliament' as the 'natural' sovereign locus of the state, and which is the antithesis of the rest of the state and its European environment, *in casu* the constellation consisting of civil servants and the EU. The use of historical references to 1814, 1905 and 1940 – as well as self-referentially to 1972! – were rampant on the no side in 1994 as well (Kvalsvåg 1999). Interestingly, at times both pros and antis acknowledge this. Reflecting on the demise of the pros three months after the fact, the head of the European Movement had this to say:

> In the fight for the majority of the Norwegian people's votes, the game was actually up when the EC changed its name to the EU. That opened things up for the final brainwash, with the concept of the union as the detergent. For conspicuous historical reasons, it is easier in Norwegian than in any other language to use the word union in order to preclude any pretence to thinking, or remove any trace thereof.
>
> (Lønning 1997 [1994]: 199)

It was no longer necessary to argue that the EC was a 'union'; it had declared it itself. The name itself warrants for the continuity where Norway's relationship to the Union is concerned – that the two entities which are referred to by that same signifier are very different indeed is of less importance. This must be a textbook example of how signifiers are more important than signifieds.

Indeed, as demonstrated above, the negative connotations of the concept of 'union' are overwhelming, for reasons which have to do with *post hoc* representations of the 'cultural' union with Denmark and the 'political' union with Sweden. Still, it would be unwarranted to conclude that Norwegian discourse on Europe is impermeable. There does exist at least one embryonic representation which challenges both the nationalist and the functionalist representations at the basic level, by challenging the idea that 'the people' is a metaphysical entity. This position arrived in the 1980s and represents the state as a mediator between societal groups which cannot be seen to institutionalise either society or nation because they should remain conceptually distinct from them. It argues, however, that the state is no epiphenomenon, but on the contrary a necessary element where the world is made to look as if it hangs together. Given the intensity of transactional flows, the evolving networks of global politics and the growing incommensurability of life worlds, there is a normative need for common spaces, and the state may be one provider of such a space. For this position, society cannot be at one with itself, but must remain unbounded and fluid. One belongs to society not first and foremost by dint of cultural homogeneity, but because of the contingence of physical presence and a certain inclination to participate in select social activities such as political debate. This representation may be called post-national, inasmuch as it does not privilege people, nation or society, but rather sees configurations of each as *ad hoc* phenomena. Whereas the emphasis of other positions is on cultural equality, this position postulates a reality of cultural difference, and has an inclination to celebrate these differences (see Eriksen 1994; Jervell 1998; Johansen 1994; Neumann 1999).

Bearers of the functionalist representation have sometimes tried to use moves from the embryonic post-national position, for example when a leading social democrat talked about European integration 'blasting the roof off the nation state' during the 1994 referendum campaign, or when talk is about how politics understood among other things as state involvement must 'follow' the intensification of transnational flows of information by intensifying political integration inside the framework of the EU. The attractiveness of the post-national representation for bearers of the functionalist representation is that it offers something which the latter lacks, namely a consistent view of why Norwegian membership in the EU may be represented as logical and necessary as a response to the fading of the nation state. The major problem for this position, which explains its continued marginality and its absence from parliamentary debates, is the difficulty of a post-national representa- tion representing a convincing national identity. The post-national representation's insistence that national identity remains one of a number of important identities even after the historical era of the nation state is not necessarily an immediately successful political move. The post-national representation is in regular evidence in newspapers, journals and books, but it has yet to permeate general political discourse.

Conclusions

The concept which is at the core of Norwegian political discourse, including discourse on Europe, is that of 'the people'. Rune Slagstad (1998: 455) maintains that 'the identity of the Norwegian system is tied to national patriotism', in the sense that every new group, class or movement which succeeded in shaping it availed itself of national patriotism. An early occurrence of this took place in the 1830s, when a marginalised part of the civil servant stratum formulated a popular (*folkelig*) patriotism which it pitted against the European-based culture of the civil servants (the terms used at the time were the patriots vs. the intelligentsia). Crucially, when this clash was reviewed half a century later, it happened in such a way that the patriots of the 1880s insisted that neither the civil servants of the 1830s nor the civil servants of their own period were patriotic or 'national' at all. This was an unwarranted, but extremely productive political move. The nation was thus made into the domain of the victorious country-based liberals, and theirs only. The tie between the part of the state which they had made their own – Parliament – and the nation was fixed. The civil servants were left with the bureaucracy, and with no legitimate coupling to the nation.

Rune Slagstad also has an answer to how this tradition became a central source of self-identification for those working against Norwegian EU membership: 'The opposition to the EC in 1972 found an argumentation which contributed to forming its identity in the works of Rokkan' (Slagstad 1998: 383). Macro-sociologist Stein Rokkan's reading of Norwegian history as a struggle between a centrally placed bureaucracy and a peripherally dispersed people served as one particularly strategic resource amongst others which could be invoked to portray a 'no' as a logical continuation of Norwegian history. This absolutely central move, which had already been taken by 'the 143' who institutionalised the nationalist representation in Norwegian discourse on Europe back in 1961, has been repeated again and again. History has only vague and dimly understood direct effects on political discourse, but it may be specifically invoked and explicitly used in order to bolster a representation's claim to be the only 'real' representation of a political collective. This is what the national representation succeeded in doing where Norway was concerned. In a situation where the electorate has been split almost exactly down the middle in two referenda, one would expect the nationalist representation's claim that 'the people' are against the EU to have been falsified by the actions of the voters. However, in Norwegian discourse on Europe 'the people' is not an electorate reducible to individual voters, but a metaphysically irreducible entity with an existence across time. This particular representation of the nation is not reducible to an electorate, and so is not directly receptive to actions taken by the electorate. In the terms of the nationalist representation, 'the people' would still be against EU membership, regardless of whether 1.2 per cent of the voters had cast their votes differently in the referendum and the electorate had consequently returned a yes vote. It is logical that bearers of the nationalist representation repeatedly said they would not bow to a yes result in the referendum, for the logic in question is a metaphysical logic, where 'the people' exists in terms of its represented history, not in terms of its actually aggregated and observable actions.

With the exception of the statist representation, which disappeared during the inter-war period, all the representations of Norway which have been in circulation since the 1840s seem to rest on a master dichotomy: on the one hand, there is the history-making Norwegian people; on the other hand, there is the state in its bureaucratic aspect. Parliament is the aspect of the state which is ideally supposed to mediate between the two. To the extent that 'Norway' is tied in with the people and 'the EU' with bureaucracy, Norway may be represented as a political project which is incompatible with Europe. Norwegian EU membership would spell the end of the hegemonic representation of Norway. The interesting thing is that the proponents of EU membership actually also embrace a people-based representation, and then fail to stave off the consequences of this for their representation of the relationship between the EU and Norway. The major trope of the pros therefore becomes 'EU membership cannot be that bad'. This was no argumentation by means of which one could expect to win the hearts and minds of the electorate. To end on a note of conjecture, neither does it seem to have some kind of as yet unreleased appeal. It remains, therefore, an unlikely candidate for bringing about change in the discourse.

One type of factor which should in principle be able to do that, however, is the material one. As argued by Christine Ingebritsen and discussed at the outset of this chapter, an economic collapse would probably exert a material pressure on discourse that would over time change the nationalist representation as well as its ability to draw in new bearers. The resulting weakening could well be strong enough for the pros to win the day due to a lack of resistance. The problem with this line of reasoning is that it is hard to see how an economic collapse of a sufficient magnitude could come about.

Inasmuch as the major strength of the nationalist representation hinges on its ability to represent itself as the will of the people, the most likely factor for change has to do with a possible change in the meaning of that term, as well as its relationship to other key terms – nation, Parliament, state, Europe and, to some extent, society. If there is an increase in the number of contexts in which 'the people' either is not relevant or is not articulated to 'Norway', but rather to, for example, 'Europe', then one should expect the relevance of that term for Norwegian discourse on Europe to lessen as well. Put differently, the more actively different parts of Norwegian society integrate with (the rest of) Europe, the more contexts there will be where the power of 'the people' does not apply. The more different parts of society integrate with Europe, the less will be the relevance of that part of discourse which involves the state and state membership. Inasmuch as the term 'the people' comes into play as the antithesis of 'the state', barring 'the state' from a context in effect means barring 'the people' as well. The problem with this way of reasoning is that, at some point, all these integrating contexts must be made relevant to the membership question in order to have an effect on it, and once the membership question comes up, then the concept of 'the people' is immediately activated. In the wake of the 1972 and 1994 referenda alike, the immediate response from the antis to *any* talk of membership was 'defend the people's no'. The force of this slogan is packed exactly in that key term: 'the people'.

In the nineteenth century, a key move of the romantic and populist nationalists was that Norway was a nation, and that the 'natural' thing for a European nation to be was a nation with 'its own' state. In the twenty-first century, the pros may argue that Norwegians are a people and a nation, and that the 'natural' thing for a European people to be is to be part of a European people with 'their own' union. Whether this will happen, or whether it will be effective is, to repeat, a matter of sheer conjecture. However, until new moves are made by the bearers of the nationalist and functionalist representations, or until new representations permeate Norwegian discourse on Europe, this little piggy is likely to remain at home.

Notes

*   Earlier versions of this paper were presented to the International Studies Association's annual conference, San Diego, 1996; to ARENA, University of Oslo, 1 December 1998; to the Norwegian Institute of International Affairs, 28 November 1999; and to workshops at the Copenhagen Peace Research Institute. I thank all the participants on these occasions, and particularly Lene Hansen and Jutta Weldes, for their comments.

1   A widespread idea in Norwegian literature, which also has its Danish adherents (e.g. Ladewig Petersen 1973: 459), is still that the incorporation never really took place.
2   What is at issue here is Koht's representation and the role it played in forging overall social democrat representations, not how this reading of the Manifesto and the First International compares with other readings. Koht does not mention, for example, that Mazzini and his followers, who availed themselves of representations of the nations curiously similar to Koht's own, were actually thrown out of the First International for this very reason. Neither does he mention that at the time he let this text be reprinted – in 1933 – Soviet communist practice on the nationality question was rather different than the reading one may find in this essay.

Norway 127

3 Numbers in parentheses are to pages in the local Hansard, the *Stortingsforhandlinger*, 6–8 June 1972, pp. 3177–421.
4 Numbers in parentheses are to pages in the local Hansard, the *Stortingsforhandlinger*, no. 36, 1–30 September, Session 1993–4. Abbreviations used are as follows: C = Centre Party; Chr = Christian People's Party; Con = Conservative; and L = Labour.
5 However, according to the later Minister of Defence, 'The Western Union has not really turned out to be more than a paper tiger'; Fjærvoll 4810; for an analysis of these two opposing representations of the WEU on the no side, see Eide 1996.

References

Aarnes, S. Aa. (1980) *Norsk Kulturhistorie*, vol. 4: *Nasjonen finner seg selv*, Oslo: Aschehoug.
Allen, H. (1979) *Norway and Europe in the 1970s*, Oslo: Universitetsforlaget.
Anderson, M. S. (1993) *The Rise of Modern Diplomacy 1450–1919*, London: Longman.
Andresen, A. F. (1994) *Opplysningsideer, nyhumanisme og nasjonalisme i Norge i de første årene etter 1814: Nytt lys på vår første skoledebatt*, KULT Report no. 26, Oslo: Norwegian Research Council.
Angell, S. I. (1994) *Frå splid til nasjonal integrasjon: Norsk nasjonalisme i mellomkrigstida*, KULT Report no. 29, Oslo: Norwegian Research Council.
Bjørklund, T. (1982) *Mot strømmen: Kampen mot EF 1961–1972*, Oslo: Universitetsforlaget.
Christensen, O. (1993) *Skiidrett før Sondre: Vinterveien til et nasjonalt selvbilde*, Oslo: Ad Notam.
Dahl, H. F. (1969) *Fra klassekamp til nasjonal samling. Arbeiderpartiet og det nasjonale spørsmål på 1930-tallet*, Oslo: Pax.
Dalhaug, O. (1995) *Mål og meninger: Målreisning og nasjonsdannelse 1877–1887*, Oslo: The Research Council of Norway.
Danielsen, H. (1998) 'Nasjonalisme i Høyre før 1905?', in Ø. Sørensen (ed.) *Jakten på det norske: Perspektiver på utviklingen av en norsk nasjonal identitet på 1800-tallet*, Oslo: Ad Notam Gyldendal.
Eide, E. B. (1996) 'Adjustment Strategy of a Non-member: Norwegian Foreign and Security Policy in the Shadow of the European Union', *Cooperation and Conflict* 31, 1: 69–104.
Eriksen, K. E. and Lundestad, G. (eds) (1972) 'Norsk utenrikspolitikk', in *Kilder til moderne historie I*, Oslo: Universitetsforlaget.
Eriksen, K. E. and Pharo, H. Ø. (1997) *Norsk utenrikspolitikks historie*, vol. 5: *Kald krig og internasjonalisering 1949–1965*, Oslo: Universitetsforlaget.
Eriksen, T. H. (1994) *Typisk Norsk*, Oslo: Huitfeldt.
Esping-Andersen, G. (1990) *The Three Worlds of Welfare Capitalism*, Princeton, NJ: Princeton University Press.
Fure, Odd-B. (1997) *Norsk utenrikspolitikks historie*, vol. 3: *Mellomkrigstid 1920–1940*, Oslo: Scandinavian University Press.
Gabrielsen, T. (1975) *Med en følelse av fellesskap: Samarbeidstanken som omskapte Europa*, Oslo: Grøndahl.
Helle, K. (1974) *Norge blir en stat 1130–1319: Handbok i Norges historie*, vol. 3, 2nd edn, Bergen: Universitetsforlaget.
Hoel, O. L. (1998) 'Ivar Aasen som opposisjonell nasjonalist', in Ø. Sørensen (ed.) *Jakten på det norske: Perspektiver på utviklingen av en norsk nasjonal identitet på 1800-tallet*, Oslo: Ad Notam Gyldendal.
Ingebritsen, C. (1998) *The Nordic States and European Unity*, Ithaca, NY: Cornell University Press.
Innst. (1972) [*Recommendation from the Foreign Affairs Committee to the Storting*] no. 277, pp. 502–32.

128   *Iver B. Neumann*

Jervell, S. (1998) *N@rge foran oppbruddet*, Oslo: Europaprogrammet.

Jespersen, L. (1984) '1600-tallets danske statsmagt', in E. L. Petersen (ed.) *Magtstaten i Norden i 1600-tallet og dens sociale konsekvenser*, rapporter til den XIX nordiske historikerkongres, vol. I, Odense: Odense Universitetsforlag.

Johansen, A. (1994) *Den store misforståelsen. 'Kulturarv' og 'nasjonal egenart' i Norges-reklame og politisk kultur: en advarsel*, Oslo: Spartacus Tiden.

Klippenberg, M. (1998) 'Ut or unionane? Den frilynte ungdomsrørsla i framvekstårene', in Ø. Sørensen (ed.) *Jakten på det norske: Perspektiver på utviklingen av en norsk nasjonal identitet på 1800–tallet*, Oslo: Ad Notam Gyldendal.

Koht, H. (1933) *Norsk vilje*, Oslo: Noregs Boklag.

Kvalsvåg, S. (1999) 'Argumentasjonsbruk i den norske EU-debatten. En sammenligning av EF-debatten i 1972 med EU-debatten i 1994', Bergen: Report no. R-9911, LOS-Centre.

Lønning, I. (1997 [1994]) '1905 og 1994 – et perspektiv på unionsdebatten', in *Fellesskap og frihet: Tid for idépolitikk*, Oslo: Genesis.

Lunden, K. (1992) *Norsk grålysning*, Oslo: Samlaget

Matlary, J. H. (1993) '"And Never the Twain Shall Meet?" Reflections on Norway, Europe and Integration', in T. Tiilikainen and I. D. Petersen (eds) *The Nordic Countries and the EC*, Copenhagen: Copenhagen Political Studies Press.

Mykland, K. (1997) 'Forord II', in E. Albrectsen *Fællesskabet bliver til*, vol. 1 1380–1536, *Danmark–Norge 1380–1814*, Oslo: Scandinavia University Press.

Neumann, I. B. (1996) *Russia and the Idea of Europe: A Study in Identity and International Relations*, London: Routledge.

—— (1998) 'European Identity, EU Expansion, and the Integration/Exclusion Nexus', *Alternatives* 23, 3: 397–416.

—— (1999) *Uses of the Other: 'The East' in European Identity Formation*, Minneapolis: University of Minnesota Press.

—— (2000) 'State and Nation in the 19th Century: Recent Research on the Norwegian Case', *Scandinavian Journal of History*, 25(3): 239–260.

Østerud, Ø. (1996) 'Norwegian Nationalism in a European Context', in Ø. Sørensen (ed.) *Nationalism in Small European States*, KULT report no. 47, Oslo: The Research Council of Norway.

Petersen, E. Ladewig (1973) 'Norgesparagrafen i Christian III's håndfæstning 1536', *Historisk tidsskrift* 12–6, 3–4: 393–464.

Rian, Ø. (1984) 'Hva og hvem var staten i Norge?', in E. L. Petersen (ed.) *Magtstaten i Norden i 1600-tallet og dens sociale konsekvenser*, rapporter til den XIX nordiske historikerkongres, vol. I., Odense: Odense Universitetsforlag.

—— (1997) *Den aristokratiske fyrstestaten*, vol. 1, 1536–1648, *Danmark–Norge 1380–1814*, Oslo: Scandinavia University Press.

Ruggie, J. G. (1998 [1993]) 'Territoriality at Millennium's End', in Ruggie *Constructing the World Polity: Essays on International Institutionalization*, London: Routledge.

Seip, A.-L. (1994) 'Jakten på nasjonal identitet', in *Nytt Norsk Tidsskrift*, 1994, 4: 281–94.

Seip, J. A. (1997 [1974]) *Utsikt over Norges historie*, Oslo: Gyldendal.

Slaatta, T. (1999) 'Europeanisation and the Norwegian News Media: Political Discoure and News Production in the Transnational Field', unpublished report, no. 36, Dept. of Media and Communication, University of Oslo.

Slagstad, R. (1998) *De nasjonale strateger*, Oslo: Pax.

Sørensen, Ø. (1983) *Frihet og enevelde. Dens Schielderup Sneedorffs Politiskeskrifter*, Oslo: Universitetsforlaget.

Sørensen, Ø. (1989) *Hitler eller Quisling?* Oslo: Cappelen.

Sørensen, Ø. (1997) *Bjørnstjerne Bjørnson og nasjonalismen*, Oslo: Cappelen.

Sørensen, Ø. *et. al.* (1995). 'Når ble nordmenn norske?', in *Revolusjon og resonnement – et festskrift for Kåre Tønnesson*, Oslo: Universitetsforlaget.

Stenseth, B. (1993) *En norsk elite: Nasjonsbyggerne på Lysaker 1890–1940*, Oslo: Aschehoug.

Storsveen, O. A. (1998) 'Evig gammel. Henrik Wergeland, P.A. Munch og historiens nasjonale funksjon', in Ø. Sørensen (ed.) *Jakten på det norske: Perspektiver på utviklingen av en norsk nasjonal identitet på 1800-tallet*, Oslo: Ad Notam Gyldendal.

Stortingsforhandlinger, no. 36, 1–30 September, Session 1993–4.

Stortingstidende, 1905/06 *[Proceedings of the Storting]*.

Stråth, B. and Sørensen, Ø. (1997) 'Introduction: The Cultural Construction of Norden', in Ø. Sørensen and B. Stråth (eds), *The Cultural Construction of Norden*, Oslo: Scandinavia University Press.

Svendsen, Å. (1998) 'Konfliktlinjer i historiefaget 1860–1905', in Ø. Sørensen (ed.) *Jakten på det norske: Perspektiver på utviklingen av en norsk nasjonal identitet på 1800-tallet*, Oslo: Ad Notam Gyldendal.

Time, S. (1998) 'Om Garborg som aktør i fortellinga om "det norske"', in Ø. Sørensen (ed.) *Jakten på det norske: Perspektiver på utviklingen av en norsk nasjonal identitet på 1800-tallet*, Oslo: Ad Notam Gyldendal.

Wæver, O. (1990) 'Three Competing Europes: German, French, Russian', *International Affairs* 66, 3: 477–95.

5   Sweden and the EU

Welfare state nationalism and the spectre of 'Europe'*

Lars Trägårdh

Introduction: the EU and the challenge to national sovereignty

Many Europeans view the EU and the move towards an 'ever closer' union with mixed feelings. While security concerns and the 'peace argument' continue to play an important role, it is evident that with the fading memory of the Second World War, the receding threat of a Third World War, and the collapse of the Soviet Union, the process of economic and political integration has increasingly come to be complicated by concerns over 'national identity'. To some extent the emergence of neo-nationalism is an expression of the increasing split between the elites, who tend to be persuaded by integrationist arguments and seduced by the promise of increased economic growth, and the masses, who are both less 'European' in their outlook and more prone to feel threatened by unemployment thought to be linked to 'globalization'.[1] Thus the political climate has pushed to the fore the latent conflict between the EU 'project' and the *survivance* of the nation, to invoke a Québecois figure of anxiety.

It is in this new, post-1989 context, that an understanding of how historically rooted conceptions of national identity inform the politics of 'Europe' becomes critical. For, as this book makes clear in the case of the Nordic countries, the degree to which Europeans feel such bouts of anxiety varies quite dramatically from country to country, ranging from the relative Euro-enthusiasm in the 'heartland' countries like France, Germany, Italy and the Benelux, via legendary British insularity and intransigence within the Union, to Swiss and Norwegian refusals to even join the EU.[2] From this perspective, Sweden has consistently proven to be one of the most Euro-negative of all the current member states.[3] A reluctant late-comer to 'Europe,' the Swedes joined the EU only in 1995 and then with only a slim majority of the population voting 'yes' after a heated and divisive debate. In fact, a considerable part of the population continues to oppose EU membership and the discourse on Europe is far more likely to express apprehension over the 'spectre of Europe' than confidence in the 'promise of Europe'. Symptomatically, Sweden was one of the few members to take a wait and see attitude towards the adoption of the Euro as a common currency, and the polls continually suggest that even though the governing Social Democratic Party has in principle embraced Swedish accession to the EMU (the European Monetary Union), the Swedes continue to be sceptical of the Euro.

How do we explain this negative attitude towards the EU on the part of the Swedes who otherwise would seem to be poised to take advantage of the benefits afforded by membership, not least given their long-standing commitment to free trade and their dependence on large, export-oriented companies? In this chapter I will seek to show that the idea of European integration poses a deep threat to the way in which many Swedes have come to understand the proper relationship between 'state', 'society', 'nation' and 'people'. That is, Swedish national identity has come to be tightly linked to the welfare state, understood not simply as a set of institutions but as the realisation of *Folkhemmet*, the 'people's home', the central organising slogan of the Social Democrats, the party which has dominated Swedish politics since 1933.

The extraordinary and lasting potency of this concept derives from the seamless way in which the two concepts of 'the people' – those of *demos* and *ethnos* – have been fused into one coherent whole. That is, it is not simply that in Sweden the democratic-Jacobin notion of the people has won out over the ethnic-cultural reading associated with, most infamously, the German experience. Rather, the Swedish concepts of *folk*, *folklighet* and *folkhem* are all part and parcel of a national narrative that has cast the Swedes as intrinsically democratic and freedom-loving, as having democracy in the blood. Thus, since to be a Swedish nationalist meant perforce that one embraced democratic values, it was possible in the 1930s for the Social Democrats to successfully harness the power of national feeling, to become 'national socialists', and fight off the challenge from domestic would-be Nazis.

Furthermore, and just as importantly, the 'Swedish model', as it came to be known, was characterised by an extreme form of statism, built on a social contract between a strong and good state, on the one hand, and the emancipated and auto-nomous individual, on the other. Through the institutions of the state the individual, so it was thought, was liberated from the institutions of civil society – the family, the neighbourhood, the churches, the charity organisations. The inequalities and dependencies associated with these institutions were to be replaced by an egalitarian social order. In this scheme the state and the people were conceived of as intrinsically linked; the people's home was a *folkstat*,[4] the state was the homely domain of national community, the context in which the ideal of solidarity could be joined to that of equality. At the same time, this Swedish ideology, with its dual emphasis on social equality and individual autonomy, was understood to be distinctly modern and highly efficient; the *welfare* of the welfare state implied not just solidarity and equality but also prosperity and progress.

Of course, this vision was, for better or worse, profoundly utopian. Still, for a moment many Swedes came to see themselves, and to be seen by others, as the most modern of peoples, the most democratic and equal nation in the world, in-habiting the very model of the future. As we shall see, this self-aggrandising and messianic discourse revolved around a number of central themes that together formed a powerful national myth. Thus 'Sweden' connoted Democracy, Prosperity, Modernity and Neutrality; Sweden was *peculiarly* democratic, its economic prowess was *extraordinary*, the success of its neutrality policy was a testimony to *special* diplomatic skills, its internationalism was informed by a *superior* moral sensibility, all expressed as a holy mission to spread the Good Message of Swedish Social Democracy to the World.

From this point of view, the left-wing supporters of the nation-statist Swedish welfare state could only imagine Europe to the south of Denmark as a backward bastion of neo-feudalism, patriarchy, hierarchy, disorder, corruption and inequality. Continental notions like federalism, subsidiarity and civil society were perceived as insidious, neo-liberal or 'papist' ideas, fundamentally antithetical to the founding principles of the welfare state. Conversely, the political parties to the right have tended to see in Europe a possibility to accomplish through the backdoor what they have consistently failed to achieve at the national level: the dismantling of the oppressive welfare state and the revitalisation of the atrophied civil society. Liberals came to see the EU as a project promoting the freedom of the market from state regulation, and the freedom of the individual from the narrow confines of Swedish egalitarianism. Social conservatives and Christian Democrats, on the other hand, imagined the restoration of the 'natural' social structures of civil society they felt had been undermined by the unholy alliance between big government and big business.

In what follows I will first outline the central national narratives, tropes and concepts that continue to enable and delimit the political debate in Sweden. Next I will proceed to analyse the post-war debate over European integration from this discursive perspective.

The two freedoms: Erik Gustav Geijer and the soul of Sweden

At first glance nationalism does not appear to have played a major role in nineteenth- and twentieth-century Swedish politics. Many would agree with Gustav Sundbärg when he wrote in his classic work on Swedish 'national character,' *Det svenska folklynnet* (1911), that:

> The small amount of patriotism, that we can observe among the Swedish people, has been of the old type, from the seventeenth century: national pride. Our people has, however, had no experience of what one during the nineteenth century has meant by national awakening. This, a people's instinctual drive to give expression to its innermost essence in every vital matter, has been completely unknown to us.[5]

Indeed, the notion that the Swedes are lacking when it comes to national(ist) sentiment is an enduring one. In an influential essay from 1984, Arne Ruth also argues for such an absence of romantic nationalism and cites several other writers who 'comment on the lack of a traditional sense of national heritage in modern Sweden' (Ruth 1984: 68). And, Ruth adds, to the extent there was such a thing as a modern Swedish nationalism, it was – in sharp contrast to the development in the other Nordic countries – 'almost exclusively an upper-class ideology' (Ruth 1984: 81). As we shall see, this is a view that requires modification, since it is neither true that nationalism was absent, nor the case that it was primarily a right-wing, upper-class phenomenon.

In fact, while it is true that national feeling was not mobilised in Sweden in the same overt and dramatic way as it was in Germany, Denmark, Norway or Finland, a rather well-defined notion of Swedish peculiarity nonetheless developed during the nineteenth century; indeed, a conception of Swedish national identity emerged during the first few decades of that century that proved both enduring and politically pregnant. The primary locus for this 'national awakening' was a loosely organised, numerically small, and relatively short-lived association called *Götiska Förbundet* ('The Gothic Society'), which was created in the wake of the loss of Finland to Russia in 1809.[6]

The society began as a rather frivolous association of young men from the province of Värmland in the middle of Sweden, many of whom were to become leading figures on the Swedish cultural scene. While the proceedings were at first carried out in a humorous spirit, the venture was eventually given a more serious direction by its leader, a minor government bureaucrat by the name of Jacob Adlerbeth, who authored the by-laws and the statement of purpose for GF and who remained the cementing force behind GF for the duration of its existence (Geijer 1845). Under Adlerbeth's leadership GF was formally founded on 11 February 1811 to serve the great 'moral-patriotic' cause.

'It is', wrote Adlerbeth (1845: 2), 'a regrettable truth that the majority of Swedes of our time have deteriorated relative to our great ancestors.' The old spirit of freedom, probity and patriotism was lost, Adlerbeth felt. The cause of this decline was foreign influence: 'corruption and vice always come from abroad'. Nature had given the Nordic peoples physical strength and courage, and they did not degenerate until they exchanged the 'seriousness and power of the North' for 'the wantonness of Southern Europe' (Adlerbeth 1845: 2). What to do, asked Adlerbeth: 'By what means can a people that throws itself upon ruin be saved?' Only, he answered, 'by recovering its original national character'. Thus, 'we have found that our highest purpose is to revive the old Goths' spirit of liberty, manliness, and common sense' (Adlerbeth 1845: 3).

While Adlerbeth's high ambitions for GF were not to be fully realised, the writings of its members would come to have considerable impact within the literary, folkloric and historical circles of nineteenth-century Sweden. They published translations of old Icelandic sagas and Nordic mythology; they produced a series of collections of folk songs; they wrote romantic poetry. However, for our purpose the most important body of work was that of the poet and historian Erik Gustaf Geijer, a man whose influence on Swedish self-understanding has been compared to that of Grundtvig in Denmark and Arndt in Germany. In his poetry, published in *Iduna*, the journal of GF, and above all in his monumental histories of the Swedish people, Geijer established an enduring narrative on Swedish national character and the historical drama through which this character was forged.

The main protagonists around whom this 'myth' was organised were the free Swedish yeoman peasant – *odalbonden* – and the king. Together they fought the good fight for personal and national freedom, against the foreign powers and domestic lords who were bent on enslaving the uniquely free Swedish peasant, on the one hand, and on submitting the nation to foreign rule, on the other. In particular the part historical, part mythical figure of Engelbrekt came to figure prominently in this account. According to legend Engelbrekt led the peasants out of the province of *Dalarna* (Dalecarlia) in a successful revolt against Danish and German overlords in the fifteenth century. In this schema, patriotism coincided with a love of personal freedom. The political and social rights of the peasants came to be associated with the 'soul of the people'. The 'national' and 'democratic' imperatives came to be inextricably fused, and with this followed the idea that the state and the people were joined in a common endeavour to safeguard the two freedoms, that of the nation and that of the individual.

Geijer could attach himself to a pre-existing trope; *odalbonden* was by the time of his writing already a stock figure just as Gothicism was a well-established tradition. For example, the poet G. F. Gyllenborg anticipated much of the discourse on freedom and the virtues of the North that were to find definitive expression in Geijer's 'Gothic' poetry. In 'Vinterqvädet' (1759) he warns the free-born Swede against the effeminacy of the South, and exhorts him to appreciate the toughening climate of the North, from which the spirit of freedom derives. Sweden is the land of heroes, never to be the wretched home of slaves ('trälars usla bo'), and he who forgets that to be born in Sweden is to be born free, his name should forever be hidden in darkness (Gyllenborg 1759; Blanck 1911: 380; Blanck 1918: 249).

The same theme was sounded by other poets, such as Oxenstierna and Sjöberg, culminating with Thorild, a writer whose works were first collected and published by Geijer himself (1819–35). In 1792–3 he wrote his 'Songs in the Gothic mood' including 'The voice of the people' and 'Songs from the days of Engelbrekt', in which he gives voice to the Gothic values with particular force:

> No one's master, no one's slave:
> That was the honor of the Goths
> Fancy names, struggles for titles
> those are the concerns of clowns
> To be free is manly virtue
> free, free, free in the land of Goths
> that is the honour of men.
>
> (Thorild 1819–24)[7]

With Thorild the discourse on the peasant is mixed with one on 'the people' in the democratic sense, and the pre-historical mythos of the *ur-bonde* and the ancient peasant democracy is overlaid with a historically specific reference to Engelbrekt and the struggle against Danish rule:

> When Engelbrekt stood up in anger
> and said: Brothers, No!
> The villains' daggers point our breast

Soon the race of heroes from Norden got hot
and the arms of a hundred-thousand peasants
pointed to the heavens, swore: No!

They said these words
in the manner of an honorable *bonde*
All Sweden's power is the power of the people
All rights are rights of the people.

(Thorild 1819–24)[8]

However, it is through Geijer that the mythos acquires its definitive form. As Blanck points out, 'the Swedish peasant as a literary figure is fixed by Geijer in a way that has since turned out to be ineradicable' (Blanck 1911: 379). In famous poems like 'Manhem' and 'Odalbonden' Geijer combines the Herderian and Jacobin notions of 'the people'. On the one hand he evokes an ancient Nordic peasant from a distant *ur*-time ('There was a time when in the North there lived a noble-minded race . . . then no one was slave or master, every *odalbonde* was a man unto himself'), on the other he presents a rather more historical figure, a political man who goes to the assembly to make the law, with the king, for the common weal (Geijer 1811). This is the peasant who works his land and fights to defend his country and his ancient personal liberties, a theme that becomes central to Geijer's historical writings. In fact, as early as 1803, Geijer wrote a prize-winning essay in which he compared the happy situation of the Swedish peasant to those of other countries. 'There is no Swedish man who is a slave', he concluded, everybody shares in the civil rights (Geijer 1923: 24).

In his two major histories of Sweden – *Svea Rikes Hävder* and *Svenska Folkets Historia* – Geijer elaborated on this motif, continuing an older tradition of the eighteenth-century historians that has become known as '*aristokratfördömandet*' ('the condemnation of the aristocracy') (Hessler 1943; Henningson 1961). The central event was, as we have noted above, the liberation from Danish rule during the time of the Kalmar Union. The rebellion led by Engelbrekt and his peasants is here cast as *the* heroic act in Swedish history, through which the peasants were saved from serfdom and the nation saved from foreign rule. Thus he viewed the king and 'the people', that is the peasants' estate, as the two pillars of the state. The villains in this story were, on the other hand, the nobles, who were willing to trade the independence of Sweden for increased personal power and wealth. The unhappy fate of Poland was, for Geijer, a warning of where unchecked aristocratic power could take a country. Geijer, like others before him, thus saw the king as the principle of unity and action, while the nobles constituted a destabilising force, driven by selfish motives, and unable to act for the common good of the nation (Hessler 1937).

The Swedish Social Democrats and the turn towards a national socialism

The influence of Geijer on the way in which Swedes have imagined themselves and their 'national character' has been enormous. His foundational myth of the Swedish nation was reproduced in textbooks that were assigned to most, if not all Swedish students by the beginning of the twentieth century, and his conception of Swedish history and Swedish national identity found expression in the writings of political figures spanning the entire ideological spectrum. Even the prominent Swedish historian Erik Lönnroth, who devoted much of his professional life to disproving Geijer's assertions, conceded that 'Geijer's conception of history, characterised by profound originality and suggestive force, entered into the imagination of the succeeding generations' (Lönnroth 1943: 1). Indeed, whether or not Geijer's interpretations are factually correct they certainly penetrated into the history books, the literature and the political discourse. As Lönnroth wistfully notes, possibly reflecting on his own rather futile efforts to debunk Geijer's tall tales, 'even a hundred years later it has not fully loosened its grip'. For someone – like Geijer – who came to history through the study of sagas, myths and folk songs, it was, perhaps, only fitting that his efforts at history have themselves turned into myth.[9]

I have elsewhere traced the reception of this myth into nineteenth- and twentieth-century historical literature and history textbooks; let me here confine myself to a few examples (Trägårdh 1993). Consider, for example, the classic, standard school text on Swedish history by Odhner (first published in 1899, and reprinted many times thereafter). Having dramatically retold the story of Engelbrekt, Odhner concludes that:

> He gave back to Sweden's *allmoge*[10] its freedom and independence, he called the towns-men and the peasants to national assemblies, he awoke the slumbering national feeling by uniting the various separate groups in order to save the nation. From his time one can talk of not simply different provinces, estates and classes in Sweden, but also of a Swedish Nation.
>
> (Odhner 1902: 97)

Such an essentialist view of Swedishness, derived from Geijer's conception of Swedish history and national character, was also common at the outset among leading figures within the fledgling workers' movement as it began to gain strength at the turn of the century. Take, for example, the Social Democrat Bengt Lidforss, who during the great general strike of 1909 lost himself in a particularly romantic-heroic vision of the Swedish working-class movement, one tinged with xenophobia to boot.[11] The working class, he wrote,

> is the marrow and core of the Swedish people, the blood inherited from the parents through innumerable Swedish generations. It is *folket* that stands up to all the managers, bosses, stockholders with mostly exotic names and of foreign descent, like the Swedish *allmogen* under Engelbrekt . . . did against the Danish lords of the past.
>
> (Björk 1946: 292)[12]

However, it was only after the collapse of the Second International and with the reforms of 1920, which finally introduced general suffrage – and thus a sense of the inclusion of the working class in the nation – that the Social Democrats began to move aggressively to mobilise the national theme. Soon after the First World War a series of books and articles appeared that signalled this new attitude on the part of the Social Democrats. In 1926 Per Albin Hansson – the leader of the Social Democratic Party and the future Prime Minister – wrote a key article called 'Sweden for the Swedes – the Swedes for Sweden' in which he begins by quoting from a slogan used at a Social Democratic election meeting in 1924: 'Long live the fatherland, that Sweden which one day will become a good home to *all* Swedes!' (Hansson 1926: 3; his emphasis). Here Hansson played with a common right-wing jingoist slogan, consciously challenging the received notion that nationalist rhetoric belongs on the political right. On the other hand, as the phrase 'one day will become' makes clear, his Swedish nation was a nation in the making, the nation of the future.

While *småfolket*, 'the little people', were still not fully accepted and Sweden was still a class society, the conditions had now changed. 'After the introduction of general suffrage', Hansson wrote, 'it is entirely up to *folket* itself how the country is run.' The conquest of Sweden for the Swedes could be accomplished through the ballot, and only lethargy and indifference stood in the way (Hansson 1926: 15–16). In this article Hansson gave voice to an early version of the idea of *folkhemmet* – 'a good home to all Swedes' as he put it in this early rendition – a concept that he was to introduce in its definitive and more catchy form two years later at the 1928 party congress. Two important mutations in the discourse of the Social Democrats that are signalled with this move should be noted, the first is a shift towards a nation-statist socialism that rejected classic Marxist hostility to the 'bourgeois state' associated with the notion that the state is destined to vanish with the arrival of communism, and the second is the tendency to replace the confrontational concept of class with the inclusive notion of the *folk*.[13]

A first phase in the process of appropriating 'the national' was characterised by the influence of the Austro-Marxists and their affirmation of the national idea as such. Younger Social Democrats like Nils Karleby and Richard Lindström wrote a number of articles and books in the mid-1920s that were directly influenced by Otto Bauer's great work on the nationality question – *Die Nationalitätenfrage und die Sozialdemokratie*. Citing Bauer, Lindström asserted that 'socialism must be built on a national basis' and that 'we must accept the nation as a given . . . to deny the nation is to deny life itself' (Lindström 1928a: 11). He agreed with Bauer that each nation has its own national character and its own peculiar 'spirit'. This represented, of course, a major revision of Marx's own view of the nation which was that it was destined for the dustbin of history, first to be fatally undermined by global capitalism and then to be swept away by world revolution.

During a second phase – culminating in the 1930s – the empty category of 'national character' was increasingly filled with a positive and concrete content that linked the notion of a Swedish 'national socialism' (Lindström) to pro-statist and pro-democratic attitudes, themes that then were developed into a full-fledged *folklig*-national doctrine according to which the Swedish-Nordic democratic tradition was an expression of the peculiar Swedish 'folksjäl' ('soul of the people').

In elaborating this theory of what we may call, paraphrasing Stalin, 'democracy in one country', the Social Democrats explicitly attached themselves to the by now traditional historical discourse associated with Geijer. This formulation of a Social Democratic version of Geijer's national narrative was deployed in direct opposition to conservative attempts at mobilising nationalist sentiments for their own political purpose.

Conservatives were attacked for attempting to usurp the national and patriotic idea and accused of being un-Swedish. Thus Lindström, for example, would argue that the Youth Section of the Conservative Party was not in touch with the 'true' Swedish national tradition.

> Our alert Swedish Youth does not desire to become the hirelings of *industriherrar* and *godsägare* (industrial lords and estate-owners). It wants to stand on *folklig* basis and thereby links up to the best traditions in our history.
>
> (Lindström 1928b: 23)

These, 'the best traditions in our history', were explicitly those of Engelbrekt and the Swedish peasants. Thus Hansson would recall the legacy of Engelbrekt – 'the man we from our childhood years have learned to see and honour as a man of the people' – the founding of the parliament, and the popular fight for national and personal freedom:

> It is a long time ago that the old peasant chief answered the calling of the *herrar* ('the lords') with a stern reminder that 'the workers are flesh of our flesh and bone from our bone'. But the same is still true. The best of democratic tradition can be found among peasants and workers. Just like the peasant class during its struggle for influence protected the *folk*-freedom, so has the working class. Here there is a common inheritance to administer.
>
> (Hansson 1935c: 112)

Thus, 'Engelbrekt and Gustav Vasa – the two great liberators of the nation and the people – became for us in school the ideals, the mighty freedom-fighters to whom we looked up and whom we wanted to follow.' This was the tradition of freedom in which the Social Democratic workers' movement was merely the last link, Hansson argued:

> The concept of freedom has over time been extended, lordship and oppression has been broken down in new areas, new *folk* groups and classes have successfully fought their own freedom fight, won equal citizenship rights, liberated themselves from slavery and slave-mentalities. Figures have been added to our gallery of heroes, a few older ones have perhaps been pushed aside, but others remain. It is warranted to speak of a tradition of freedom in our country, independent of the changes in society.
>
> (Hansson 1935e: 132–33; see Figure 5.1)

Figure 5.1   Svenska folkets väg är folkfrihetens och demokratins väg
'The way of the Swedish people is the way of democracy and national freedom.'
The image mixes the colours of the Swedish flag – blue and yellow – with the red
of socialism, invoking a national socialism. The ladder suggests an upward
progression towards Social Democracy, each step inhabited by famous leaders
from Swedish history, including Engelbrekt and Hjalmar Branting (the first Social
Democratic Prime Minister).

Source: Swedish Labour Movement Archives and Library (Arbetarrörelsens Arkiv och Bibliotek)

Thus, he concluded: 'you have a tradition to safeguard, a duty to fulfill towards the
present and the future. In this matter as in all: Be Swedish!' Indeed, Hansson
claimed, 'our Swedish people is essentially democratic. It loves freedom and hates
oppression' (Hansson 1935f: 131). That is, democracy in Sweden was not simply a
matter of ideology or of dry constitutional arrangements, but was rooted in the very
soul of the people:

> It is with every reason that we Swedes are proud of our country. It is a country
> of *folk* freedom and *folkligt* self-government, where democracy is rooted not merely
> in the constitution, but also in our traditions and in the disposition of the *folk*.
> (Hansson 1935g: 137)

These words were spoken during the early 1930s just as the Social Democrats and
the Peasant Party formed a lasting popular/populist alliance under the banner of

Folkhemmet, and it is with the peasant–worker alliance of 1933 that the Social Democratic deployment of the Geijerian trope reaches its fullest form. The old pitting of a nationally-minded king and patriotic and freedom loving peasant against the treacherous and faithless lord, is reinvented: the aristocrats of old become the industrialists and capitalists of today, the peasants are joined by the workers as the true representatives of the *folk* and the nation. As in the German right-wing nationalist imagination the Jew is equated with cosmopolitan capitalism, so for Swedish left-wing nationalists the capitalist elite is viewed with enduring suspicion as not sufficiently national or patriotic, a trope that we will be able to pursue well into the contemporary debate over the EU in Sweden.

Central to this nationalist turn of the Swedish Social Democrats was a general shift after 1929 from *klass* (class) to *folk* as the key, organising concept (Trägårdh 1990: 42–5). That year Hansson wrote an important essay in the leading Social Democratic journal *Tiden*, entitled 'Folk och klass' ('Folk and class'), in which he explicitly embraced the notion that the party must project itself as a party of the people, so as not to be trapped within the exclusionary and adversarial language of class and class struggle. Showing a fine understanding of the power of words, Hansson wrote that 'the class struggle might be an ever so horrible fact', a fact that must not, however, blind us to the superiority of the *folk* concept as a propaganda tool:

> There is something much more exciting about the thought that we are fighting for the *folk*. To such an appeal everybody will listen; in the coming together of the *folk* most of us want to be a part.
>
> (Hansson 1935a: 46)

Indeed, such sentiments led Hansson further and further towards a truly all-embracing national(ist) position. If the initial move was to include both peasants and workers as bona fide members of the *folk*, joined in a common struggle against *herrarna*, by 1935 even this residual notion of class conflict was eliminated. In yet another speech featuring Engelbrekt, given on the occasion of the 'Day of the Peasant', he declared that 'it was "*gemenskapen*" (community/unity) among the Swedes that Engelbrekt wanted to bring about. Today it is also true that popular-national (*folkligt nationella*) aspirations can have no other goal' (Hansson 1935d: 264). Although there is much that separate us into groups and classes, 'in the midst of all that, "gemenskapen" still spills forth; the nation is one and the people is one, we live together and are dependent on each other' (Hansson 1935d: 265).

The list of all the different people whose efforts all add to the common good of the national community is telling – and utterly unlike any a Social Democrat would have produced ten years earlier: the peasant, the worker, the teacher, the thinker and the leader, the fisherman, the shopkeeper, the housewife. Of course, this rather high-strung nationalist rhetoric must be read against the developments in Germany, where just a few years earlier the Protestant peasants and many other sections of the *Volk* had overwhelmingly voted for Hitler, making the failure on the part of the German Social Democrats to harness and appropriate the national feeling only too apparent.

Still the tone and language of Hansson is striking as he plays with the deep ambivalence of the *folk* concept; one moment the *folk* is fighting *fogdar* and *herrar*, the next moment the great *folkhem* is invoked. Together these references form a 'Geijerish' discourse, part mythical, part historical, on the founding of Sweden and the essence of Swedishness, to which Hansson attaches – at the tail end – himself, the Swedish working class and the Social Democratic Party. In this conception – *folkhemmet* – the historically rooted identification of the national with the democratic came together with singular power, *ethnos* and *demos* merging in what came to be the central metaphor of the national socialist Swedish welfare state. The Social Democrats were in the process transformed from a marginal party of the unpatriotic, internationalist left into the dominant and eminently national party, and it was their version of Swedish national identity that came to be the hegemonic one. Further-more, this was a hegemonic position that soon was to transcend the realm of political rhetoric and utopian visions: from 1933 until the present with but short periods out of power, the party has ruled and therefore shaped the construction of modern Sweden, its institutions as well as the national myths.

Statist individualism: social democracy and the Swedish social contract

While the success of the Social Democrats in playing the national card is most often seen in a positive light, as a kind of vaccination against right-wing, ethnic national-ism, it has in recent years become fashionable to paint this picture in more sombre colours. Not only has Social Democratic enthusiasm for social engineering been decried, but with the recent debate highlighting the record-setting rates of forced sterilisation carried out in the name of national health, the *folkhem* has been portrayed as illiberal and disrespectful of individual rights to a degree unheard of outside the domain of fascist regimes (Zaremba 1999).[14]

This brings us to the question of the relationship between the individual and the state, for the nationalism of the left is not just rooted in an essentialist notion of a democratic Swedish 'soul of the people', but also in a statism that links social equality, national solidarity and individual autonomy to the beneficial power of the state. Indeed, 'democracy' is in Sweden built on a basis fundamentally different from the one associated with the development of liberal democracy in the 'West' where, broadly speaking, it grew out of gentry and bourgeois opposition to the absolutist state.

In England, the story of parliamentary democracy is the story of successful gentry resistance to the king in the name of defending and preserving the 'ancient English liberties'. In France and Germany, 'civil society' and the 'public sphere', as Koselleck and Habermas have shown, formed as a response to absolutism, as a free social space for (critical) moral and increasingly political discourse (Koselleck 1988; Habermas 1989). The institutions of bourgeois civil society – at first secret or semi-legal societies, later officially sanctioned if still feared by the state – became the locus for social and political utopianism, for the production and dissemination of public opinion, and came to serve as a powerful 'fourth estate'. Furthermore, as Charles Taylor has argued, the development of a modern, Western democratic political culture was a process that entailed the universalisation and democratisation of the rights and sensibilities once peculiar to the noble members of society, the gradual mutation of aristocratic privilege into human and civil rights. It was a process of raising formerly downtrodden members of society to the level of the privileged, of granting recognition and aristocratic-cum-human dignity to all (Taylor 1994).

In Sweden, on the other hand, the ethos of modern democracy is informed by the legacy of the unique position of the Swedish peasantry. Because the Swedish peasantry largely escaped feudalism and even retained its rights to be represented as a separate estate in the *riksdag*, it could play a role unparalleled elsewhere. In particular, it allowed for an enduring alliance between the quasi-absolute monarchy and the peasant estate against the common enemy, the nobility. Thus the Swedish gentleman class never came to play the same leading role as was the case elsewhere in Western Europe. The consequence was that the Swedish political culture came to be cast in a mould very different from that of other Western democracies.[15] Far from generalising noble or bourgeois privilege, the organising principle was that of levelling, of eliminating rather than extending privileges and special rights. Ultimately it was a process of universalising the egalitarianism of the peasant community, of reducing noble and bourgeois 'rights' until there were but 'peasants' – 'the people' – left. If in the West the ideal type was the honorable gentleman, in Sweden it was the modest peasant (Zaremba 1987).

It was the luck and, some would claim, the political genius of the Swedish Social Democrats to be able to tap into this potent tradition, half myth, half institutional reality, during the high age of statist nationalism after the First World War. Thus, during the famous 'deals' between the peasants' and workers' parties during the early 1930s, the Social Democrats managed to shoulder the mantles of both monarchical statism and peasant populism by becoming, on the one hand, the Party of State and, on the other, the Voice of the People. The time-honoured tradition of seeing the king/state as an ally against the upper classes, mutated and deepened with the democratisation of the political system and the coming to power of the workers' and peasants' parties. Instead of seeing 'civil society' as a crucial repository of freedom and protection against the power of the state, the state was seen as having a legitimate and decisive role to play in eradicating inequalities and the remaining privileges of the upper classes.

Swedish political culture can thus be said to be democratic rather than liberal. It is characterised by centralised power and uniformity as well as by an ancient tradition of inclusive, participatory democracy. It offers the peasant communes broadly defined access to the democratic process even as it places rather narrow limits to the possibility of diverging from the communal consensus. In sharp contrast to Continental Europe, the social contract on which the welfare state was built is one between the individual and the state at the expense of the intermediary institutions of civil society, such as the family, and private and voluntary organisations. The latter are associated not with pluralism and freedom, but with demeaning private charity, unequal patriarchal relations, and informal (ab)uses of power. In Sweden the state is instead conceived as the liberator of the individual from such ties of dependency, an order of things I have termed 'statist individualism' (Trägårdh 1997). In other words, 'freedom' has in Scandinavia come to be extremely 'positive' rather than 'negative', and it is hardly surprising that a liberal critic like Maciej Zaremba has been able to argue convincingly that Sweden lacks dramatically in the area of civil and individual rights (Zaremba 1992). The state –individual alliance has allowed for relatively equal positive freedoms – 'social rights' – at the expense of individual liberty and free choice. Indeed, if we want to define Scandinavian political culture in terms of broader intellectual currents, it is Rousseau and the notion of general will, rather than Montesquieu's notion of separate powers, or Locke's liberal suspicion of excessive state power, that proves enlightening. Turning to the *Social Contract* one finds a passage that in many ways could serve as the motto for at least the Swedish welfare state:

> The second relation is that of the members of the body politic among themselves, or of each with the entire body: their relations among themselves should be as limited, and relations with the entire body as extensive, as possible, in order that each citizen shall be at the same time perfectly independent of all his fellow citizens and excessively dependent on the republic – this result is always achieved by the same means, since it is the power of the state alone which makes the freedom of its members.
>
> (Rousseau 1968: 99)

While this position is one that tends to alarm readers of a more liberal bent, and partly for good reason, it is for many Swedes, as indeed it was for Rousseau, part and parcel of an outlook that holds that the informal and unchecked power of families, churches and charities is much the greater evil than the formal, distant and politically controllable power of the state (Trägårdh 1997). As one defender of the Swedish welfare state has noted:

> Few welfare states are as consistently based on the idea of individual autonomy as is the Swedish. Virtually all of our welfare programmes are tied to the individual person, not to the family or to the job as is the norm in other Western countries . . . the struggle for full employment . . . follows the principle that each person should have power over his or her own life . . . The delivery of welfare services through the public sector rather than within the family has constituted a process of emancipation . . . the pressure on the family has decreased . . . The dependency on other family members has diminished as the performance of many, often instrumental tasks have been placed outside the family domain.
>
> (Antman and Thorvaldsson 1994: 24)

Not least has this perspective informed Social Democratic gender policy in Sweden, where the autonomy of women in relation to men has been gained largely through the provision of day-care, on the one hand, and the encouragement of female participation in the labour market, on the other. Thus, in so far as Swedish national identity is tightly linked to the welfare state, the emphasis should be equally on 'welfare' and the 'state'. A decoupling of nation and state would appear to be wholly foreign to the Swedish political tradition; indeed it would be hard to even formulate in intelligible terms. Indeed, as critics of Swedish 'statism' like to point out: the terms nation, state and society are in Swedish virtually synonymous. This must be understood against concepts like subsidarity and federalism, so central to the Christian Democratic model for the EU, a model fundamentally based on precisely the separation between the (cultural) nation, the (civil) society and the (political-economical) state.

Missing in Sweden is the kind of critique of the state that has become common among leading leftist thinkers on the Continent and in Britain who are not only suspicious of any talk of 'healthy' nationalism,[16] but who also tend to view statism, in Habermasian terms, as the 'colonisation' of civil society by the state. Not so in Sweden where, as we shall see, it has been the 'bourgeois' parties on the right and the conservative-libertarian think tank Timbro who have tried to mobilise the rhetoric of 'civil society' in an attempt to associate the Swedish welfare state with the totalitarian regimes to the East and the dangers of excessive state power and big government. Conversely, left-wing opposition to Europe is rooted in both worries about a lack of an egalitarian, democratic tradition in Europe south of Denmark, and in a concern that harmonisation of social policies will spell the end of Swedish-style statist individualism in favour of the dreaded Christian Democratic alternative, returning the individual to the care and capriciousness of civil society.

Nationalism of the right

What about the nationalism of Swedish Conservatives and the radical right during this period? In general the turn of the nineteenth century was characterised by an outburst of national romantic feeling, deepened by a sense of national crisis akin to that which followed Russia's conquest of Finland in 1809 (Björk 1946). Decades of emigration to America were followed by the loss of the last vestige of Sweden's Great Power legacy as Norway broke away from the union with Sweden in 1905. This prompted concerned patriotic Swedes to organise a public commission to explore what had gone wrong with the Swedish national character. A number of literary and quasi-political tracts calling for national rejuvenation were subsequently written by conservative intellectuals and poets (Sundbärg 1911).

While the conservatives also relied on the tradition of national-romantic history associated with Geijer, they tended to focus more on the glory of the Swedish kings, especially the Vasa kings – from Gustav I Vasa, through Gustav II Adolf, to Karl XII – than on the power of the proto-democratic peasants' estate. Similarly, in the case of Engelbrekt, emphasis was placed on his role as the saviour of the nation rather than that of the protector of the liberty of the peasants. However, they never could fully escape the rather narrow confines of the Geijerian trope, with its dual celebration of king and peasant. This dilemma facing conservative nationalists is well illustrated by the biography on Engelbrekt written by Henrik Schück, the foremost Swedish historian of literature of his time. In the dedication Schück writes that he is seeking to draw the picture of what he calls 'the first Swede', and the entire book in fact reads like one extended celebration of Sweden and Swedishness (Schück 1916: 1). Few men have meant more for Sweden than Engelbrekt, insists Schück. He laid the groundwork for 'the free, independent, *Swedish* Sweden' (Schück 1916: 209; his emphasis). He was the great *folkhöfdingen* ('folk chief'), whose aim it was to ensure that the crown remained in Swedish hands (the king should be an 'infödd folklig konung', a 'native, *folklig* king'), whose power should rest on the cooperation of all the classes of the people, who would rule according to ancient Swedish laws.

Schück's fundamentally conservative nature shows through when he asserts, somewhat improbably, that Engelbrekt was not a demagogue who 'sought to egg on the different social classes against each other' (Schück 1916: 212). Instead of using violence and therefore risking civil war, he always chose the way of legal measures: 'His policy was to unite Sweden, both against the outside, against Denmark, and internally, against the perils of class struggle' (Schück 1916: 213). His way, then, was the way of generating political consensus and promoting national unity. What we see here is, of course, a statement that has as much, if not more, to do with the times in which Schück himself wrote than with the times of Engelbrekt. What quite probably was on his mind was the power and political agenda of the Swedish Social Democrats who at the time of writing – 1916 – could still be imagined as a 'revolutionary' party. Ironically, Schück's own vision of a Swedish society in which *allmogen* plays a central role without using violence in fighting *herrarna*, largely coincides with the (later) Social Democratic *folkhem* idea; the *folk* rules, in a sense of *folk* that simultaneously asserts the democratic and national principles, in a way that to be sure favours the 'broad segments of the people' but without denying other classes their part and place.

The national monarchy was thus one of the main points on Engelbrekt's agenda. What was more important than anything else was, he writes, that 'Engelbrekt gave us a Swedish *fosterland* ("motherland")'. It was Engelbrekt's great contribution to develop the 'unreflecting hatred of the *allmogen* against the brutal foreign lords into a more and more conscious love of a free, independent Sweden ruled by law' (Schück 1916: 215). But, his conservative predilections notwithstanding, Schück also notes a second theme, namely 'the broad democratic basis of the new state'. Thus Engelbrekt sought to abolish the '*stormansvälde*' (rule of lords) in favour of a system in which lord and *allmoge* worked together: 'Every peasant had the same rights as the lord', and 'the law recognised no class above the peasants' (Schück 1916: 213). Through the *riksdag* Engelbrekt saved the Swedish peasant estate and prevented it from sinking into serfdom, a threat that had seemed only all too real during the rule of foreign lords:

> Engelbrekt gave [the Swedish peasant] back a place in the political struggle; this raised his self-esteem, and the war of liberation, when one *fogdeborg* (lord's castle) after another fell by the axes of the peasants, taught them that the Swedish peasant estate was a power which did not have to submit to the pretensions of the lords. The Swedish *allmogen* therefore emerged, thanks to Engelbrekt, freer and stronger from the class-struggles of the Middle Ages than either the Danish or the German.
>
> (Schück 1916: 214)

Significantly Schück's celebration of ancient freedoms and democratic traditions was derived not from an embrace of abstract democratic principles and
theories, but rather from the organic connection he perceived between the national
and democratic themes in the story of Engelbrekt. Schück's democratic sentiment was, in a sense, merely an aspect of his intense love of Sweden and all things
Swedish.[17]

The central concept of *folkhemmet* was also subject to contestation. In fact, it was
originally coined and used by conservative intellectuals and political figures, some
twenty years before Per Albin Hansson and the Social Democrats successfully
appropriated it. The earliest citation is a reference from 1896 in the newspaper
Göteborgs Handels- och Sjöfartstidning. In the article the word *folkhem* refers to a place
that provides a reading-room, a larger space for lectures, music programmes and
teaching along with a café 'with cheap food and non-alcoholic beverages', where
'poorer people against a modest fee can gain access to books, newspapers and writing
material'. There are, the journalist observes, 'several such *folkhem* in Stockholm'
(*Göteborgs Handels- och Sjöfartstidning* 1896: 3).

A decade later two further instances can be cited, the first one by the conservative
politician Alfred Petersson from Påboda (1909), the second by the prominent bishop
Manfred Björkquist (1912) (*Göteborgs Handels- och Sjöfartstidning* 1959: 12; *Svenska
Dagbladet* 13 July 1989, 3 and 13 September 1976). However, the more well-known
coinage is that of the influential conservative political scientist Rudolf Kjellén, who
in 1912 deployed the word as a distinct political concept in an article called
'Nationalism and Socialism'. False prophets who divided the nation needed to be
unmasked, he wrote; 'only on the basis of its own traditions can Sweden be made
into that happy *folkhem* that it is meant to be' (Kjellén 1915: 56).

Kjellén linked the idea of a *folkhem* to another new term that he had coined two
years previously, that of *national socialism*. Anticipating the national socialism of the
German Nazis and echoing similar arguments by his contemporary German
conservatives who promoted what they called a 'German socialism', that is a
socialism of national unity devoid of class struggle, he spoke positively about the
workers' movement and the collectivism that he saw as a valuable aspect of
socialism. However, he opposed the ideas of 'class' and 'class struggle,' which he felt
weakened the nation:

> Thus the Socialism of the Socialist Party reduces this idea [of solidarity] to the
> working class. Extend this idea to embrace the whole of the *folk* – think of a
> *national socialism* [his emphasis] instead of a class socialism – and what is
> dangerous to society becomes a wonderful societal power.
>
> (Kjellén 1915: 22)

Throughout the 1920s and 1930s further unsuccessful attempts were made by
conservatives to establish a right-wing reading of the *folkhem* slogan, as well as its close
relative, *folkgemenskap*, a direct translation of the German *Volksgemeinschaft*.[18] In
particular the youth-wing of the Conservative Party, *Svensk Nationell Ungdom* (SNU),
was active in competing with the Social Democrats over who was the rightful voice

of the people and the nation. Eventually, the SNU turned down the road of Nazi-inflected nationalism and was cut loose from the Conservative Party itself.

Subsequently, neither it, nor the various official Nazi parties in Sweden met with significant success. These would-be architects of Swedish right-wing nationalism had to face the problem that the very moment they raised the nationalist banner they were also forced to contend with the already existing Geijerian myth of Swedish national character. And this was a myth that in its *concrete substance* proved hard to reconcile with the basic thrust of radical right-wing, anti-democratic nationalism along the lines familiar elsewhere in Europe (outside of Scandinavia) since the story of the Swedish nation was at heart a celebration of democracy and freedom.

This point becomes clearer if we take a closer look at an essay from 1942, entitled 'The Swedish Line', in which the Conservative John Cullberg attempts to analyse what is 'Swedish' in the context of the dual threat of fascism and communism. 'Two things', he writes, 'have lately with increasing clarity appeared to us as inalienable (*oförytterliga*) values for Swedish societal life: freedom and law-bound order. And we have understood that the two indissolubly belong together' (Cullberg 1942: 575). According to Cullberg, Swedes can make the claim that these universal human values in a sense are specifically Swedish traits: 'No other people's history is in the same way as that of the Swedish the history of a free people.' He continues to note the themes with which we are now familiar: no serfdom, the threat to Swedish *allmoge* that was fought back, how personal freedom was linked to a liberal constitution that allowed '*folkets vilja*' ('will of the people') to have a decisive influence on the rule of the land.

Cullberg then goes on to note the conservative, historical character of this order: 'This [order] is by no means, like it is in many other countries, a creation of modern democratic ideas; rather it is rooted in *uråldriga* (ancient) Swedish societal traditions.' Swedish freedom, that is, 'has always lived and flowered in the protection of the Swedish Law', and Cullberg traces it back through the Middle Ages back to old regional laws – from the thirteenth century – back to the '*germanska rättssamhället*' ('the Germanic society that was ruled by law').[19] Therefore,

> when we now fairly unanimously reject the idea of a reconstruction of society, which is foreign to Swedish disposition, is it not due to conservative rigidity and anxiety about trying new ways. Rather, it is because freedom under lawful order mark Sweden's way through the bewildering terrain of history.
>
> (Cullberg 1942: 576)

Cullberg's musings capture well the dilemma confronting Swedish Conservatives. Given the hegemony of Geijer's national myth, there was little room for an anti-democratic, nationalist, popular/populist position. He could not but give homage to the Swedish tradition of 'freedom' and 'democracy' even if he did so in historicist rather than rationalist, Enlightenment terms.

If, then, the nationalist road was foreclosed, what we see developing in Sweden instead, beginning in the 1930s, is the beginnings of a right that is an advocate of the free market, the rule of law and individual (first and foremost property) rights.

This division between a nationalist left and a free market right has, in fact, endured to the present day, even though the *nationalism* of the left, as we shall see, is complicated and partly hidden by a simultaneous enthusiasm for *internationalism* in the (limited) form of development aid and high-profile involvement in the UN and other international organisations.

From history to modernity: the birth of the 'Swedish model'

Swedes and foreign observers were quick to juxtapose the economic and political success of post-1933, Social Democratic Sweden with the contemporary collapse or crisis of democracy elsewhere. As early as 1935 Per Albin Hansson could be heard declaring that 'Democratic *Norden* can serve as a model for people in other parts of the world' (Hansson 1935b: 220) and one year later Marquis Childs mythologised the notion of a 'peculiarly' democratic Sweden in one of the internationally most influential books ever published about Sweden, namely, *Sweden: The Middle Way*, a book that came to define Sweden for a generation of Americans (Childs 1936).

However, while the fundamental perception of Sweden as the home of democracy and equality remained central, the rise of the 'Swedish model' during the post-1945 period entailed something more, and rather different, than the idea that the Swedes were exceptionally gifted when it came to the business of making democracy work (Lawler 1997). The overt nationalism of the Social Democrats soon faded as nationalism in general was increasingly discredited in the context of the Second World War and the Holocaust. Whereas the poster we examined earlier (Figure 5.1) emphasised the historical link between the Social Democratic workers and Engelbrekt and his peasants, later Social Democratic posters, such as the one included here ('The People of the Future votes for the Workers' Party' – Figure 5.2), evoke a rather different image of Sweden. Here the focus is on the steady march from 'poverty to affluence' (Koblik 1975), on the transformation of Sweden into the 'prototypical modern society' (Jenkins 1969; Thomasson 1970; Ruth 1984). Utopian social engineering was joined to the celebration of national democracy even if, as we shall see, the latter remained a potent trope.

The idea that Sweden is especially 'modern' has roots that predate the construction of the Social Democratic welfare state. As Arne Ruth has noted, even during the heyday of national romanticism, which coincided with rapid industrialisation and social upheaval, Swedish right-wing nationalism was progressive rather than backward looking: 'Compared to the Wagnerian cultural pessimism that accompanied the industrial breakthrough in Germany, it stood out as almost a champion of rationality' (Ruth 1984: 81). Thus industrial skill and strength came to be seen as central – not antithetical – to national renewal. Special talent for engineering and hard work came to be seen as quintessential Swedish virtues, and as early as 1916 the influential essayist Ludvig Nordström envisioned Sweden as 'a model country for the world', being a particularly 'excellent race', a 'well-balanced people geared for progress', endowed with a sense for 'good organization; sound political instincts, and some of the world's best engineers' (Ruth 1984: 83).

Figure 5.2 Framtidsfolket
'The People of the future vote for the workers' party (The Social Democrats)'

Source: Swedish Labour Movement Archives and Library (Arbetarrörelsens Arkiv och Bibliotek)

The great symbol of Sweden's love affair with all things rational, utilitarian and modern has become the famous Stockholm Exhibition of 1930. Much more than just a showcase for functionalism in modern architecture and design, it has come to represent a more general turn towards rational planning, functionality and engineering in its broadest sense, including, of course, very much the idea that society, too, could be properly designed so as to maximise the welfare of its population.

This was an attitude that was adopted by leading Social Democrats, who turned from the romance of socialist revolution to the far more practical task of building the welfare state. As Magnus Ryner notes, Swedish Social Democrats identified with 'the unambivalent modernity of Americanism, which contrasted with the ambivalence of inter-war Europe' (Ryner 1998). The Social Democratic Youth Federation, SSU, played a particularly important role in this transformation. As the historian Henrik Berggren has shown, the SSU was spectacularly successful in mobilising new members during the 1920s and 1930s, partly by playing on the linkage between 'youth', 'youthfulness' and 'modernity'. Central to the rhetoric of the SSU was an embrace of the very attitude that the Stockholm Exhibition stood for: 'Only by accepting the inevitability of change, only by affirming industrialism, capitalism and mass culture, could one hope to exploit these forces in the service of creating a good society', as Berggren summarises the ethos of the SSU (Berggren 1995: 205). The socialist youth was, as they put it, 'the youth of reality', bravely facing an ever-changing world, less concerned with a static vision of a socialist utopia and more prone to see their task in terms of engineering modernity.

Befitting a nation imagined as 'the people of the future', it was thought that there was little to learn from the past. The celebration of Swedish democracy as a function of 'deep' history gave way to a vaguer, ahistorical and essentialist sense of superiority: Sweden as a 'model' of modernity to be emulated (though rarely equalled). Indeed, the primary function of the past was to serve as a negative counterpoint to the ever-more glorious, modern present. In a provocative essay on the treatment of history as a subject in post-war Sweden, Henrik Berggren recollects a history textbook from his boyhood in which Greta, the young heroine in the story (called 'In the Old Days'), is given the opportunity to travel back in time. An interesting experience, of course, but as Berggren notes it was unclear what, if anything, could be learned from this. Indeed, the primary purpose of this pedagogical exercise seems to have been to instil a sense of gratitude for having been born into the welfare state. No doubt we would all react like Greta, by soon demanding to be returned to modernity: 'I have had enough now, says Greta. I want to go back to our time . . . Back to our house with central heating and cooked food and telephone and radio and television and all the other things we have' (Berggren 1993: 21–2).

Another manifestation of this lack of historical consciousness in post-Second World War Sweden is the relative absence of monuments and memorials around which the citizens can organise a collective, national memory. As the ethnologists Jonas Frykman and Orvar Löfgren have noted, compared to most countries in Europe, Sweden is a barren landscape in this regard (Frykman 1991). However, there is more to it than that, for there are indeed monuments and national icons, just not the kind of statues of leaders or war memorials familiar to students of collective memory on the Continent. The historian Kjell Jonsson once told a story from his youth in Sundsvall, a port city in northern Sweden, that is instructive in this regard. Sitting by the dock, he would watch the ships being loaded, setting off for foreign lands with the products of the great Swedish export firms like Volvo and SKF. Then, he remembered, he felt proud to be Swedish (Frykman 1991: 169). And, as Jonas Frykman notes, Swedish literature and film of the twentieth century is filled with electric trains, high voltage electric lines, piston engines and factory smoke stacks. These are the true national monuments of modern Sweden. The scientists, the engineers, the workers were all imbued with the same spirit, the spirit of modernity. Represented not, to be sure, in the Soviet social-realist vein, flamboyant and overdrawn, but as the epitome of Swedish sobriety and rationality. Just as the French have tended to identity Frenchness with civilisation, so the Swedes have identified the modern with the Swedish: 'While the French attitude was that anyone could become a *citoyen* who simply was sufficiently civilised, so the Swedes thought that those who were modern enough surely thought as a Swede would' (Frykman 1991: 169). And so, just as the French had been bent on their (in)famous *mission civilatrice* during the high age of imperialism, so the Swedes came to imagine themselves on a mission to modernise and rationalise the world by way of setting an edifying example, by becoming the very model of modernity.

Thus the mythos of the Swedish model revolved around two motifs, one looking backwards, one looking forwards. On the one hand Sweden was, since time immemorial, the home of freedom, equality and democracy. On the other it was the most modern of nations, a modernity that ultimately derived from the economic and technological prowess of the Swedes. Central to the idea of the modern was *välstånd* ('prosperity'), if a prosperity tamed within the ideological framework of *välfärd* ('welfare'). Significantly, the Swedish word for welfare, *välfärd* (as in *välfärdsstat*, 'welfare state'), contains a dual emphasis on prosperity and equality. This is a point that becomes particularly clear if one compares it to the English term 'welfare', a notion that is negatively tainted by its association with dependency and social policies aimed at dealing with poverty (as in 'welfare queens'). *Välfärd*, by contrast, suggests universal prosperity at a solid middle-class level, while it simultaneously implies a value system that eschews glaring inequalities of income and conspicuous displays of personal wealth. But while 'equality' as an identity-marker is often emphasised in the case of modern Sweden, prosperity is, in fact, of equal importance.

By the 1960s Swedes had come to see themselves as not only the most democratic and most equal *folk* (Dahl 1984), but also as one of the richest peoples in the world. Indeed, the regular publication of the current position of Sweden in the world GDP rankings had become a matter of great concern in the Swedish public debate, and the more recent crisis in Sweden during the early 1990s cannot be properly understood without taking into account the drastic slippage Sweden had experienced in this regard. As we saw in the case of Kjell Jonsson's childhood musings about the sources of Swedish national pride, Volvo, more than Engelbrekt, had by the 1960s come to symbolise post-war Sweden. The political idea of *folkhem*-as-democracy was over time transformed into that of the welfare state, of what Tage Erlander, the long time prime minister who served after Per Albin Hansson and before Olof Palme, called the 'strong society' (*det starka samhället*), a project that was, by comparison, a profoundly material, even economistic enterprise. Big Business and Big Labor worked hand in hand with the Good Corporatist State for the Greater Good of the People. It should be stressed, however, that prosperity was not merely a matter of satisfying personal material needs, not even simply a sign of individual or class status. Rather, a high GDP became a matter of national pride, indeed, of *national identity*.

For a long time these two strains within the mythos co-existed without much tension. Progress *à la Suédoise*, it seemed, involved precisely *both* constant economic expansion *and* an equally constant increase in equality. The latter became, in fact, the instrumentalised meaning of democracy in an increasingly bureaucratised and paternalistic welfare state. Thus '*ökad jämlikhet*' – 'increased equality' – became one of the most common political slogans of the Social Democrats of the 1960s and 1970s. At the same time, equality came to be appreciated as a matter of *rationality*, not merely as a purely *ethical* goal; inequality, like feudalism, was backward and economically counterproductive, as much as it was morally reprehensible.

However, as we shall see when we turn to the more recent debates over the EU, once Sweden's economic position was weakened after 1970, followed by a loss of control over the national economy in the context of economic liberalisation in the 1990s, the contradictions between the economistic and egalitarian ethos and identity would become more apparent. Indeed, this tension at the heart of the Social Democratic narrative on modern Sweden would inform the deep and continuing split within the party with respect to the EU.

Neutrality and internationalism

However, aside from 'democracy', 'modernity' and 'prosperity', there is a fourth symbolic-discursive element that has played a crucial role in the debate over Swedish involvement in European integration, namely 'neutrality'.[20] As we will see, the notion of a 'conservative' and 'capitalist' Europe has often been contrasted with a Sweden that was imagined to be more 'moral' in its behaviour, not only at home, but also in its foreign policy. While others – especially the Great Powers – conducted themselves in a manner more befitting a Bismarck or a Metternich, the Swedes ostentatiously rejected the amoralism of *Realpolitik*. From Dag Hammarskjöld and Folke Bernadotte to Olof Palme, and indeed including even Carl Bildt, the Swedish way has been one of whole-hearted support of binding international law, expressed in a language steeped in a deeply moralist vision of a new world order, one fashioned in the image of Swedish rationality, democratic values and social engineering. On the one hand, this took the form of the policy of neutrality and non-alignment through the refusal to join military-political alliances dominated by Great Powers. This meant first and foremost a rejection of membership of NATO, but it had important ramifications when it came to the possibility of joining the EEC/EC/EU as well. On the other hand, it found expression in support of various failed attempts at Nordic cooperation, an enthusiastic embrace of the UN, and a vociferous display of sympathy for the peoples of the Third World and their struggle against colonialism and Cold War, Great Power machinations.

By the early 1960s Swedish intellectuals were seriously debating the rather self-satisfied notion that Sweden was the 'world's conscience'. The leading writer Lars Gustafsson, in an attempt to deepen the discussion, argued that in fact Swedish 'Third Worldism' should be understood as a new and central aspect of Swedish national identity. Indeed, he argued, 'if Swedish patriotism exists nowadays, it consists of our desire to make ourselves heard in the connection with which this new solidarity confronts us' (Ruth 1984: 71). That is, as Ruth summarises, internationalism acquired the status of national ideology: 'Equality at home and justice abroad have come to be regarded as complementary and mutually supporting values' (Ruth 1984: 71).

This conception of a special Swedish gift for handling international conflicts in a rational, lawful and peaceful manner was fuelled partly by what was widely seen as a wise settling of two potentially explosive conflicts: first, in 1905, when Norway separated from the union with Sweden, and second during the 1920s when the question arose of what to do with the Finnish islands of Åland, whose population is Swedish speaking. In both cases Sweden acted in a manner that has been perceived as giving priority to lawful and peaceful conduct, even if that meant giving up what many might have thought to be a legitimate claim from a strictly national point of view, especially in the case of recognising Finnish sovereignty over the Åland islands.

This vision of Sweden as particularly adept at handling potentially explosive situations has underpinned and inspired many ambitious initiatives when it comes to foreign aid, peacekeeping missions and disarmament schemes. The most eloquent and well-known proponent of this ideology was Olof Palme, whose passion for foreign policy in this spirit became legendary. The most dramatic example was possibly his trenchant critique of the United States' war in Vietnam, but the same line of thinking was evident in his equally strong condemnation of the Soviet invasion of Czechoslovakia. In an essay from the early 1980s on 'Sweden's Role in the World', Palme summed up his view of the goal of Swedish foreign policy as befitting a developed and non-aligned nation:

> To secure in all situations and in the ways we choose ourselves, our national freedom of action in order to preserve and develop our society within our frontiers and according to our values, politically, economically, socially and culturally; and in that context, to strive for international détente and peaceful development. The realization that durable peace and détente are possible is a concept fundamental to social-democratic foreign policy since the beginning of the 1920's . . . The same concept has guided us as we have shaped our foreign policy with regard to the Third World in the 1960s and 1970s. We have taken a stand for national freedom and independence . . . As a small state we have as our goal a world in which the principles of sovereignty and non-intervention are fully respected. This has also made it possible for Sweden, albeit to a modest extent, to build bridges between South and North in a period marked by crisis and the risk of polarization.
>
> (Palme 1982: 244–5)

This quote makes clear the connection between 'national freedom' and the preservation of 'our values' and the support for 'small states' in general and Third World countries in particular. In both cases the fundamental principle is that of respect for national sovereignty. The 'internationalism' of Palme was not a matter of collapsing the world of nation-states into a World Federation, but rather a vision of a global order based on the right of all nations to create their own 'people's home', broadly understood.

This attitude found expression in a preference for, at the one extreme, a global approach when it came to trade and supra-national organisations; GATT and the UN were frameworks within which Sweden found its place with natural ease. This global perspective was, at the other extreme, complemented not only by an insistence on the sanctity of neutrality and the sovereignty of the nation-state, but also by a fondness for various Nordic – usually failing – cultural, economic and security arrangements. Indeed, the Nordic countries appeared as less problematic and more 'natural' partners because they were perceived as culturally and ethnically close. In this scheme of things, Europe did not figure, being simultaneously too close and too different. As the historian Mikael af Malmborg summarises the debate over European integration between 1945 and 1959: 'Norden, the world, and nothing in between', (Malmborg 1994) an attitude that would remain salient well into the debates over EU membership in the 1990s.

Sweden and the 'four Ks'

The European question was rather marginal to the Swedish debate until Harold Macmillan in 1961 decided to hand in a British application for EEC membership. Since the Swedish economy was dominated by industrial firms who depended on their access to an international market, the Social Democrats had for a long time favoured free trade even as they rejected closer political, military or even economic integration that would pose a threat to 'neutrality', leading to the decision to join the looser EFTA free trade area rather than the proto-federalist EEC. Thus, since a British departure from EFTA would have affected Sweden directly, an intense discussion ensued in Sweden, especially and most importantly within the Social Democratic Party, which totally dominated the political scene, remaining in power continuously from 1933 until 1976.

In this debate Sweden was continually cast in the trope of democracy, equality and solidarity, while 'Europe' was pictured, especially by the Social Democrats and the left at large, in terms of the so-called 'four Ks': *konservatism, kapitalism, katolicism, kolonialism* (Conservatism, Capitalism, Catholicism, Colonialism).[21] That is, 'Europe' was cast as the conceptual opposite of 'Sweden'. It was the realm of untamed capitalism, it suffered from the legacy of colonialism, its social policies were informed by backward notions rooted in catholic social thought, and it was politically dominated not by Social Democratic parties but by Conservatives of different shades.

A particularly influential book in this debate was *We and Western Europe*, co-authored by the famous economist Gunnar Myrdal, in which the Swedish welfare state was compared with the EC. Symptomatically Myrdal described the EC as a collection of states 'with a more primitive form of social organisation than ours' (Ekström *et al.* 1962: 33). Elaborating, Myrdal continued by arguing that:

> it is above all the securely Protestant countries that have progressed eco-nomically and in all other ways . . . In so far as political democracy can be thought of as part of 'European culture', then we must remind ourselves of its weakness in the countries south of Scandinavia on the European continent with the possible exception of Holland (although the division between Catholics and Protestants is problematic and among other things is expressed in the fact that the country for long periods of time lacked a government). That democracy is far more self-evident, unshakable and efficient in the Anglo-Saxon immigrant countries and in Scandinavia we all know.
>
> (Ekström *et al.* 1962: 33)

That the Protestant north is more democratic and more economically advanced was thus 'self-evident', as was the 'weakness' in this respect displayed by the Catholic countries to the south. Similarly, another important contributor to the debate of the early 1960s, the economist Claes-Erik Odhner, commissioned by LO (the National Confederation of Labour Unions) to analyse the question of EC membership, noted the wider context within which the economic debate was located. Referring to the values that make up the 'basic political and social attitudes' of a political culture, Odhner alerted the reader to a contemporary Europe 'dominated by conservative governments', wedded to what he called, citing the Norwegian academic Ragnar Frisch, the 'unenlightened rule of capital'. Many of the European countries, he continued, do not fulfil even the most 'elementary requirements for qualifying as democratic systems' (Odhner 1962: 72). Furthermore, the religiously and politically fragmented working-class movement, he argued, would seem to call in question the prospect for a 'progressive political, economic and social development' (Odhner 1962: 73).

This pessimism when it came to a continental counterforce capable of battling the 'strong power of unenlightened capital' notwithstanding, Odhner still accepted, however reluctantly, the fact that, as he laconically remarked, 'Sweden is in Europe'. Thus he suggested that time may in fact be on the side of those who argue for a more assertive policy, taking the European bull by the horns in an attempt to shape rather than defensively react to the process of European integration. In this Odhner anticipated the unenthusiastic decision by the Social Democrats, some thirty years later, to apply for membership of the EU in the name of market access and 'co-rule'.

Another typical contribution from the left from this period was that of Enn Kokk, a central figure within the Social Democratic party. Kokk rejected the EC, which did not represent a 'true' internationalism, although he, again in the name of economic realism, advocated a limited form of free trade association. Echoing Myrdal and Odhner, Kokk emphasised the 'undemocratic' character of both the EC member states and the structure of the EC itself. Painting a portrait of a conservative Western Europe, where even nominal socialists and social democrats were found wanting, Kokk recounted the details of how capital and papism rule in West Germany, Italy and France. In Germany big capital dominated, with influential lobbies in Bonn and Brussels, huge corporate profits and (too) low taxation. Kokk added for good measure that 'corruption seems to be widespread' (Kokk 1962: 130). Furthermore, denazification had not been carried out with any degree of enthusiasm, he wrote, and German nationalism remained unchanged; even Willy Brandt was going soft when it came to demands by the German *Vertriebene* (refugees) from the lost eastern territories. Indeed, German Social Democracy had lost much of its radicalism and socialist authenticity, Kokk felt, and he disapprovingly quoted from the party programme according to which the SPD 'in christlicher Ethik, im Humanismus und der klassichen Philosphie verwurzelt ist' (is rooted in Christian ethics, humanism and classical philosophy).

Similarly, the political culture of 'arch-Catholic' Italy, dominated by an alliance between the Christian Democrats and the Fiats and Olivettis, as well as that of Gaullist France, was determined to be worryingly lacking in 'democracy'. Indeed, in France the political situation was so bad according to Kokk that the extent to which 'France is democratic even in the liberal sense' appeared in his view as rather uncertain (Kokk 1962: 134). Even in the Benelux countries the tendency was the same, with, again, 'the Catholics obstructing the work of the labour movements', and all manner of ethnic and linguistic confusion reigning, compounded by the presence of refugees from former colonies, the latter in itself a testimony to a dubious past with respect to the democratic heritage (Kokk 1962: 134). Thus, in conclusion, Kokk felt that the emerging picture of contemporary Western Europe was *dyster* (gloomy) indeed:

> Today's Franco-German combination, an alliance between General de Gaulle and Dr Adenuer at the forefront of a Catholic, conservative and capitalist Western Europe is a disquieting creation. Today Western Europe is, in spite of the 'dynamic' EEC, a politically dead landscape.
>
> (Kokk 1962: 135)

The discussion was, as it turns out, cut short by a speech given by Prime Minister Tage Erlander on 22 August 1961 in which he closed the door to full membership in the name of neutrality. In view of the still exceedingly strong Swedish economy, the issue of 'prosperity' remained a muted one; as Erlander noted, 'the central question is, of course, foreign policy' (Andrén 1975: 53). However, as always when the notion of 'neutrality' is deployed in Swedish political discourse, there was more going on than first meets the eye. After providing a close reading of the Treaty of Rome in terms of Swedish neutrality policy, Erlander expands the scope:

> In this country we have been able to pursue a policy which, in some respects, has been of a pioneering nature even from an international point of view and which has been supported by a great majority of the people. It is not surprising that we should have doubts about acceding to international agreements which can be expected to considerably restrict our chance to pursue this policy.
>
> (Andrén 1975: 54)

The reference to a 'pioneering' policy that must not be compromised through the accession to 'international agreements' is clear; free trade, yes, a loss of sovereignty that would threaten the building of the welfare state, no. As Nils Andrén has argued, implicit in the speech was the 'idea of Sweden as a sheltered asylum, happily embarked on comprehensive social experiments and jealously protecting herself against harmful influences from abroad' (Andrén 1975: 54).

At the time the pro-Europe forces were overwhelmingly concentrated on the political right in Sweden, among the economic liberals in the Liberal and Conservative parties, who could imagine the EEC as a way to limit the growing presence of the Swedish state in an era of high welfare-statism, for whom the EEC was associated with lower taxes and less constraints on the private sphere at large. As the leader of the Conservatives, Gunnar Hechscher, remarked in reference to

Erlander's speech: 'It would not be quite so easy for the Swedish government to pursue socialist policies in the context of cooperating with countries with different ideological traditions' (Ohlsson: 1993). However, voices like Heckscher's were far and few between, and it would not be until the rise to pre-eminence of a more radically neo-liberal leadership within the Conservative Party – Gösta Bohman and his protégé Carl Bildt – after 1970, and particularly in the 1980s and 1990s, that this perspective was to become truly legitimate, not to mention influential.

In the event, the debate of 1961–2 was a bit of a false alarm. As Andrén notes, 'Sweden's European moment of truth had in fact not arrived in 1961', saved as the Swedes were by de Gaulle's veto against British EEC membership (Andrén 1975: 54). The case was, however, reopened when de Gaulle departed from the scene in 1969 in the wake of the upheavals of May 1968. This time, the stakes were higher since both Britain and Denmark (and Norway, it seemed for a moment) resolutely made their move from EFTA to the EEC. At the time, since the Euro-federalist forces found themselves at a relative low point, Olof Palme, who had replaced Erlander in the same year, initially seemed to have toyed with the idea of a closer association, perhaps even membership.

Nonetheless, the anti-European front soon mobilised and raised objections, most of which followed the pattern set from the debate of 1961–2, while the yes-side also anticipated some of the newer arguments that would come to inform the debates in the 1990s. In the post-1968 atmosphere that reigned, the tone of the debate was harsher than in the early 1960s, and the internationalist argument linked to a critique of the EEC as neo-imperialist and insufficiently considerate of the needs of the Third World gained greater prominence. Conversely, Bohman, now the leader of the Conservatives, introduced a line of argument that would become more and more important as the Swedish economy began to falter, namely that Swedish corporations might have to choose to leave Sweden if they were denied access to the European market on equal terms, a sentiment for which he had full sympathy. To this Palme in turn replied, with irony, that it was sad to hear such arguments from a man like Bohman, hailing as he did from 'a party that once was our most nationalistic'. It would not hurt, Palme went on, 'with a bit of ordinary patriotism and civic spirit' (Palme 1971). That is, echoing his comrades from the 1930s, Palme played the national card by associating patriotism with the defence of the democratic and solidaristic welfare state.

The upshot of the debates of 1970–1 was yet another rejection of the membership option, announced by Palme in March 1971, although a free trade agreement with the EEC was signed in July 1972 and went into effect in January 1973. Furthermore, this decision was largely in harmony with the trend suggested by the opinion polls. Thus the share of those who were for membership slipped from 59 per cent in April 1970 to 31 per cent in December that same year, while the percentage of those against rose from 18 to 27 per cent. Particularly important was the drastic drop in the yes-side among Social Democratic voters, from 56 per cent to 21 per cent (Ohlsson 1993).

The radicalisation of the left and the revolt of the business community

It would take another dozen years or so before the debate was rekindled again. This time the context was, however, fundamentally different. The EEC was changing, rising from the depths of 'eurosclerosis', transforming itself from a European *Economic* Community, via a European Community into a European *Union*, with all the federalist implications those name changes implied, not least in the minds of the champions of national sovereignty. This is not the place to rehearse this story in detail, but let us simply note a few landmarks: the White Paper of 1985, the Single European Act of 1986 and the Maastricht Treaty of 1991.

The deepening of the EU project raised the stakes further, of course, and would in and of itself have strengthened the arguments of the no-side against the idea of membership. At the same time, however, the fall of communism in 1989 meant that the Swedish neutrality policy, especially in the strict sense of that term, suddenly appeared to many as quaintly anachronistic in the new post-Cold War context. Furthermore, the 1980s saw the rise of neo-liberalism and increasingly influential calls for the deregulation of the economy and the dismantling of the corporatist regime that underpinned the Swedish welfare state.

However, as crucial as these external developments may have been, even more important was the domestically engineered breakdown of the historical compromise between labour and capital that had been established in 1938 ('the Saltsjöbaden agreements'). At the discursive level the collapse occurred in two stages. First the Social Democrats underwent a radicalisation beginning in the 1960s as a new generation rediscovered the young Marx and pondered the depths of the alienation that seemed inherent to the Taylorist and Fordist production regimes. Less enamoured with functionalism and social engineering, less likely to accept a sub-ordinate position within the hierarchical structures of big business, less concerned about 'mere' survival than the generation which had experienced the depression, and radicalised by the Vietnam War into a fresh anti-capitalist, anti-imperialist world-view, a new potent political force emerged to the left of the Social Democrats and the LO. As a new 'moral economy' emerged, one that introduced notions of gender equality, eco-socialism and a renewed emphasis on workplace and economic democracy, the Social Democrats were pushed into initiating a number of reforms that fundamentally would challenge the very premise of the agreements of 1938. The most controversial proposal envisioned the establishment of so-called 'wage-earner funds' that would require companies to set aside some of their profits in funds to be used by unions to buy stocks. The result in the long term would have been the gradual socialisation of the major Swedish firms, and as the historian Tim Tilton has pointed out, this idea 'was not presented as just another incremental reform . . . it was heralded as the beginning of a new and more distinctively socialist epoch' (Tilton 1990: 229). While these proposals were never fully realised, they led to an acrimonious political struggle that lasted seven years, from 1976 to 1983, when a weak version of the wage-earner funds was set up, which was in turn dismantled by the Conservative government under Carl Bildt in 1992.

In the second phase, the business community responded to the radicalisation of the left by a turn to neo-liberalism, starting with the appointment of Curt Nicolin as the director of the SAF (Swedish Employers Association) in 1978. The climate of distrust became endemic, and the SAF began to unilaterally withdraw from the corporate social contract on which the 'people's home' rested, a move that was completed by January 1992. From an institutional perspective this was dramatic enough, but here I would like to focus on the effects of the new orientation of the SAF on the discursive landscape in Sweden.

The central innovation was to introduce an anti-statist discourse that hitherto had been virtually non-existent in Sweden, if we discount the anarcho-syndicalist left.[22] The central vehicle for conceptual creativity on the right was a think tank, the Timbro Institute, which was established in 1978. Timbro was funded by the business community as an alternative to the established academic institutions, which were perceived as dominated by the leftist 'intelligentsia', and quickly became an increasingly important player in setting the agenda and defining the terms for the Swedish public debate during the 1980s.[23]

By 1992 writers associated with Timbro had managed to inject the idea of 'civil society' into the Swedish political language (Trägårdh 1995 and 1999). The concept was an import from Eastern Europe where it referred to the sphere in which dissidents mobilised against the coercive communist state. In the context of this state-versus-society dichotomy, the Swedish Social Democratic state was associated with excessive state intervention – the 'command economy' – in the market and in the so-called 'small world' of voluntary organisations, neighbourhood associations, families and friends. The latter sphere was linked to freedom, independence and civic virtue, while the former was associated with bureaucracy, inefficiency and dependency.

The coinage and successful introduction of this neologism was all the more remarkable since, in fact, the distinction between state and society has been more or less absent in the Swedish language. Indeed, the conflation of the two terms is indicative of just how thoroughly the corporatist order had come to penetrate Swedish society: the favourite term for the 'welfare state', for example, has not been *välfärdsstaten*, but *välfärdssamhället* ('the welfare *society*'). Symptomatically, when the conservative sociologist Hans Zetterberg launched an ambitious project at Timbro to study and critique the Swedish welfare state, his term of preference was *socialstaten*, 'the social state'. This was, of course, an attempt to get away from the positive associations to 'community' and welfare-as-prosperity-and-equality that were triggered by the word *välfärdssamhället*. *Socialstaten*, by contrast, was meant to conjure up visions of an oppressive or at least bureaucratic social(ist) state.

The EU debate during the 1990s: the people's home versus 'Europe'

The attack on the legitimacy of the (Social Democratic) state, which took off during the 1980s, was directly linked to the campaign on the part of the SAF to promote Swedish membership of the EU. By undermining the legitimacy of and confidence in the nation-statist, corporatist regime, the pro-EU arguments could gain in force. Central to this rhetorical strategy was the insertion of a wedge right where the Social Democratic 'myth' of modern Sweden was perceived to be most vulnerable, that is, in the gap that separated *free trade internationalism* from *welfare state nationalism*. Prosperity, it was argued, depended on deregulation and a truly open economy: the choice had to be made between welfare statism that over time would lead to economic stagnation, and a relative dismantling of the welfare state in order to ensure economic growth.[24]

The narrative that linked (social) democracy, modernity and neutrality depended on the generation of sufficient wealth to allow *välstånd* (prosperity) and *välfärd* (welfare as equality and solidarity) to co-exist. What the pro-EU forces supported by the business community attempted, with considerable success, was to establish the idea that wealth production now depended on Sweden joining the EU and that, conversely, a failure to do so would lead to a mass exodus by Swedish companies with a consequent and drastic reduction in the living standards of ordinary Swedes. Whatever the validity of neo-liberal economic theory, it is clear that Timbro and the SAF were quite successful in their attempt to set the terms for the political debate. Specifically, they managed to push economic thinking as such into the fore, and increasingly economics gained prominence in the public debate, reflected in the steady growth of the sections dealing with economic issues in the leading daily newspapers.

With the financial and economic crises that characterised the 1990s – the collapse of the currency, negative growth rates, and most especially the explosion of unemployment that took place after 1990 – this perspective gained further in credibility, and it was against this backdrop that the decision to apply for membership of the EU was made by the Social Democratic government under Ingvar Carlsson on 26 October 1990.[25]

While this decision appears in retrospect to many as unavoidable, it was at the time experienced as something of a shock given the legacy of repeated assertions to the effect that Swedish neutrality policy was inconsistent with membership. Indeed, even Carl Bildt, the leader of the most Euro-enthusiastic of all the parties, had ruled out full membership as late as July 1989, citing neutrality as the obstacle. Predictably, in many quarters this turn-around was seen as a deep betrayal of long-held national values; as giving in to the neo-liberal ideology that had gradually acquired a near hegemonic status among economists, business people and the leadership of the political parties to the right of the Social Democrats. What followed was an intense political battle leading up to the referendum on EU membership in November 1994, a debate characterised by a dramatic resurgence of the left-nationalist narrative on the part of the defenders of national sovereignty and the welfare state, on the one hand, and an unholy alliance of the neo-liberal right and the economistic wing of the Social Democratic Party, on the other. As one author put it in a 1992 book title, the lines were drawn in a struggle that pitted 'The People's Home against Europe' (Stråth 1992).

The 'bourgeois' yes-side: For a European civil society

On the yes-side the dominant argument was very much the one we have encountered already in our discussion of how the SAF moved towards a neo-liberal discourse, one that turned on the rejection of the 'over-regulated' corporatist welfare state and the embrace of the EU as a way to institutionalise a new, pro-business economic order. The speech given by the then Prime Minister Carl Bildt to the EU Commission in November 1991, under the heading 'Sweden – from a reluctant to an enthusiastic European', is indicative. Bildt provided a brief historical survey of why Sweden had until recently chosen to stay outside the European integration project: neutrality, economic success, 'far-sighted investments in social reforms', all adding up to a certain mentality with respect to Europe that he summarised as follows:

> It was possible in the Swedish debate on our policy towards European integration to find people who would claim that Sweden represented some superior form of society which should not be unduly endangered by co-operation with supposedly less developed European nations. For a long time the dominant forces in Swedish politics tended to see Sweden as a country which, through its so-called 'third road' policies could build bridges between East and West, not only in terms of security, but also in terms of finding some kind of compromise between the two competing social and economic systems.
>
> (Bildt 1991a)

Bildt then went on to argue that 'it goes without saying that there is no longer any room for this sort of policy'. On the one hand, 'no one wants to be a compromise between a system which has turned out to be a success and another that has turned out to be a historic catastrophe'. On the other, Bildt concluded, the 'third road' policies had failed miserably as domestic economic policy, and Sweden had lost its former leading position as an economic power-house and was now sadly 'lagging behind'.

Along with the Liberal Party, the Conservatives under Bildt's leadership consistently promoted a positive vision of EU membership. They explicitly claimed the mantle as 'the European Party', as Bildt put it. Together with the Liberals, Bildt launched what was polemically called '*den enda vägens politik*' – the politics of the only possible way – a reference, of course, to the 'third way' of the Social Democrats as well as to the post-Cold War, 'end of history' notion that now there was only one way, the way of the free market.[26] It was really just a matter of relaying the objective truth. Thus argued Carl B. Hamilton, a leading financial expert in the Liberal Party, 'it would be absurd to believe that more jobs would be created if we say no to the EU' (Hamilton 1994) and in a similarly condescending way Göran Tunhammar, the head of the SAF, likened the task of the employers to that of a parent, who had to patiently 'explain the importance of European integration to their workers and their families' (Tunhammar 1994).

The alternative to the 'only way' was the failed way of Swedish Social Democracy, a particularly flagrant case of 'eurosclerosis', as it was put in the official 'yes to EU' pamphlet put out by the Conservative Party:

> Sweden is perhaps one of the worst examples of eurosclerosis. We have to a greater extent than other European countries made the mistakes that the EU is now in a serious way trying to correct: a rigid labour law, a complicated and expensive work environment bureaucracy, overly generous social insurance schemes, shortened work time, extended vacations and a lowered retirement age, and finally disastrously high taxes on wealth, capital gains and income, which have gradually worked to eliminate more and more jobs in the private sector.
>
> (Moderaterna 1994: 15)

Still, sensitive to the crassness of this out and out economical perspective, if not to the arrogant tone of many of the Euro-friendly technocrats, Bildt and the Conservatives also liked to emphasise the 'peace' argument, often hailed as the number one reason for voting yes. The EU had been and would continue to be a guarantee that not only prosperity but also peace would reign in Europe. Exit polls taken after the referendum showed that these three issues – the economy, employment and peace in Europe – were, indeed, the reasons most often cited by those voting yes.

Furthermore, Bildt tried to balance his obvious enthusiasm for Europe by invoking a federalist vision of multiple identities. As the title of his 1991 memoir *Hallänning, svensk, europé* suggests, he fashioned himself not only as a European, but also as a Swede, and, most cosily, as a member of his local province Halland on the Swedish west coast (Bildt 1991b). Nonetheless, as he put it in the title of the final chapter of that book: 'Europe is the future!' By this he meant that 'Europe' now – in the post-1989 period – stands for a new post-socialist development in the realm of ideology, 'a new ideological synthesis', which he calls a 'humanistic renaissance after a century dominated by a materialistic ideology', that is, by 'socialism' of one kind or another. He identified as the two key concepts in this new synthesis 'civil society' and 'subsidiarity', two ideas that focus on the freedom of the individual and the primacy of local and natural communities against the more or less totalitarian ambitions of the state. The concept of civil society, he argued, stood for 'a society of citizens as opposed to a society dominated by the state' (Bildt 1991b: 312):

> In the context of the Swedish debate, which has been raging in the recent decades, it translates into the pitting of a libertarian against a collectivist conception of democracy. While in the libertarian view of democracy the freedom of the individual is decisive, it is the political system and the unimpeded rule of the majority that is most important from the point of view of the collectivist conception of democracy.
>
> (Bildt 1991b: 311)

Therefore, Bildt concluded his book, to be partners in the building of 'the new Europe' meant to share in the 'realisation of a common political programme based on the primacy of individual freedom, the rule of law, the principle of subsidiarity and the free market' (Bildt 1991b: 318).

The Liberals, for their part, tried to soften their image by off-setting their hard economic arguments with continued support for certain social-liberal measures that linked them to the Social Democrats: labour market policies, gender equality, ecology, work place environment and safety, for example.[27] This was true for the party's leader Bengt Westerberg in particular, whose support for gender equality – so central to the modern, post-1970 mythos of Social Democratic Sweden – even got him named 'honorary woman of the year' in 1994.[28] Westerberg's more 'human' profile was also expressed in his critique of the undercurrent of xenophobia that characterised some of the wilder claims of the no-side. As he observed in the Swedish Parliament in November 1994:

> There have been cases of extraordinary exaggerations in the argumentation of the no-side, for example cases of intolerance and fear of the culturally different, which are wholly unacceptable for a liberal.
>
> (Westerberg 1994: 8)

Westerberg continued by alluding to anti-Catholic comments made by a member of the Social Democratic government, a concern echoed by Bildt who on a separate occasion remarked that:

> This election campaign has shown that the kind of basic prejudices that exist in all societies are quite prevalent in Sweden as well. As I continue to travel abroad, I will from now on be ashamed to be a citizen of a country where a minister [the Minister of Agriculture, Margareta Winberg] has tried to capitalise on anti-Catholic prejudices in the way she has.
>
> (Holmberg 1994)

By raising the issue of an ugly nationalism, Westerberg and Bildt sought to undercut the potential charge that they, as part of a cosmopolitan elite, as latter-day nobles, did not care enough for the 'people' and lacked a simple, honest sense of patriotism, as Palme had charged in 1971. Westerberg especially could do so with a great deal of credibility since he had for years been a champion of the rights of immigrants and refugees. Furthermore, since the campaign coincided with the war in former Yugoslavia, it was relatively easy to put less careful proponents of welfare state nationalism on the defensive; no one wanted to be caught in the company of Le Pen or Milosevich. Thus the well-known anthropologist Ulf Hannerz warned that xenophobia coloured the EU debate; behind the arguments displaying an obsessive worry about the fate of *snus*,[29] the strict Swedish drug and alcohol policy and *allemansrätten*[30] if Sweden were to join the EU, there lurked a general fear of the 'other' (quoted in Öhrström 1994). Similarly the respected economic historian Mauricio Rojas, himself a refugee from Pinochet's Chile, warned against narrow-minded visions of a homogenous *folkhem*; for him yes to Europe meant yes to a liberal, pluralistic and tolerant Europe where individual rights were more important than the sanctity of the nation (Rojas 1994).

Whereas both liberal and conservative voters overwhelmingly voted yes, in the case of the two remaining bourgeois parties yes- and no-voters were relatively evenly split. The Centre Party, with its environmentalist wing and a historical link to the Social Democrats and the construction of the *folkhem*, was and remains critical of what they perceived as the centralism of the EU project. With its roots as a peasants' party, it saw itself as representing the people of the countryside, and in geographical terms the vote was dramatically split between the sparsely inhabited and no-voting north and the yes-voting and urban south. While often working in tandem with the Social Democrats on the basis of their common historical identity – harking back to the 1930s – as the 'movement' parties representing 'the people', that is, the peasants and the workers respectively, the Centre Party diverged from the Social Democrats in its anti-industrial, anti-urban, some would even say anti-modern sentiments.[31] Much like the anti-EU wing of the Social Democrats, the Greens and the Left Party, the no-wing of the Centre Party tended to distrust the EU as being too pro-market and pro-business and not sensitive enough to ecological issues and the needs of the little people of the marginalised countryside. Reflecting a certain lack of decisiveness due to the intra-party split,[32] the Centre Party demanded new referendums in the case of remaining central issues, such as any changes in the neutrality policy, joining the EMU, or other matters requiring further whittling away at the foundation of national sovereignty (Carlgren and Hansson 1994).

The Christian Democrats, on the other hand, could reasonably claim to be the most naturally European party of them all. Thus, as Niels Arbøl argued in a book on Christian Democracy in Europe, European integration was from the very beginning intimately associated with leading Christian Democrats such as Konrad Adenauer, Robert Schuman and Alcide de Gasperi (Arbøl 1992). These were politicians who rejected nationalism in favour of Christian universalism (or at least Europeanism), who championed the institutions of civil society in opposition to the Conservative and Socialist romance with the strong state, who embraced federalism, decentralisation and the principle of subsidiarity. On the other hand, given the strength of the statist tradition as well as the prevalent suspicion that continental Christian democracy really meant 'Catholicism', these were arguments that could easily backfire, and therefore the Christian Democrats, like the Centre Party, kept a relatively low profile during the campaign leading up to the referendum.

What the Christian Democrats under their leader Alf Svensson represented was, at any rate, the solidaristic, social conservative side of the right. They were far more likely to speak in a language that emphasised solidarity and community, to show concern that the EU must not simply become a marketplace where winners gain and losers suffer. Thus, during a 1992 meeting of the European Peoples' Party (EPP) – the all-European Christian Democratic Party – Svensson openly declared that the Conservative parties in Scandinavia were founded on neo-liberal values quite foreign to the humanist and Christian ideas central to Christian Democracy (Arbøl 1992: 299). Conversely, Svensson declared, citing from the platform of the EPP, that his party stood for human dignity and Judeo-Christian values such as solidarity, 'meaning protection for the weakest in our society and the world at large' (A. Svensson 1994: 13). This attitude was well represented by another leading light in the party, the physician Jerzy Einhorn, himself a refugee from Hitler's Germany, for whom the EU was closely linked to a vision of peace, community and solidarity with the old, weak and sick (Einhorn 1994). However, for the Christian Democrats such care and protection was properly the function of the institution of civil society, not of the state.

The no-side: for a Swedish nation-state

In the opposite corner from Bildt stood the left-wing, no-side, composed of the Greens, the Left Party and half of the Social Democratic grassroots, including a majority of the LO members. Arguing vehemently against giving up national sovereignty, they conjured up vivid images of the cultural differences between Sweden (and Norden), on the one hand, and Europe on the other (Agrell 1992). The left-leaning organisation '*Nej till EG*' ('No to the EC') relished linking prostitution, drug-liberalism, sexism, elitism and the 'democratic deficit' to the EU. As the titles and images of the pamphlets distributed during the 1993 campaign suggest, 'Europe' was equated with a 'bordello' or 'a women's trap', and 'Brussels-power' (i.e. the power of a bureaucratic elite) was contrasted with '*folkstyre*' ('rule of the people'). (See Figures 5.3–5.5).

This vision of 'Europe' was contrasted with the democratic, solidaristic and national welfare state. As Göran Greider, a leading voice of the anti-EU forces within the Social Democratic Party, declared: 'I believe in the nation-state', arguing that 'democracy assumes a sense of community'. By contrast, he claimed, to create a so-called 'European human being' would amount to nothing 'but the setting loose upon the world yet again of the unruly beast' associated with the pre-democratic times prior to the French revolution and the construction of the modern, democratic nation-state (Greider 1993: 16). In 'Europe' the market would rule, and the weak would be left to fend for themselves as the *Gemeinschaft* of the nation-state gave way to the *Gesellschaft* of a cosmopolitan federation.

A similar note was struck in the pamphlets distributed by the Left Party. Thus the nation-state, it was argued, 'is in Sweden intimately associated with democracy' (Jacobsson 1997) and 'Swedish membership in the supra-national and undemocratic European Union would mean for us a considerably inferior form of democracy' (Vänsterpartiet 1994a: 4). The EU was a neo-liberal project that had 'developed in an artificial manner without popular/national (*folklig*) support' (Vänsterpartiet 1994b: 23):

> The EU is inextricably interwoven with Western European Big Capital. The history, structure and future development of the EU, as detailed in the Maastricht Treaty, speaks its own, clear language. To vote No to Swedish membership in the EU is part of the struggle against the growing power of international capital.

> (Vänsterpartiet 1994c: 23)

Figure 5.3   Bordell Europa
'Brothel Europe.' Here the European Union is linked to liberal attitudes and laws
with respect to prostitution, suggesting a lack of respect for women.

Source: Robert Nyberg

The principle of subsidiarity was also attacked by the Left Party. The concept,
they inform the reader in one of their election campaign broadsides, is 'coined
by a Catholic pope' (Vänsterpartiet 1994d: 6) and 'derived from the authoritarian
Catholic social doctrine, meaning "submission" or "secondary"' (Vänsterpartiet
1994b: 23). It is also argued that subsidiarity has been mistakenly translated in
Denmark and Sweden as *närhetsprincipen* ('closeness principle'), thereby suggesting
that it has to do with decentralisation and grassroots democracy. In fact, claimed
the Left Party, it has nothing to do with the democratic idea of decentralisation
(power from below), rather it is but a rhetorical ruse to cover up the true nature of
subsidiarity, that is, the 'submission' to central rule from Brussels (Vänsterpartiet
1994b: 5 and 1994e: 7–8). Furthermore, it is a concept that is central to the continental welfare system, one that places a very un-Swedish emphasis on the family.
Whereas in Sweden the individual is the basic unit,

> in the EU countries legislation takes the family as its point of departure. This
> is what is called 'familism'. It is in this perspective we must understand the so-
> called subsidiarity principle.

(Vänsterpartiet 1994d: 6)

Figure 5.4 Är EG en kvinnofälla?
'Is the EC a women's trap?' The gender equality of Sweden is contrasted with the backward state typical of continental Europe, with the mother staying behind in the kitchen while the father is off to work.

Source: Robert Nyberg

Thus subsidiarity has nothing to do with democratisation, but in fact serves to throw women, children and the elderly back into the hands and mercy of the patriarchal family, and submit the local community and the nation to the rule of the Euro-elite in Brussels.

Responding to critics who branded them as nationalists, Göran Greider and other anti-EU campaigners emphasised that nationalism comes in 'good' as well as sinister forms. Thus Rolf Karlbom, a historian at the University of Gothenburg, wrote in an anti-EU periodical that those who accuse the no-side of narrow nationalism miss the point that Swedish national identity – and thus Swedish nationalism – is historically linked to democracy, solidarity and humanity. 'There is no reason', he notes, 'to be ashamed of Swedish history. It is not a matter of national romanticism or of chauvinistic patriotism to point out that next to Switzerland, Sweden has the most ancient tradition of popular rule.' Quoting approvingly from a pamphlet from the 1930s, Karlbom suggested that this propensity for 'people power' amounted to a 'deeply rooted spirit of the people' (Karlbom 1993: 14).

Indeed, a few years after the referendum, the still active 'No to EU' organisation organised a series of demonstrations, during which the struggle of Engelbrekt and

Figure 5.5   Folkstyre eller Brysselmakt?
'People's power or Brussels power?' Swedish popular and egalitarian democracy
is contrasted with the elitist rule of experts and bureaucrats in Brussels.

Source: Robert Nyberg

Gustav Vasa against foreign rule and feudal oppression of the 'little people' was
re-enacted in a modernised version. Conjuring up a vision of the EU as a latter day
version of the Kalmar Union,[33] the Brussels bureaucrats and the bosses of the
multinational firms were identified with the foreign bailiffs and lords against whom
the brave Swedish peasants had revolted in the name of national independence and
personal freedom. The message was clear: it was time for the people to rise up once
more and defeat yet another infernal attempt to deprive them of their ancient rights
in the name of a union that would only serve the interest of the privileged 'Euro-
class'.

Another important element in the iconography of the no-side was the figure
of Norden. Jörgen Bengtsson, a founder of the organisation 'Alternativ till EG', thus
argued that Norden – as opposed to the EU – was a 'natural' *gemenskap* ('community'
in Tönnies' sense of *Gemeinschaft*), with a common history, culture, religion, linguistic
affinities and economic development. Norden, he claimed, 'constitutes a *folklig*
community and is relatively speaking ethnically homogeneous', where people 'think
more or less the same, have the same lifestyle and temperament, have a sense of
belonging together, and have a similar view of important human and social questions'
(Bengtsson 1993: 12–13; 1992). Specifically, Bengtsson argued, 'Norden stands for a

unique social model', one that involves a taxation-financed, universal welfare state, a high level of general education, a tradition of egalitarianism, a strong position for women and minorities, active labour market policies, and a well-developed tradition of *folkstyre* (rule of the people) (Bengtsson 1993: 13–14). By contrast, the EU was viewed, in the words of Greider, as a 'club for the executives of the multinational corporations' and a fundamental threat to the welfare state and the 'Nordic' social contract.

The notion that Swedish women had achieved a greater degree of gender equality became another central argument, one that was intimately linked with the defence of the strong state threatened, as we have already seen in the Left Party pamphlets cited above, by the Catholic principle of subsidiarity. Only the state, it was argued, could deliver women from the oppressive conditions that characterised 'civil society', a sphere characterised by hierarchical and patriarchal structures. The EU was described as a 'women's trap', where women had little access to state-financed day-care, were thus unable to work, and became as a consequence dependent on men (Eriksson 1993). Furthermore, 'Europe' was associated with prostitution, a theme that formed part of a broader attack on the loose morals of the (Catholic) Europeans, who indulged in drugs and free alcohol in the most un-Swedish of ways (Månsson and Backman 1993). Thus the elimination of internal borders envisioned by the Schengen agreements was cast as a threat to national sovereignty at the moral level (Karlsson and Torstensson 1995).

At the same time, Schengen was blamed for erecting too much of a wall in relation to non-Europeans. Thus Per Gahrton, a leading member of the Greens and one of the most vociferous debaters on the no-side, claimed, in a common turn of phrase, that the EU was but 'fortress Europe', an association of ex-colonial powers still steeped in neo-colonial attitudes towards the developing world. He bemoaned the passing of the active Swedish neutrality policy championed by Palme. True internationalism, Gahrton projected, would end with Swedish entry into the EU:

> Sweden has a long tradition of independence and neutrality, Sweden has spoken with a loud voice on the world scene. Not everybody has liked this. Some have wanted to silence the Swedish voice of solidarity in the world. And so it will be if Sweden becomes a province of the European Union.
>
> (Gahrton 1994)[34]

For the no-side, then, social justice, equality, solidarity, individual autonomy, gender equality, freedom to show solidarity with the poorer countries of the world, all this depended on the continued existence of the nation-state. Solidarity could develop only within the imagined community of the nation, only a democratic state could guarantee the survival of the nation, without a people's home the individuals would exist only as atoms in the heartless world of the market and the so-called civil society.

The Social Democratic yes-side: prosperity above all

While the arguments and the discourse used by the conservative-liberal yes-side and the left-wing no-side were both predictable and straightforward, the position of the Social Democratic Party was more complex since it was split between a no and a yes contingent. Given the sheer size of the party, as well as its legacy as the party of government for most of the post-1933 period, the arguments made by the yes-side within the party were in fact pivotal. It is widely recognised that had Ingvar Carlsson not been able to sway a large minority of the SAP rank and file to follow him, the referendum vote would have gone the other way. Carlsson's task was daunting, he had to convince reluctant SAP voters to abandon the long-cherished ideas still promoted by the no-side within the party. The relative success on the part of the SAP leadership was no mean feat. How did they do it?

To understand the historical and discursive context of the Social Democratic yes position, we need to return to our analysis of the central narrative on Swedish national identity. While the no-side latched on to one side of the discourse on Swedish exceptionalism, playing up the dire consequences of abandoning national sovereignty and the policy of neutrality (Greider 1993; Johansson 1994; Åkerman 1994),[35] the yes-side organised their argument around the other side of the narrative, that of modernity and economic prowess. The welfare state project was, after all, not simply about equality but also about prosperity, and prosperity was not only about individual self-interest but also a matter of national pride. Thus the arguments about the economic effects of EU membership were intimately linked to the crisis of the Swedish economy, which in turn was perceived as a crisis of (Social Democratic) national identity.

To a degree, then, a certain paradoxical harmony between the agenda of the Swedish business community and the Social Democratic 'modernists' is apparent. The two sides share a discourse on modernity, on efficiency, on prosperity, on macho notions of Swedish quality and competitiveness, conceptions, as we have seen, with deep historical and discursive roots. Both sides thus see economic growth as a central objective, and herein lies, of course, a potential for rapprochement in the construction of a neo-corporatist social contract.

Nonetheless, their positions on the proper relationship between the EU and the Swedish welfare state differed fundamentally. Although some of the Social Democratic proponents of EU membership simply noted that Sweden had to accept the reality of the EU,[36] most sought to go beyond the defeatist, fatalistic position of those who bought into the teleology of the 'only way',[37] and they did so by redirecting the self-confident, messianic impulse so central to Swedish identity onto the broader European stage. Leading Social Democrats like Ingvar Carlsson, Mona Sahlin, Allan Larsson and Leif Blomberg argued that membership of the EU represented an opportunity to take on the responsibility of shaping EU policy in crucial areas like employment and social policy, indeed, Larsson argued, the EU itself was already moving away from the politics of 'the only way'.[38] In making this rhetorical gesture, these Social Democrats directly challenged the notion, popular among both the Conservatives and the EU opponents on the left, that the EU was a 'rightist' project.[39] Some, like Carl Lidbom, even chided the nay-sayers for raising the anti-Catholic, quasi-nationalist banner:

> It would be a pity if Sweden were to end up outside the European integration project because Margareta Winberg managed to scare people by invoking the

spectre of Catholics and the Vatican, or because Astrid Lindgren made people believe that in the EU countries animals are not considered 'living creatures but merely trade goods'.[40]

(Lidbom 1994b)

This is what set the Social Democrats' yes-side apart from the Conservatives, Liberals and Christian Democrats; far from seeing EU membership as the defeat of Social Democracy, they projected a vision of a Europe refashioned in the image of Social Democratic Sweden. Thus, where the Conservatives of Bildt saw the EU as a way to diminish the space for the political manipulation of the free market, the Social Democrats spoke in terms of re-establishing a lost balance between politics and the market. Since capital had already gone international, so must the state in order to level the playing field and give lost power back to the 'people'. As Ingvar Carlsson said in the Swedish Parliament after the vote:

> It is now clear that both Finland and Sweden will enter the European Union. In a few days it is also possible that Norway will join the band of Nordic countries in the EU . . . This would provide us in Norden good opportunities to leave our imprint on the common European policies. Norden has much to offer in the way of common interests and values. I am thinking about the Nordic commitment to the environment, to gender equality and to social welfare.
>
> (Carlsson 1994)

Carlsson went on to stress the importance of pressing the EU to make greater commitments beyond the EU itself, not least in Eastern Europe, and continued by noting that:

> When Sweden becomes a member of the EU a new democratic dimension opens up for us in Sweden. Swedish Social Democracy will work to make Europe a living democracy where the equal worth of all humans and participation become the basis for politics. Politics shall be used as an instrument to balance the market forces.
>
> (Carlsson 1994: 3)

Here one can also observe a telling difference in how Swedes, Danes and Norwegians conceive of the relationship between Norden and Europe. While many people in all three countries appear to be convinced of the superiority of the Nordic Way, this is an attitude that is expressed rather differently from country to country in the debate over the EU. As Kresten Schultz Jørgensen, the editor of the Danish Social Democratic daily *Aktuelt*, put it in an interview on Swedish radio: the Danes are 'schizophrenic' in that they are flattered to be sitting with the big EU boys (having a 'little brother' complex) even as they are filled with a pompous, introverted and vaguely xenophobic sense of self-satisfaction and superiority. This, Jørgensen argues, is in sharp contrast to the Swedes who tend to approach the EU with a (possibly self-delusional) sense of confidence, seeing in the superiority of the Swedish model something to bring to the EU, rather than merely a vulnerable asset threatened by EU membership (Jørgensen 2000). Here the assertive Swedish 'big brother' identity works in a way quite different from the 'little brother' syndrome that Jørgensen associates with Danish attitudes, allowing Swedish Social Democrats to project onto the European scene domestic utopian schemes, thus at least on the rhetorical level reconciling the ideology of welfare state nationalism with the transnational European project.[41]

Since the referendum, the wisdom of joining the EU has seemingly been confirmed by the rapid recovery of the Swedish economy. By the fall of 1999 a new sense of national pride had begun to emerge, organised not around the figure of the welfare state, but in the image of Ericsson and the explosive growth of the Swedish information technology sector and the so-called 'new economy'. And in January 2000, the Executive Committee of the Social Democratic Party, after a long period of hesitation and debate, finally decided to recommend that Sweden join the EMU:

> Through cooperation within the European social democratic movement we will ensure that the common currency – together with economic co-ordination and a European growth strategy for increased demand and greater investments – can lead to economic growth, jobs and stability.[42]

This emergence of the 'New Sweden' was symbolically recognised in the winter and spring of 2000 when *Newsweek* (2000) as well as *The Financial Times* (2000) prominently featured Sweden as the new economic wonder, proclaiming Stockholm as the Internet capital of Europe, noting that the Swedes had now surpassed even the Americans when it comes to per capita computer ownership and usage. In the same period, minister after Social Democratic minister could be seen visiting New York where they repeated the mantra about the 'New Sweden', the Sweden of 'entrepreneurs'. And at home, as Swedish interest rates plunged below the German ones, Swedish editorial writers celebrated as if the Swedes had won the Soccer World Cup:

> Yesterday at 10.36 Sweden definitively left the chaotic economy of the 1990s. At that moment the Swedish interest rate dipped below the German one. It is a great occasion. Only a few years ago . . . no one believed in Sweden. Today everybody believes in Sweden – and for good reason . . . Last week the Financial Times celebrated the Swedish miracle. Stockholm is a global centre. 'Sweden' nowadays connotes the future, the trendy and the vital.
>
> (*Expressen* 2000)

Conclusions

What, one might ask, of the state? And what happened to the 'people's home'? The Social Democrats' facility for claiming the current successes of Swedish private business as their own is remarkable. Indeed, ever since the happy coincidence in the

1930s of Social Democratic arrival into power and the end of the Depression, there has been a tendency to conflate economic growth with Social Democratic managerial skills. Yet, the jury is still out on whether the current euphoria over the rebounding economy will translate into a stable neo-national identity comparable to that of the *folkhem* ideology of the age of high-welfare statism. For one thing, suspicion of 'papist' Europe lingers on and commitment to the welfare state remains strong. The polls continue to indicate that the Swedes remain the most Euro-negative of Europeans and support for the EMU, never strong, has been getting weaker. Furthermore, the anti-EU, pro-welfare state Left Party continues to grow significantly in strength and this flocking of (former?) Social Democrats to the Left Party suggests a deepening split between the pro-EMU and EU party leadership and the more nationally minded rank and file. Indeed, the weakness of the Euro combined with the heady sense that Sweden is, once more, Number One, could easily enough translate into a feeling that Sweden could do very well without joining the EMU. After all, many of those who reluctantly voted yes in the 1994 referendum did so under duress at a time when the economy was in a shambles and EU membership seemed like a bitter but necessary pill to take.

On the other hand, one might speculate that within the paradigm of 'modernity' and 'prosperity' a shift is occurring from the ethos of statist social engineering towards that of free market entrepreneurship, which still retains a distinctly national(ist) flavour. In a recent speech on 'The Renewal of Sweden: Economy, Education and Research', the Minister of Education, Thomas Östros, thus argued that the state is more important than ever.[43] In a global economy based on information technology, the key to both individual and national development is education. Only the state can guarantee that all citizens are provided with the opportunity to join the new economy, Östros argued, and through the state collective resources can be invested where they will have the greatest impact, in the universities. The vision thus invoked suggests a new national, social contract, parodied in a scathing 1 May cartoon in the pages of *Aftonbladet*, the Social Democratic daily (see Figure 5.6): in partnership with private business, the Swedish State will turn the Nation into one giant Silicon Valley, and the citizens into an army of stockholders.

By way of conclusion, let us return to the same editorial writer who wallowed in the success of the 'New Sweden' above. Noting that the success of today was linked to the sacrifice of the past, he continued:

> The transitions made during the 1990s were not simply a matter of fiscal belt-tightening, but also a matter of a powerful breaking away from a world-view which had stifled Sweden for decades. Capitalism was finally accepted as the best economic system, the entrepreneur became a celebrated public figure, the state ceased to grow and its share of the economy even began to shrink, deregulation and privatisation gave power to the market, and membership in the EU crushed the narrow-minded and suffocating *folkhem* nationalism.
>
> (*Expressen* 2000)

Figure 5.6   Folkrörelse
'Popular (national) movement.' The cartoon mocks the new ethos of the Social Democratic Party by depicting the 1 May demonstration under the banner of economic growth. Instead of red flags, we see the flags of Telia, the newly privatised Swedish telephone company, in which some one million Swedes have now invested by buying stocks (popularly called *folkaktier* – people's stocks).

Source: Leif Zetterling

Yet, this very editorial was, of course, nothing if not a celebration of national prowess, of Sweden as, yet again, the most modern and most successful of nations. The People's Home is Dead – Long Live the People's Home.

Notes

*   An early version of this paper was funded through and presented to the Convenor Group on Challenges to Sovereignty at the Center of German and European Studies and the Center of Slavic and East European Studies, both at the University of California, Berkeley. I would also like to appreciatively acknowledge grants given by the American-Scandinavian Foundation and Barnard College, as well as additional assistance provided by the Copenhagen Peace Research Institute, which made possible the subsequent research on which this article is based. I would also like to thank those who at various points have read and critiqued the manuscript: the members of the Convenor Group at Berkeley, the members of the Willen seminar at Barnard College, Roland Anrup, Henrik Berggren, Erik Berglöf, Pascale Montadert, Lisa Tiersten and last but not least my indefatigable editor, Lene Hansen.

1   This split often takes a regional form, pitting the urban(e) modernists against the
    rural rustics. This was dramatically evident in the Swedish case, with the yes-voters
    concentrated in Stockholm, Gothenburg and the populous south, while the rural
    hinterlands, including the sparsely populated northern two-thirds of Sweden, voted
    massively 'no'.
2   Indeed, even the French came very close to voting no in the Maastricht referendum.
3   See, for example, the European Commission (1999: 41–3), which indicates that the
    Swedes are more unhappy with the EU than are the citizens of any other member state.
    Also see Barkman (1999) in which the author reports on the findings from *Eurobarometer*
    no. 50, which indicates that the Swedes and the British are those who are most attached
    to their national, as opposed to European, identity.
4   The concept *folkstat*, that is, 'people's state', was used by leading Social Democrats in
    Sweden, influenced by the Germans, before it was replaced by the 'warmer', more
    communitarian notion of *folkhem*. See for example Engberg (1945: 307).
5   'Den lilla patriotism, som vi kunna igenfinna hos vårt svenska folk, har varit av den
    gamla arten, från 1600-talet: nationalstoltheten. Däremot har vårt folk helt och hållet
    gått miste om hvad man under 1800-talet menat med nationell väckelse. Denna
    folkens instinktiva strävan att i hvarje lifsyttring gifva uttryck åt sitt eget innersta väsen,
    det har varit något för oss obekant' (Sundbärg 1911: 3).
6   The Goths were one of the nomadic tribes that invaded Europe during the time when
    the Roman Empire went into terminal decline. Swedish writers, beginning with
    Johannes Magnus in his *Historia de omnibus gothorum sveonumque* (1554), constructed a
    rather fantastic tale to the effect that the Goths originally came from Sweden (along
    with much else that was great and good . . .).
7   Ingens herre, ingens träl: Det var Göthers Ära. Pråligt namn och Titlars gräl, Må en
    Narr besvära. Wara Fri är Manna-dygd, Fri, Fri, Fri i Göthers bygd! Det är Karlars
    Ära.
8   När Engelbrekt stod up i harm, Och sade: Bröder, Nej! Hvar Nidings dolk se mot vår
    Barm! Strax Nordens hjeltars Ätt blef varm, och hundratusend Bönders Arm Svor,
    sträckt mot himlen: Nej Då har han dessa Orden sagt, på ädelt Bonde-sätt: All Sveriges
    Magt är Folkets Magt, All Rätt är Folkets rätt.
9   As with many other national myths, this is a story that contains a measure of truth. The
    Swedish peasants were indeed unique in that they not only kept the land, escaped
    feudalism and serfdom, but even retained political representation both at the national
    level – as the fourth estate – and at the local, village level – in the form of self-
    government. As Michael Roberts (1967: 4–5) has put it: 'It may well be true that the
    idealization of the yeoman peasant by such writers as E. G. Geijer has been proved
    to have but a shaky historical basis', yet in the final analysis 'it is still safe to say that
    the peasant in medieval Sweden retained his social and political freedom to a greater
    degree, played a greater part in the politics of the country, and was altogether a more
    considerable person, than in any other western European country.'
10 *Allmoge, allmogen* refers to the peasants, the 'little' people.
11 Lidforss is well known for his anti-Semitic views.
12 The quote from Lidforss is taken from Staffan Björk (1946), and in the footnote where
    he cites this quote Björk furthermore observes that 'Social democratic propaganda often
    made use of Engelbrekt.' And this is in reference to the period around 1900, which
    again suggests the deep roots of this left-wing, national discourse (Björk 1946: 344).
13 In practice many Swedish Social Democrats were from the very outset both nationally
    minded and pro-statist, reflecting both the stability of the Swedish state and the legacy
    of inclusion of the lower estates. Nonetheless the party was during its first few decades
    under the heavy influence of the German Social Democrats and it was only during the
    1920s that they began to elaborate a more resolutely autonomous position in their
    ideological and theoretical writings. Furthermore, during the early decades of the

party's history, the state was relatively hostile to the workers' movement and most workers were still denied the right to vote. Thus the importance of the suffrage reform of 1920.

14 Also the Foucauldian turn within social science has meant that more research has been done on the 'discipline and punish' aspects of the welfare state as a 'normalising' project. See, for example, the various dissertations coming out of Tema Barn at the University of Linköping under the leadership of Bengt Sandin.

15 I am making a broad, comparative and structural argument here, and in doing so I perhaps exaggerate the weakness of the Swedish nobility. As Michael Roberts, Nils Runeby and others have shown, the aristocracy was at times quite powerful, not least during the seventeenth century before Charles XI famously cut the power of the nobles through the so-called 'reduction' scheme, whereby the Crown re-appropriated a large portion of the land granted to the nobles during the previous century. Furthermore, during the eighteenth century – the so-called 'Age of Liberty' – the nobles dominated the parliament at the time when the Crown was relatively weak. Nonetheless, even then the peasants retained their freedoms and even increased their land-holdings. In the final analysis, especially from a comparative perspective, my point stands.

16 Not that Swedish leftists are particularly comfortable with being branded as nationalists. Indeed, the nationalism of the Swedish left is largely unspoken, even invisible, hidden behind a discourse on the welfare state, *folkhemmet*, solidarity, equality, etc. This is made all the more plausible since nationalism in Sweden is, in its left-wing as well as right-wing versions, so intimately tied to the state, more than to notions of race or culture.

17 That is, one might speculate that had the national narrative – as was the case in Germany – posited a tension between democratic values and the 'essence' of the national spirit, one could imagine that he would have chosen the nation over democracy.

18 The conservative genealogy and connotations of the *folkhem* concept in fact disturbed some leading Social Democrats. Thus Arthur Engberg, a future minister, wrote in 1929 a series of articles criticising Per Albin Hansson for his usage of the 'new' concept, and he specifically referred to Kjellén's earlier and, in Engberg's view, highly suspect use of that same term (Engberg 1929).

19 The centrality of law in Swedish society has often been noted. The fact that the peasants themselves formed the jury and used the courts to a great extent deepened the respect for the law. Since no one was above the law, it was not viewed merely as an instrument of administration or oppressive exercise of power from above. For a discussion of these and related issues, see Eva Österberg (1992).

20 For an analysis of the origins and early development of Swedish 'neutralism' and the peace movement, see Bert Mårald (1974).

21 An alternative version of the 'four Ks' is *konservativa europa, kapitalets europa, kartellernas europa och det katolska europa* (Conservative Europe, the Europe of Capital(ism), the Europe of the Cartels, and Catholic Europe) (Misgeld 1990; Stråth 1992: 208).

22 Interestingly, the syndicalists were among the few groups in Sweden who supported the idea of a united Europe after 1945. The syndicalists were in favour of a large federal order with power devolved downwards to the local level. They criticised the Social Democrats for both their statism and their nationalism (Malmborg 1994: 138–40).

23 In fact, while I am not familiar with any quantitative research on this matter, the perception that Swedish academia is dominated by, if not a leftist intelligentsia, at least by professional academics more or less closely affiliated with the Social Democratic Party, is probably not too far off the mark, particularly in the social sciences. At any rate, the Timbro Institute has provided diversity to an intellectual milieu sorely lacking in pluralism.

24 See, for example, the chapter on 'A dynamic Europe' in the 'Book of facts' put out by the Conservatives, in which the EU is associated with faster economic growth, while

economic stagnation and high rates of unemployment are traced to 'inflexible labour markets' particularly characteristic of 'countries which have for long periods of time been ruled by socialist governments' (Moderaterna 1994).

25 After decades of very low unemployment, the rate jumped from 1.8 per cent in 1990 to 9.8 per cent in 1994, not counting those who were in various types of labour market programmes.

26 This notion drew on Francis Fukuyama's influential 'end of history' thesis (Fukuyama 1992).

27 'We in Sweden have much to learn and gain from membership in the EU, but we also have much to offer. Our experience and know-how when it comes to labour market policies, gender equality, environmental policies, the workplace environment, anti-drug policies, means that we arrive far from empty-handed' (Westerberg 1994: 28).

28 During a *Kvinnor Kan* ('Women know how to') convention in 1994, when he was offered this honour by Ann-Britt Grunewald.

29 A kind of snuff tobacco that is peculiar to Sweden.

30 The cherished right of all Swedes to wander freely in nature, even on privately owned land.

31 Prior to the rise of the Swedish Greens (Miljöpartiet), the Centre Party was home to the environmentalists and the 'back to nature' movement, dating back to the 1970s (Holmberg 1998).

32 Due to this split, the party leadership chose to play it safe by largely remaining outside the limelight during the debate. As one commentator noted: 'The Centre Party chairman, Olof Johansson, made himself almost invisible' (S. Svensson 1994: 2).

33 The Kalmar Union was the union of Denmark, Norway and Sweden under the Danish Crown that was formed in 1397, against which Engelbrekt led a successful rebellion in 1434.

34 Also see Vänsterpartiet (1994b: 14–15). For another EU critical view on the neutrality issue, see Agrell (1992). Also see Åström (1999).

35 Another leading no-voice among the Social Democrats was Margareta Winberg.

36 See for example Carl Lidbom (1994a), even though Lidbom too, ultimately, is encouraging a more offensive approach to the EU.

37 The notion bandied about by the Conservatives and the Liberals, that in the post-Socialist era, there was only one way, that of liberal democracy and the free market.

38 In particular a document produced jointly by the EU Social Democrats – 'Put Europe to work' ('Sätt Europa i arbete') – was cited. See also Larsson (1994a, 1994b and 1994c) and Blomberg (1994).

39 For examples of how the Left Party explicitly denied the validity of this argument, see their pamphlet (Vänsterpartiet 1994c).

40 Astrid Lindgren, cited by Lindbom, is the much loved and highly influential author of children's books, who in this context became known for her passionate support of animal rights and her critique of the treatment of slaughter animals in the EU. On Sweden, EU and the treatment of animals from an EU critical perspective, see Per Jensen (1992).

41 Jørgensen did not discuss the cases of the Norwegians or the Finns in this interview. However, the Norwegian debate on the EU is in this context even more defensive than the Danish, since many Norwegians appear to be highly sensitive when it comes to the discourse on 'union' due to their self-understanding as a newly liberated former Danish and Swedish colony.

42 Announcement from the Executive committee of the Social Democratic Party from 14 January 2000.

43 Talk given by Östros on 18 February 2000 at the Swedish Consulate General in New York.

178   *Lars Trägårdh*

References

Adlerbeth, J. (1845) 'Stiftelseurkunden jemte stadgarna för det göthiska förbundet', *Iduna*, 11.

Agrell, W. (1992) 'Farväl till svensk neutralitet', in W. Agrell *EG/EU – till vilket pris?*, Stockholm: LTs förlag.

Åkerman, N. (1994) 'EU avskaffar vår välfärdsstat', *Dagens Nyheter*, 16 October.

Andrén, N. (1975) 'Sweden and Europe', *Cooperation and Conflict*, 10.

Antman, P. and Thorvaldsson, K.-P. (1994) *Hur förena jämlikhet med individens frihet?: om välfärdens mål och organisering*, Stockholm: Brevskolan, LO.

Arbøl, N. (1992) *Ett nytt Europa: Kristdemokrater visar vägen*, Stockholm: Samhällsgemenskapens förlags AB.

Åström, S. (1999) 'Neutralitet dödförklarat som begrepp', *Dagens Nyheter*, 20 June.

Barkman, C. (1999) 'Svensken ingen europé', *Dagens Nyheter*, 4 October.

Bengtsson, J. (1992) 'Statsförbundet Norden – ett alternativ till Europeiska unionen', in W. Agrell, *EG/EU – till vilket pris?*, Stockholm: LTs förlag.

—— (1993) *Alternativ till EG: Ge Norden en chans!*, Hudiksvall: Alternativ till EG.

Berggren, H. (1993) 'I skuggan av det förflutna', *Moderna Tider* 37, 4.

—— (1995) *Seklets ungdom*, Stockholm: Tiden.

Bildt, C. (1991a) 'Sweden – from a Reluctant to an Enthusiastic European', remarks made at the office of the Commission of the European Communities in Bonn, 12 November.

—— (1991b) *Hallänning, svensk, europé*, Stockholm: Bonniers.

Björk, S. (1946) *Heidenstam och sekelskiftets Sverige*, Stockholm: Natur och Kultur.

Blanck, A. (1911) *Den nordiska renässansen i sjuttonhundratalets litteratur*, Stockholm: Bonnier.

—— (1918) *Geijer's Götiska diktning*, Stockholm: Bonnier.

Blomberg, L. (1994) 'Arbetarrörelsen måste ta ansvar för utformningen av EU-politiken', *Svenska Dagbladet*, 1 March.

Carlgren, A. and Hansson, K. (1994) 'Folkomrösta om varje EU-steg', *Dagens Nyheter*, 21 November.

Carlsson, I. (1994) *Riksdagens protokoll 1994/95: 28*, 23 November, Stockholm: Swedish Parliament.

Childs, M. (1936) *Sweden: The Middle Way*, New Haven, Conn.: Yale University Press.

Cullberg, J. (1942) 'Den svenska linjen', *Svensk Tidskrift*.

Dahl, H. F. (1984) 'Those Equal Folk', *Dædalus* 113, 1.

Einhorn, J. (1994) 'Ett ännu viktigare val', *Dagens Nyheter*, 23 September.

Ekström, T., Myrdal, G. and Pålsson, R. (1962) *Vi och Västeuropa*, Stockholm: Raben & Sjögren.

Engberg, A. (1929) 'Folkhemmet', *Social-Demokraten*, 15 September.

—— (1945) 'Fosterlandskärleken', *Tal och skrifter*.

Eriksson, M. (1993) *Är EG en kvinnofälla?*, Göteborg: Nej till EG.

European Commission (1999) *Eurobarometer*, March.

Expressen, editorial, 16 May 2000.

Financial Times 'Country Focus: Nordic Region', 25 January 2000.

Frykman, J. (1991) 'Modernitet som svensk mentalitet', in W. Agrell (ed.) *Nationell säkerhet utan gränser*, Stockholm: Allmänna förlaget.

Fukuyama, F. (1992) *The End of History and the Last Man*, New York: The Free Press.

Gahrton, P. (1994) *Handbok för EU-tvivlare*, Stockholm: Ordfronts förlag.

Geijer, E. G. (1811) 'Manhem' and 'Odalbonden', *Iduna*, 1.

—— (1845) 'Berättelse om Götiska Förbundets stiftelse och verksamhet', *Iduna*, 11.

—— (1923) *Samlade Skrifter, Del 1: Essayer och avhandlinger 1803–1817*, Stockholm: Norstedt.

Göteborgs Handels- och Sjöfartstidning 1896, no. 83.

Göteborgs Handels- och Sjöfartstidning 1959, no. 81.

Greider, G. (1993) 'Jag tror på nationalstaten', *Kritiska Europafakta*, no. 26, Göteborg: Nej till EG.

Gyllenborg, G. F. (1759) 'Vinterqvädet', in *Årstiderna*.

Habermas, J. (1989) *The Structural Transformation of the Public Sphere*, Cambridge, Mass.: MIT Press.

Hamilton, C. B. (1994) 'Högre arbetslöshet om vi inte går med i EU', *Dagens Nyheter*, 3 March.

Hansson, P. A. (1926) *Sverige åt svenskarna – svenskarna åt Sverige*, Stockholm: Tiden.

—— (1935a) 'Folk och klass', in *Demokrati*, Stockholm: Tiden.

—— (1935b) 'Nordisk demokrati', in *Demokrati*, Stockholm: Tiden.

—— (1935c) 'Land skall med lag byggas', in *Demokrati*, Stockholm: Tiden.

—— (1935d) 'På bondens dag', in *Demokrati*, Stockholm: Tiden.

—— (1935e) 'Frihet och självtukt', in *Demokrati*, Stockholm: Tiden.

—— (1935f) 'Demokrati eller diktatur', in *Demokrati*, Stockholm: Tiden.

—— (1935g) 'Tal till Sveriges flagga', in *Demokrati*, Stockholm: Tiden.

Henningson, B. (1961) *Geijer som historiker*, Uppsala: Svenska bokförlaget.

Hessler, C. A. (1937) *Geijer som politiker*, Uppsala: Geber.

—— (1943) '*Aristokratifördömandet*', Särtr. ur Scandia 15.

Holmberg, C. (1998) *Längtan till landet*, Göteborg: Historiska Institutionen vid Göteborgs Universitet (Avhandlinger från Historiska Institutionen i Göteborg nr 20).

Holmberg, M. (1994) 'Gallskrik och kaos i jalägret', *Dagens Nyheter*, 14 November.

Jacobsson, K. (1997) *Så gott som demokrati*, Umeå: Boréa.

Jenkins, D. (1969) *Sweden: The Progress Machine*, London: Robert Hale.

Jensen, P. (1992) 'Sverige, EG, djurhållningen och maten', in W. Agrell, *EG/EU – till vilket pris?*, Stockholm: LTs förlag.

Johansson, S. (1994) 'EU vill ha arbetslöshet', *Dagens Nyheter*, 20 January.

Jørgensen, K. S. (2000) in an interview on Swedish Radio P1, 'God morgon världen', 30 April.

Karlbom, R. (1993) 'Lång svensk folkstyrelsetradition', in *Kritiska Europafakta*, no. 26, Göteborg: Nej till EG.

Karlsson, K. and Torstensson, G. (1995) *Schengen – Öppna gränser för knarket och höga murar mot flyktingar*, Göteborg: Folkrörelsen nej till EU.

Kjellén, R. (1912) *Politiska Essayer*, vol. 1, Stockholm: Geber.

—— (1915) *Politiska Essayer*, vol. 2, Stockholm: Geber.

Koblik, S. (ed.) (1975) *Sweden's Development from Poverty to Affluence*, Minneapolis: University of Minnesota Press.

Kokk, E. (1962) 'Världen, vi och Västeuropa', in *Förändringens vind*, Stockholm: Raben & Sjögren.

Koselleck, R. (1988) *Critique and Crisis*, Cambridge, Mass.: MIT Press.

Larsson, A. (1994a) 'Europa överger den enda vägen', *Dagens Nyheter*, 9 September.

—— (1994b) 'Folkomröstning kräver inte tystnad', *Dagens Nyheter*, 27 February.

—— (1994c) 'Tänk om, Sten Johansson', *Dagens Nyheter*, 29 January.

Lawler, P. (1997) 'Scandinavian Exceptionalism and European Union', *Journal of Common Market Studies* 4, 35: 565–94.

Lidbom, C. (1994a) 'Fel syn på EU inoms', *Dagens Nyheter*, 5 August.

—— (1994b) 'Förödmjukande utanförskap', *Dagens Nyheter*, 11 November.

Lindström, R. (1928a) *Socialism, nation och stat*, Eskilstuna: Folket.

—— (1928b) *Flaskbarnet: En skrift om Sveriges nationella ungdomsförbund och dess verksamhet*, Eskilstuna: Folket.

Lönnroth, E. (1943) 'Den svenska riksdagens uppkomst', *Scandia*.

Magnus, J. (1554) *Historia de omnibus gothorum sveonumque*.

Malmborg, M. af (1994) *Sverige och den västeuropeiska integrationen 1945–1959*, Lund: Lund University Press.

Månsson, S. and Backman, S. (1993) *Bordell Europa*, Göteborg: Nej till EG.

Mårald, B. (1974) *Den svenska freds- och neutralitetsrörelsens uppkomst*, Stockholm: Akademiförlaget.

Misgeld, K. (1990) 'Den svenska socialdemokratin och Europa från slutet av 1920-talet till början av 1970-talet', in B. Huldt and K. Misgeld (eds) *Socialdemokratin och svensk utrikespolitik: från Branting till Palme*, Stockholm: Utrikespolitiska Institutet.

Moderaterna (the Conservative Party) (1994) *Ja: en faktabok om moderaterna i Europa*, Stockholm.

Newsweek (2000) 'Stockholm: Hot IPOs and Cool Clubs in Europe's Internet Capital', *Newsweek*, 7 February (international edition).

Odhner, C.-E. (1962) *Sverige i Europa*, Stockholm: Raben & Sjögren.

Odhner, C. T. (1902) *Lärobok i fädernslandets historia*, Stockholm: Nya tiden.

Ohlsson, P. T. (1993) *Gudarnas ö: om det extremt svenska*, Stockholm: Bromberg.

Öhrström, L. (1994) 'Främlingsrädsla färgar EU-frågan', *Dagens Nyheter*, 5 January.

Österberg, E. (1992) 'Folklig mentalitet och statlig makt', *Scandia*, no. 58.

Östros, T. (2000) Talk given by Östros at the Swedish Consulate General in New York on 18 February.

Palme, O. (1971) *Riksdagens protokoll*, no. 137, 2 December, Stockholm: Swedish Parliament.

—— (1982) 'Sweden's role in the World', in B. Rydén and W. Bergström (eds) *Sweden: Choices for Economic and Social policy in the 1980's*, London: Allen and Unwin.

Roberts, M. (1967) *Essays in Swedish History*, Minneapolis: University of Minnesota Press.

Rojas, M. (1994) 'Invandrarna behövs i EU', *Dagens Nyheter*, 4 November.

Rousseau, Jean-J. (1968) *The Social Contract*, New York: Penguin.

Ruth, A. (1984) 'The Second New Nation: The Mythology of Modern Sweden', *Dædalus* 113, 1.

Ryner, J. M. (1998) *Neoliberal Globalization and the Crisis of Swedish Social Democracy*, Working Paper SPS no. 98/4, Florence: European University Institute.

Schück, H. (1916) *Engelbrekt*, Stockholm: Gebers.

Stråth, B. (1992) *Folkhemmet mot Europa*, Stockholm: Tiden.

Sundbärg, G. (1911) *Det svenska folklynnet*, Stockholm.

Svenska Dagbladet (1976) 13 September.

—— (1989) 13 July, p. 3.

Svensson, A. (1994) *Riksdagens protokoll 1994/95: 28*, 23 November, Stockholm: Swedish Parliament.

Svensson, S. (1994) 'Swedes Vote Yes to Membership in the EU', *Current Sweden*, no. 408.

Taylor, C. (1994) *Multiculturalism*, Princeton, NJ: Princeton University Press.

Thomasson, R. (1970) *Sweden: Prototype of Modern Society*, New York: Random House.

Thorild, T. (1819–1824) *Thomas Thorilds samlade skrifter, vols 1–3*, ed. Erik Gustaf Geijer, Uppsala and Stockholm.

Tilton, T. (1990) *The Political Theory of Swedish Social Democracy: Through the Welfare State to Socialism*, Oxford: Clarendon Press.

Trägårdh, L. (1990) 'Varieties of Volkish Ideologies', in B. Stråth (ed.) *Language and the Construction of Class Identities*, Göteborg: Dept of History, Gothenburg University.

—— (1993) 'The Concept of the People and the Construction of Popular Political Culture in Sweden and Germany, 1800–1933', unpublished dissertation, University of California at Berkeley.

—— (1995) *Civilt samhälle kontra offentlig sektor*, Stockholm: SNS.

—— (1997) 'Statist Individualism: On the Culturality of the Nordic Welfare State', in B. Stråth and Ø. Sørensen (eds) *The Cultural Construction of Norden*, Oslo: University of Oslo Press.

—— (1999) 'Det civila samhället som analytiskt begrepp och politisk slogan', in E. Amnå (ed.) *Civilsamhället*, Stockholm: SOU.

Tunhammar, G. (1994) 'Folkomrösta i juni', *Dagens Nyheter*, 7 January.

Vänsterpartiet (1994a) *Alternativ till EU-medlemskap*. Stockholm: Vänsterpartiet.

—— (1994b) *Program för en alternativ europapolitik*, Stockholm: Vänsterpartiet.

—— (1994c) *Europeiska Unionen: socialistiskt eller nyliberalt projekt?* Stockholm: Vänsterpartiet.

—— (1994d) *Frågor och svar om EU nr. 2: Kvinnorna och EU*, Stockholm: Vänsterpartiet.

—— (1994e) *Frågor och svar om EU nr. 3: Demokratin*, Stockholm: Vänsterpartiet.

Westerberg, B. (1994) *Riksdagens protokoll 1994/95: 28*, 23 November, Stockholm: Swedish Parliament.

Zaremba, M. (1987) 'Byalagets diskreta charm eller folkhemmets demokratiuppfattning', in Sekretariatet för Framtidsstudier, *Du sköna gamla värld*, Stockholm: FRN-Framtidsstudier.

—— (1992) *Minken i folkhemmet*, Stockholm: Timbro.

—— (1999) *De rena och de andra: om tvångssteriliseringar, rashygien och arvsynd*, Stockholm: DN.

6   Finland in the New Europe

A Herderian or Hegelian project?

Pertti Joenniemi

This chapter examines the background of Finland's linkage with Europe and European integration. The aim is, in particular, to enquire into the reasons for the ease with which re-orientation has taken place during recent years. Why is it that Finland stands out as the only one among the Nordic countries that has largely managed to stay aloof from the category of 'reluctant European'?

It is claimed that the answer resides mainly in Finland's history and the multiplicity of the national project. Finland appears, at first sight, rather integrated and with a tight state–nation nexus. However, it turns out – if studied over time – that both categories have a history of their own, the nation has preceded the state and there has been a considerable flexibility in their relationship. This flexibility stems to a large extent from a certain duality in the Finnish concept of the nation: it may be divided into a soft and cultural nation on the one hand and one linked to the power political state on the other. There is the *Kulturnation* as well as the *Staatsnation*. The former leans primarily on Herderian departures whereas the latter rests first and foremost on a Hegelian heritage. This duality allowed for a rethinking of nation and state on separate levels once 'Finland' was faced with the challenge of European integration. In this context, Finland's Nordic orientation is also explored and it is viewed – to some extent in contrast to the other Nordic countries – as one of the factors that adds to its flexibility and which underpins the loose territorial linkage that has been utilised in a further immersion in Europe.

An exceptional case

The ambivalence and popular disquiet that have over recent years marked both the Danish and Swedish relationship to the EU – not to mention those of Norway and Iceland – has not to any major degree been mirrored by the Finnish position. In fact, Finland stands out as the only Nordic country that has been able to assume a positive orientation to European integration without triggering the response that national identity is being threatened. There has therefore been little need for Finland – due to a relatively solid domestic support – to aspire to exemptions or foreclose participation in view of a deepening and broadening of European integration.

The active taking part and the policy of being an EU member who aims for a quite central position is something of a surprise considering that Finland preferred, during the years of the Cold War, to stay on the sidelines of European politics. Lining up with grand institutional endeavours has usually not been seen as a Finnish virtue; Finnishness has mostly been conceptualised as a culture of opposition and resistance, exemplified by the myth of Lalli – a figure articulating fierce opposition towards early efforts to bring Christianity to Finland. The legend of fighting bravely the Winter War against the Soviet Union strengthens similar images, and the low profile vis-à-vis Europe during the Cold War could thus be presented in positive terms as tapping into a longer Finnish tradition. For some time Finland participated in EFTA as an associate member and eventually concluded a free trade agreement with the EC in 1972. Economic necessities have traditionally been kept separate from more political and security-oriented concerns, and economic considerations have taken a secondary place if they have risked colliding with political ones. The line pursued remained rather cautious for a long time and was clearly less internationalist and engaged than the one adopted by the Nordics in general (Heiskanen 1988: 5).

Becoming an EU member was viewed, as late as the end of the 1980s, as inconceivable. Prime Minister Harri Holkeri, for one, found reason to stress in November 1990 that 'Finland's neutrality constitutes the corner stone in the protection of our living, our independence, our sovereignty and our national existence.' He concluded, arguing in quite traditional and state-centred terms, that 'submitting to the EU's foreign policy and giving in to the demands of a joint defence would imply that Finland voluntarily abandons its independence and becomes part of a major power' (cited by Pekonen 1993: 49).

Yet the issue of EU membership was injected into Finnish politics at the beginning of the 1990s. Somewhat unexpectedly – due to changes in the external environment – the country had to take a stand and the intention to apply for entrance was announced in March 1992. Actually, in a speech given in Bruges the same year President Koivisto went much further than Sweden in setting the terms for membership when he indicated that Finland was ready to accept the Maastricht Treaty on the European Union in total. It stands to reason – taking into account the past record – that Finland's rather swift and at least in some respects successful transition has been regarded, by many observers, as surprising. The prudence, patience and self-reliance often associated with Finland vanished into thin air. The sudden reversal of the policies pursued has thus been difficult to explain, at least if one stays with the rationalist and interest-based arguments commonly used in the context of analysing Finland's foreign and security policy.

Many of the explanations employed have been based on the idea that Finland has simply been escaping its past, that it wanted to liberate itself from its dependency on Moscow and the Soviet Union, and that it was therefore – in opting for a more secure future – eager to join the Union. It is argued that the previous *Ostpolitik* – with a wait-and-see attitude towards European integration – has been traded for a new *Westpolitik* to avoid any further abandonment by the West. The referendum yielding a clear support for membership has been interpreted, along these lines, as constituting a vote for the West in general and not specifically for the Maastricht Treaty. Securing a position within the Western camp has been seen as Finland's prime objective, and it has been held that a Western standing – which assures a certain form of protection – is more central than any politico-economic sub-stance (Arter 1995). It is argued along these lines that joining the EU was basically a decision taken by the foreign policy leadership and that it was executed in a centralised fashion. These rather state-centred explanations further tend to assume – at least implicitly – that 'the Finns' did not really know, nor cared to know, what the EU was in reality about; they wanted to be on board anyhow due to reasons of statist security and arriving 'home'. Becoming a member has been seen – by some observers – as weighing more heavily than utilising membership once part of the EU. This line of argument has also been conducive to doubts concerning Finland's preparedness to fully abide by the fundamentals of supranational integration.

These explanations seem, however, to rest, for the most part, on a set of problem-atic assumptions. The assertion that the foreign policy leadership made use of its centralised decision-making capacity seems to hold true to a considerable degree, but should also be placed in perspective. Holding a referendum reflected in and of itself a profound change in the previously highly elite-oriented foreign policy culture, and it showed that major foreign and security policy questions could no longer legitimately be decided by state leaders alone (Karvonen and Sundelius 1996: 258). The power to decide rested, in the end, with the nation rather than the state, and much suggests that the nation used this opportunity in a rather self-reliant manner, that is, people formed their opinion on terms of their own. As to the argument that the population went along with the leadership due to a lack of either knowledge or interest, the Finnish debate prior to the referendum seems to contradict such claims. A study by Pertti Pesonen shows that the Finns have been rather well informed – once the issue of European integration became acute – about the essence of the European Union (Pesonen 1998: 8). Second, the Finns did not simply follow 'the' leadership: a broad spectrum of alternatives were in fact presented within the political debate. Out of the major political parties the National Coalition (conservative) and the Social Democrats were clearly in favour of membership while the Agrarian Centre Party – then a major government party – adopted a more hesitant view. The Greens were deeply divided on the issue and the Left Alliance was clearly against joining the EU (Tiilikainen 1996: 119).

Issues pertaining to the past or identity-related concerns had a modest standing in the debate and the themes of security and defence did not stand out in any distinct way. Instead of arguing that Finland joined the Union due to reasons of security, one could claim that the move became possible with an increasing non-concern for statist and territorial security. Security turned less state-centred than previously, and as to the security of the nation – which had become the prime concern – there was a cultural heritage and production which allowed that question to be dealt with.

Yet some state-related concerns became quite central. There were worries about the fate of Finnish 'independence' since sovereignty might be compromised within the EU. These doubts were countered by the pro-EU argument that Finland had, in fact, always associated itself with Western values, such as liberal democracy and market economy, and EU membership was therefore a logical continuation of Finnish political traditions. The sceptics also expressed concern for the impact of membership on the welfare state, and the debate preceding the referendum became very much a discussion of various concrete issues such as the impact of EU membership on the standard of living, agriculture or employment. The discussion also reflected concerns about the loss of tax money, the high costs of membership, and the rather bureaucratic nature of the EU. Moreover, there was a keen interest in the amount of power that could be potentially exercised within the EU institutions as well as the additional influence gained by moving from participation in the European Economic Area (EEA) to full membership. Opposition was stronger among women who feared that membership would lead to a deterioration of their social and employment rights, and among those living in the northern parts of the country who feared discrimination as a result of the increasing centralisation of power that partnership in the EU would presumably entail (Tiilikainen 1996: 120). Instrumental concerns appear in sum to have been more central than nationalist arguments.

Since Finland became a member of the EU in 1995 it has become evident that the goal has not been to downplay the eastern dimension in an attempt to secure a position within the western camp. Contrary to what those explaining Finland's pro-EU attitude as a result of a wish to 'join the West' would lead one to believe, Finland's stance within the EU has not been one of either/or, but a 'both/and' searching for an option beyond a bifurcated East–West construction. This has shown itself most clearly in the area of foreign and security politics where the expression 'non-alignment and independent defence' has remained central despite membership of the Union. Finland accepts the recent decision to furnish the EU with a peacekeeping capacity, but remains reserved about endeavours of going further towards some forms of collective defence. When it comes to 'hard' security, Finland still prefers to remain aloof rather than become an integral part of the Western structures. The door to NATO has been open, but there has been a distinct lack of willingness to use that option. Hence the policies pursued do not give the impression of Finland being hampered or determined by the past in any narrow sense (Browning 1999). The commitments that flow from membership have not been viewed as something superficial and secondary to the (assumed) protection offered by the EU but have been regarded as a serious undertaking. Instead of alignment and NATO membership, various ideas of bridge-building towards the Baltic countries as well as towards Russia have come to the fore (Törnudd 1996). In its 1997 report on Finland's security policy, the government stressed that 'Finland has made an active contribution to the Union's joint strategy on Russia, which aims at building a lasting partnership between the Union and a democratic Russia' (Ministry of Foreign Affairs 1997). The attitudes have been quite pragmatic and EU membership *per se* does not appear to have a high value. The aim has mostly been articulated as one of counteracting marginality – or to put it differently, using the option of combining the peripheral with centrality once the opportunity emerges – and increasing Finland's own centrality to the extent that is possible for a small country located at the fringes of Europe. It has been thought that Finland should 'be part of where decisions are made'.

'Yes' to membership

The, by Nordic standards, pro-integration climate was evidenced – following an extensive debate – by a clear 'yes' with 57 per cent of the votes in favour of membership in the consultative referendum in October 1994. Parliamentary approval of membership followed in November, and after ratifications the treaty on accession to the European Union came into force at the beginning of 1995. In contrast to what the more traditional explanations could lead one to believe, the public support for membership has stood the test of being confronted with the realities of European integration. The support for membership has by and large remained at the same level, or declined only modestly: opinion has not tilted against the EU in the same fashion as in Sweden (Pesonen 1998: 12; Törnudd 1996: 62).

Finnish membership has, since the referendum, been taken for granted and there has been almost no discussion about revising the decision to join nor any successful attempts to question the legitimacy of Finland's membership. Instead attention is devoted to the various issues that flow from membership, such as the question of a joint European currency, and handling the Presidency of the Union during the latter half of 1999.

Popular backing has been strong enough for the government to announce that Finland would join the single currency by the 1999 deadline laid down by Maastricht. This stance was supported not only by the Conservatives and Social Democrats, but also by the Left Alliance and the Greens, the two additional members of the 'rainbow government'. In the case of the Left Alliance the decision was preceded by a vote among its membership indicating that the support for the integration process, including a deepening of the EU, has grown over time as the Left Alliance and the Greens were quite reserved about Finland's membership of the EU in the debate preceding the referendum in 1994.

The government's pursuit of a pro-integration policy within the EU has been legitimised by what has often been depicted as the substantial results Finland has achieved. For example, on the question of enlargement Finland worked in favour of Estonia's membership, as it was assumed that at least one Baltic country would be included among the front-runners; Sweden and Denmark on the other hand argued for the inclusion of all three Baltic countries. The recommendation of the Commission and the end result at the Luxembourg summit in December 1997 was to include Estonia in the first group of potential new members, in other words a decision which was closer to the Finnish than the Danish or the Swedish postures (Vesa 1998: 58), although the other two Baltic countries later qualified for candidacy. In the field of monetary issues, the Finnish currency turned out to be more stable than those of the other Nordic countries, and this has been seen – at least prior to the more recent decline in the value of the Euro – as another indication that the policies of active participation have yielded a dividend.

Another indication of success, regarded as quite important at least by its Finnish proponents, consists of the Northern Dimension initiative which was accepted by the European Council in December 1998. The foreign ministers of the Union came together – jointly with the Baltic countries, Poland, Iceland, Norway and Russia

– at an informal meeting in Helsinki in November 1999, and the EU's summit in Helsinki in December 1999 took stock of the results and asked the Commission to prepare an action plan – approved in Feira in June 2000 – with the aim of linking the TACIS (Technical Assistance to the Commonwealth of Independent States) programme closer to the Northern Dimension (Forsberg 1999). Sweden organised a similar high level meeting to review the results during its presidency in 2001.

The EU's adoption of the Northern Dimension shows that 'northernness' has been brought onto the EU's agenda. Such a signifier allows actors, in particular Finland, to assume a northern identity instead of choosing from a menu consisting only of easternness and westernness. At a more general level, Finland appears to have succeeded in initiating a discourse on the relationship between the EU and its periphery. This might allow Finland to become an active bridge-builder, instead of just remaining a bridge used by others, by inserting a concept on the European agenda which opens up for the advancement of cooperative relations in the northernmost parts of Europe. Particularly important in this respect might be the creation of future regional connections with Russia, that is, the opening up of a kind of backdoor for closer relations with the EU, allowing for parts of Russia to become Europeanised. The Union will, for its part, clarify the interests, policies and priorities in the region during the process that Finland has initiated (Ojanen 1999: 14–16).

The lack of popular disquiet and the air of self-confidence that have over the recent years characterised Finnish EU policies have attracted attention abroad, particularly in the neighbouring Nordic countries. 'Determined policies have for the first time since 1945 provided Finland with a core position in European politics – as the only Nordic country' argues Nils Morten Udgaard (1998), a foreign affairs specialist in the Norwegian daily *Aftenposten*. The Danish Prime Minister remarked in the context of the Danish referendum on the Amsterdam Treaty in June 1998 that if the outcome were 'no', Finland would turn into an increasingly important partner. He thought that Finland – due to its central position within the EU – could mediate crucial contacts. Major parts of the Swedish press – and particularly the political opposition – have highlighted Finnish achievements, occasionally even presenting Finland as an example which Sweden should follow. Not least the Finnish joining of the EMU has attracted attention. In view of the long-standing Swedish image of itself as the Nordic 'big brother', this change in perceptions is quite unprecedented. It has not been commonplace to argue in the Swedish debate that Finland would be more European, competent and more skilful in its policies than Sweden, rather to the contrary. A major Swedish daily went as far as arguing that the traditional roles seem to have been revised: Finland has turned into something of a role model for Sweden to copy in European politics.[1]

Explaining the Finnish case: elites, interests and identity

No doubt Finland's rather smooth transformation into a full-fledged European player within a relatively short period stands out as something unexpected.

However, besides the attention devoted to Finland in the Nordic media and policy world, the Finnish case has not attracted much research and the question of Finnish distinctiveness has not been singled out for any closer inspection and analysis. Research has so far mainly consisted of surveys covering the period of entrance and Finland's initial years as an EU member, and has been quite descriptive (Tiilikainen 1993 and 1996). Lauri Karvonen and Bengt Sundelius have been among those few scholars who have taken a more theoretical approach to the Finnish change (Karvonen and Sundelius 1996: 258). Their analysis singled out Finnish flexibility, and as an explanation of the rapid transformation they pointed to the skills of the Finnish foreign policy leadership. They argued that this leadership has, due to tradition, a centralised decision-making capacity which many state leaders would envy.

To take another example, Raimo Väyrynen (1993) examines the significance of elite bargains in the context of Finland joining the Union. He argues that the business elite took the initiative by investing in Western Europe during the 1980s thereby creating an interdependence which later pushed the political leadership into accepting the idea of membership. The deep economic crisis at the beginning of the 1990s exacerbated the need to integrate more closely with the European Community, to receive new impulses for the economy, to support the stability of the *markka* and, in the worst case, to bail out the Finnish economy (Väyrynen 1993: 44). The argument is, in short, that the leadership was forced by economic factors to accept the option of membership.

Väyrynen's interest-oriented argument certainly embraces a number of essential factors in Finland endorsing European accession. The growing economic inter-dependence that resulted from the policies pursued by the private sector, combined with the decline of the eastern market and the depth of the economic crisis that Finland encountered during the beginning of the 1990s narrowed down the options available to the political leadership. This explanation – part of liberal inter-governmentalism – might illuminate crucial reasons why Finland turned into a member country, but it fails to account for the active way in which the accession has been utilised. If the leadership was more or less forced into accepting member-ship, then what explains the manoeuvring of Finland into one of the front-runners of European integration policies once the threshold of membership had been passed? Economic imperatives or elite bargains alone can hardly explain this. Moreover, this explanation leaves questions about the popular mood unanswered. Denmark and Sweden are faced with largely similar structural conditions, but public opinion in those countries has stayed reserved about the process of European integration. Väyrynen's approach explains the orientation of the state and it covers some of the interplay among the political elites, but it appears to surpass the crucial impact of identity-related and cultural questions, and more broadly the state–nation nexus, on Finland's position towards the EU.

We can begin the analysis of the importance of these issues by examining Christine Ingebritsen and Susan Larson's effort to explain Finland's accession – and Norwegian resistance – to European integration (Ingebritsen and Larson 1997). Ingebritsen and Larson include interest-oriented factors as well as factors pertaining to national identity, and their comparative study highlights some distinct differences between the two countries. Their analysis departs from the fact that the political leaderships in both countries were confronted with well-organised interest groups, but notes that the process also entailed the introduction of new ideas into the domestic discourses as well as a redefinition of national identity. In the Finnish case the latter aspect was not much of a concern, they argue, and the debate could therefore focus on more practical and pragmatic issues of a political and economic nature. The Finns readily accepted, the two authors conclude, a reconstruction of their national identity as 'European'. They did not feel very European to start with, but they accepted that such an ingredient of Finnish identity would in all likelihood become increasingly important in the future as a precondition for an active participation in the construction of 'Europe'.

In the case of Finland, interest-based arguments could thus be combined with concerns for identity while the opposite turned out to be true for Norway. The Norwegian government had to withdraw its application for membership as interests and national identity clashed, thus yielding a 'no' in the referendum. The Norwegian debate showed a much stronger preoccupation with issues of identity with the no-side constructing the 'Union' as a threat to national identity. The conclusion offered by Ingebritsen and Larson is that 'Finns defined their interests as Europeans, whereas Norwegians were deeply divided about their relationship to Europe and Europeanness' (Ingebritsen and Larson 1997: 215). Finland and Norway differ in how they see themselves as nations in relation to the rest of Europe, and, in turn, how their national identity is affected by the EU. The relationship between Finnishness and Europeanness has a sufficient degree of complementarity whereas the relationship between Norwegianness and Europeanness is much more problematic. What looked positive and acceptable in Finland turned in many cases, viewed through the prism of identity, into something negative in Norway. Different images of identity provided different understandings of national interests with Finland having more leeway than Norway as the identity of the nation was not seen to be threatened. The two countries reacted differently when exposed to postmodern challenges which loosened up the state–nation relationship and provided room for other political categories to emerge on the political stage.

Ingebritsen and Larson's study no doubt embraces essential aspects of both Finland's accession to and the Norwegian rejection of the Union – and a similar analysis could perhaps be extended to cover Denmark and Sweden as well. Their approach is, furthermore, not in contradiction with Väyrynen's but complements it in crucial manner by going beyond liberal intergovernmentalism. Väyrynen's interest-oriented and rationalist approach which focuses on the postures and interplay within national elites can be broadened by combining it with Ingebritsen and Larson's non-materialistic factors.[2]

Another angle from which to pursue the importance of national identity is through the question of societal strength, or – employing the terminology of Barry Buzan, Ole Wæver and Jaap de Wilde (1998) – of societal security. Adopting this theory one could argue that the Finns felt sufficiently strong identity-wise to be able to cope with the idea of becoming part of the EU whereas the Norwegians were far more insecure on this score. The domestic sphere allowed and provided room for Finnish visions of a Europeanised future as these visions spurred rather than endangered the formation of an acceptable 'self'. The opposite turned out to be true in the case of Norway and to a lesser extent in the case of Denmark and Sweden where reconciling national identities with Europeanness has been a more difficult endeavour. It could hence be argued that the Finnish 'secret' underlying the active EU policies consists of a kind of societal strength which implies that issues pertaining to identity have not become central, at least not in a negative manner. Or to articulate it in the terminology used by Ole Wæver: the society has not become securitised independently of the state (Wæver 1995). This line of argument does not imply, however, that identity constitutes something less significant for the Finns, nor does it mean that Finnish national identity would be somehow fixed and strong in the sense of being insensitive to any impulses from the external environment. Issues pertaining to identity are certainly important and significant for the Finns, even if the move towards Europe does not appear to undermine societal security.

The Finnish state is allowed to aspire to closer links with Europe and take part in the process of integration as the nation feels sufficiently at home, although at a different level, in the new Europe. This implies that not only the concept of the state but also that of the Finnish nation may resonate – or at least not clash – with 'Europe'. Being increasingly confronted with the task of relating to 'Europe' does not force the nation to deny its vision of itself. The flexibility and ability of the nation to cope with an increasing number of impulses from the external environment has enabled the state to pursue rather active Europe-oriented policies, and the European platform has been used without the state being drastically inhibited by the nation feeling destabilised or threatened.

The line of argument pursued by Ingebritsen and Larson pays attention to the fact that the burden of adaptation does not only rest with the state; it equally concerns the nation, and the Finnish case seems to confirm Etienne Tassin's argument that '[T]he struggle for Europe begins with a struggle inside each nation' (Tassin 1992: 189). Finland appears to have been able, with regard to these inner struggles over national identity under changing circumstances, to cope with a considerable number of challenges both at the level of the state and at the level of the nation.

A break with the past

This, then, raises the question why. Why does the Finnish nation not want to better shield itself from any closer linkages to 'Europe', and what explains the ease of the relationship?

It appears that issues of identity have not turned into a major concern within the debate over European integration, neither before nor after the referendum. Finland has not been deprived of any central symbols, there have been no major debates about the need to preserve its identity, to shield its culture or to cling to institutions which are deemed essential for the country to remain 'Finland'. The issue has been mentioned, but the atmosphere has not been an alarmed one and the 'No to the EU' movement, which had some success in the context of the referendum in 1994, has since led a shadowy existence. A rather straightforward and instrumental approach combined with an ability to accept 'facts' – sometimes linked with Finnishness – seems to yield results. And yet there is a radical break with the past. The need to define much more concretely and inclusively the country's position vis-à-vis European integration is one aspect of a broader challenge to redefine itself internationally after the demise of the Cold War and the disappearance of the Soviet Union. Significant changes have also occurred within the domestic setting with the remnants of a class society giving place to a rather diffuse but extensive and omnipresent middle class.

The necessity to adapt to the existence of a problematic big power neighbour has declined, and the link between the external and the internal settings – which used to be rather central and tightly controlled – has become quite diffuse. The previously very strong nexus between the state and the nation may be questioned and doubts can also be raised about the tradition to aspire to a broad consensus – in general and in the sphere of foreign affairs in particular – and the habit of incorporating, if possible, any deviant views. These alterations could be interpreted as signs of increasing disorder and fragmentation, but they can also be viewed as liberating oneself from previous straitjackets and demands for conformity.

Both possible interpretations are, it seems, to some extent valid. There are worries that 'Finland is such a young nation-state that even signs of minor fragmentation cause concerns among those located at the centre of the culture' (Allardt 1988: 30), but the views in favour of liberation seem nevertheless a bit stronger. Although it is somewhat difficult to offer very generalised conclusions on the basis of a plurality of trends it can, for example, be observed that attitudes towards refugees and immigrants have become more relaxed and there is a promotion rather than a restriction of regional initiatives which illustrates a move towards more decentralised political structures. Other political levels than just the state level have been gaining ground. In becoming increasingly oriented towards the international, the state appears to be interested in turning over a number of tasks to sub-national actors. Boundaries that were previously divided have in many cases been transformed into interfaces which unite rather than separate. Importantly, the Karelian question – a border dispute between Finland and Russia – has been constructively reopened through a de-sacralisation of territory. This has allowed the issue to transform – albeit the debate continues – from a divisive, statist territorial dispute into a matter of transborder cooperation. The latter aspiration provides Finland with a porous (although still regulated) eastern border, and this trend is apparent along the eastern border more generally. Various 'soft' kinds of security issues enter the agenda but they do not imply a return to previous territorially based constellations as most of them have to be tackled by cooperation across the border (Joenniemi 1998).

Some questions have nonetheless surfaced about the very meaning of 'Finland'. The intelligentsia who have historically occupied a core position in the construction of 'Finland' have experienced a loss as the dual tasks of safeguarding the statist relations in view of the challenges posed first by Russia and later by the Soviet Union, and of mediating between the state and the nation have declined in importance. The meaning of Finland as a project and the intelligentsia's central location is no longer taken for granted in the same way as before. What was understood as a mission of historical proportions is no longer there. Risto Alapuro, a Finnish sociologist, depicts the process – in very broad terms – as a story of modernisation that has been drastically undermined (Alapuro 1989: 204).

This implies that questions such as 'who are "we" and what is "our" place in the new context' have to be addressed in a new fashion. One has to step beyond the previously tight state–nation nexus, and this also opens up new tasks for the intelligentsia. The state does not offer the same firm anchorage as before and the previous consensus pertaining to the nexus between neutrality and independence is becoming less credible and interesting. While the independence of the country and national identity were for long maintained by the rather strict moves of exclusion, with Finland being defined by what it was not, the basic move in the new Europe consists increasingly of inclusion. For Finns one would assume this to be a particularly tough challenge, given the creed of the Finnish national movement, as formulated in the nineteenth century by one of its leaders in a terse sentence, 'We are no longer Swedes, we do not want to become Russians, so let us be Finns' (Jakobson 1992: 1; Joenniemi 1993a: 36). Now this double negative and position in-between has, it seems, been substituted with a far more positive and inclusive approach towards Europe, but it still leaves us with the question as to how this was so easily accomplished.

The construction of a nation

The process of Europeanisation involves challenges to traditional notions of sovereignty, and as a consequence questions often emerge about the bond between the state and the nation. In the Finnish case this bond has traditionally been understood to be quite tight, and seen as natural and organic in essence. It is also telling that the concepts of nation, people and citizen are quite undifferentiated in linguistic terms (*kansakunta, kansa, kansalainen*), although it may be noted that the nation (*kansakunta*) appears to have derived from people (*kansa*). These properties have made 'Finland' resistant towards efforts of deconstruction. The concepts of state and nation have been fused to such a degree that it has appeared meaningless to tear them apart and present them as two separate spheres with different histories.

A closer analysis reveals, however, that the two concepts are indeed distinct from each other and have their separate historical backgrounds. Both the nation and the state are in the Finnish case relatively young, although the nation precedes the (Finnish) state. As there was no Finnish state to start with, the endeavour turned into one of writing the history of the nation (with people as the key organising concept). This development has not, however, been a linear one, despite the advancement of such arguments (Alapuro 1988), nor does the nation date back to some ancient history as nationalistic historians have claimed. Finland is, in fact, one of the youngest nations and nation-states among current EU members.

The construction of the Finnish nation took place at the beginning of the nineteenth century when the opportunity as well as the need to launch a national project surfaced after the Finnish War of 1808–9 waged between Sweden and Russia.

Consequently, the Finns could abandon the Swedish *riket*. A new entity emerged, largely with the consent of the local elite, as the previously Swedish province became a part of Tsarist Russia. Up until that point the Finns – to the extent that the concept of 'Finns' was there in the first place – had been Finnish-speaking inhabitants of Sweden.

The new ruler, Emperor Alexander I, lent his support to the idea of a Finnish nation and established the Grand Duchy at the diet in Porvoo (Borgå). He solemnly proclaimed the elevation of the Finnish people to the rank of a nation and promised to respect the culture, habits and the institutions of the new entity, and Finland was thus granted an autonomous position under the Emperor's personal rule. The aim of providing the Finns with leeway was not, however, a reflection of the Emperor's liberal inclinations; there were political motivations involved. Tsarist Russia had an interest in borders being drawn against Sweden in the sphere of identities as well as territorially, and there was also a need for some window dressing vis-à-vis the rest of Europe – Finland could potentially mediate and channel Central European economic and cultural experiences into the relatively backward Russia which was dearly in need of such stimulus. Russia's *Realpolitik* motivation has been seen as one of pacifying a newly conquered territory by granting it political concessions at a time when the turmoil of the Napoleonic Wars made the European situation unstable. Moreover, there was space for yet another entity in the context of a multi-national Russia as the Russian empire was not about producing homogeneity and displacing local identities.

This opportunity was swiftly utilised by the Finns. One of the aims of the Finnish political elite was to create a central administration of its own, to preserve the governing bodies and laws that originated with the Swedish rule and to attain a national economy which was prosperous enough to provide a certain standard of living for the people in the duchy. It also wanted to hook into the western market, penetrate the Russian one and – if possible – mediate between Russia and the rest of Europe (Paasivirta 1978). All this sought to single out Finland as something special within the Russian state. This 'special' was articulated above all through language and literature: *Kalevala*, a collection of folk poems in the Finnish language that provided the nation with a mythical 'Golden Age', achieved a considerable standing. But there was little room for conceptual expansion and self-articulation in any statist sense. An open call for a politically independent Finland would have been in danger of running into severe difficulties: Finland could not explicitly take the form of a (political) state as this would immediately have clashed with the Russian one. The new entity could, however, cautiously link up with certain modern ideas, among them nationality as represented by a certain *Bildungsbürgertum*, a term with obvious civilisational connotations.

The option of creating a political unit was thus provided by Russia, and Matti Klinge (1980, 1982) has argued that Finland was made rather than born and that this creation was not at all self-evident, let alone inevitable:

> the construction of national identity became possible and even desirable not merely because of the interests of elites in Finland, but also because of the

strategic interests of Russia, for it was realised that the loyalty of the people was best guaranteed by means of local elites and traditions.

(Klinge 1980: 243)

Anssi Paasi claims, along similar lines, that 'Despite its autonomy, Finland was above all a territorial expansion of Russian military power and from the Russian point of view a safety zone for St. Petersburg' (Paasi 1996: 83). Finland was, in his view, for a long time a state-nation rather than a nation-state, or a political nation based on bureaucratic practices (Paasi 1996: 87).

The Finnish elite hence set itself the goal of constructing a national identity within the framework of an imperial Russia. It purported itself as a nation but refrained from a clear-cut statist project and the question of territorial delineation. There was inclusion as Russia was accepted as the primary political environment in the sphere of statist politics, but exclusion in terms of language, culture and a considerable part of the bureaucratic policies. There were no efforts to reject contacts – along the lines of the French Revolution – with the Russian nobility or to revolt against Russia. Instead, the strategy was one of alignment, of anticipating issues that might lead to friction, and of adaptation instead of assuming a profile of brave resistance. The Finnish elite aimed, in short, to create a nation by utilising its position within a rather semi-feudal constellation. Finnish historiography started to draw distinctions in various directions and portrayed the Finns as the original inhabitants of the land. Meanwhile, Sweden was kept at a distance by claiming that the Finns had suffered oppression at the hands of a colonising Swedish aristocracy (although both arguments can be disputed: see Østergård 1997: 55).

The nation thus took the form of a loose cultural entity unfolding in a non-statist manner (Tommila 1990: 99). Instead of being presented as a community created by relations of blood or by a tight nexus between the people and the soil, the nation was depicted as coming into being by growth and development; language on the other hand could not be emphasised due to the existence of a Swedish-speaking minority. The policy of pragmatic adaptation pursued by the so-called Fennomanes – a rather reformist grouping – was quite successful in the sense of avoiding strict moves of exclusion in the statist sphere. This provided the Finns with images of loyalty towards the Emperor and Russia, and helped to avert uprisings, revolts and violence, generally typical for the development of nationalist movements in the early nineteenth century.

Lining up with Enlightenment

The concept of the nation emerged to signal the unity of the people and took primarily the shape of a Herderian *Kulturnation*. The nation was not conceived as a political nation but as a cultural one with emphasis on language, rule of law, competent administration, civil development and economic progress. The Finns were delineated as a group of people among other groups within a broad multi-national formation. Nationality was, as a consequence, primarily conceived of in terms of a territorial location (defined in regional terms) linked to certain ideal type images of landscapes rather than demarcated places with clear borders (Häyrynen 2000). It was, in this sense, pre-political more than political in essence.

The concept of the Finnish nation was above all an emancipatory one (Apunen and Rytövuori 1982). Nationality was depicted as a uniting factor, one that super-seded all cleavages pertaining to estate, class, language or geographic location; 'Finland' would provide unity in the context of plural identities. The purpose of the Finnish nation was conceptualised – in the presentations of its main advocates such as Johan Vilhelm Snellman, a philosopher and a statesman – as one of reflecting more general trends of modernity and development.

This is to say that nation-building was, in the first place, not a process of drawing borders or staying aloof from others in order to form a distinct and territorially bounded 'we'. Instead, it boiled down to a kind of selective modernity. Developing the economy, making progress in the sphere of technology by constructing water-ways, railways or roads, or investing in culture was uncontroversial, whereas aspiring for a political state was not. Hence Finland was represented in terms of inevitable progress (although conceptualised as civilisation rather than Enlightenment, the latter containing a number of features that clashed with empire-building), linking in with the general spirit of the era and showing others which way to follow.[3] These aspirations to become exemplary and stay in tune with what was timely in terms of general – primarily European – trends linked the nation to a certain universalism and broader civilisational aims. Yet there was little idealisation as the Finnish nation was at least as much spurred by the prevailing conditions than by any voluntarism or spiritual motivations.

The general ideology underpinning the project implied that the constituting forces and the very purpose of the nation were located outside and not within the nation itself, that is, the nation got its meaning through representing certain more general trends which had more to do with time than place. In any case, the Finnish nation did not emerge as a self-enclosed and tightly delineated entity but as a way of linking in with and representing development at large. It was not there in the first place because of specific political aims or particular histories.

The nation was conceptualised, not as something unique and distinct, but as a vehicle for the expression of higher ambitions of humankind – this provided a close linkage between the nation and 'Europe'. The task was thus not one of defending a certain individual nationality but to remain linked to the broader currents of development which provided room beyond any strict delineation of political space. International relations were thereby conceptualised as moves of opening up and linking in with both Russia and Europe. They were seen in terms of integrative and cooperative action and less as a sphere imbued with conflicts and the exercise of repressive power.

The very aim of the nation was – according to the small group of founding fathers – to be better, more advanced, more democratic and more western than Russia in general. Yet it had to be part of the whole (Russia), to constitute a measure of progress and a proof that change was at least possible, if not inevitable. The nation – a concept that now incorporated the people but not the state – expressed itself through its cultural achievements, not through aspirations for (political) statehood.

The nation was, in other words, conceived as being quite different from the state (in contrast to those concepts of nation which contain an implicit linkage to the state), with culture and political power constituting separate spheres. The aim of the Finnish leadership was to assure the support of the people against an entity, namely Russia, which could turn hostile if the Finnish project were pushed too far. This situation dictated that the nation could not be conceptualised as the basis for an independent state, and hence the nation had to be seen as located on a level of its own. It was allotted the task of paving the way for a symbolic sphere that signalled unity, one that the Finnish nation could then utilise for self-fulfilment, while simultaneously indicating a difference to 'Russia'. The nation was to provide space for Finland's subjectivity as a cultural entity, and to do so without fusing into a state, or running into conflict with the statist entities already in place. Many of the elements in the thinking of the founding fathers were Hegelian – and their inspiration came mainly from German thinking – but the stress on the nation and its cultural base opened up for Herderian rather than Hegelian impulses (Pulkkinen 1999: 128).

The attitude towards the state – both as a concept and as a concrete formation – was rather practical and pragmatic. The state was not viewed as an anti-nation to be resisted if it did not bend to the needs of the nation. The nation was there for different things and its aim was to grow as a cultural entity. As a consequence there was little to be gained from engaging oneself in political struggles over statehood, resisting 'foreign' authority, fighting repression, achieving a tight territorial basis or drawing divisive borderlines between 'us' and 'them'. The prevailing ideology reflected both moves of inclusion and exclusion, but with the latter aspect being relatively soft and leading to a certain openness (Saukkonen 1999: 204). The attempt to avoid closing down political space in any limited nation-state fashion explains why J. V. Snellman, in articulating conceptualisations which became hegemonic, opposed all political manifestations of sympathy towards Sweden (i.e. against Russia), or towards the Poles who resorted to armed struggle.

Nationalism was thus not in conflict with feeling loyalty towards the Emperor and the Russian state. Initially, the contest was not about statehood, sovereignty or political freedom in any narrow fashion as the nation was constituted, in the first place, by communality, language, culture, landscapes and historical experiences serving as arguments for a common (Finnish) fate. The impact of Enlightenment ideology was visible, but in a moulded and cultural manner allowing Finland to evolve in a very specific way. For example, claims along French lines supporting strong individuality and citizenship were missing, as individuality was basically seen as selfishness (Manninen 1986: 17). The task of the Finnish nation was thus not to provide the backing and platform for free individuals to develop, and the ultimate basis of the nation did not, as in France, consist of the individuals choosing to belong to it. Nationality was perceived as resting on an objective (cultural) ground as well as providing a linkage to larger historical and civilisational projects: the ethnic and civic dimensions of Finnish nationhood did not coincide.

In Hans Kohn's (1967) distinction between Western and Eastern conceptions of the nation, Finland obviously belongs to the Eastern (that is the not-so-modern) category. The downplaying of the individual and the upgrading of the historical and collective nation, one furnished with historic missions, is easily understandable as there was little space within Tsarist Russia to introduce notions that would have turned the individual, as a citizen, into a constitutive figure. Separate Finnish citizenship would have required drawing borders and it would have singled out Finland in a statist sense. Staying with nationhood – in a broad, cultural and collective sense – allowed Finnishness to unfold independently of statehood as a way of going, under the prevailing circumstances, beyond questions of statehood. The nation was not there to resist some particular state, nor to conquer a state of its own. Linking to a Western, more politicised conceptualisation of the nation would have placed Finland on a collision course with the Russian 'motherland' and deprived Finland of the role of mediating, in a milder form, some of the thoughts of the Enlightenment, individualisation and urbanisation which originated with the French Revolution.

A Hegelian turn

Although Finland initially emerged as a cultural nation, the concept of a *Staatsnation* soon entered the picture. Herderian ideas of the nation clashed towards the end of the nineteenth century with Hegelian departures, that is, the understanding that the primary purpose of a nation is to form a state in order to test its viability in a contest between similar entities on the interstate arena. In this clash the Hegelian views proved so successful, particularly as the Russian rule had turned increasingly repressive, that a state-centred representation of Finland over time got the upper hand. The concept of a nation became increasing fused to the concept of the state and Finland gained the features of an ordinary state–nation construction.

Much of Finnish historiography shares the ideology of this Hegelian departure; either Finland has been presented as a state-nation almost from the very beginning of the Russian period – with a disguised state of its own in the form of a central administration – or the process has been presented in a finalistic manner as if the aim of nation-building was always to end up with a state of one's own, that is, that even if the state did not yet exist the sole purpose of the political project was to create one. The moves of inclusion and exclusion have been rather strict in such writings, thereby trying to contribute to a 'pure' and geographically predicated form of political landscape. The stress on the importance of language, culture and civilisation remained, but the reading became rather state-centred. Finland was no longer depicted as the eastern edge of Europe but seen as part of a Europe standing aloof from Russia.

The abandonment of the previous constellation – as the Hegelian views turned increasingly hegemonic – did not imply that 'Finland' became a place where everybody living there could express themselves freely.[4] As with many other 'late' states, the tolerance for difference declined and the efforts to keep the nation together – for example in the sphere of religion – increased in importance. Conformity, it was thought, was needed for the nation to be able to distinguish itself from other similar formations. As a consequence, questions of language, class or location within an East–West constellation became conflictual. The Finnish-speaking part of the population – consisting mainly of peasants and the countryside – and the Swedish-speaking administration, upper classes and the coastal population became pitched against each other. The matter of being western, in contrast to the easternness of Russia, became important and fuelled internal class-based conflicts within Finland. The emergence of a significant left wing in 1907 (in the general election the Finnish Social Democrats became the largest socialist party in Europe) was hence understood as something 'foreign' and 'eastern'. It represented a (political) concept of the people which was seen as unwarranted and deeply divisive by the more conservative forces.

The emancipatory concept underlying 'Finland' was still significant at the turn of the century when the nation was mobilised to counteract the ambitions of the Tsar. The Tsar's administration tried to restrain Finland's autonomy and to repress the new, radical ideas – including civic freedom – of the Enlightenment which penetrated Russia, to some extent through Finland. A far-reaching parliamentary reform with universal suffrage was, however, carried out. Once installed, the parliament got a Finnish-speaking majority and the left gained a political platform. In general the nation became much more politically conscious, territorially linked and far better organised.

The views remain divided in Finland as to how this history should be written. The key question is whether the Finns achieved their political victories through resistance, which included a general strike in 1905, or whether autonomy came about as a consequence of revolutionary movements in Russia, international political conditions, and skilful Finnish political conduct (Polvinen 1971; Apunen and Rytövuori 1982: 72). It is in any case important to note that the nation was not mobilised to act against its own state, that is the Finnish administration. The aims of the various civic movements that emerged after the turn of the century were to contribute to the formation of a Finnish state which should be something more than just the administration already in place. The prevailing ideology was thus quite different from the one assumed by similar movements, for example in Sweden (Stenius 1998). Whereas the Swedish civic movements held a very critical attitude towards the Swedish state and formed parts of a counterculture, the Finnish ones resisted the policies of the Russian state with the aim of substituting the Russian state with a Finnish one. The protests from below, to the extent that they existed, were not directed against the (Finnish) state but became fused with the endeavours of providing the nation with a state of its own in a truly Hegelian spirit.

After Russia's military defeat in the First World War and the subsequent revolution, Finland gained independence in December 1917. At the same time conflictual aspects associated with the class division inside the nation increased to such a degree that a bitter civil war broke out between the 'Whites' and the 'Reds' in 1918. On the one hand, the war was a reflection of the increasingly repressive understandings of the Finnish nation and, on the other, it spurred developments that further fortified such notions. Nationality turned into something far less cultural and was much more strictly delineated in terms of ethnicity and territoriality.

Similar changes occurred in the way civilisation was understood. It was conceptualised, with the transformation from Herderian to Hegelian thinking, in a far more narrow and exclusive manner than previously. In some instances it turned missionary and expansionist and Finnishness became a vehicle for border-drawing and the introduction of rather sharp territorial delineation between 'us' (sameness) and 'them' (otherness). Finland purported itself to be an outpost of Western civilisation and stepped into what John Agnew and Stuart Corbridge have called 'the territorial trap' (Agnew and Corbridge 1995: 79). Medvedev argues that 'In an attempt to break out of [Russian] space, Finland came up with a structured and delineated territory' (Medvedev 1998: 18). A sword and a war trumpet became the prime national – or rather statist – symbols surpassing the previous ones of a Kantele (a traditional Karelian musical instrument) and a plough.

The flexibility of the earlier years grew thin, and the nation was increasingly conceptualised in ethnic terms by contrasting Finnishness with Russianness. Russia was in many ways orientalised and made into an alien Other, and instead of Finland mediating Enlightenment civilisation to Russia, the idea was to stay away from the inherent forces of darkness. 'In the cosmology of Finnish statehood, Russia is the primordial, pre-national, pre-conscious condition, something that precedes Finnish national consciousness, the darkness from which the nation (a piece of light and Enlightenment) is born' (Medvedev 1998: 6). Interaction eastwards came largely to a halt, the border turned into a divisive one and the aim of the politics pursued was to preserve a distance to the eastern neighbour now depicted, in public discourse as well as in official documents, as an eternal enemy (Hietanen and Joenniemi 1982). The country developed a fortress mentality and a feeling of being a strategic and cultural outpost of the West. Hence Finland turned into a state-nation *par excellence* with an emphasis on statehood instead of the previous one on nationhood (Paasi 1996). It became primarily a *Staatsnation* with increasingly weak features of a *Kulturnation*, although the two conceptualisations continued to co-exist.

A reversal of the trend

The pre-eminence of the Hegelian conceptualisation prevailed up to the Winter War of 1939–40 and the Continuation War of 1941–4. After the Second World War a debate emerged over how to cope with the Soviet Union in the new geopolitical situation. This debate was concerned not only with the wars and Finnish–Soviet relations, but with the character of international politics more broadly as well as with the nature of Finland as a political configuration.

No doubt the Hegelian power state had grown stronger during the early years of independence when the emancipatory endeavours had taken the back seat. The pre-eminence of the power state contributed to some extent, albeit in a limited fashion, to Finland getting entangled in two wars with the Soviet Union. The power political state did not cause the clash but implied a particular mentality and a certain inability to cope with and respond to external signals. Various external factors weighed more heavily, it appears, than the internal transformations of the Finnish nation-state or the emergence of the Hegelian power state and it would be an overstatement to claim that Finland had been at the mercy of some particularly war-prone forces. True, there had been a semi-fascist movement in the 1930s threatening a take-over of the state and preaching the resort to repressive measures against domestic as well as international – that is Soviet – communist forces, but measures were found to deal with this challenge. The movement bowed in the end to pressure from President Svinhufvud, the threat could be handled within limits of the established political system, and there was no need for any extraordinary measures.

After the war the legitimacy of Soviet policies towards Finland came up, and various modes of explanation clashed fiercely. Was it inevitable that Finland would become drawn into the war with the Soviet Union (siding with Germany during the Continuation War) or could this have been avoided by pursuing more conciliatory policies? What were the Soviet intentions when it referred to imperative security needs and demanded political and territorial concessions from Finland?

The *Realpolitik* school has viewed power as a question of dominance whereas a softer position has tended to regard power in terms of social competence. The latter position has been far more critical about the Finnish policies prior to and during the wars, but the *Realpolitik* school has also been strongly present in the public and scholarly debates.[5] The explanation offered by the *Realpolitik* position was one of Finland having drifted into the wars by and large against its own will but then having fought ferociously and bravely once the realities of war were encountered. Furthermore, it was thought – along Hegelian lines – that the alliance between the state and the nation had stood the test of war.

Some space was, however, available for views which were close to those of the early years of nation-building. The previous emphasis on the Hegelian power state was thus replaced by a movement towards the Herderian nation celebrated in the nineteenth century. This is to say that when evaluating the defeat of the Continuation War, one did not have to construct an entirely new project. The new elements therein could be conceptualised and experienced as a return to something familiar, as the *Kulturnation* was provided with a second opportunity to constitute the 'real' Finland.

President Paasikivi was a central figure in implementing the reversal from the Hegelian power state to the Herderian nation. He linked up with earlier, Herderian traditions and argued that 'now the pen has to restore what the sword has broken', thereby siding with the more critical views concerning the background of the two wars with the Soviet Union. This line was a cautious one of minimal gestures, security was recognised as a core issue, but the idea was to handle it primarily by political and societal means. It was explicitly assumed that the Finnish–Soviet relationship – in line with the previous Finnish–Russian one – could be based on mutual trust. The Paasikivi line, later to be followed by President Kekkonen, had strong emancipatory flavours from the very beginning, although it was implemented in a top-down and rather authoritarian manner (Apunen and Rytövuori 1982: 79).

The conceptualisation of the state in terms of power was downplayed – although the result was not an anti-power state along the lines of post-war Germany – and the policies pursued were those of coping and adapting to the external realities (Mouritzen 1988). The efforts to internationalise remained modest and the foreign policy leadership aimed at staying aloof from the Scandinavian humanitarian internationalism undertaken by Denmark, Norway and Sweden. This policy was one of staying in-between within a Europe consisting of the East and the West, keeping a low profile and pursuing a policy based on a strict instrumentalism which avoided idealist stances as well as protests on controversial issues (Apunen and Rytövuori 1982: 70).

This foreign policy was complemented by internal efforts to bolster societal strength. The task was again one of coping with a variety of necessities but utilising wherever possible whatever space was left open. The state and the nation worked in liaison as the need to stick together and safeguard the nation's unity was felt to be of utmost importance. Much energy went into the nation unfolding in the spheres of culture and economy: cultural facilities were developed throughout the country and a pragmatic rationalism in the economic area led to the pursuit of policies of economic growth, welfare and development. The nation should prosper and leave its mark despite the hindrances in the sphere of foreign policy.

These trends in Finnish thinking showed some similarity with those of post-1945 Germany, although the reversal from Hegelian concepts back towards Herderian ones was milder and more cautious. The trauma of the two wars also spurred some self-critical thinking in Finland. Having partly sided with Germany in the Continuation War, various restrictions on Finland were incorporated into the Peace Treaty of Paris in 1947 in the attempt to eradicate the root causes of its assumed proneness to war. However, the measures imposed on Finland were far milder than the reshuffling that took place in the German case. For Finland, the year 1945 marked both rupture and continuation: thinking did not come to a halt with viewing the power political state as a problem to be handled and a danger to be minimised (Wæver 1990). Some wartime politicians were sentenced as war criminals and certain right-wing organisations were outlawed as the new leadership wanted to demonstrate the will and capacity to settle the wartime scores without outside interference. Stability and cooperation were projected by the fact that the country was governed by broad popular coalitions, including at some juncture also the People's Democrats (a combination of socialists and communists) and, second, by the low levels of interest and investment in the armed forces during the post-war period. The applied formula was one of unanimity, for example in the form of broadly based centre-left governments, and despite some discord, one could speak of 'unity in diversity' (Alapuro 1994: 320).

One of the aims of these policies was to check the state and to assure that it remained in proper hands. The state and the nation were to some extent viewed as separate entities entrusted with the responsibility of balancing each other out. This was done in order to assure the existence of a stable and healthy political system, but the process of formal restructuring was not taken very far. There were no efforts in the Finnish case to rewrite the constitution, to insert a constitutional court located above ordinary politics, to introduce further democratisation or to decentralise power by introducing a federalist political system with strong local entities, that is, to provide space for categories that reach beyond the Herderian/Hegelian nexus. Little reason was also found to clarify further the division between the executive, legislative and judicial branches of power as well as to ensure their independence from each other. There was a strengthening of the nation – the wars themselves had already contributed to this, for example by reducing suspicions that some parts of the left would turn subversive once the opportunity arose – but this did not imply that the state was deprived of power in any drastic way.

There certainly was a conceptual tension between the traditions of the *Staatsnation* and the *Kulturnation* in the post-Second World War period, but the clash stayed within limits. The nation did not turn into any separate *Kulturnation* but remained largely one of *Staatsnation*, although with considerable stress on the latter aspect of nation. The conceptualisation of the nation in emancipatory terms, once central to Finland's self-understanding, was again allowed the front seat. Aspirations for growth, development and a furthering of civilisational aims favoured the nation, but the state – stripped of some of its power political features – was also granted some tasks within this context. The need to play the Finnish state against the nation was hence conceived as modest.

One step back, two steps forward

Post-war Finland is also comparable to Germany as being a broadly recognised success story. Finland has encountered occasional difficulties such as a deep recession at the beginning of the 1990s, but it has, in general, done rather well. Finnish achievements look particularly dramatic if compared with those of the Soviet Union, a neighbouring country and one of the victors of the Second World War. The Soviet project crumbled and the state disappeared while Finland goes on as a rather prosperous and well-functioning nation-state. The return to the more emancipatory departures of the formative years of the Finnish nation has no doubt contributed to this. This move provided the flexibility – that is a conciliatory foreign policy, broadly based governments, relatively easy access for the younger generations into positions of power, etc. – needed to cope with various external and internal challenges. The duality that underlies Finland as a nation-state has turned out to be a valuable resource to be drawn upon during periods of transition.

However, the question has emerged whether the national project continues to rest on its previous foundations, whether the challenges that gave it meaning – above all the external threats – are still there and to what extent the basis of 'Finland' has to be fundamentally reconsidered. The nation-state is at the centre of a contest between different views and representations and some confusion concerning Finland's position on the European map. Should Finland retain most of her post-war essence, could the country turn into a project that is less of a state but articulates itself increasingly as a nation through economy and culture, or does the entire project, that is, both the state and the nation, have to be renewed by providing breeding ground for categories such as regions? Does Finland lose with the demise of the Cold War, which provided the option of being 'in-between'? Finland was somehow an object of curiosity due to the Finnish–Soviet relationship and it was often admired as a small capitalist country able to cope with a big socialist neighbour. Will Finland be able to adjust and find its place in the new Europe, a Europe which might leave Finland as a small and insignificant actor somewhere on the outskirts of power and influence? Is Finland located on the brink of Europe, or does it stand out as an entity in-between, providing bridges for Russia to also be part of the new Europe?

All of these views have been presented and dealt with in the debate over the future of Finland in an integrating Europe. Much points to a profound break and a period of transformation. The external threats to security are far less severe and they are not expected to threaten the independence of the country through, for example, large-scale military invasion. As exemplified by the various peacekeeping endeavours, the concept of security no longer provides ground for strict divisions into an internal and external sphere, and security becomes increasingly linked to the EU and European integration. External necessities are not connected with the internal need for adaptation in the same way as during the post-war period. The communists have, moreover, largely disappeared from the domestic political scene, the Left Alliance which has a seat in the government plays fully along with the ordinary rules of parliamentarianism and democracy, and the green movement has turned into an established political force both in parliament and within government.

One important shift consists of the increasing internationalisation the state has undergone through EU membership, another of the internal decentralisation where a devolution of political and economic power from the state and the central administration to the regional and local levels of administration has taken place. There are clear indications that the longing for strict unity and conformity – along Herderian/Hegelian lines – has declined and more tolerance for diversity has appeared. The grip of the state and the influence of a homogenising national culture have become less tight. This leaves more space for regional and local cultures which in turn enable the Finns to adopt a calmer attitude towards the process of internationalisation (Heiskanen 1988: 4). There is no need for any far-reaching self-discipline – sometimes interpreted as censorship or 'Finlandisation'. Likewise, the need for a strong top-down approach to politics which should ensure that domestic developments stay within the limits set by the harsh external conditions has declined as well. All this implies, however, that the Finns need to re-think their place in the world. There is, in contrast to the Cold War years, too much openness in the air and questions have surfaced about who 'we' are and the meaning of the national project (Alapuro 1994: 321; Joenniemi 1992 and 1993b; Lehtonen 1999).

Finland: Nordic or northern?

Finland had to specify, at the beginning of the 1950s, its international position when the question surfaced whether it could join the Nordic Council together with Denmark, Iceland, Norway and Sweden. The decision was to postpone membership, and Finland became a member of the Nordic Council only some three years later, in 1956.

The question was then one of who 'we' were. The relations with the Soviet Union had a clear priority, but could the eastern relations be complemented with Nordicity in a distinct in-between position? Not just the external realities caused some hesitation towards the Nordic. Scandinavianism had been viewed with suspicion during the Tsarist period and it also conflicted with the Hegelianism of the early years of independence. Later, during the inter-war period, and as part of the drive towards homogeneity and conformity, there was a strong drive to reduce the Swedishness of the country and construct it as purely Finnish and Finnish-speaking. However, the experience of the wars considerably reduced the intensity of this friction. There was more room for the concept of the Finnish nation to unfold (and it had more strength to do so). Moreover, the inclinations of the state and the nation coincided to allow the Swedish-speaking part of the population to establish stronger relations across the borders of the nation-state. As to the state, the question of joining the Nordic Council was comprehended as a favourable move in foreign and security policy terms. Nordic cooperation was valued as it was expected to contribute to the removal of Finland from great power conflicts and to strengthen the country's profile as a 'third' standing between the blocks. It would add to an image of Finland as a peaceful Nordic country in an area of reduced tension.

However, in joining the Nordic Council Finland insisted on special treatment. To insure that the move towards Nordicity would not hamper relations eastwards, Finland demanded that matters pertaining to security should not be on the joint Nordic agenda. Initially, the line pursued in the context of the Nordic Council remained rather cautious, but Finland became over time a full-fledged and active member of Nordic cooperation, although the banning of an institutionalised Nordic dialogue on matters of security remained at least formally intact until the end of the 1980s. In general membership turned out to be unproblematic and did not burden Finland's eastern relations.

Already during the late 1960s the Nordic countries had had to formulate a stand on whether to approach the EEC and join European integration or to turn to Nordic cooperation as an alternative option. The decision on whether Norden should take another step on the ladder of integration and establish a free trade union was a difficult one for Finland. The idea of negotiations was accepted, however in the end Finland was unable – partly for internal reasons – to come out in a positive vein. It was feared that a Nordic move could hamper relations with the Soviet Union but there was also the worry that a Nordic choice might stand in the way of later accession to the EEC.

The view of Nordicity as a civilisational alternative to Europe – one that has been more clearly discernible in Iceland, Norway and Sweden than in Denmark – has not been shared by Finland. The two spheres and identifications are not seen as standing in opposition to each other as has sometimes been the case in the other Nordic countries. The Finns do not conceptualise Norden as a demarcation from Europe: a democratic, Protestant, progressive and egalitarian North against a Catholic, conservative and capitalist Europe (Sørensen and Stråth 1997: 22). Instead, it has been seen as a move to open up rather than close down and carve out a separate sphere, that is, as something that runs parallel to and in line with Europeanisation. It has been comprehended as a non-statist, non-security and non-territorial form of community. There has been a feeling of Nordicity: Finland has more than 600 years of common history with Sweden, and the cultural heritage this experience has brought about assures such a stance (Engman 1994: 63). Finland's Nordic orientation can also be dated to the 1930s when the pincers of Stalin and

Hitler provoked dreams of a Nordic community of destiny, and more concretely spurred a Nordic grouping of neutrals (Sørensen and Stråth 1997: 16). Somewhat later Finland became involved in different forms of bottom-up cooperation, activities that constitute an essential part of Nordicity, during the Winter War of 1939–40. A considerable number of Scandinavian communities and popular organisations then tried to help Finland during a period of strain and hardship.

Finland is firmly Lutheran (with a small orthodox minority) and has culturally, socially and economically very many features in common with the other Nordic countries. The main language of the country, Finnish, deviates, no doubt, considerably from the Scandinavian languages. It is part of a group of finno-ugric languages which differ from both the Scandinavian and the Slavic ones in terms of vocabularies as well as grammar (Allardt 1989: 13).[6] Finland's easternness, the links with Russia and then the Soviet Union, a relatively authoritarian form of government as well as the fact that the Finns were not originally part of the discourse on Scandinavianism have raised further doubts as to whether Finland belongs to the Nordic family (Jansson 1989: 113). On a more general note, it has been relatively easy for Finns to cope with Nordicity, another loosely bounded nation-feeling and a horizontal type of identity premised on culture. The problems have not been conceptual but political, and to a large degree it has been possible to overcome the latter obstacles, too.

It appears that Finland's Nordicity has over the years stood the test of time and that previous doubts have largely evaporated. Finland has had a profile of its own, being perhaps more pragmatic and less ideological about Nordic cooperation, and the concept of Norden has been sufficiently broad and flexible to incorporate this.

However, the debate on where Finland belongs is by no means over. There have been claims that Finland might be on its way to substituting Nordic cooperation with closer ties towards the EU. There have also been voices in the domestic Finnish debate suggesting that Finnish Nordicity was necessitated mostly by the Cold War. As that period has been left behind, Finland might now reconsider its position and link in with Europeanness without any mediating positions. The value of Nordicity has, according to this line of thinking, drastically declined. Why study the Swedish language if the alternative is French or German, languages which offer a more direct inroad into European affairs and influence? The Finnish language has itself gained more international connotations siding now increasingly with the Estonian one (Sundberg 1997: 203). Why spend energy on keeping Nordic cooperation alive when there is the option of investing the same resources in influencing broader European politics?

These questions have not surfaced with any major strength and have remained a cause for concern mainly among the Swedish-speaking community in Finland. This community feels somewhat entrenched as Finland now has more leeway to move in a western and eastern – or for that matter northern – direction. However, there has not been any major reason for concern: Nordicity is being re-valued but this does not imply a devaluation. Nordic cooperation has, on the contrary, retained its importance, although its meaning has obviously undergone some changes with the upheavals of the post-Cold War years.

Finland has supported a restructuring of Nordic cooperation and a turn away from an internal orientation and towards a focus on joint external challenges. Nordicity has thereby increasingly assumed the nature of statist cooperation vis-à-vis the nearby environment or Europe at large, although grassroots movements are also trying to follow suit, for example in the form of Nordic associations being established in the Baltic countries as well as in St Petersburg, Murmansk and Kaliningrad. It has become evident that Finland remains Nordic, although in the Finnish case Nordicity is part and parcel of a more general Europeanness. This implies that it has been relative easy for Finland to join the EU without this being understood as a betrayal of Nordicity. There have been voices arguing for Nordic cooperation as an alternative to EU membership – including a previous Minister for Foreign Affairs and leader of the Centre Party, Paavo Väyrynen (1994) – but these views have been less pronounced than the ones in the other Nordic countries, and the relationships between Nordic and European forms of integration have not caused much concern in the Finnish EU debate (Arter 1995: 382–3). It has been at least as important to consider the consequences of European integration for the eastern border, and whether Nordicity has any role to play in this regard.

This is a relevant concern as experiences suggest that Finland is increasingly achieving an eastern dimension of cooperation. The relationship with the Baltic countries and particularly with Estonia is growing rather close and the border with Russia has also become more permeable. This border is no longer strictly divisive in the way it used to be, it mediates instead a considerable amount of cooperation and contacts. This allows Finland to link up with its pre-independence history from when it was an autonomous part of Tsarist Russia and to function as a meeting place and a bridge – and to turn in the best of cases into a bridge-builder – between Russia, Norden and the more central parts of Europe. It has again become beneficial to be located quite far to the west if seen from the east, and very much to the east if seen from the west. What is sometimes viewed as remote and peripheral can in other contexts be utilised and marketed, as has even been the case more recently with Finland's rather northern – and almost arctic – location. Furthermore, the interpretations concerning the repressiveness of the Russian period have become destabilised with the policies of Russia and the Emperor vis-à-vis Finland being seen in a somewhat more favourable light (Klinge 1997).

Finland's Europeanisation seems to bring with it, more generally, a multiplication of identities and a far broader menu that the one that was available during the years of the Cold War. The utilisation of northernness in the context of the Northern Dimension is a case in point. Finland has turned into a full-fledged European, Nordic identity is still there and some of the continuities – though in many cases thought of as having been lost – have resurfaced to provide a cooperative substance to the country's easternness. Linking up with St. Petersburg might, for example, turn out to be an important move provided that the metropolis gets going and turns into a resource that Russia makes use of when approaching Europe (Joenniemi 1996). The increased fuzziness of the eastern border and the playing with northernness in the context of the EU do not immediately undermine Norden, but they nevertheless raise questions about what Norden means as a concept and as a political project under the current conditions. The appearance of northernness, a marker loaded with ambiguity and therefore open to a variety of interpretations, might be particularly challenging in this regard. Nordicity is more firmly defined, it has a distinct basis in the Nordic councils, and it has stood for an endeavour to stay aloof and to be 'better' than the rest of Europe. It is hence not very applicable when the aim is to turn boundaries into outer-oriented and fluid frontiers within a more flexible and multi-centred Europe.

By way of conclusion

It is obvious that the Herderian and Hegelian approaches to politics and the formation of nation-states, as well as their relationship to one another, are much more nuanced than the one depicted in this chapter. The two approaches do not stand markedly in opposition to each other. However, it seems also clear that much can be achieved by contrasting a soft Herderian nation with a Hegelian power state – and, for that matter, by looking beyond these two prime categories. The construction of a crude dichotomy appears to be rather helpful in depicting certain key features of Finland's development, first as a soft Herderian nation and then increasingly as a Hegelian power state which, finally, turned into a more sophisticated configuration.

This dynamism indicates, among other things, that Finland has not been a straightforward and cumulative project, one that took off as a nation leaning on soft Herderian departures later to assume the shape of a tight Hegelian state-nation where the state was the major expression of the collective identity of the entity. The wars prevented such a pattern from growing even stronger and space was instead opened up for a return to Herderian inclinations. There is a certain parallel here with German developments, and it is no coincidence that the two concepts employed in this analysis also point – both in their linguistic form and in their history – in the same direction. Anyhow, they appear to have some applicability in the Finnish case as well.

The duality and flexibility underlying the national project implies that there is much in the new post-Cold War Europe that Finland can relate to. Europe may be depicted as both old and new. The old assures that there is space available not only for the Finnish state but also for the nation. These moves are not those of either/or – as viewed for example by Heikki Patomäki (1994) in one of the contributions to the debate. They are premised on inclusion to be followed by non-categorical moves of (re)closure which do not in any strict sense play various categories of political space against one another. The ethnic-genealogical can, to some extent, be kept separate from the civic-territorial. Conceptualisations of time (in the Finnish case history) appear again as important as those of space in anchoring the national project. Some challenges are brand new but some may also be recognised and coped with on the basis of earlier traditions, and there appears to be sufficient balance between the old and the new for the challenges to remain digestible.

Some central elements of Finland as a political (statist) project had to be abandoned in the course of transformation – including for a large part the one of neutrality – but these losses do not seem to cut very deep. The politics of neutrality has, in the case of Finland, had a tactical rather than an identity-related character. The employment of such a posture has not stood out as a constitutive move that expresses the essence of the Finnish nation-state as it has in the case of Sweden (see Chapter 5 in this volume). Moreover, the state seems to be able to cope with stronger international influences, a more assertive nation and the growing importance of categories such as regions and regionalisation.

Some of the practices developed during the post-war period have simply been skipped but others have retained their value. Finland has, in many instances, been able to meet the new by mobilising and reactivating traditions that originated during the early years of nation-building. The whole national project was coined rather late and had a rather invented nature, but this has not amounted to a search for some grand narrative providing 'Finland' with a firm and unambiguous grounding, and national identity has as a consequence taken on a certain lightness. There has not been – as Finland has often been defined by what it is not (a kind of non-Sweden or non-Russia) – any sacrosanct narrative of a *Homeland*, one that would now be endangered by a *Return to Europe*. There is no firm image of a 'Finland' now clashing with a firmly defined 'Europe'. Instead, the flexible and non-crystallised nature of 'Finland' provides room for manoeuvre – and this seems to set Finland apart from Denmark and Sweden, not to speak of Norway. Only a country that approves and sees some positive sides in having a somewhat marginal and loosely defined position is able to coin, it seems, initiatives based on such an unconventional claim that there is a northern way of being European, that there is a third way and a northern dimension to the EU.

There have certainly been challenges involved, but its appears that there exist quite a number of reasons why Finland has been able to feel – to a reasonable degree – at home in the new setting. It has been possible to grasp that linking up with broader European developments does not only constrain and impose restrictions; it also enables the opening up of new possibilities as well as the clearing of paths needed for traditions to become once again alive. Such a constructivist reading might explain some of the ease of the Finnish adaptation despite the fact that many traditions have been challenged. This is particularly true for elements such as the aspiration for conformity that suppressed individuality, the significance of agrarian values to the definition of 'the people' and the relationship between the nation and the people. Increasingly distinctions have to be made between an ethnic group (i.e. Finns) and a political community (the nation), or between those persons possessing rights within this community (the citizens).

However, there seems to be a considerable dose of continuity as well. External challenges may activate certain mechanisms that help to blend the familiar with the foreign, leading to a tolerance for a certain dissonance. The nation does not – in being at 'home' precisely because of these challenges – have to turn overtly defensive; it is not deprived of its essence and the option of being itself. 'The new nationalism seems yet one more manifestation of the plurality of opinions in present-day Finland', argues Risto Alapuro (Alapuro 1999: 120). The nation may also come across new and liberating ways of self-articulation – such as northernness in the context of proposing a Northern Dimension for the EU – or feel stronger because of being allowed to utilise some of its more traditional resources based not only on a Herderian and civilisational reading of Finland itself, but also of 'Norden' and 'Europe'.

The formative years of nation-building provided Finland with a competence to cope with a situation where the task is not one of defending and clinging to what is already there but to tune in to the new and the changing. Responding to such challenges ties in with the Herderian traditions of the country. Past experiences may explain why the nation does not feel overly threatened by the prospect of a changing link to the state – with the state becoming increasingly international and growing perhaps weaker. The task is again one of emancipation, development and renewal under changing conditions. And more particularly, the leap from being linked with a multinational empire having its centre in St Petersburg to a Brussels-centred European Union is, after all, not that large.

Political authority may also be dispersed in the process of becoming European, and this without the nation panicking due to fears of having its identity undermined. Past experiences, and the flexibility of the nation–state nexus, make Finland cope reasonably well with considerable changes in both the external and the internal environments. There is the possibility of encountering Europe not only as a strong state but also as a nation, or to put it differently, a pluralistic Finland appears to be able to cope with an increasingly pluralistic Europe. The weakening as well as internationalisation of the state may be interpreted as a drastic loss if viewed from a Hegelian point of view, but if seen in a Herderian perspective such a trend may provide Finland with increasing room to express what could be comprehended as its true and original nature: a northern entity which contains Russia, the Nordic countries and considerable parts of Europe. Finland retains its meaning and articulates itself increasingly as a nation in the context of an integrating Europe, one that also includes Norden. The growing distance to the state is not seen as fatal as Finland during its formative years had to articulate itself and create a subjectivity outside of statist structures and to some extent even in opposition to statism. Past experiences of having to express itself in rather pragmatic and non-statist manners appear to be an asset in view of the challenges of Europeanisation and globalisation.

A European Union of the nation-states – and perhaps even a development in a federalist direction – will be acceptable from a Finnish point of view as long as there is space for the nation to unfold. However, a European Union resting on a joint identity would be perceived as quite problematic. An 'empire-type' of Europe – allowing a certain plurality – is acceptable whereas a homogeneous and uniform Europe is not. There has to be sufficient room for a national/local identity, and seen from this perspective a Europe of regions could well be in line with Finnish traditions. These traditions correspond with region formation in the shape of the Baltic Sea region or the Barents Euro-Arctic region, or – for that matter – developing Nordic cooperation to constitute a European region. Likewise, the idea of an EU qualified by a Northern Dimension fits this pattern. In general, the institutional conditions are not that decisive as long as there is space for Finnishness as one 'dialect' among the European 'languages'.

Notes

1 *Svenska Dagbladet*, 16 Nov. 1996. It should be added that the Swedish reactions certainly also tie in with domestic concerns and clashes over the policies to be pursued vis-à-vis the EU.
2 Ingebritsen and Larson do, however, view identity as being more central than material factors as it precedes and shapes the definition of national interests (Ingebritsen and Larson 1997: 210).
3 Some of the currents reflected, however, more Romantic aspirations of defending the countryside and the traditional rural values against emerging urbanisation and industrialisation.
4 Which could have been expected as the nation-state was very much depicted as a joint Finnish project in contrast to being part of Russia.
5 There has not been anything resembling the German *Historikerstreit* critical reviewing of one's own past.
6 There exist, however, considerable similarities in the semantic structures between the Finnish language and the Scandinavian ones.

References

Agnew, J. and Corbridge, S. (1995) *Mastering Space: Hegemony, Territory and International Political Economy*, New York: Routledge.
Alapuro, R. (1988) *State and Revolution in Finland*, Berkeley: University of California Press.
—— (1989) 'The Intelligentsia, the State and the Nation', in M. Engman and D. Kirby (eds), *Finland: People, Nation, State*. London: Hurst.
—— (1994) *Suomen synty paikallisena ilmiönä 1890–1933* (The Creation of Finland on the Local Level), Tampere: Hanki ja jää.
—— (1999) 'Social Classes and Nationalism: The North-East Baltic', in M. Branch (ed.) *National History and Identity*, Studia Fennica, Ethnologica 6, Finnish Literature Society: Tampere, pp. 111–21.
Allardt, E. (1988) 'Yhteiskuntamuoto ja kansallisvaltio' (Form of Society and the Nation-State), in K. Eskola and E. Vainikkala (eds) *Maailmankulttuurin äärellä* (At the brink of a worldwide culture), Nykykulttuurin tutkimusyksikkö: Jyväskylän yliopisto, pp. 15–34.
—— (1989) 'Suomi pohjoismaisena yhteiskuntana' (Finland as a Nordic Society), in *Suomi Pohjoismaana* (Finland as a Nordic Country), Helsingin yliopisto, Studia Generalia, Kevät/Spring, Yliopistopaino: Helsinki, pp. 3–14.
Apunen, O. and Rytövuori, H. (1982) 'Ideas of "Survival" and "Progress" in the Finnish Foreign Policy Tradition', *Journal of Peace Research* 14, 1: 61–83.
Arter, D. (1995) 'The EU Referendum in Finland on 16 October 1994: A Vote for the West, not for Maastricht', *Journal of Common Market Studies* 33, 3: 361–87.
Browning, C. (1999) 'Coming Home or Moving Home? Narratives in Finnish Foreign Policy and the Re-interpretation of Past Identities', *UPI Working Papers*, Helsinki: Finnish Institute of Foreign Affairs.
Buzan, B., Wæver, O. and de Wilde, J. (1998) *Security: A New Framework for Analysis*, London: Lynne Rienner.
Engman, M. (1994) 'Är Finland ett nordiskt land?' (Is Finland a Nordic Country?), *Den jyske Historiker*, 69–70: 62–7.
Forsberg, T. (1999) 'Soft Means to Hard Security: Finland and the Northern Dimension of the European Union', seminar paper presented at, "Regional Security in Border Areas of Northern and Eastern Europe", Pskov, 6–8 July.

Häyrynen, M. (2000) 'The Kaleidoscopic View: The Finnish National Landscape Imagery', *National Identities* 1, 2: 5–19.

Heiskanen, I. (1988) 'Europeanism and Finnish Culture', in *Yearbook of Finnish Foreign Policy 1987*, Helsinki: Finnish Institute of International Affairs.

Hietanen, A. and Joenniemi, P. (1982) 'Varustelu, kieli ja maailmankuva: Puolustusrevisionin ja parlamentaaristen puolustuskomiteoiden mietintöjen tarkastelua' (Armament, Language and a World View: Exploring the Defence Committee Reports), *Rauhaan tutkien* 3, 1: 18–45.

Ingebritsen, C. and Larson, S. (1997) 'Interest and Identity: Finland, Norway and the European Union', *Cooperation and Conflict* 32, 2: 207–22.

Jakobson, M. (1992) *Finland Seeks Membership in the European Community*, Helsinki: Finnish Features.

Jansson, J.-M. (1989) 'Pohjolan tulevaisuus kulttuuriyhteisönä' (Norden's Future as a Cultural Community), in *Suomi pohjoismaana* (Finland as a Nordic Country), Helsingin yliopisto, Studia Generalia, Kevät/Spring, Yliopistopaino: Helsinki, pp. 111–19.

Joenniemi, P. (1992) 'Finland på jakt efter mening' (Finland in Search for Meaning), *Dagens Nyheter*, 5 December.

—— (1993a) 'Euro-Suomi: rajalla, rajojen välissä vai rajaton?' (Towards a European Finland: On the Border, Between the Borders or Borderless?), in P. Joenniemi, R. Alapuro and K. Pekonen *Suomesta Euro-Suomeen* (From Finland to a European Finland), Research Report 53, Tampere: Tampere Peace Research Institute, pp. 13–48.

—— (1993b) 'Suomen kaksinaisluonne: Herderin vai Hegelin maa?' (The Finnish Duality: Herder's or Hegel's Country?) in P. Joenniemi, R. Alapuro and K. Pekonen *Suomesta Euro-Suomeen* (From Finland to a European Finland), Research Report 53, Tampere: Tampere Peace Research Institute, pp. 63–92.

—— (1996) 'Finland, Europe and St. Petersburg in Search for a Role and Identity', Studia Slavica Finlandensia, Tomus XIII (Yearbook of the Institute for Russian and East European Studies), Helsinki, pp. 101–8.

—— (1998) 'The Karelian Question: On the Transformation of a Border Dispute', *Cooperation and Conflict* 33, 2: 183–206.

Karvonen, L. and Sundelius, B. (1996) 'The Nordic Neutrals: Facing the European Union', in L. Miles (ed.) *The European Union and the Nordic Countries*, London: Routledge.

Klinge, M. (1980) 'Poliittisen ja kulttuurisen Suomen muodostuminen' (The Formation of the Political and Cultural Finland), Suomen kulttuurihistoria II. Helsinki.

—— (1982) *Kaksi Suomea* (The Two Finlands), Helsinki: Otava.

—— (1997) *Finlands historia 3. Kejsartiden* (Finland's History 3. The Tsarist Period), Helsinki: Schildts.

Kohn, H. (1967) *The Idea of Nationalism*, London: Macmillan.

Lawler, P. (1997) 'Scandinavian Exceptionalism and European Union', *Journal of Common Market Studies* 35, 4: 565–94.

Lehtonen, T. (1999) *Europe's Northern Frontier: Perspectives on Finland's Western Identity*, Porvoo: The Finnish National Fund for Research and Development (SITRA).

Manninen, J. (1986) 'Porvarillisen hegemonian juurista' (On The Roots of Bourgeois Hegemony), *Teoria ja politiikka: Tiedonantaja*, January: 16–18.

Medvedev, S. (1998) *Russia as the Subconsciousness of Finland*, UPI Working Paper 7, Helsinki: The Finnish Institute of International Affairs.

Ministry of Foreign Affairs (1997) *Security in a Changing World: Guidelines for Finland's Security Policy*. Report by the Council of State to the Parliament, 17 March 1997, Helsinki: Publications of the Ministry for Foreign Affairs 8/1997.

Mouritzen, H. (1988) *Finlandization: Towards a General Theory of Adaptive Politics*. Aldershot, UK: Avebury.

Ojanen, H. (1999) 'How to Customise Your Union: Finland and the Northern Dimension of the EU', in *Northern Dimensions: Yearbook of the Finnish Institute of International Affairs*, Helsinki: Forssa: The Finnish Institute of International Affairs.

Østergård, U. (1997) 'The Geopolitics of Nordic Identity – From Composite States to Nation-States', in Ø. Sørensen and B. Stråth (eds) *The Cultural Construction of Norden*, Oslo: Scandinavian University Press.

Paasi, A. (1996) *Territories, Boundaries and Consciousness: The Changing Geographies of the Finnish-Russian Border*, Belhaven Studies in Political Geography, Chichester: Wiley.

Paasivirta, J. (1978) *Suomi ja Eurooppa* (Finland and Europe 1808–1914), Helsinki: Kirjayhtymä.

Patomäki, H. (1990) 'Suomi ja suomalaisuus arviotava uudelleen' (Finland and Finnishness has to be Re-evaluated), *Helsingin Sanomat*, 4 August.

—— (1994) 'Paluu vuosisadan vaihteeseen?' (A Return to the Beginning of the Century?), *niin & näin* 3, 2: 48–9.

Pekonen, K. (1993) 'Suomen representoiminen EY-puhunnassa' (Representations of Finland in the Debate on the EEC), in P. Joenniemi, R. Alapuro and K. Pekonen, *Suomesta Euro-Suomeen* (From Finland to a European Finland), Research Report 53, Tampere: Tampere Peace Research Institute, pp. 49–62.

Pesonen, P. (1998) 'The Finns and the Swedes in the European Union', in P. Pesonen and U. Vesa, *Finland, Sweden and the European Union*, Research Report 77, Tampere: Tampere Peace Research Institute, pp. 5–36.

Polvinen, T. (1967 and 1971) *Venäjän vallankumous ja Suomi I–II* (The Russian Revolution and Finland), Helsinki: Otava.

Pulkkinen, T. (1999) 'One Language, One Mind', in T. Lehtonen (ed.) *Europe's Northern Frontier: Perspectives on Finland's Western Identity*, Helsinki: PS-kustannus.

Saukkonen, P. (1999) *Suomi, Alankomaat ja kansallisvaltion identiteettipolitiikka* (Finland, The Netherlands and the Politics of Nation-state Identity), Helsinki: Suomalaisen Kirjallisuuden Seura.

Sørensen, Ø. and Stråth, B. (eds) (1997) 'Introduction: The Cultural Construction of Norden', in Ø. Sørensen and B. Stråth *The Cultural Construction of Norden*, Copenhagen: Scandinavian University Press.

Stenius, H. (1998) 'Folkrörelserna skapade olikartade politiska kulturer' (The Civil Movements Created Different Political Cultures), in R. Alapuro, K. Smeds, I. Liikanen and H. Stenius (eds) *Den finska folkrörelsen*, Stockholm: Nordiska museet.

Sundberg, J. (1997) 'Har EU-Finland kantrat österut?' (Has the EU-Finland Moved Eastwards?), *Finsk Tidskrift*, no. 4: 198–210.

Tassin, E. (1992) 'Europe: A Political Community?', in C. Mouffe (ed.) *Dimensions of Radical Democracy: Pluralism, Citizenship, Community*, London: Verso.

Tiilikainen, T. (1993) 'Det finländska folket inför det historiska beslutet- EG-opinionens utveckling i Finland från 70-talet till medlemsförhandlingarna', in J. Bingen and R. Lindahl (eds) *Nordiske skjebnevalg?*, Oslo: Europa-programmet.

—— (1996) 'Finland and the European Union', in L. Miles (ed.) *The European Union and the Nordic Countries*, London: Routledge.

Tommila, P. (1990) 'Suomalaisen identiteetin muotoutuminen 1800-luvun alkupuolella' (The Formation of the Finnish Identity in the Beginning of the Nineteenth Century), Societas Scientiarum Fennica, Sphinx, Yearbook 1988 of the Finnish Society of Sciences and Letters, Series B, Papers and essays, Helsinki, pp. 97–106.

Törnudd, K. (1996) 'Ties that Bind to the Recent Past: Debating Security Policy in Finland within the Context of Membership of the European Union', *Cooperation and Conflict* 31, 1: 37–68.

Udgaard, N. M. (1998) 'Finlands tause triumf over historien', *Aftenposten*, 7 May.

Väyrynen, P. (1994) 'Europeisk union eller Nordisk gemenskap?' (The European Union or a Nordic Community?), *Nordisk Kontakt*, no. 7–8: 4–11.

Väyrynen, R. (1993) 'Finland and the European Community: Changing Elite Bargains', *Cooperation and Conflict*, 28, 1: 31–46.

Vesa, U. (1998) 'Legitimacy Pressures upon Finland and Sweden', in P. Pesonen and U. Vesa, *Finland, Sweden and the European Union*, Research Report 77, Tampere: Tampere Peace Research Institute, pp. 41–61.

Wæver, O. (1990) 'With Herder and Habermas: Europeanization in the light of German Concepts of State and Nation', Working Paper 16, Copenhagen: Center for Peace and Conflict Research.

—— (1995) 'Danish Dilemmas: Foreign Policy Choices for the 21st Century', in C. Due-Nielsen and N. Petersen (eds) *Adaptation and Activism: The Foreign Policy of Denmark*, Copenhagen: DJØF Publishing.

7   Conclusion

Lene Hansen

The past four chapters have sought to give a detailed analysis of, first, the historical formation of the basic conceptual constellations which structure the debates on European integration in the Nordic countries, and, second, the main positions and problematiques surrounding the referenda in the 1990s. This concluding chapter will, first, discuss whether there are any significant similarities and differences between the ways in which the four countries have approached Europe as well as between the conceptual constellations which have structured the national debates. The chapter then moves on to suggest which theoretical lessons we might draw from our cases and how the challenge from liberal intergovernmentalism presented in the Introduction might be addressed. The chapter ends by suggesting what the future might hold for the debate on European integration and for the importance of 'Norden'.

Comparing conceptual constellations

The first and most striking finding was the difference between the heated debate, and very slim margins in the referenda, in Denmark, Norway and Sweden on the one side, and the, by comparison, relative ease with which Finland accepted EU membership on the other. As was pointed out in the Introduction, polls have shown that the Finns, on average, are about as (dis)pleased with the EU as are the Danes (with Sweden showing an even more negative attitude), but the difference between 'the reluctant three' and Finland is not only that the level of support for integration is on average higher in Finland, but that the EU has failed to attract the same kind of critical attention.

In Chapter 6 Pertti Joenniemi explained the, from a Nordic perspective, unusual Finnish pro-integrationism as a consequence of

> a certain duality in the Finnish concept of the nation: it may be divided into a soft and cultural nation on the one hand and one linked to the power political state on the other. There is the *Kulturnation* as well as the *Staatsnation*. The former leans primarily on Herderian departures whereas the latter rests first and foremost on a Hegelian heritage. This duality allowed for a rethinking of nation and state on separate levels once 'Finland' was faced with the challenge of European integration.

The first phase of major importance for the formation of this constellation was Finland's period under Tsarist Russia. The transfer from Sweden to Russia facilitated the creation of 'Finland', as an entity with both a certain amount of political autonomy at the administrative level and a cultural national identity formulated along Herderian lines. As Joenniemi points out, to strive for independence was under those conditions an almost unthinkable project, and this led the nation 'to provide space for Finland's subjectivity as a cultural entity, and to do so without fusing into a state, or running into conflict with the statist entities already in place'. When Finland gained independence in 1917 it was as a by-product of the Russian defeat in the First World War and the subsequent revolution, yet at this point, a Hegelian understanding of the nation, and its relationship to the state, had gained force. This Hegelian understanding implied that the nation was fused to the state, and that the state should be a strong and powerful one, ready to 'test its viability in a contest between similar entities on the interstate arena'. But the Hegelian turn had not fundamentally eradicated the Herderian tradition which was partly restored after the Second World War when 'The state and the nation were to some extent viewed as separate entities entrusted with the responsibility of balancing each other out.' The outcome was not, however, a complete reversal to a Herderian past, but a tension, or flexibility, in terms of which concept of the nation was privileged. This conceptual constellation appears to have been loosened even further after the end of the cold war where Joenniemi argues that 'The grip of the state and the influence of a homogenising national culture have become less tight.'

The final conclusion is thus that the dual existence of the Herderian and the Hegelian conceptions has allowed Finns to conceive of the cultural nation and the state nation separately; and that the Finnish *Kulturnation* can exist comfortably inside the EU as long as the EU is not deliberately trying to enforce a common cultural European identity. One could add that the Hegelian element, which manifested itself in a top-down style of foreign policy during the cold war, might have led to more support for the idea that the government is in incontestable charge of foreign policy than in the other Nordic countries. Finland lacks, in other words, the accentuation of 'the people' as an anti-elite construction which, as we will return to below, is a key characteristic of the debate in Denmark and Norway. What the Finnish case seems to suggest is that countries whose conceptual constellations imply a difference between the cultural and the political nation fare a better chance of avoiding the legitimacy debate for as long as the EU does not try to build a uniform cultural identity. European integration can thus remain unproblematic at high levels of political integration – Joenniemi suggests that even federalism might be acceptable in the Finnish case – granted that it stays within the realm of the political and the economic.

If we turn to the three sceptics, there is a striking similarity between Denmark and Norway. Not only did they choose similar policies at the institutional level during the cold war – both became members of NATO and both sought to join the EEC – but their basic conceptual constellations also have crucial elements in common. This, of course, is not too surprising considering that a national movement had started to make its impact in Denmark even before Norway was lost to Sweden in

1814, and later on, that a community of Danish and Norwegian romantics came together in Copenhagen in the 1830s and 1840s (see p. 12). So while Norwegian nationalism developed in part through a rejection of what was seen as an alien Danish influence, it nevertheless took a form and developed a discursive structure which was quite similar to the Danish one.[1] Both the Norwegian and the Danish constellations consist of a cultural conception of the nation to which is coupled the central concept of 'Folket'; as Neumann argues in Chapter 4, by the 1840s '"the people" were thus installed as a key referent of the nation'. This romantic nationalist position became hegemonic in Norway, but as in Finland, it was not until the turn of the century that a political programme to link the nation to the state was established and the call for an independent state was convincingly made.

The path towards a nation-state was quite different in Denmark. The nationalist movements in Finland and Norway had begun in a distinctly Herderian manner, stressing the question of cultural identity, not least language, but leaving the question of political autonomy initially unanswered. Denmark, on the other hand, was a dynastic state where the first forms of modern popular identity were patriotic, loyalty to the king and to the realm, in a gradually emerging political nation. However, the later dominant construction of the nation, which crystallised after the traumatic defeat in 1864, drew on cultural, Herderian traits, and its inner core was 'the people' who had the potential to be articulated in opposition to the elite. This anti-elite figure started out as an aspect of the national-liberal movement, but it was inherited by the Social Democrats who made the working class the centre of 'the people'. A similar development took place in Norway, where 'In the course of the 1930s, a representation emerged where the workers' movement defined itself not only as the core of the people, but as the arena where that core could enter an intimate relationship with other working strata of the people, particularly the farmers.' But when the Social Democrats came into government, they could not eradicate the potential anti-elite element, which could then be turned against them.

The consequence of this constellation for the debate on European integration in Norway and Denmark has been that 'the people's' anti-elite connotation can be successfully mobilised by the no-side; and the debate has – with a few exceptions – left the basic conceptual constellation unchallenged. The privilege of 'the people' to decide over the nation, and then, over the state, formed the first crucial component behind the no-side's success. The role of 'the people' implied both in Norway and in Denmark that the government's recommendation of a 'yes' (which in the case of Denmark was shared by the majority of the political and financial establishment) was turned against the government itself. The Norwegian no-side was 'able to represent the fact that the state was harnessed to the yes cause as positively confirming that it was not only different from the people, but actually opposed to them'. The second element of the no-side's success stems from the tight link between state and nation which has made it very difficult to de-link the cultural and the political level – as in Finland – and to conceptualise the EU in non-state terms. This has given the debate a distinctly statist character where all agree on the desirability of the nation-state, and of a Europe of the nation-states, but where the no-side has held that the EU is a federalist (meaning statist) project, whereas the yes-side has argued that this is not actually the case, that the EU is still 'only' an inter-governmental form of cooperation taking place between sovereign states. Thus despite the economic and governmental resources at the yes-side's disposal, it was on the whole forced into a reactive rather than a proactive position within the debate.

The anti-elite figure in Denmark and Norway was an important source of strength for the no-side, but other aspects of the discursive structure need to be included in order to understand what it is that the no-side presents as threatened by EU integration. What is the content of the nation/state to be protected? There are two important aspects. One is national identity: the impossibility of de-linking the political and the cultural nation implies that almost any political construct at the European level can be seen as a threat to the nation. The other aspect is the welfare state, and among the roots for this threat image is the category of Norden (implicitly or explicitly). It is almost seen as inherent, as constitutive of modern Norden to be more welfare state oriented than others. Therefore, irrespective of what 'facts' are presented about the actual size of pensions or the safety of employment across Europe, it is assumed in the Nordic countries that integration and harmonisation can only mean less of the welfare state.

Turning to Sweden, it is clear that in this case too the *Folket* figure prominently. Lars Trägårdh, in Chapter 5, argues that in Swedish discourse 'the people' involves a fusion of both *demo* and *ethnos*, and that 'the state and the people were conceived of as intrinsically linked; the people's home was a *folkstat*'. This development was tied to the hegemonic position of the Social Democratic Party, which also, as in Norway and Denmark, tapped into the national discourse of the nineteenth century and co-opted the concept of 'the people'. The dominant conceptual constellation thus became one where *Folkhemmet* represents a harmonious link between 'state' and 'people'. If we compare Sweden with Denmark and Norway, we find that all three countries' political discourses feature 'the people' as a central concept, but that the distinct anti-elite, and potential anti-state, connotations in Norway and Denmark are not found to the same extent in Sweden.

The Swedish constellation is also the tightest and least flexible of the four countries in the sense that it involves a fusion between 'state' and 'people'; the Finnish constellation has a duality between the cultural and the political nation, and the Norwegian and the Danish ones include the potential anti-elite/anti-state construction of 'the people'. The Norwegian and Danish constellations formed the starting point for both pro- and anti-integrationists, and the Finnish constellation has so much flexibility that it was able, according to Joenniemi's analysis, to cope with the dramatic transformation of the end of the cold war and the entrance of Finland into the EU. The Swedish Social Democratic *Folkhemmet* constellation, on the other hand, allowed for less manoeuvre and it is perhaps not surprising that it is in Sweden that we find the clearest example of a rearticulation of the basic con-stellation. Trägårdh describes how the Timbro Institute initiated 'an anti-statist discourse that hitherto had been virtually non-existent in Sweden'. This discourse invoked the concept of 'civil society' to create a division between 'state' and 'society' which had been collapsed by the hegemonic *Folkhemmet* construction. This de-linkage was then part of the argument why one should be in favour of Swedish membership of the EU: constructing more room for 'civil society' was required and the EU, with its continental political tradition, would help this process along. The second element of the liberal and conservative pro-European strategy in the early 1990s was to point to Sweden's poor economic performance and to argue that the route to recovery was through membership of the EU.

This attempt to de-link state and society did, of course, constitute a major challenge to the Swedish Social Democrats, but it did not prevent them from deciding on a pro-membership course and the common conceptual turf of the two yes-sides became the economic necessity argument: 'The welfare state project was, after all, not simply about equality but also about prosperity, and prosperity was not only about individual self-interest but also a matter of national pride.' The no-side, on the other hand, argued that the EU was fundamentally different from Sweden and that membership would threaten all the virtues of the welfare state, in sum that the *Folkhemmet* construction would be put under extreme pressure if the Swedish state 'joined Europe'.

It is obvious that economic arguments played a major role in the Swedish debate, as they did in the Danish ones in 1972, 1986 and 2000. Our argument is not therefore that 'material interests' are of no importance for the debates on integration, but that economic reasoning might be used more or less frequently, that it might figure prominently in some countries, but not equally so in others. Or, that the financial state of affairs might provide one side with an advantage in terms of mobilising the economic argument, that is, everything being equal, if a country is doing well economically, there will be less pressure for changing the current situation (as in Norway in 1994 and Denmark in 2000) than if the economic situation is seen as problematic (as in Finland and Sweden in the early 1990s).

A comparison of Denmark and Sweden shows that the economic rationale might be tied more or less explicitly to the construction of national identity. Lars Trägårdh points out that the argument that Sweden needed to improve its economic performance – and that this required EU membership – was intimately tied to the construction of Swedish national identity in terms of modernity and economic prowess.[2] All countries wish, of course, to see their economy do well, and so does Denmark, but the Danish yes-side's argument about the economic benefits of EU or EMU membership did not to the same extent as in Sweden tie itself to a basic element deemed crucial to Danish national identity. The conclusion is thus that while economic arguments matter, it is not that they are made *in opposition* to national identity, but that national identity might entail a specific *economic* dimension. Thus, it is the structure of identity that defines the scope and form of economic rationality – not vice versa.

Theoretical reflections

Before turning to the specific claims made by liberal intergovernmentalism which were singled out in Chapter 1, let us briefly recapitulate our main theoretical claims. We argued in Chapter 2 that one can understand the national debates on the EU through an identification of the basic constellation of key collective concepts, which most often include 'state', 'nation', 'society' and 'the people'. Our argument is in this respect a *structuralist* one inasmuch as we claim that these conceptual constellations structure the debate on Europe.[3] The Danish debate, for example, has depicted a pro-integration 'Europe as intergovernmental cooperation' on the one side against a 'Europe as federalist superstate' on the other. Both of these constructions of Europe draw upon a conceptual constellation at the basic Danish level which links state and nation tightly together and where the nation is identified along the lines of a classical *Kulturnation*. But this strong emphasis on structure notwithstanding, ours is not a deterministic structuralism. Established conceptual constellations are structural starting points which actors need to consider and address even if they wish to change them, but these structures *can* be put under pressure, as is shown by Lars Trägårdh's analysis of the conservative rearticulation of the Swedish welfare state enshrined in *Folkhemmet*. While we ascribe a high degree of stability to conceptual constellations, they are also considered susceptible to pressure, in particular if domestic or external events are seen as leading to a national crisis and a call for change.

Some readers might nevertheless find the case studies rather deterministic in leaving too little room for registering current change as well as for envisioning it in the future. As argued in Chapter 2, our understanding of poststructuralism operates with a dual emphasis on structures – which necessarily implies a certain degree of stability – as well as on the principled openness and contestability of discourses. Yet, striking the proper balance between stability and contestability in a concrete analysis is often quite difficult, in particular when presenting both the historical formation of the basic state–nation constellation as well as a detailed interpretation of the current debate on Europe in just one chapter. As a consequence, the analysis of the debate, shifts and differences between the main positions at level 3, that is the concrete manifestations of European integration policies, might be underdeveloped. Not only might this give the impression of a too neatly organised set of 'yes' and 'no' positions, it might also underplay the extent to which minor positions within the debate might be building up pressure for transformation at the deeper levels.

But a more principled defence against determinism might be connected to our understanding of predictability and agency. As Ole Wæver points out in Chapter 2, if a system is under severe pressure, there is a drive towards change at a deeper level and with our structural model we are capable of predicting which transformations at level 2 will be more likely than others. Our theory identifies, in other words, a set of structural possibilities at levels 2 and 3, but which possibilities are ultimately articulated, and which become hegemonic, depends on the creative forces of political agency.

If the change in question is located at level 1, the basic state–nation constellation, predicting the exact outcome of a potential change is very difficult indeed. One might as a general rule presume a tendency towards keeping some aspects of the basic constellation in place – for example to reconstruct the link between state and nation and modify the concept of the state, while keeping the conceptualisation of nation in place – but this is still only broadly suggestive, and cannot qualify as a prediction in the stricter sense applicable to change *within* a structure. We cannot tell those engaged in the political debate precisely which reconstruction of state, nation, people, society and so on is going to be successful in the future.

Although, it has been our purpose in this book to present a structural theory and apply it to a set of case studies, it is worthwhile reiterating that both the reproduction and the transformation of structures are carried out by political agents striving to generate support for their policies in the face of a multitude of challenges and possibilities. Our contribution to those directly engaged in the political process is an understanding of where the major blocks to new policies are located. This, however, is not to suggest that the best advice would always be to avoid those and 'play it structurally safe'; in some cases external developments might be so significant that ducking the question of more fundamental change will be counter-productive. One's policy will be increasingly questioned due to its inability to incorporate, for example, the speed and depth of European integration, and in the meantime political opponents might construct a more convincing policy that does address this issue.

The analyses in Chapters 3 to 6 focus on presenting empirically and historically rich accounts of how key concepts have come to pose certain restrictions on how 'Europe' can be debated. Iver Neumann's analysis of Norway and Pertti Joenniemi's of Finland discuss, and criticise, alternative rationalist attempts to explain these countries' position vis-à-vis European integration. But we have not carried out actual tests of our theory, either against alternative rationalist explanations or of hypotheses deduced from our theory. From a rationalist, liberal inter-governmentalist point of view it is, however, a central question how our analysis compares in terms of explaining the position each country has taken on the question of European integration.

Let us, therefore, turn briefly to the central liberal intergovernmentalist claims made by Ingebritsen and Moravcsik, which we presented in the Introduction. Ingebritsen's central conclusion was that 'The diverging paths to Europe conformed to the specificities of sectoral politics' (Ingebritsen 1998: 115). Making a materialist claim, Ingebritsen argues that 'Differences in economic export structures and what Europe offers each state can explain why some states were more positive than others to European Community membership' (Ingebritsen 1998: 169). Norway had the resources to stay aloof whereas Finland and Sweden were too dependent on European markets to say 'no'. This implies that 'The political process of integration was, as I have argued throughout, decided by a partnership between governments and economic interest groups in which the public had a limited voice in the outcome' (Ingebritsen 1998: 168). But even if the negotiations preceding entrance into the Union were conducted by governments who were strongly influenced by economic interest groups, it is still the case that membership – and thereby 'the package' which has been negotiated – needed to be approved by the public. And as the negative outcomes in Norway and Denmark, and the close race in Sweden, show, this is by no means a formality for the Nordic governments.

So why did we get different results in the Nordic EU-related referenda? It would seem that the very small margins in Norway and Sweden have been toned down in Ingebritsen's conclusion in favour of the final 'yes' or 'no' result. Yet, as both numbers were very close to the critical 50 per cent it seems justified to claim that, statistically speaking, the outcome could have gone either way in both countries. The biggest difference in terms of the populations' view of the EU runs therefore not between Norway and the rest of the Nordics, but between Finland on the one hand and the 'reluctant three' on the other. But despite the overwhelming support in favour of membership amongst the economic and political leadership in Sweden and Denmark roughly half of the population voted 'no' to Maastricht and the EMU in Denmark, and membership in the case of Sweden. Put differently, if sectoral interests were so constitutive for the policy towards Europe as claimed by liberal intergovernmentalism, one would have predicted a much firmer 'yes' in these two countries. Especially since both the government and the major opposition parties advocated in favour of acceptance.

Our analysis leads us to argue that while Ingebritsen's assumptions would seem to be confirmed in the case of Finland, one might also explain Finland's pro-integration position by its flexible and dual construction of the nation. This has allowed a separation of the political and the cultural, so that political integration at the European level could be supported without this leading to the fear that national identity might be threatened in cultural terms. Denmark, on the other hand, is characterised by a conceptual constellation which makes it very difficult to follow precisely this separation. We would argue, furthermore, that although the outcome in Sweden was a 'yes', to characterise Sweden as an enthusiastic, or even an unproblematic European, would be an exaggeration. Even if the materialist reasons Ingebritsen points to should make Sweden strongly in favour of integration, it has been a problem for the government in the 1990s to convince the electorate of this policy. Lars Trägårdh's analysis points out that the tightness of the Swedish conceptual constellation could explain both the liberal-conservative attempt to articulate an alternative as well as the high degree of reluctance after the approval of membership: the dominant constellation has tied 'the people' closely to the Swedish state, and if there are any doubts whether this 'contract' is threatened inside a more liberal Europe, it is likely to meet with substantial opposition. Ingebritsen's analysis of Norway was, finally, problematised by Iver Neumann who pointed out that the oil resources were not a part of the debate in 1972 and that they cannot therefore explain the 'no' in the first referendum. What our analysis has shown is in short that the correlation between the economic interests and governmental stance on the one side and public opinion on the other does not run as smoothly as claimed by Ingebritsen's rationalist framework.

One of liberal intergovernmentalism's strongest claims is that 'important social groups' influence states' policy towards Europe. This claim is specified in more detail by Moravcsik who argues that:

> The most fundamental influences on foreign policy are, therefore, the identity of important societal groups, the nature of their interests, and their relative influence on domestic policy. Groups that stand to gain and lose a great deal *per capita* tend to be the most influential.

> (Moravcsik 1993: 483)

Our research seems to suggest two critical comments concerning this link between 'important social/sectorial/economic groups', on the one hand, and the outcome in referenda on the other, at least in the Nordic context. There was, with the possible exception of Norway, strong support in favour of membership or a 'yes' to Maastricht amongst the economically important groups. These groups clearly thought that it would be in their own interests, as well as probably in the national interest, to secure a 'yes'. If Moravcsik and Ingebritsen were right, one would assume that with the substantial amount of money and 'information' these economic and political leaders poured into the campaigns, the result should be a clear 'yes'.

Our analysis has shown, however, contrary to the expectations of liberal intergovernmentalism, that this unity at the elite level *contributed* to the 'no', at least in Denmark and Norway, rather than to a 'yes'. Furthermore, the argument that a 'no' would cause economic hardship, and political isolation, seemed to have insufficient impact on the debate. Our analysis argues that this was no coincidence, but can be explained by the discursive structures in Norway and Denmark that construct 'the people' in potential anti-elitist and anti-state terms. The no-sides managed to activate this construction in making the argument that the rallying of 'powerful forces' was conspicuous in and of itself – and that 'objective' economic analysis should be considered part of an attempt to intimidate the voters. Finally, economic arguments are inserted in a general rhetorical figure that pitches rational against emotional arguments. This scheme is used by some yes-sayers to denounce 'no'-arguments, but it is – in different forms – equally used by the no-side to present economic arguments as dubious expressions of narrow materialism and egotism.

To point to the importance of discursive structures is not, however, to claim that material factors, or interests, have no impact. Obviously, it makes a difference that in the Norway of the 1990s oil resources made it possible for the no-side to fence off economic arguments in favour of integration to a different extent than in the Danish context. There might in other words be different degrees of freedom for a particular argument to be made, dependent on the perception of the country's economic strength and ability to prosper independently of membership of the EU or the EMU. But our contention is, nevertheless, that the discursive structure built upon the basic conceptual constellation provides an alternative 'structure' through which the arguments about material interests need to be presented. Material interest can therefore only act through these structures. In some cases, as in Denmark and Norway, these discursive structures might in fact be so trickily designed that the advancement of material interests is precisely what triggers opposition to integration.

But the anti-elitism of 'the people' is not the only factor that complicates the link between economic/material interests and powerful groups on the one hand and their ability to influence the public on the other. Another complication stems from the uncertainty surrounding the definition of these very material interests: it is not uncommon to find heated discussions of whether predictions by governments, trade unions, or employers' associations are in fact reliable. This contestation is, of course, spurred in part by 'the people's' distrust of 'their' elites, but the outcome is in any case that an objective definition of material interests, costs and benefits becomes the point of contestation. If we turn to the second and last claim made by Moravcsik, namely that 'Liberal theory suggests that fundamental constraints on national preferences will reflect the costs and benefits to societal actors; where these are weak, uncertain or diffuse, governments will be able to pursue broader or more idio-syncratic goals' (Moravcsik 1993: 494), our conclusion is not that we have proven liberal intergovernmentalism to be wrong on this point, but that the very assessment of costs and benefits has become politicised to the extent where they cannot be determined with any certainty. And it is this politicisation – which is neither diffuse nor certain – which prevents the governments from pursuing their 'idiosyncratic goals' in the field of European integration.

A look to the future: Europe and Norden

European integration is likely to remain a key foreign policy issue in Norden for the foreseeable future. Denmark probably takes the prize as the country with the most frequent and intense debate on Europe; the 'no' in the EMU referendum in September 2000 was at first taken as an indication that referenda should be avoided for at least a couple of years, unless the EU came up with new treaties which, due to a transfer of sovereignty, required a new referendum. Yet, only a month later, the first discussions of the non-membership of the WEU and EU defence co-operation started to surface, raising questions about whether the exception on participation in defence policy should be the next in line for a referendum. Certainly, having referenda on EU questions has now been established as a practice to such an extent that future treaties are likely to be subjected to referenda whenever there is even a small indication that sovereignty might be transferred.

Sweden has made a convincing economic recovery after the shock of the early 1990s, but the political and financial leaderships have not been successful in terms of making their pro-integration orientation drip down into the larger electorate. Polls continue to show that Sweden harbours the most sceptic population of EU members, and with the recent rejection of the EMU in Denmark, one would suspect that there will be governmental reluctance to announce a referendum on the EMU in the immediate future. And accession to the EMU without a referendum would, in the light of the high level of scepticism, be unlikely.

Finland and Norway, finally, are currently the least 'EU-debating' countries in Norden: Finland, as integration is not seen as particularly problematic, but, rather, as described by Joenniemi, a chance for Finland to manifest itself in terms of regional politics and as the bridge to the (potentially huge) Russian market; Norway, since the second 'no' has resulted in a consensus that a new referendum would require a 'new situation', or at least something which can be constructed in such terms. In any case, since Norway's possible entrance would demand a referendum, Denmark has developed the referendum as a political practice, and Sweden would be likely to have one prior to accession to the EMU, Norden will continue to be a region with a high frequency of referenda and with an ensuing tendency to make European integration a politicised issue.

But what of 'Norden' itself? Our decision to focus on the debates on the EU in the Nordic countries was, of course, informed by the assumption that the four countries were, indeed, part of 'Norden', yet 'Norden' itself is a political category whose form and survival is dependent on being sustained through practice. If we take the debates on the EU as one form of practice, we have found that 'Norden' does continue to play a role in Sweden and Denmark, not most prominently as a concrete institutional alternative, although that is occasionally advanced as a possibility by the most EU-critical voices, but as a particular identity. 'Norden' is juxtaposed to 'the EU', with the former being a natural, organic community amongst equally democratic, environmentalist, pro-women's rights, etc. nations – the EU by contrast is the opposite of all these (good) things. 'Norden' is in short used as a significant marker to identify 'us' against 'Europe'. This construction has strong historical roots stretching back to the mid-nineteenth century and it was therefore both a logical and a powerful move of the no-side to enlist this figure in its political argument. The yes-side was as a consequence put in a position where it needed to articulate a 'Nordic programme' of its own – simply declaring 'Norden' null and void would require too deep a discursive change and was probably deemed too difficult to be accomplished – and its choice was to point to 'Norden in Europe', to underline that with 'the Nordics' inside the EU one could, for the first time since 1972, be reunited. Nordic identity was discursively acknowledged, but the difference to 'Europe' was toned down compared with the no-side.

In Norway, it appeared to be the yes-side which most vocally tried to articulate 'Norden' in its favour. Finland, again, differed not only in having had much less of a contestation of full EU membership (including the EMU), but also in its more ambiguous relationship with 'Norden' primarily due to the element of anti-Swedism which has been part of Finnish national history. The most prestigious Finnish initiative has thus evolved more around 'the Northern dimension' in an attempt to build a bridge to the Russian and Baltic east than it has tried to reinvigorate Norden in its classical form.

'Norden' continues to play a role in the debates on Europe, but to what extent it will remain a powerful move is an open question. Its historical roots are both a resource of strength and a potential limitation, and there is no guarantee that the romantic 'Norden' construction of the nineteenth century is going to make a successful transformation to the globalised twenty-first century where routes of travel, education and TV follow no particular Nordic pattern.

Notes

1   This similarity was of course also spurred by the influence of German, Herderian thought in both of the national settings.
2   The emphasis on modernity is also a strong feature of Finnish national identity; see Joenniemi's analysis.
3   And it might even have relevance for other foreign policy debates as well, such as alliance and security policy (Agersnap 2000).

References

Agersnap, L. (2000) 'Fra Dagsorden til Verdensorden: En poststrukturalistik analyse af Danmarks udenrigspolitiske identitet', MA thesis, University of Copenhagen.

Ingebritsen, C. (1998) *The Nordic States and European Unity*, Ithaca, NY: Cornell University Press.

Moravcsik, A. (1993) 'Preferences and Power in the European Community: A Liberal Intergovernmentalist Approach', *Journal of Common Market Studies* 31, 4: 473–524.

Index